THE GREAT BOOK OF CLASSIC CUISINE

First published in Germany under the title *Unser Bestes Kochen & Backer*

This 1990 edition is published by Weathervane Books, distributed by Outlet Book Company, Inc.,
a Random House Company, 225 Park Avenue South, New York, New York 10003,
by arrangement with Ceres-Verlag R.A.

Printed and bound in Hong Kong

Library of Congress Cataloging-in-Publication Data
Dr. Oetker (Firm)
[Unser Bestes. English]
The great book of classic cuisine / Dr. Oetker.
p. cm.
Translation of: Unser Bestes.
ISBN 0-517-69951-6
1. Cookery, European. I. Title.
TX723.5.A1D7 1990
641.594—dc20 90-35135
CIP

ISBN 0-517-69951-6
8 7 6 5 4 3 2 1

THE GREAT BOOK OF CLASSIC CUISINE

DR. OETKER

WEATHERVANE BOOKS
New York

CONTENTS

Sauces

Fish

Meat

Poultry

CONTENTS

CLASSIC CUISINE

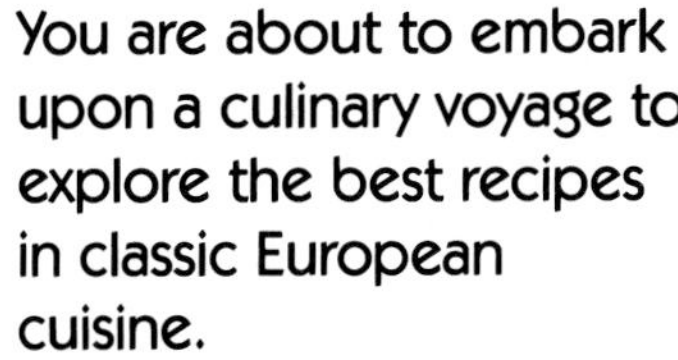

You are about to embark upon a culinary voyage to explore the best recipes in classic European cuisine.

Whether you prefer to read a cookbook word for word, browse for inspiration, plan elaborate menus, or simply enjoy looking at the attractively photographed dishes, *The Great Book of Classic Cuisine* will stimulate your culinary imagination.

Hundreds of recipes, cooking tips, and enticing ideas guarantee you a comprehensive guide to good cooking and eating. *The Great Book of Classic Cusine* is a work of lasting value for today's cooks and for generations to come.

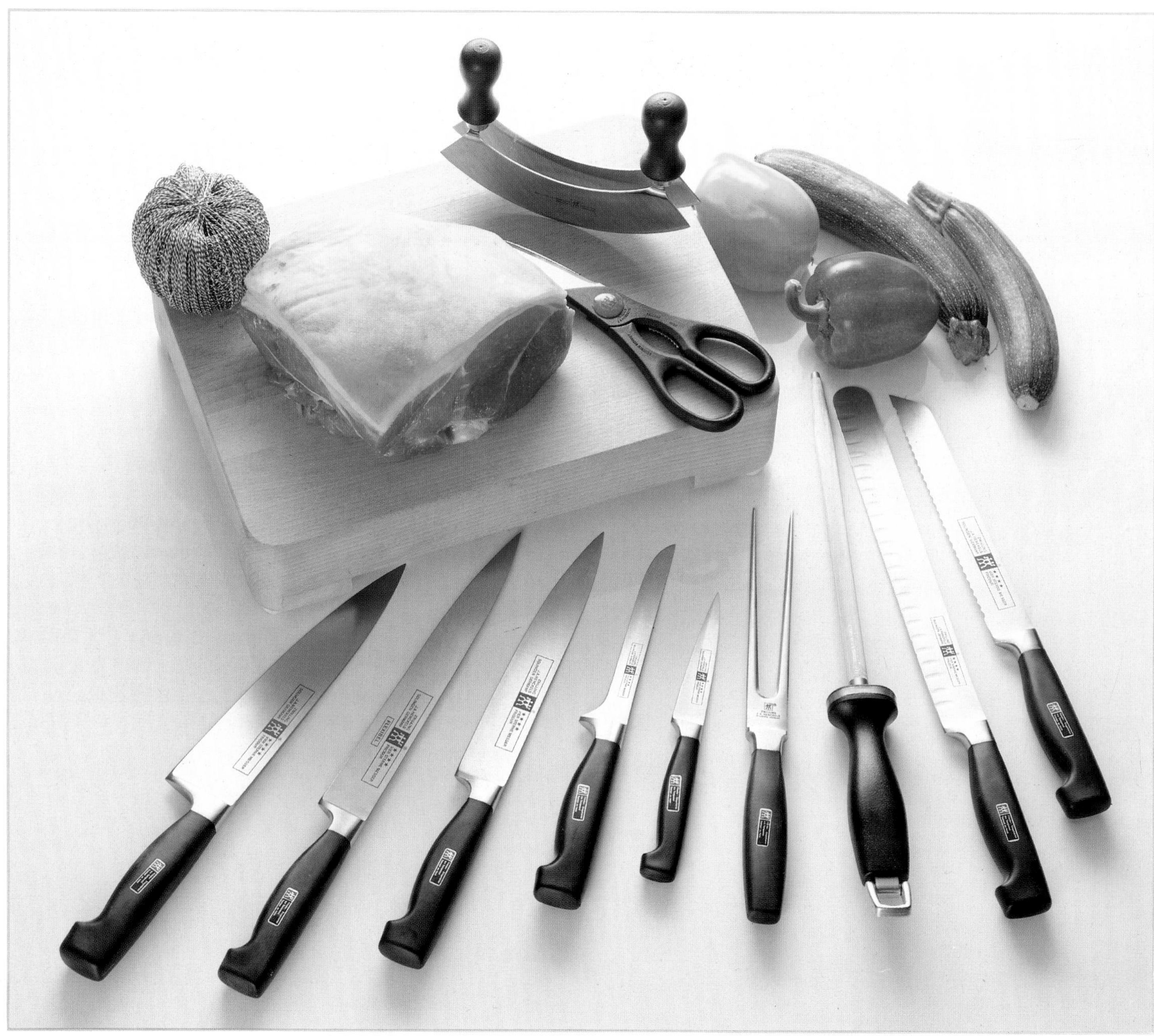

This attractively photographed selection of knives and cooking utensils illustrates some of the many practical and handsome tools available for use in the kitchen. Shown from left to right are: a cook's knife; ham knife; meat knife; boning knife; garnishing knife; meat fork; sharpening steel; serrated meat knife; and bread knife. Above: kitchen scissors and mincer.

Pots and pans are an essential part of any kitchen. This photograph displays an elegant assortment of kitchen equipment selected to illustrate some of the basic cooking tools needed for a small household. Shown in the photograph are: a pressure cooker; assorted frying pans and saucepans; a heavy-bottomed casserole dish; a stock pot; a double boiler; and an oven-proof casserole or soufflé dish.

GLOSSARY OF COOKING TERMS

Al Dente: Firm to the bite, not soft or mushy. Used to describe vegetables or pasta.

Au Gratin: Having a browned or crusted top, often made by topping with bread crumbs, cheese, or a rich sauce and passing under the broiler.

Bake: To cook foods by surrounding them with hot, dry air. Similar to roast, but the term baking usually applies to bread, pastries, vegetables, and fish.

Bard: To tie thin slices of fat, such as pork fatback, over meats with no natural fat cover to protect them while roasting.

Béchamel: A sauce made by thickening milk with a roux.

Beurre Manie: A smooth paste made by blending equal parts of raw butter and flour.

Beurre Noir: Butter heated until it is dark brown and then flavored with vinegar.

Bind: To thicken a liquid by boiling it with a binding agent.

Blanch: To cook an item partially and very briefly in boiling water. Usually a preparation technique, as to loosen skins from vegetables, fruits, and nuts; to partially cook french fries or other foods; to prepare for freezing; or to remove undesirable flavors.

Boil: To cook in water or other liquid that is bubbling rapidly at a temperature of about 212°F at sea level and at normal pressure.

Braise: (1) To cook covered in a small amount of liquid, usually after preliminary browning. (2) To cook certain vegetables slowly in a small amount of liquid without preliminary browning.

Broil: To cook (broil) and brown through direct radiant heat from above the food, with or without the addition of fat.

Caramelization: The browning of sugars caused by heat.

Chop: To cut into irregularly shaped pieces.

Clarified Butter: Purified butterfat, with water and milk solids removed.

Consommé: A rich, flavorful, seasoned stock or broth that has been clarified to make it perfectly clear and transparent.

Court Bouillon: Water containing seasonings, herbs, and usually an acid; used for cooking fish.

Croquette: Food that has been pureed or bound with a thick sauce, made into small shapes, breaded, and fried.
Deep-fry: To cook submerged in hot fat.
Deglaze: To swirl a liquid in a frying pan or other pan to dissolve cooked particles or food remaining on bottom.
Demiglaze: A rich brown sauce that has been reduced to half its original volume.
Double Boiler: A pot that rests over another pot containing boiling water; used for preparing delicate sauces and custards or for melting chocolate without burning it.
Dredge: To dip food items in flour, beaten eggs, and bread crumbs immediately before frying or deep-fat frying.
Dressed: (1) Poultry in market form: killed, bled, and plucked. (2) Fish in market form: viscera, scales, head, tail, and fins removed.
Dry-heat Cooking Methods: Methods in which heat is conducted to foods without the use of moisture.
Fillet, Filet: (1) Meat: boneless tenderloin. (2) Fish: boneless side of fish. (3) Chicken: boneless breast of chicken. (4) The act of removing the bones from meat, fish, or chicken.
Flambé: To pour a small amount of brandy or other high-percentage alcohol liqueur onto food, ignite, and allow to burn off.
Glaze: (1) A stock that is reduced until it coats the back of a spoon. (2) A shiny coating, such as a syrup, applied to a food. (3) To make a food shiny or glossy by coating it with a glaze or by browning under the broiler or in a hot oven.
Grill: To cook (broil) and brown through direct radiant heat from below the food, with or without the addition of fat.
Julienne: (1) To cut into small, thin strips about ⅛ x ⅛ x 2½ inches. (2) To garnish with foods cut in this manner.
Marinate: To soak a food in a seasoned liquid.
Meringue: A foam made of beaten egg whites and sugar.
Mince: To chop into very fine pieces.
Mirepoix: A mixture of rough-cut or diced vegetables, herbs, and spices used for flavoring.
Pan-broil: To cook uncovered in a frying pan or skillet without fat.
Pan-fry: To cook in a moderate amount of fat in an uncovered skillet.

Parboil: To cook partially in a boiling or simmering liquid.
Parcook: To cook partially by any method.
Pilaf: Rice or other grain product that has first been cooked in fat and then simmered in a stock or other liquid, usually with onions, seasonings, or other ingredients.
Poach: To cook very gently in water or other liquid that is hot but not actually bubbling, about 160°F to 180°F.
Puree: (1) A food product that has been mashed or strained to a smooth pulp. (2) To make such a pulp by mashing or straining a food.
Reduce: To cook by simmering or boiling until quantity is decreased; often done to concentrate flavors.
Roast: To cook foods by surrounding them with hot, dry air, in an oven or on a spit over an open fire.
Roux: A cooked mixture of equal parts flour and fat.
Sauté: To cook quickly in a small amount of fat.
Sear: To brown the surface of a food quickly at a high temperature.
Shock: To pour cold water over cooked, hot food items.
Shred: To cut into thin but irregular strips, either with the coarse blade of a grater or with a knife.
Simmer: To cook in water or other liquid that is bubbling gently, at about 185° F to 200° F.
Soufflé: A light, fluffy, baked egg dish consisting of a base (such as a heavy white sauce) mixed with egg yolks and flavoring ingredients into which beaten egg whites are folded just before baking. May be sweet or savory.
Stew: (1) To simmer a food or foods in a small amount of liquid that is usually served with the food as a sauce. (2) A dish cooked by stewing, usually one in which the main ingredients are cut into small pieces.

1

2

3

Stock: A clear, thin (that is, unthickened) liquid flavored by soluble substances extracted from meat, poultry, and fish, and their bones, and from vegetables and seasonings.
Strain: To pass cooked food items or raw, pureed foods through a sieve.
Sweat: To cook in a small amount of fat over low heat, sometimes covered.
Truss: To tie poultry into a compact shape for cooking.
Wash: (1) To brush or coat a food item with a liquid such as egg wash or milk. (2) The liquid used in this procedure.

FREEZING FOOD

A well-stocked freezer can provide a feast for unexpected guests, as well as a regular source of prepared foodstuffs, packed in appropriately sized portions, for those times when it is not possible or convenient to prepare a meal from scratch.

Rather than relying on prepackaged commercial dinners for a meal after a hard day at work, why not use your freezer wisely, and stock it with healthy, economical dishes prepared under more leisurely conditions?

You can freeze almost all foodstuffs. Here are some suggestions for preparing food for the freezer.

Vegetables, such as the broccoli shown, are first cleaned and washed (photograph 1), then blanched. The vegetable is placed in a sieve set in boiling water for 2 to 5 minutes (photograph 2) to destroy any surface bacteria and deactivate enzymes. The sieve and contents are then immediately plunged into cold water to stop the cooking process (photograph 3). Place the vegetables in a plastic freezer bag or container; date and label for future use.

Fruit can be frozen raw. It is first washed and patted dry. Peel and core apples and pears and cut them into pieces, then blanch them or they will become brown and look unappetizing. It is also possible to freeze fruit with sugar. Simply mix in a few tablespoons of sugar before placing in dated and labeled freezer containers.

Raw meat may be frozen whole, but it is better to freeze meat in serving-size portions. Remove the meat from its store packaging and wrap tightly in aluminum foil before freezing. Date and label the package. Meat should not be kept in the freezer for more than three months.

Raw poultry should be prepared so that it is oven-ready. Remove the store packaging and any offal. Rinse the poultry with cold water and pat dry with paper towels. Wrap tightly in aluminum foil; date and label the package. Poultry should not be kept in the freezer for more than three months.

4

Fish should be gutted and cleaned before freezing. Freeze only fish that has been freshly caught. Wrap in aluminum foil; date and label the package. Fish should not be kept in the freezer for more than three months.

Bread, rolls, pastries, and cakes all freeze very well. Bread and cakes may be sliced into individual portions that need less time to thaw. Wrap well to guard against the formation of ice crystals.

Prepared dishes should be stored in tight-sealing freezer containers. Decide ahead of time how you will portion the prepared dish (individual or family-size servings); date and label the containers. Prepared dishes should not be kept in the freezer for more than three months.

5

HERBS AND SPICES

HERBS

There is nothing quite as special as the flavor of fresh herbs. Fresh herbs, naturally, have a stronger, more aromatic taste than their dried counterparts. Depending on seasonal availability, herbs may be used alone or in combinations, in almost every sort of savory dish or sauce, to greatly enhance the natural flavoring of the food.

Some herbs freeze well. Although they may turn black in the freezer (basil, for example), their flavor is fully preserved and available for use in sauces and stews.

Many cooks who have become used to fresh herbs prefer to grow their own for year-round availability and easy use.

The following pages illustrate many common, and some uncommon, herbs and spices.

When using herbs from your own garden, pick them just before they are to be used.

To keep herbs fresh in the refrigerator, wrap them in aluminum foil and store in the vegetable crisper.

Storing herbs in a dish or glass of water causes valuable vitamins, as well as flavorings, to be lost in the water.

Always rinse fresh herbs under cold, running water before use.

Be sure to chop herbs just before they are to be used to ensure that the full flavor and value are preserved.

BASIL

This intensely aromatic herb, also known as the "royal herb," originated in Asia and is widely cultivated today. Basil is particularly delicious in tomato-based sauces and dishes, and is also the principle ingredient of pesto, an Italian green sauce.

SAVORY

Savory grows abundantly in the countries around the Mediterranean Sea. Both the leaves and the stalk of savory are used for flavoring. Savory is used in preparing all sorts of beans, stews, and lamb dishes, as well as sauces.

BORAGE

Borage is a mild herb that goes very well with cucumbers and pickles. It is often used for seasoning salad dressings.

DILL

Sweet-smelling dill is ideal in preparing salads, light sauces, fish, and crabs. The feathery leaves are chopped into fragments, or the entire stalk may be used whole as a garnish.

TARRAGON

Tarragon has been one of the most popular herbs to be cultivated in France and Italy. Only the small leaves of tarragon are used for flavoring. Indispensable as a seasoning in Béarnaise Sauce, this rather strong herb goes well with poultry and fish and any sauces created for these.

WATERCRESS

Watercress is eaten whole, for both the tender stems and small green leaves are delicious. Used in salads, served alone, or as seasoning for light sauces or clear soups, this herb has a delicate flavor.

LOVAGE

Lovage is an excellent herb for flavoring stews, sauces for meat, and for cooking peas and beans. This herb was very popular with cooks in ancient Rome.

MARJORAM

Marjoram originated in the Mediterranean countries. Only the leaves, which have a strong flavor, are used as a seasoning. Marjoram is recommended for hearty stews, ham dishes, soups, and stuffed poultry.

PARSLEY

Parsley is one of the most common and widely available fresh herbs. Common, or curly-leafed, parsley has a milder flavor than the broad, smooth-leafed Italian parsley. Parsley leaves are often used as a garnish, but the stems and leaves should be used in preparing stocks and soups to achieve full flavoring.

ANISE

Fresh anise has a mild, licorice-like flavor. It goes well with green salads, cucumber dishes, and in light soups and stews.

ROSEMARY

Rosemary has a piquant, spicy, slightly bitter flavor. It is usually used to season roasted or grilled meat and fish. Rosemary is perfectly suited as a flavoring for lamb, chicken, zucchini, and tomatoes.

SAGE

Sage has a hearty, strong flavor, and should be used in moderation. It is used in cooking fish, liver, lamb, and pork, and also as a secondary seasoning for tomato sauces.

SORREL

Sorrel may be prepared by itself as a vegetable or pureed and served as a sauce. The tender leaves are used to flavor soups and sauces, fish dishes, poultry, or roasts.

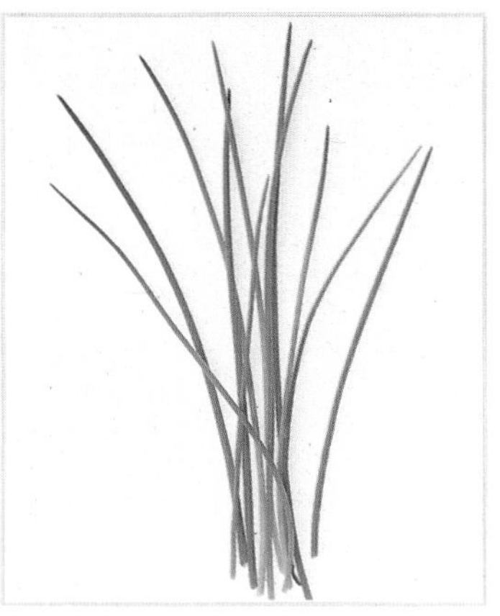

CHIVES

The chive has a fresh, delicate, oniony flavor, and is found in a wide variety of dishes, including stews, mixed salads, herbed butters, tomato sauces, and soups. Chives mix well with all sorts of herbs, and make an attractive garnish when freshly chopped.

CELERY

Celery may be used in almost all food dishes. It is available as whole seeds, ground, or as salt, and is an excellent flavoring for stocks, stews, salads, dressings, seafood, and vegetables.

THYME

This aromatic herb, of which there are many different varieties available, is most commonly sold as "common" thyme. Thyme is used to season meat, poultry, sauces made with red wine, and tomato and mushroom dishes.

ORPINE

The rather acid, aromatic leaves of orpine are sometimes used to flavor fresh salads or soups.

LEMON BALM

Lemon balm is a variety of mint. The leaves have a spicy lemon flavor, and are used to season salads, poultry, and veal, as well as light sauces and soups. Lemon balm may also be used to garnish many sweet dishes.

CAYENNE PEPPER

Cayenne pepper is made from the ground pods of a special variety of hot red pepper. The pepper pods are dried and ground to produce this fiery spice, which should be only used in very small amounts.

TURMERIC

This yellow spice, cultivated in India, is related to ginger. It has a hot flavor and a trace of acidity. Turmeric is good for seasoning sauces, stews, and marinades.

CURRY

Curry consists of 12 to 15 (or more) different spices, usually a mixture of chili, cloves, coriander, cumin, ginger, mustard, pimiento, and other seasonings. Curry is used in preparing meat, fish, poultry, and vegetable dishes.

FENNEL SEED

Fennel may be purchased as seeds or ground to a powder. Used principally to flavor certain types of holiday cookies and pastries, it also makes an interesting seasoning for fish vegetables, salads, and sweet dishes.

GINGER

The ginger plant forms tuberous roots that may be used fresh, preserved in syrup, dried, or powdered. This hot spice is suitable for seasoning poultry, lamb and other meat, as well as gingerbread, spiced cookies, and cakes.

CARDAMON

Cardamon is used in much the same way as cinnamon and cloves for seasoning baked desserts and meat dishes. It is also delicious in marinades and barbecue sauces.

CORIANDER

Coriander seeds are used whole or ground. This spice is an excellent seasoning for stews and vegetables such as cabbage.

CUMIN

Cumin is a classic flavoring used in cheese and unleavened bread. Whole or ground cumin seeds are also frequently used for marinades, and in chili and tomato sauces.

HERBS AND SPICES

CARAWAY SEED

Whole or ground caraway seed is used to season stews, soups, rye bread, cheese, marinades, and certain vegetable dishes.

BAY LEAF

Dried or fresh bay leaves make excellent flavoring for fish stews, roast meats, marinades, and vegetable soups.

MACE

The outer coat of the nutmeg is called mace. Available dried and ground, this pleasingly aromatic spice is excellent as a pie seasoning. It may be used wherever nutmeg is found as an ingredient.

NUTMEG

Nutmeg is the fruit of the evergreen nutmeg tree that grows in tropical regions. This spice is used to season many vegetables, white sauce, and certain cookies and pastries.

CLOVES

The clove is the dried bud of the tropical evergreen clove tree. Ground or whole, strong-flavored cloves are used for seasoning meat and vegetables. Because of the strength of this spice, whole cloves are usually removed from a dish before serving.

PAPRIKA

Spicy paprika is mainly grown in Hungary, Bulgaria, Greece, and Spain. The pepper pods are dried and ground in different varieties to produce sweet or hot paprika. This spice makes an excellent seasoning for all types of savory dishes.

PEPPER

Pepper is cultivated mainly in India, Indonesia, and Brazil. This important seasoning consists of the small, round fruits of a climbing plant, whose husk ripens from green, through red and black, to a yellowish white. All of these types of pepper are available whole or ground. White pepper is the hottest variety, while black pepper has the spiciest flavor.

ALLSPICE

These reddish brown berries are dried and ground, or sold whole. The flavor is a combination of cinnamon, nutmeg, and clove. Allspice is used to season meat dishes, but is mainly found in spiced cakes and cookies, as well as fruit pie fillings.

SAFFRON

Saffron is taken from the yellow stamens of a crocus-like plant. It is difficult to harvest and so is expensive. A mild spice widely used in Mediterranean cuisine, saffron also turns any food it seasons a bright yellow color.

MUSTARD SEED

Whole mustard seed is used in preparing marinades, fish stews, and pickles. Ground mustard seed produces mustard powder, used as the principle component of all types of mustard.

SESAME SEED

This plant, which produces pods with little, oval seeds, grows in the tropical regions. The seeds are available whole or crushed, and have a nutty flavor. Lightly toasted sesame seeds are often sprinkled on vegetables or salads, but are most often used as a flavoring in bread.

SOY POWDER

The soy bean is the basic ingredient for soy sauce and soy paste. Soy flour is used as an ingredient in bread, rolls, soups, and sauces. Roasted soy beans make an excellent and nutritious snack food.

STAR ANISE

Star anise has the same flavor as anise seed, and both spices may be used interchangeably. Anise is particularly effective as a flavoring for cookies or sprinkled on sponge cakes. Star anise also makes an attractive garnish for desserts.

VANILLA BEANS

Vanilla beans provide us with vanilla extract, a seasoning widely used in baking and desserts. You can make vanilla sugar by aging a vanilla bean or two in a sealed container of refined sugar.

JUNIPER BERRIES

Dried juniper berries are suitable for seasoning sauces and stocks, meat or fish dishes, and cabbage. They are also used for flavoring gin.

CINNAMON

The small cinnamon tree is a bay leaf plant. Cinnamon is the dried inner bark of the tree. Ceylon cinnamon is mildly spicy and has a light color. Cassia is slightly bitter and darker. Cinnamon is sold in sticks or ground to a powder. It is used for desserts, added to drinks or coffee, and, in small quantities, as a seasoning for meat and seafood.

CLASSIC CUISINE

From puff pastries to paté and terrine, appetizers make a light, delicious introduction to an elegant lunch or dinner. The appetizer shown here is a salad of avocado, button mushrooms, shrimp, and caviar dressed with a cream marinade.

QUEEEN VOL-AU-VENTS

Yield: 6 servings
For the pastry shells:
1 package frozen puff pastry, thawed
1 egg yolk, beaten
For the filling:
½ cup diced cooked veal
½ cup diced cooked chicken
½ cup quartered mushrooms, sautéed
½ cup diced pickled beef tongue
For the white sauce:
1 small onion, peeled and diced
2 tablespoons butter
1 tablespoon flour
1⅔ cups chicken stock
1 cup heavy cream
1 teaspoon salt
1 tablespoon lemon juice
1 tablespoon Worcestershire sauce

1. Puff pastry is needed to make the delicate crispy cases for this vol-au-vent. It is difficult to make puff pastry, so this recipe uses a prepared frozen puff pastry. Packaged puff pastry contains 3 to 5 slabs of puff pastry.

2. Separate the slabs of puff pastry (photograph left), and thaw for 20 minutes at room temperature. Brush every second slab with beaten egg white, lay slabs on top of each other, and press lightly with a rolling pin. Puff pastry must always be rolled from the outside edges—this ensures that the dough bakes evenly. Cut circles of dough, using round 2-inch and 3-inch cookie cutters. Lightly knead the remaining dough together and roll it out to about ⅛-inch thickness.

3. Cut 3-inch bases and 2-inch tops from the rolled dough. The round cutters must be sharp. Blunt cutters press the edges of the dough together, and prevent it from rising properly.

4. Rinse a baking sheet with cold water and place the pastry bases on it. Brush the tops of the bases with beaten egg yolk, being careful that the yolk does not run over the edges of the pastry. Place the tops onto the bases.

5. Brush the surfaces of the pastry with egg yolk. Prick the dough several times with a fork.

6. The photograph above shows the finished vol-au-vents. Before they are baked, the puff pastry must stand for 15 minutes. Bake the pastry in a preheated 400°F oven for about 15 minutes, or until golden brown. To make the filling (photograph left), finely dice ½ cup each of boiled veal and boiled chicken. Mix with ½ cup quartered, braised mushrooms and ¼ cup pickled and diced beef tongue. Refrigerate.

7. To prepare a white sauce, sauté 1 small diced onion in 2 teaspoons butter until the onion is transparent. Whisk in 1 heaped tablespoon flour and sauté for 10 more minutes. Add 1⅔ cups chicken stock and simmer for 20 minutes. Boil 1 cup whipping cream until it is reduced by one half and stir into the stock mixture. Stir this into the meat mixture. Season with 1 teaspoon salt, 1 tablespoon lemon juice, and 1 tablespoon Worcestershire sauce. Spoon some of the filling into each vol-au-vent.

SALMON TERRINE

Yield: 4 to 5 cups

2 tablespoons butter
1 small onion, peeled and finely diced
2 salmon fillets (about 1 pound), skin and bones removed
3 slices fresh white bread, crusts removed and cubed
1 egg, beaten
Salt
White pepper
Grated nutmeg
1-½ cups whipping cream
1 tablespoon chopped fresh dill
Butter for greasing

1

Melt the butter in a heavy frying pan and sauté the onion over low heat until transparent, stirring constantly; do not allow the onion to brown. Remove from the pan and let cool, reserving the butter.

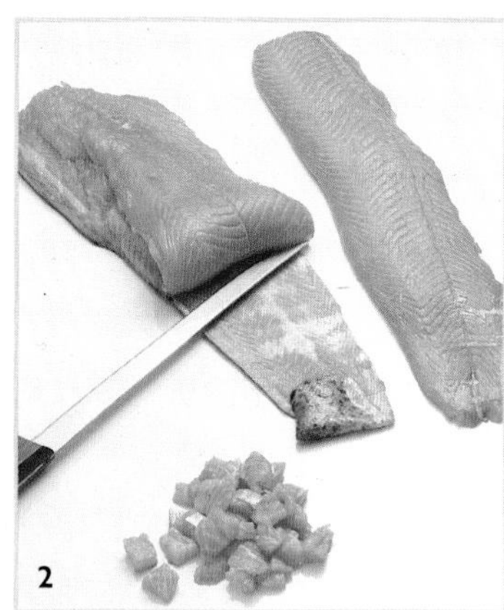

2

Place one of the salmon fillets, covered, in the refrigerator; dice the other fillet.

3

Mix the diced salmon with the onion, melted butter from the frying pan, and bread cubes. Add the egg, 1 teaspoon salt, and a pinch of pepper and nutmeg. Pour in the cream, cover, and refrigerate for at least 1 hour.

4

Puree the cold mixture, a little at a time, in a blender, then put the puree in a small bowl. Work quickly so the puree remains cold; if it warms, the puree will become lumpy.

5

Fill a large bowl with crushed ice. Place the bowl of puree in the bowl of ice. Stir the puree with a spatula until smooth and shiny. Fold in the chopped dill and season with salt and pepper to taste.

6

Thoroughly grease a 4-cup, long terrine mold with butter. Pour in half of the puree and smooth with a spatula, forcing the air bubbles out of the mixture. Remove the salmon fillet from the refrigerator and salt lightly. Place the salmon in the mold and cover with the remaining puree; smooth with a spatula.

7

Fill a large baking pan with water and heat the water to 200°F. Place the mold in the pan of water, making sure that the mold is about ¾ submerged in the water, that is, that ¼ of the depth of the mold is still above the water level. Cover and cook for 50 minutes in a 200°F oven. Remove from the oven and let cool (photograph above).

To serve, unmold the terrine, slice and arrange on a plate (photograph right) with lettuce and a vinaigrette dressing.

HAM MOUSSE

Yield: 6 to 8 servings
⅓ package gelatin
1 cup light Veal Stock (see Index)
¼ cup boiled ham
Salt
White pepper
1 cup whipping cream
Meat consommé aspic, for garnish

Follow the step-by-step instructions to prepare this delicious mousse.

Dissolve the gelatin in lukewarm water. Add the veal stock and set aside.

Puree the ham in a blender or food processor for 2 minutes, or until very smooth. Gradually add the veal stock mixture. Strain out any pieces of ham and season with salt and pepper. Let the mixture cool but not set.

Whip the cream until stiff peaks are formed and fold gently into the mousse, a little at a time, using a large spatula. Cover and refrigerate until set.

To serve, place 2 tablespoons of the mousse on each plate and garnish with pieces of meat aspic.

LEEK AND CHEESE FLANS

Yield: 4 servings
1½ cups flour
¼ cup unsalted butter
Salt
4 to 6 tablespoons water
1 small egg
½ cup Béchamel Sauce (see Index)
2 tablespoons grated Emmenthaler cheese
2 tablespoons whipped cream
3 leeks, cut in julienne strips and blanched in salt water
2 strips cooked bacon
2 slices Emmenthaler cheese

Follow the step-by-step instructions to prepare this elegant appetizer.

Blend the flour, butter, and salt in a food processor until just mixed. Add the egg and 1 tablespoon of water at a time until the mixture forms a ball. Cover the dough with plastic wrap and refrigerate for 1 hour.

Heat the Béchamel sauce in a saucepan and add the grated Emmenthaler and whipped cream. Stir in the leeks and bacon.

Roll the dough out on a floured board and line 4 individual tart pans with it. Refrigerate for 15 minutes, then bake in a preheated 425°F oven for 10 minutes. Remove from the oven and cool.

Place the cheese slices in the tart pans and spoon the leek mixture on top. Bake on the highest rack in a 450°F oven about 12 minutes, or until golden brown.

MARINATED PEPPERS

Yield: 4 servings
1 small red pepper
1 small yellow pepper
1 small green pepper
Salt
Pepper
2 cloves garlic, peeled and crushed
3 sprigs parsley, chopped
Juice of ½ lemon
6 tablespoons olive oil

Preheat the oven to 500°F. Roast the peppers on an oiled baking sheet for 15 minutes, until the skins become black and blistered. Place the peppers in a paper bag for 5 minutes. Peel off the skins, halve the pods, and remove the seeds and white cores, reserving any juice. Cut the peppers in 1-inch strips and arrange on a plate. Season with salt and freshly ground pepper.

Sprinkle garlic and parsley over the peppers. Combine the lemon juice, reserved pepper juice, and olive oil and pour over the peppers. Marinate for 2 hours before serving.

MARINATED EGGPLANT

Yield: 6 servings
1 large eggplant, sliced
1 tablespoon olive oil
Salt
½ cup plum tomatoes, strained and seeded
2 cloves garlic, peeled and crushed
Pepper
½ teaspoon dried oregano
⅛ cup parsley, chopped

Sprinkle the eggplant well with salt and set aside for 30 minutes to drain; rinse and dry well.

Heat the oil in a frying pan and sauté the eggplant slices until golden, turning occasionally. Add the tomatoes and garlic and season with salt, freshly ground pepper, and oregano. Bring to a boil, then transfer the eggplant mixture to a plate; cool at room temperature.

To serve, sprinkle with parsley.

SWEET AND SOUR PEARL ONIONS

Yield: 8 to 10 servings
1½ pounds pearl onions, peeled
4 cups salt water
½ large red pepper, cubed
1 cup wine vinegar
½ cup water
1½ cups sugar
Cloves
1 teaspoon mustard seeds
1 tablespoon pickling spice

Cook the onions in boiling salt water for 1 minute; drain. Put the onions and pepper cubes in prepared jars.

Combine the wine vinegar, water, sugar, cloves, and mustard seeds in another saucepan and boil for 5 minutes; remove from the heat. Stir in the pickling spice, then pour the mixture over the vegetables. Let cool, seal with foil or screwtop lids, and store in a cool place.

MARINATED BEANS

Yield: 8 servings
1 large onion, peeled and diced
Salt
2 cloves garlic, peeled and crushed
Pepper
½ teaspoon dried oregano
4 tablespoons red wine vinegar
5 tablespoons olive oil
½ cup parsley, chopped
1 (1-pound) can red kidney beans, drained
1 (1-pound) can garbanzo beans, drained

Sprinkle the onion with salt and let stand for 10 minutes. Add the garlic, mustard, freshly ground pepper, oregano, vinegar, oil, and parsley. Pour the liquid over the beans and refrigerate for 2 to 3 hours before serving.

STUFFED AVOCADOS

Yield: 4 servings
2 medium ripe avocados
3 tablespoons lemon juice
2 tablespoons walnut oil
Salt
Pepper
1 tablespoon chopped dill
8 ounces smoked salmon, thinly sliced

Cut the avocados in half and remove the pits. Scoop out the avocado meat with a melon baller, leaving a little remaining in the skin. Sprinkle the avocado balls with lemon juice, to prevent discoloration.

Combine the remaining lemon juice, oil, salt, pepper, and dill. Add the salmon and avocado balls and place in the avocado shells. Let the avocados stand for at least 1 hour before serving.

WHITE HERRING

Yield: 4 servings
$\frac{1}{4}$ cup sweet white wine
1 green cooking apple, peeled and cut in 4 slices
4 white herrings
4 tablespoons cranberries
3 tablespoons whipping cream

Heat the wine in a saucepan and stew the apple for 10 to 15 minutes. Let the apple cool in the wine.

Drain, reserving the wine, and place the apple on a plate.

Roll up the white herrings and stand them on the apple slices. Place 1 cranberry in each herring.

To serve, mix the cream with a little white wine and spread over the fish.

STUFFED MUSHROOMS

Yield: 8 servings
1 large can snails (24 pieces)
24 large mushrooms
1 carrot, peeled and finely chopped
1 scallion, finely chopped
3 cloves garlic, peeled and crushed
3 tablespoons softened butter
3 tablespoons parsley, chopped
Salt
Pepper
Juice of ½ lemon

Place the snails and juice in a saucepan and simmer for 5 minutes; drain.

Remove the stems from the mushrooms and coarsely chop, reserving the caps. Mix the chopped mushrooms with the carrot, scallion, and 1 crushed garlic clove. Melt the butter in a frying pan and sauté the vegetables for 3 to 5 minutes.

Place the mushroom caps, with the opening facing up, in snail dishes. Fill with the vegetables and place a snail on top.

Combine the remaining garlic, softened butter, parsley, salt, pepper, and lemon juice and spread the mixture over the stuffed mushrooms. Bake in a preheated 400°F oven for 20 minutes.

STUFFED TOMATOES WITH FISH MOUSSE

Yield: 2 to 4 servings
1 salmon fillet, with skin and bones removed
2 egg yolks, chilled
8 small tomatoes
Salt
Pepper
1 tablespoon butter
1 tablespoon lemon juice
For the sauce:
1 tablespoon lemon juice
2 tablespoons olive oil
4 tablespoons whipping cream
Salt
Pepper
Cayenne pepper
¼ teaspoon Dijon mustard
1 tablespoon fresh basil leaves, finely chopped

Rinse the fish in cold water and pat dry. Place the fish in the freezer while preparing the tomatoes.

Slice off the tops of the tomatoes and hollow out. Place the tomato shells in a shallow ovenproof dish and season with salt and pepper. Brush with melted butter and cook in a preheated 350° F oven for 10 minutes.

In the meantime, quickly puree the cold fish in a blender or food processor. Add the egg yolks, salt, pepper, and lemon juice and pass the mixture through a food mill.

Remove the tomato shells from the oven and pipe the fish filling into them using a pastry tube with a smooth tip. Cut the tomato lids in penny-sized slices and place on the fish mousse. Bake in a preheated 325°F oven for 30 minutes.

To serve, mix the sauce ingredients together and pour the sauce over the tomatoes.

ASPARAGUS VINAIGRETTE

Yield: 4 to 6 servings
1 pound green asparagus, tied in 4 bundles
Salt water
½ teaspoon sugar
1 teaspoon butter
½ teaspoon honey
2 tablespoons sherry vinegar
Pepper
½ teaspoon Dijon mustard
4 tablespoons walnut oil
5 fresh basil leaves, cut in fine strips

Cook the asparagus, sugar, and butter in salt water for 10 minutes. Drain, reserving the liquid, and arrange on serving plates.

Combine the honey with 1 tablespoon of the reserved asparagus water. Add the vinegar, salt, pepper, and mustard and mix well. Stir in the oil and add the basil leaves.

To serve, pour the sauce over the lukewarm asparagus.

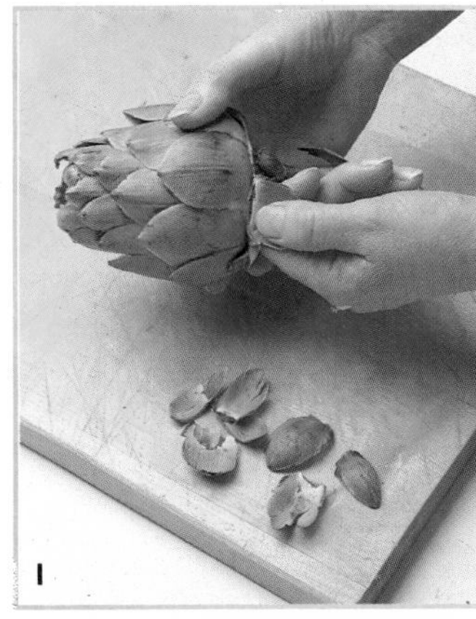
1

2

3

4

ARTICHOKES VINAIGRETTE

Yield: 4 servings
4 artichokes
Lemon juice
Salt
For the vinaigrette:
1 shallot, peeled and crushed
3 tablespoons red wine vinegar
Salt
Pepper
1 pinch sugar
6 tablespoons olive oil
1 tablespoon parsley, chopped
1 small tomato, skinned, seeded, and diced

Wash the artichokes and remove the outer leaves (photograph 1). Cut off the top quarter and stem of the artichokes with a sharp knife; trim the pointed ends of the leaves with scissors until the ends are even. Rub each cut edge with lemon juice.

Put the artichokes in boiling salt water and simmer over low heat for 30 minutes, or until tender. Remove with a slotted spoon (photograph 4) and drain, with the bases up.

To make the vinaigrette, mix the shallot, vinegar, salt, pepper, sugar, olive oil, and parsley together. Add the diced tomatoes.

To serve, place each artichoke on a separate plate with a bowl of vinaigrette.

SALMON CARPACCIO

Yield: 4 servings
10 ounces fresh salmon, without skin or bones
Coarse salt
White pepper
Juice of 1 lime
2 tablespoons olive oil
1 tablespoon whipping cream
2 tablespoons sour cream
3 tablespoons caviar
1 small head lamb's lettuce

Slice the salmon diagonally in ¼-inch strips and arrange on chilled plates. Mix the salt, pepper, lime juice, and olive oil together and sprinkle over the salmon slices.

To serve, combine the whipping cream, sour cream, and caviar. Top each plate with a spoonful of the caviar cream and garnish with leaves from the lettuce that have been thoroughly washed and drained.

BEEF CARPACCIO WITH MUSTARD SAUCE

Yield: 4 servings
5 to 8 ounces fillet of beef, trimmed and slightly frozen
Salt
Freshly ground pepper
Watercress
½ teaspoon Dijon mustard
2 tablespoons balsamic vinegar
2 tablespoons olive oil

Cut the beef in paper-thin slices with an electric knife. Sprinkle 4 plates with salt and pepper and place the beef on top. Garnish with watercress.

Stir the mustard, vinegar, salt, and pepper together and add the olive oil. Serve the meat and sauce separately.

MARINATED MUSHROOMS

Yield: 6 to 8 servings
3 cloves garlic, peeled and quartered
8 tablespoons olive oil
5 tablespoons chicken stock
Juice of ½ lemon
1 bay leaf
8 white peppercorns
½ teaspoon salt
1 pound mushrooms, quartered
Fresh basil leaves for garnish

Bring all of the ingredients except the mushrooms and basil to a boil in a saucepan. Reduce the heat and simmer for 20 minutes. Add the mushrooms and continue simmering for 10 minutes. Remove from the heat and cool to room temperature. Transfer the mushrooms and liquid to a covered container; refrigerate for 1 to 2 days.

Before serving, arrange the mushrooms on a plate and garnish with basil leaves.

SHRIMP SALAD WITH SORREL SAUCE

Yield: 6 to 8 servings
1 large celery root, peeled and sliced
Salt
2 avocados, peeled and diced
15 to 20 cooked and peeled shrimp
½ cup peanuts
1 tablespoon sunflower oil
For the sauce:
½ cup sorrel
¼ cup whipping cream
Juice of ½ lemon
Pepper
Salt
2 drops Tabasco sauce

Blanch the celery root in boiling salt water for 12 to 15 minutes, or until tender. Drain and cut in small cubes. Mix the avocados, celery root, shrimp, peanuts, and oil together. Set aside.

Wash the sorrel and remove the stalks. Reserve a few leaves for the plates and cut the rest in fine strips. Combine the strips with the cream, lemon juice, pepper, salt, and Tabasco sauce.

To serve, arrange the sorrel leaves on plates, pour the sauce over the greens, and place the shrimp on top.

ARTICHOKE BOTTOMS WITH EGG CREAM

Yield: 6 servings
Yolks from 3 hard-boiled eggs
1 tablespoon butter
1 tablespoon whipping cream
1 tablespoon buttermilk
2 anchovy fillets
2 teaspoons capers
Pepper
Grated nutmeg
½ teaspoon dried thyme
1 can artichoke bottoms, drained
8 black olives, halved

Puree the egg yolks in a blender or food processor with the butter, cream, buttermilk, anchovies, capers, and 2 teaspoons of caper liquid. Season to taste.

To serve, pipe the egg mixture on the artichoke bottoms using a pastry tube with a jagged tip. Garnish with black olives.

1

2

3

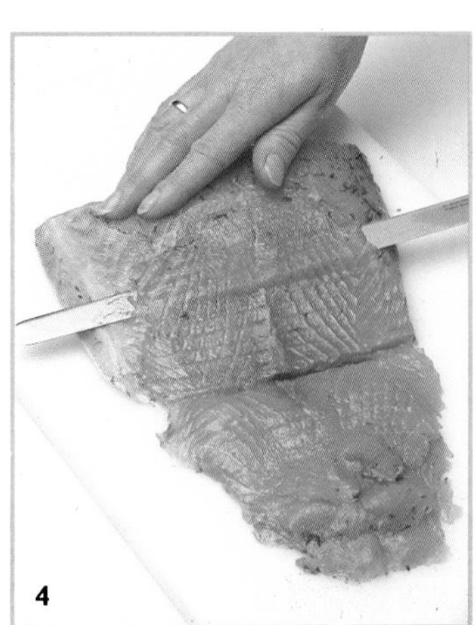
4

SALMON WITH MUSTARD SAUCE

Yield: 8 to 10 servings
1 pound salmon, with skin and bones removed
5 coriander seeds, crushed
1 tablespoon sugar
1½ teaspoons freshly ground pepper
1 teaspoon coarse salt
2 bunches fresh dill, roughly chopped
For the mustard sauce:
1½ tablespoons hot mustard
1 tablespoon sugar
2 tablespoons wine vinegar
5 tablespoons olive oil
1 tablespoon finely chopped fresh dill
For serving:
A few inner leaves of romaine lettuce
½ teaspoon red peppercorns

Halve the salmon lengthwise and remove all bones (photograph 1). Mix the coriander, sugar, pepper, and salt together and rub the inside of the fish with the mixture. Sprinkle the dill over the salmon (photograph 2). Place the halves back together and wrap firmly in plastic wrap. Flatten the salmon with a board or weights (photograph 3) and refrigerate for 2 days, turning several times. Scrape off the herbs and cut the salmon diagonally in very thin slices (photograph 4).

Stir the sauce ingredients together with a whisk.

To serve, arrange the salmon on individual plates with a little sauce and some lettuce leaves; sprinkle with red peppercorns. Serve the remaining sauce separately.

CHINESE CABBAGE

Yield: 4 to 6 servings
1 medium Chinese cabbage
8 ounces beef or pork tenderloin, cut in ¼-inch strips
3 small oranges, peeled
1 grapefruit, peeled
1 cup seedless red grapes, halved
7 tablespoons mayonnaise
1 tablespoon brandy
Salt
Pepper

Cut the cabbage leaves in 1-inch strips, then wash and drain them. Separate the oranges and grapefruit into segments, removing the white membranes and seeds and reserving the juice. Arrange the fruit and the cabbage strips in a bowl.

Mix the mayonnaise, reserved orange and grapefruit juice, and brandy together; season to taste.To serve, pour the sauce over the fruit and cabbage.

PICKLED FISH

Yield: 4 servings
8 to 10 ounces angler fish, sea trout, or salmon fillets, bones and skin removed
Salt
Pepper
Juice of ½ lemon
1 small ripe avocado, peeled and diced
1 cup button mushrooms, finely sliced
1 small plum tomato, diced
½ teaspoon red peppercorns
Fresh mint leaves

Cut the fish in very small cubes and place in a shallow dish. Lightly season with salt and pepper and a little of the lemon juice. Cover with plastic wrap and refrigerate for 2 hours.

Sprinkle the diced avocado with the remaining lemon juice.

To serve, place the fish in the center of a plate and arrange the avocado, mushrooms, and tomato in circles around it. Sprinkle with red peppercorns and garnish with mint leaves.

VEAL AND PARMA ROLLS

Yield: 4 servings
4 thin veal scallops (about 4½ ounces each)
Pepper
1 clove garlic, peeled and crushed
4 slices Parma ham
8 fresh sage leaves
1½ tablespoons ice-cold butter
2 tablespoons olive oil
½ cup beef stock
5 tablespoons Marsala wine or sherry

Lightly pound the veal slices until slightly flattened. Season with pepper and rub with garlic. Place 1 slice of ham and 2 sage leaves on each veal scallop. Roll up tightly and fasten with toothpicks.

Heat 1 tablespoon of butter and the olive oil in a frying pan and sauté the rolls on all sides. Add the stock, cover the pan, and cook slowly over low heat for 20 minutes. Remove the rolls from the pan, take out the toothpicks, and cover the meat to keep warm.

Reduce the pan juices to ¼ cup. Add the Marsala or sherry; bring to a boil and reduce by half. Remove from the heat and add the remaining butter, a little at a time.

To serve, cut the veal rolls in ½-inch slices and serve with the sauce.

SHRIMP IN CREAM CURRY

Yield: 4 servings
1 tablespoon butter
4 small scallions, cut in thin rings
12 shrimp, peeled and deveined
½ tablespoon mild curry powder
½ cup dry white wine
¼ cup whipping cream
2 tablespoons buttermilk
Salt
1 pinch cayenne pepper
1 tablespoon pistachio nuts, chopped

Heat the butter in a frying pan and sauté the scallions until softened. Add the shrimp and sauté 2 to 3 minutes, until they turn pink. Remove the shrimp and keep warm.

Sprinkle the curry powder into the pan and heat briefly. Add the wine and boil rapidly until the liquid is reduced by half. Stir in the cream and buttermilk, and season with salt and cayenne pepper.

To serve, arrange the shrimp on individual plates and cover with sauce. Sprinkle with chopped pistachios.

TURKEY ROLLS IN WINE SAUCE

Yield: 4 servings
4 very thin slices turkey breast
2 teaspoons savory mustard
1 cup spinach, blanched briefly and drained
3 small carrots, cut in julienne strips
Pepper
1½ tablespoons clarified butter
½ cup dry vermouth
½ cup whipping cream

Brush the turkey slices with mustard and cover each slice with spinach leaves and 3 carrot sticks. Season lightly with pepper. Roll up the turkey slices and fasten with toothpicks.

Heat the clarified butter in a heavy frying pan and sauté the rolls on all sides. Pour off the fat and add the vermouth. Cover the pan and cook over low heat for 15 minutes. Remove from the heat and keep warm.

Boil the pan juices until reduced by half and stir in the remaining mustard and the cream. Pour the sauce into a warm serving dish.To serve, slice the turkey rolls and arrange decoratively on a plate and top with the sauce.

CHICKEN BREASTS IN ORANGE SAUCE

Yield: 8 servings
4 boneless chicken breasts, skinned and sliced
1 tablespoon flour
4 tablespoons peanut oil
4 shallots, peeled and finely chopped
½ teaspoon curry powder
½ cup freshly squeezed orange juice
½ cup chicken stock
3 tablespoons cold butter
Fresh mint leaves
1 orange for garnish

Coat the chicken breasts lightly with flour. Heat the oil in a frying pan and sauté the chicken on all sides over high heat for 2 to 3 minutes. Add the shallots and reduce the heat to the lowest setting. Continue cooking until the shallots are transparent. Add the curry powder, orange juice, and stock; cover and simmer for 20 minutes. Remove the chicken from the pan and keep warm.

Reduce the liquid until it is thick enough to coat the back of a wooden spoon. Remove from the heat and stir in the butter, a little at a time.

To serve, arrange the chicken on warmed plates and cover with the sauce. Garnish with mint leaves and orange segments.

SNAILS

Yield: 6 servings
4 tablespoons softened butter
5 tablespoons whipping cream
2 cloves garlic, peeled and crushed
1 shallot, peeled and crushed
2 tablespoons mixed chopped fresh rosemary, tarragon, thyme, and parsley
Salt
Lemon pepper
2 tablespoons lemon juice
2 medium plum tomatoes, skinned, seeded, and diced
2 cans snails (24 pieces in each)

Mix 3 tablespoons of butter with the cream. Add the garlic, shallot, chopped herbs, salt, pepper, and lemon juice. Knead the mixture thoroughly and set aside.

Melt the remaining butter in a saucepan and warm the tomatoes gently.

In another saucepan, heat the snails in their liquid. Drain the snails and place in 4 small oven-proof dishes. Add the savory butter-cream and diced tomato.

To serve, broil briefly, until browned.

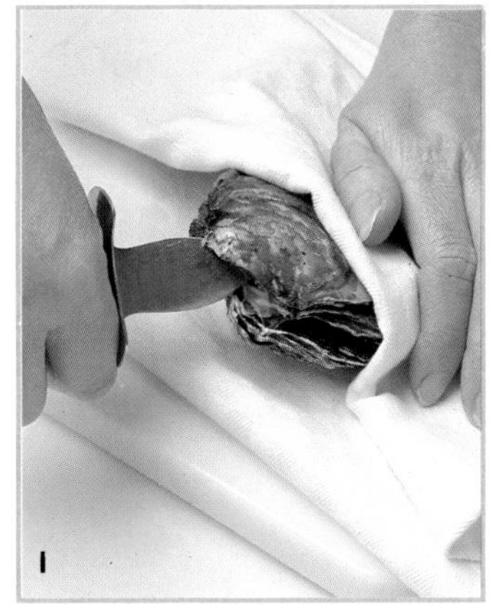
1

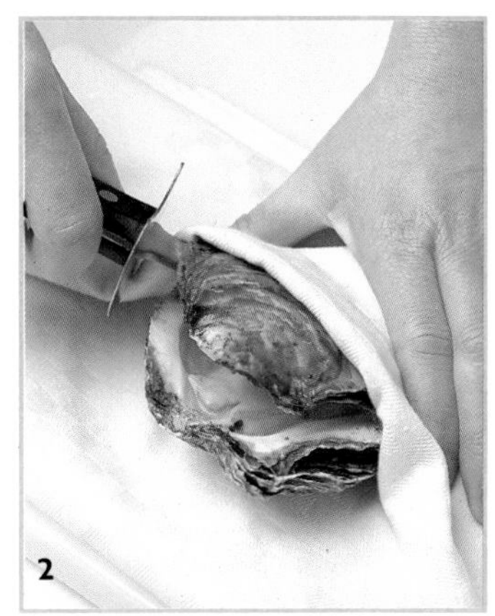
2

3

4

GRILLED OYSTERS

Yield: 4 to 6 servings
18 oysters
3½ tablespoons softened butter
2 tablespoons ground almonds
1 clove garlic, peeled and crushed
3 full sprigs parsley, chopped
Juice of ½ lemon
1 tablespoon brandy
Freshly ground pepper
1 tablespoon almond flakes

Put the oysters on a work surface with the domed side facing down. Place an oyster knife on the pointed side of the oyster, where it hinges, and force the shell open by turning the knife (photograph 1). Separate the shells using the knife (photograph 2).

Mix the butter and almonds together. Add the garlic, parsley, lemon juice, brandy, and pepper. Cover the oysters with the almond butter (photograph 4) and sprinkle with almond flakes. Broil until golden brown.

SHRIMP CRÊPES

Yield: 8 servings
For the crêpes:
Peanut oil
¼ cup flour, sifted
¼ teaspoon salt
3 eggs
½ cup milk
2 tablespoons melted butter
For the filling:
1 tablespoon butter
1 tablespoon flour
1 cup milk
2 tablespoons lemon juice
Salt
Cayenne pepper
1 pinch curry powder
1 egg white
16 shrimp, peeled and deveined
2 tablespoons grated Emmenthaler cheese
½ cup melted butter
Sesame seeds for garnish

To make the crêpes: stir the flour, salt, eggs, milk, and melted butter together quickly until a smooth, runny batter is formed. Set aside for 1 to 4 hours.

Brush a small frying pan with oil and pour 1 small ladle of batter into the pan. Quickly spread the batter evenly by tilting the pan. Sauté for about ½ minute, or until the upper surface begins to set. Turn the crêpe over and cook the other side. Transfer to a plate and cover with waxed paper. Prepare 7 more crêpes in the same manner.

To make the filling, melt the butter in a frying pan and sauté the flour until it turns pale yellow. Add the milk, stirring well with a whisk. Boil the sauce for 5 minutes, stirring constantly. Remove from the heat and cool for 10 seconds, then beat in the egg yolk. Add the lemon juice, salt, cayenne pepper, curry powder, shrimp, and cheese.

Spread the mixture on the crêpes and roll up. Place the crêpes side by side in ovenproof dishes; brush with melted butter and sprinkle with sesame seeds. Bake in a preheated 425°F oven for 20 minutes.

CRÊPES À LA PHILIPPINE

Yield: 8 servings
For the batter:
1/4 cup flour
1/4 teaspoon salt
3 eggs
1/2 cup milk
2 tablespoons melted butter
1 tablespoon vegetable oil
For the filling:
1 tablespoon vegetable oil
8 ounces fillet of beef, cut in julienne strips
1 cup string beans
1 medium carrot, cut in julienne strips
1 small leek, cut in julienne strips
1 small can bamboo shoots, cut in julienne strips
8 green leaf lettuce leaves
For the sauce:
1 tablespoon sugar
1 tablespoon soy sauce
1/2 cup vegetable stock
1 tablespoon white wine vinegar
1/4 teaspoon salt
1 teaspoon cornstarch mixed with 2 tablespoons of cold water

Make 8 crêpes following the instructions in Shrimp Crêpes (see previous recipe). Keep warm.

To make the filling, heat the oil in a frying pan and quickly sauté the meat; remove from the pan and keep warm. Add the beans, carrot, leek, and bamboo shoots to the pan and sauté for 3 minutes, or until crisp; remove and keep warm. Spread the lettuce leaves on the crêpes. Cover with the meat and vegetables and roll up.

To make the sauce, bring the sugar, soy sauce, stock, vinegar, and salt to a boil in a saucepan. Add the cornstarch mixture, stirring constantly until the sauce has thickened.

To serve, place the crêpes on individual plates and serve the warm sauce separately.

BUCKWHEAT BLINIS WITH CAVIAR

Yield: 4 to 6 servings
1/2 cup flour
1/2 cup buckwheat flour
1 1/3 cups milk
3 egg yolks
1 teaspoon salt
1 pinch sugar
1 1/2 tablespoons melted butter
3 egg whites, beaten until stiff
1 tablespoon butter
1 tablespoon oil
1/2 cup whipping cream
1/3 cup salmon caviar or Beluga-malossol caviar
Dill for garnish

Sift the flours together. Add milk, egg yolk, salt, sugar, and melted butter and mix until smooth. Set aside for 1 hour, then fold in the egg whites.

Heat the butter and oil in a frying pan. Add the batter a spoonful at a time, pressing it flat, and sauté on both sides; remove from the pan and keep warm.

Serve the blinis topped with cream, caviar, and dill.

HAM PASTRIES

Yield: 8 to 10 servings
For the dough:
1½ cups flour
1 teaspoon baking powder
½ teaspoon salt
3½ tablespoons cold butter
5 tablespoons sour cream
1 egg
For the filling:
1 tablespoon butter
1 medium onion, peeled and diced
1 cup mushrooms, chopped
1 cup cooked ham, finely diced
3 tablespoons fresh dill, finely chopped
1 cup cooked rice
Salt
Pepper
1 egg, separated
2 tablespoons milk

Combine the flour and baking powder and sift into a bowl. Add the salt, butter, sour cream, and egg and mix quickly until smooth, using the dough hook attachment of a mixer. Knead the dough, then wrap in foil and refrigerate for at least 1 hour.

To make the filling, melt the butter in a frying pan and sauté the onion until softened. Add the mushrooms and cook over high heat, stirring constantly, until all liquid has evaporated.

Combine the ham, dill, and rice and add to the onion-mushroom mixture. Season with salt and pepper to taste.

Roll out the dough on a floured surface until ½-inch thick and cut out 8 to 10 4-inch circles. Put some of the filling on each dough round. Brush the edges of the dough with egg white, then fold the dough to form half circles. Press the edges together firmly with a fork.

Place the pastries on a baking sheet lined with parchment baking paper. Combine the egg yolks and milk and brush the top of the pastries with the mixture. Bake at 350°F for 30 minutes or until browned.

HALIBUT PUFF PASTRIES

Yield: 6 to 8 servings

1 pound smoked halibut, skin and bones removed, finely chopped
3 tablespoons fresh dill, chopped
1 package frozen puff pastry, thawed
1 egg white, beaten
1 egg yolk, beaten
2 tablespoons milk

Mix the chopped fish and dill together. Roll out the puff pastry sheets individually and cover half of each sheet with the fish filling. Brush the edges of the pastry with the egg white and fold over, pressing the edges together firmly. Cut the pastry into fish shapes. Shape the pastry remnants into fins and decorations, and position on the pastry fish; brush with egg white to seal in place.

Place the pastries on a baking sheet lined with baking parchment. Brush the tops of the pastries with the egg yolk and milk. Bake in a preheated 425°F oven for 20 minutes. Serve warm, with sour cream.

MUSHROOM AND NUT PIES

Yield: 6 to 8 servings

Butter
1 package frozen puff pastry, thawed
½ cup sliced mushrooms
½ cup ricotta cheese
3 tablespoons feta cheese
¼ cup walnuts, chopped
3 egg yolks

Grease 6 small pie or tart pans with butter. Roll out the puff pastry sheets to ⅛-inch thickness and cut out circles about a third larger than the diameter of the pans. Line the pans with the pastry circles.

Sauté the mushrooms for 3 minutes in a 1 tablespoon oil. Stir the cheeses together with the nuts, mushrooms and all but 1 teaspoon of the egg yolks. Spread the cheese mixture on top of the pastry circles. Cut the pastry remnants in thin strips and make a trellis pattern over the filling. Beat the remaining 1 teaspoon of egg yolk with 1 tablespoon of water and brush the pastry strips with the mixture.

Bake the pies on the lowest rack in a preheated 425°F oven for 30 minutes.

MINIATURE PIZZAS

Yield: 8 to 10 servings
For the dough:
4 cups flour, sifted
1 package dried yeast
1 teaspoon salt
4 tablespoons olive oil
½ teaspoon sugar
1 cup lukewarm water
For the topping:
8 medium tomatoes, sliced ¼ inch thick
14 ounces mozzarella cheese, sliced
18 pitted black olives
6 anchovy fillets
1 teaspoon dried thyme
3 tablespoons olive oil
1 pound shrimp, shelled and deveined
1 egg
2 tablespoons whipping cream
Salt
Pepper
3 tablespoons chopped parsley
¼ cup Parmesan cheese, grated

Dissolve the yeast and sugar in the water. Add the salt and olive oil. Mix in the flour ½ cup at a time, and knead to form a smooth dough. Place on a floured bread board and knead again thoroughly. Dust the dough with flour, cover, and leave in a warm place until doubled in volume. Knead the dough again quickly, forming a long roll. Cut the dough in 12 equal pieces and roll each one into a circle, about ⅛-inch thick, leaving the edges a little thicker than the centers. Place the dough circles on a greased baking sheet.

Cover 6 of the pizza shells first with tomatoes, then with mozzarella, olives, and anchovies. Season with thyme and sprinkle with olive oil. Cover the remaining pizza shells with the shrimp. Stir the egg and cream together and spread over the shrimp. Sprinkle with salt, pepper, parsley, and Parmesan cheese. Bake the pizzas in a preheated 425°F oven for 20 minutes and serve hot.

CHEESE TARTLETS

Yield: 4 servings
For the dough:
½ cup flour, sifted
¼ teaspoon salt
3 tablespoons cold butter
2 tablespoons cold water
For the topping:
1 cup ricotta cheese
3½ tablespoons butter, softened
1 tablespoon flour
Salt
Pepper
2 small eggs
1 clove garlic, peeled and finely diced
2 tablespoons parsley, chopped
2 tablespoons pine nuts
1 thick slice baked ham, diced
6 fresh sage leaves

Mix the dough ingredients together quickly to make a smooth dough. Refrigerate for 30 minutes. Roll out the dough to ¼-inch thickness on a floured bread board and line 4 small, greased tart pans (diameter 4 inches) with the pastry.

To make the topping, stir the cheese, flour, salt, pepper, and softened butter together. Gradually stir in the eggs. Add the garlic and parsley to half of the cheese mixture and fill 2 of the tart pans with this mixture. Sprinkle with pine nuts, pressing them in slightly.

Put the remaining cheese mixture in the other 2 tart pans. Spread the diced ham over the cheese and lay the sage leaves on top. Bake the tarts in a preheated 400°F oven for 15 to 20 minutes. Serve lukewarm.

SMOKED FISH PASTE

Yield: 4 to 6 servings
2 smoked trout fillets, cut in bite-sized pieces
7 tablespoons butter, softened
3 tablespoons sour cream
2 tablespoons lemon juice
Salt
Freshly ground pepper
Watercress
½ teaspoon red peppercorns

Puree the trout in a food processor and mix with the butter, sour cream, and lemon juice. Season with salt and pepper to taste and refrigerate for 1 hour.

Arrange the fish paste on 4 plates. Garnish with watercress and sprinkle with red peppercorns. Serve with toasted croutons.

SHRIMP PASTE

Yield: 4 servings
30 to 40 cooked shrimp, peeled and deveined
Juice of ½ lemon
½ cup whipping cream
Pinch of horseradish
Freshly ground pepper
2 to 3 tablespoons parsley, chopped
Watercress

Set aside 12 shrimp and puree the rest in a food processor. Stir the shrimp puree with the lemon juice until smooth and season to taste with horseradish and pepper. Stir in the parsley and refrigerate for 1 hour.

To serve, arrange the shrimp paste on 4 plates and garnish with the reserved shrimp and watercress.

RAW BEEF PUREE

Yield: 4 servings
2 tablespoons butter
2 shallots, peeled and finely chopped
1/4 cup parsley, finely chopped
1 1 pound fillet of beef, finely minced
1 tablespoon mustard
Cayenne pepper
Salt
4 to 5 tablespoons chives, finely chopped

Melt the butter in a frying pan and sauté the shallots and parsley. Remove from the heat and combine with the meat, mustard, cayenne pepper, and salt. Refrigerate for 30 minutes.

To serve, arrange the beef on 4 plates and garnish with the chives.

VEGETABLE TERRINE

Yield: 10 to 12 servings
2 large carrots, peeled and cut into 1 inch
½ pound broccoli, divided in florets
2 large red peppers
½ cup milk
3 teaspoons vegetable stock
Cayenne pepper
3 small egg yolks, beaten
2 packages unflavored gelatin
½ cup whipping cream
Curry powder

Cook the carrots and broccoli separately in salt water until cooked but firm, about 12 minutes for carrots and 5 minutes for broccoli. Roast the peppers on an oiled baking sheet in a preheated 500°F for about 15 minutes, until the skins become dark and small bubbles form. Remove from the oven and place in a paper bag for 5 minutes. Peel off the skin, halve the peppers, and remove the seeds. Puree the carrots, broccoli, and peppers separately and let cool. Stir a teaspoon of stock in each puree and season with cayenne pepper.

Beat the egg yolks in the top of a double boiler over boiling water until light and creamy. Dissolve the gelatin according to the package directions, then add to the egg yolks. Fold the cream into the mixture and season to taste with salt, pepper, and a pinch of curry powder. Divide the mixture evenly in 4 bowls; add the carrot puree to one bowl, the broccoli puree to another, and the pepper puree to the third bowl. Mix well and season to taste.

Grease a 4-cup terrine mold with butter. Layer the mixtures from each bowl, spreading until smooth; allow the terrine to cool after each layer. Chill overnight in the refrigerator.

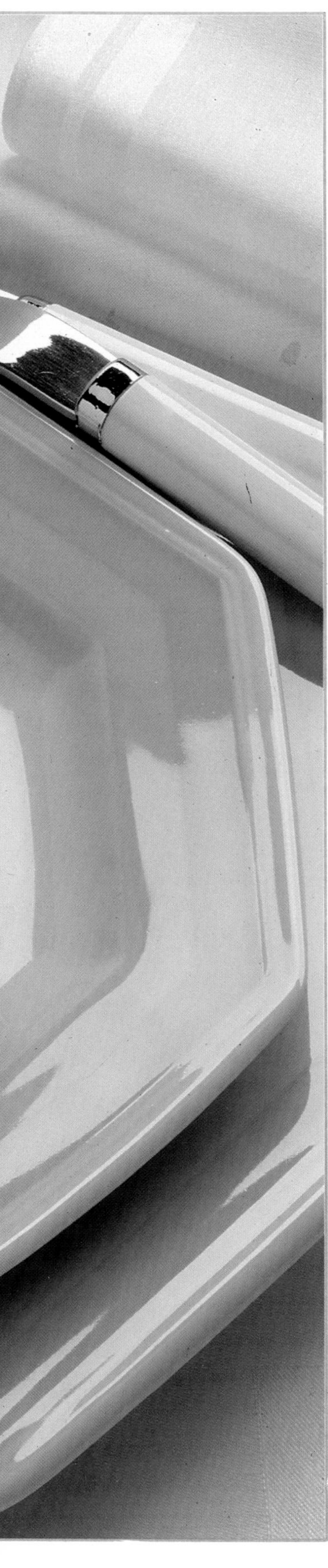

MIXED FISH TERRINE

Yield: 8 to 10 servings
2 salmon fillets, skin and bones removed
2 turbot fillets, skin and bones removed
2 egg whites
1 large carrot
1 large zucchini
Salt
¾ cup cold whipping cream
Pepper
Cayenne pepper
Curry powder
2 tablespoons lemon juice

Set aside 1 thick slice of the salmon and turbot. Puree the rest of each fish separately in a blender or food processor, adding 1 egg white to each. Refrigerate the fish slices and the purees.

Slice wide strips from the carrot and zucchini using a potato peeler. Blanch the strips in boiling salt water, then plunge into cold water and drain. Grease a 4-cup terrine mold with butter and line it with the vegetables strips.

Stir half of the cream into each of the fish mixtures and season with pepper, cayenne, and curry powder. Spoon the turbot mixture into the terrine mold and lay the reserved fish slices on top. Cover with the salmon mixture, spread until smooth, and top with the remaining vegetable strips. Cover the terrine and place in a water-filled baking pan (water should reach halfway up the sides of the mold). Poach in a preheated 300°F oven for 1 hour. Cool at room temperature, then refrigerate for 12 hours.

Serve with a sauce of whipping cream seasoned with salt, pepper, lemon juice, and finely chopped basil leaves.

CHICKEN LIVER TERRINE

Yield: 8 to 10 servings
1 pound butter
1 large apple, peeled and cut in small 1 inch pieces
2 shallots, peeled and quartered
½ cup port wine
½ teaspoon thyme
½ teaspoon marjoram
1 pound chicken liver, cut roughly in pieces
1 cup whipping cream
2 eggs
Salt
½ teaspoon pepper
1 teaspoon cayenne pepper
Chopped pistachio nuts
Orange segments

Melt 1 tablespoon of the butter in a large frying pan and sauté the onion and apple until tender. Add the port and herbs and boil until half of the liquid has evaporated; let cool.

Puree the liver and apple mixture in a blender or food processor. Melt the remaining butter over low heat and add to the puree with the cream and eggs. Strain the puree through a fine sieve, season to taste, and place in a 4-cup terrine mold. Cover and place the mold in a baking pan filled with water (water should reach halfway up the side of the mold). Poach in a 300°F oven for 45 minutes. When done, it should spring back when touched. Cool at room temperature, then refrigerate for 12 hours.

To serve, scoop out portions with a spoon that has been dipped in hot water, and place on a plate. Garnish with orange segments and chopped pistachio nuts. Serve with a hot sweet sauce made from orange marmalade, orange juice, and cayenne pepper.

HAM PIE

YIELD: 10 to 12 servings

1 pie pastry, see below
1 ½ pound pickled pork leg, without bones
½ pound bacon
2 large onions
2 tablespoons unsalted butter
½ cup dry red wine
2 eggs
¼ cup pistachio nuts
⅔ cup sour cream
Salt
Pepper
1 teaspoon pimiento
1 teaspoon freshly grated nutmeg
½ pound pickled, boiled ox tongue
1 egg, separated
2 tablespoons whipping cream
1 envelope unflavored gelatin
1 cup port wine

Prepare the pie pastry according to the recipe and refrigerate.

Dice the pork and bacon, then process with the coarse and fine blades of a food processor. Refrigerate the meat mixture.

Peel and dice the onions and sauté in the butter until the onions are transparent. Add the red wine and boil until the mixture thickens, about 5 minutes. Remove from heat and cool. Add the onion-wine mixture to the meat mixture, stir in the eggs, pistachio nuts, and sour cream. Season with salt and pepper to taste. Refrigerate.

Cut the pickled tongue into ½-inch strips.

Grease a 9 inch × 5 inch loaf pan. Roll out about ¾ of the pie pastry on a floured bread board to a 12 inch × 7 inch rectangle and about ⅛-inch thick. Make a 4-inch slice in each corner of the pastry. Carefully fit the pastry into the loaf pan and press it lightly against the sides (photograph 1). Spoon the filling into the pastry to a depth of about 1 inch. Lay the strips of tongue in the middle (photograph 2). Spoon the remaining filling over the tongue and spread it smooth. Fold the extra pastry over the filling. Roll out the remaining pastry to ⅛-inch thickness and place over the top of the loaf (photograph 3). Cut holes in the top pastry to allow the steam to escape.

Cut small leaf shapes from the remaining pastry. Beat the egg white and brush it onto the surface of the pastry. Place the leaves in an attractive pattern on the top of the pastry.

Make 2 rolls of aluminum foil to fit the steam vents in the pastry. Place them into the steam vents in the pastry to form "chimneys" (photograph 4). Beat the egg yolk and cream together and brush over the pastry.

Bake the pastry in a preheated 400°F oven for 15 minutes, then reduce oven to 350°F and bake for 35 minutes. Cool to room temperature, then refrigerate while making wine jelly.

To make the wine jelly, dissolve the gelatin according to package directions. Stir in the port wine. Place the gelatin mixture bowl into an iced water bath and stir until it begins to set.

Pour the wine jelly into the pie through the "chimneys." Refrigerate the pie to set the gelatin.

PIE PASTRY

Yield: 1 9-inch pastry

1 ½ cups flour
1 teaspoon salt
1 cup cold butter
1 small egg

Sift the flour and salt into a bowl and quickly mix the butter and eggs into the flour with a fork until a smooth dough forms. Roll out the dough and press into a 9-inch pie plate. Refrigerate until use.

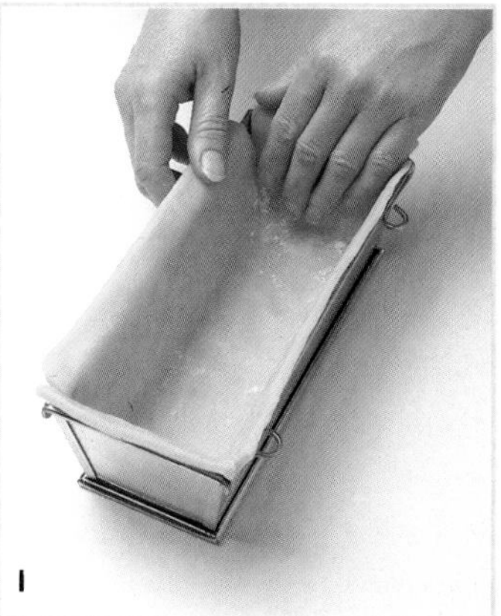

1

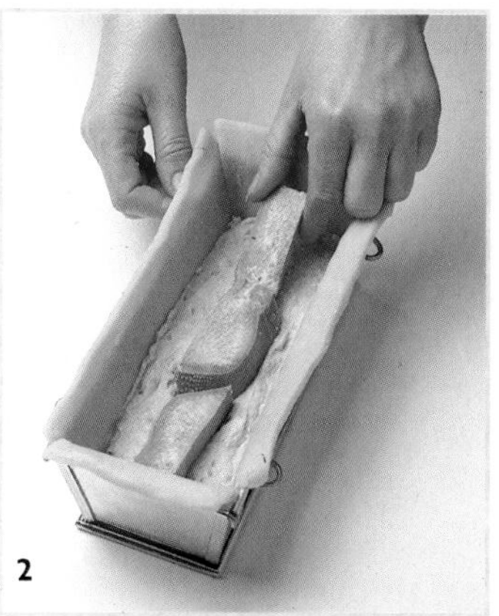

2

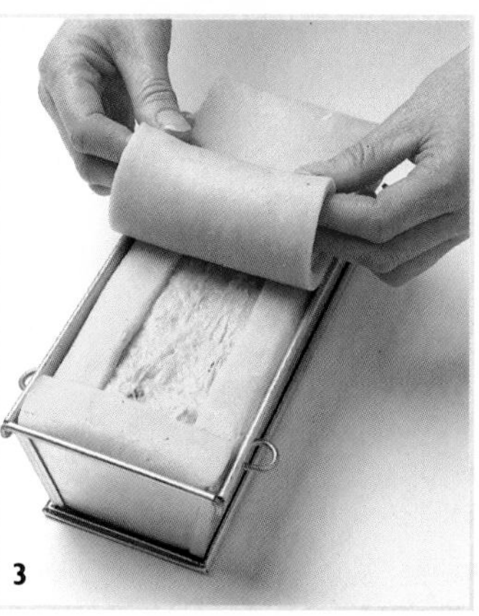

3

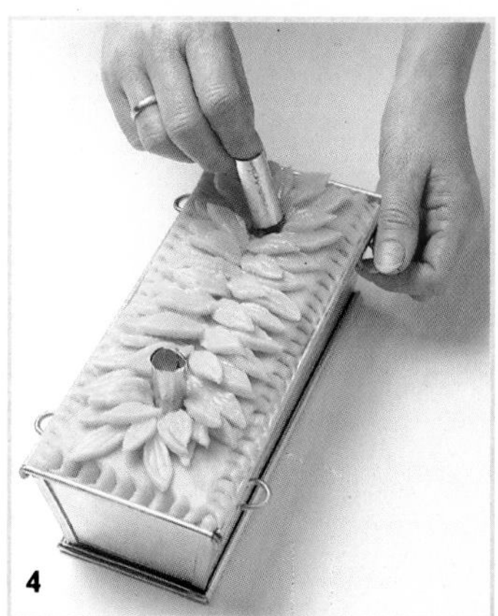

4

CLASSIC CUISINE

Soup can be served hot or cold, as a first course or as a meal in itself. The best foundation for a soup is a homemade stock prepared from meat, fish, or vegetables. Soup stock can be prepared in bulk and stored in the freezer so it will be available whenever needed. Soups served for a first course should be light, such as bouillon or cream soup. Main course soups are much heartier, and often have as ingredients dried peas, beans, or other vegetables.

Broth, or bouillon, is an extract made from meat, bones, vegetables, herbs, and seasonings. Preparing a broth is not complicated, although it is time-consuming, but it is well worth the effort.

1

2

3

4

BASIC STOCK

Yield: About 3 quarts
2 pounds beef shank and rump bones (with meat trimmings)
1 ½ pounds round bone (with meat trimmings)
1 boiling chicken, cut in large pieces
12 to 16 cups water
2 large carrots
1 bunch parsley leaves and stems, finely diced
2 leeks
¼ celeriac, diced
1 celery stalk, diced
2 tablespoons dried thyme, or 2 stalks fresh thyme
2 onions, peeled
2 cloves
1 bay leaf
1 clove garlic

Layer the beef, bones, and chicken in a stockpot (photograph 1). Cover with cold water (photograph 2) and bring to a boil. Skim off the foam with a slotted spoon (photograph 3). Continue skimming until only a white foam, consisting of tiny air bubbles, forms.

Wash the vegetables and herbs. Tie the carrots, parsley, leeks, celeriac, celery stalk, and thyme (photograph 4) together, and put the bouquet garni in the stockpot. Stick a clove in each onion (photograph 5) and put the onions in the stockpot with the rest of the ingredients (photograph 6). Bring to a boil again, then reduce the heat to low and simmer the stock for 6 to 8 hours. Line a large colander or sieve with a piece of cheesecloth and pour the stock through it (photograph 7), reserving the broth.

5

6

7

8

A number of soups can be made from this basic stock, including the following:

Meat Broth, shown in photograph 8, is a very rustic soup, which can be served with added ingredients such as soup noodles, marrow bones, and strips of vegetables. The fat content of the broth is traditionally not removed.

Bouillon is a finer version of a meat broth. The basic broth has had the fat skimmed off and has been enriched with delicate ingredients such as floating dumplings or vegetables cut in julienne strips.

Consommé or clear soup is also known as bouillon, but the bouillon has been cooked for another hour with soup greens and beef, and then strained through fine mesh. Consommé is served with the fat removed and is stronger in flavor than the basic stock. It tastes best with additional seasonings such as stiffly whipped cream flavored with curry powder.

Consommé can be clarified with a mixture of tartar and egg white.

Clarified consommé is a darker and more flavorful soup than consommé and is frequently served as an appetizer.

Soups can be given many nuances of flavor by using different herbs and seasonings. Herbs should be put in a muslin bag and cooked with the soup for 10 minutes; if the herbs are left in too long, the soup will have too strong a flavor.

Seasoning is the key to making a really delicious soup. It is best to start with a small amount of seasoning at first, adding more later if necessary. Nutmeg, saffron, cayenne pepper, Tabasco sauce, soy sauce, pimiento, cinnamon, curry, ginger, mace, and paprika are all seasonings that can be successfully used in soups.

2

3

4

A dash of cognac, brandy, or sherry also adds a gourmet touch to consommé.

Fat can be removed from soups and broths in two ways: in the first method, a highly absorbent paper towel is pulled lightly over the surface of the soup while the soup is hot. The towel absorbs the fat (photograph 1). This process should be repeated until all the fat has been removed from the soup. In the second method, the soup is allowed to cool, uncovered, and then is placed in the refrigerator. Cooling causes the fat to rise to the surface. The fat is then lifted off with a spoon and can be used for frying or braising or discarded.

To clarify broth:
For each 4 cups of lukewarm broth, cut 2 large carrots and celery stalks in fine strips and sauté them in 2 tablespoons of oil until glazed. Allow the vegetables to cool and mix with 3 egg whites that have been beaten to soft peaks (photograph 2). Add the mixture to the broth and immediately turn the heat up to the highest setting. Stir continuously and gently in a circular motion, using a broad wooden spoon, to prevent the egg white from sticking. Stop stirring as soon as the egg white starts to cook and begins to float to the surface (photograph 3). Remove from the heat and gently pour the broth through a cheesecloth to strain the soup.

Broth can be stored in tightly sealed containers in the refrigerator for 3 to 5 days. To store in the freezer, pour the cold broth into freezer containers leaving room at the top for expansion (liquid expands as it freezes) (photograph 4).

A meat or fish stock should never be heavily seasoned with salt or other spices during preparation or storage. Stocks that have been salted will become saltier when reduced or frozen. As a general rule, add seasonings when soup is prepared for serving.

Fish soup tastes considerably better when prepared from a basic fish stock. Fish stock can also be made into sauces.

For fish stock, use the heads, bones, fins, and skin of a white fish, such as flounder or grouper.

FISH STOCK

Yield: About 3 quarts
4 tablespoons butter
1 small carrot, sliced
2 small onions, diced
2 leeks, cut in rings
4 tablespoons butter
2 pounds fish scraps from cod, halibut, flounder, or sole (or a mixture of these)
12 cups water
1/4 cup parsley
2 stalks fresh thyme
1/2 cup fennel, chopped
4 celery stalks
1 bay leaf

Melt the butter in a stockpot and sauté the carrot, onions, and leeks until transparent, stirring constantly (photograph 1). Carefully wash the fish, removing the gills, and place in the stockpot; add cold water to cover (photograph 2). Tie the parsley, thyme, fennel, celery, and bay leaf together to make a bouquet garni. Add the bouquet garni to the pot and bring the water to a boil. Skim off the foam that rises to the surface. Reduce the heat and simmer for 30 minutes. Strain the stock through cheesecloth, then return to the stove and boil 15 minutes longer. Clarify the fish stock as directed in the "To Clarify Broth" section.

CREAM OF SWISS CHARD SOUP

Yield: 6 servings
3 cups chicken stock
2 heads swiss chard, washed and stalks removed
Pepper
Grated nutmeg
1 large onion, peeled
1 tablespoon butter, softened
1 tablespoon flour
1 cup whipping cream
¼ cup Roquefort cheese, cut in small pieces
Chopped parsley or chives for garnish

Bring the chicken stock to a boil in a saucepan and add the swiss chard, pepper, nutmeg, and onion. Reduce the heat and simmer until the onion is soft. Puree the soup to a fine consistency in a blender or food processor. Return the soup to the saucepan and bring to a boil again.

Combine the butter and flour, and shape into 1-inch balls. Gradually add the balls to the boiling soup and cook, stirring constantly, for 5 minutes, until the balls have completely dissolved. Add the cream and cheese and stir until well mixed.

To serve, garnish the soup with chopped parsley or chives.

TENDER POTATO SOUP WITH AVOCADO

Yield: 6 to 8 servings
1 pound potatoes, peeled and diced
4 cups beef stock
Pepper
Cumin to taste
3 to 4 sprigs parsley
½ teaspoon lemon peel, grated
1 cup sour cream
1 large ripe avocado, peeled and sliced

Place the potatoes, stock, pepper, and cumin in a large saucepan and bring to a slow boil. Cook for about 30 minutes, until the potatoes are soft. Puree the soup in a blender with the parsley and lemon peel.

Return the soup to the saucepan and heat gently; do not boil again. Add the sour cream and avocado slices and cook for 3 minutes.

To serve, ladle the soup into 4 warmed bowls and sprinkle with pepper.

CREAM OF ENDIVE SOUP

Yield: 6 to 8 servings
1 tablespoon butter
2 heads endive, chopped in wide strips
4 cups meat or vegetable stock
¾ cup cooked rice
¼ cup whipping cream
1 tablespoon lemon juice

Melt the butter in a large saucepan and cook the endive for 3 minutes. Add the stock and rice; bring to a boil. Reduce the heat to low and simmer for 30 minutes.

Puree the soup to a fine consistency in a blender or food processor. Return the soup to the pan and reheat. Add the cream and lemon juice. Serve hot or cold.

Tip: Any kind of lettuce can be substituted for the endive.

CREAM OF OLIVE SOUP WITH GARLIC SALAMI

Yield: 6 to 8 servings
1 tablespoon olive oil
4 large onions, peeled and sliced
4 cups water
2 sprigs fresh thyme
1 cup green olives stuffed with almonds
¼ cup peeled almonds
2 cups dry white wine
¾ cup garlic salami, sliced
⅓ cup goat cheese,cubed

Heat the oil in a heavy saucepan and sauté the onions until transparent. Add the water and thyme and simmer for ½ hour; strain the stock.

Puree a quarter of the stock, the olives, and almonds in a blender or food processor. Place the puree, wine, and remaining stock in a saucepan and cook until heated through.

To serve, ladle the hot soup into 4 warmed bowls and garnish with salami slices and cheese cubes.

CREAM OF MUSSEL SOUP

Yield: 6 to 8 servings
2 large onions, peeled and cut in rings
1 teaspoon oregano
2 tablespoons thyme
1 clove garlic, peeled and finely chopped
¼ cup dry white wine
4 cups water
Salt
Pepper
2 pounds mussels, cleaned, beards removed
6 large tomatoes, peeled, seeded, and pureed
1 cup whipping cream
Worcestershire sauce
Basil leaves

Place the onion, oregano, thyme, garlic, wine, and water in a saucepan and bring to a boil. Add the mussels, salt, and pepper and simmer for 3 to 5 minutes, or until the mussels have opened. Strain the cooking liquid through cheesecloth and set aside. Remove the mussels from their shells, discarding any that have not opened; keep warm.

Heat the reserved cooking liquid and the tomatoes in a saucepan. Add the whipping cream and season to taste with salt, pepper, and Worcestershire sauce. Stir in the mussels. Heat thoroughly, but do not boil.

To serve, ladle the soup into warmed bowls and garnish with basil leaves.

1

2

CREAM OF RED PEPPER SOUP WITH TURKEY BREAST

Yield: 6 to 8 servings
2½ tablespoons butter
1 pound red peppers, seeded and finely pureed
2 large onions, peeled and finely diced
2 tablespoons flour
4 cups stock
3 cups whipping cream
2 teaspoons sweet paprika
½ teaspoon red pepper
Salt
1 cup smoked turkey breast, skin and fat removed, and cut in julienne strips

Melt the butter in a frying pan and sauté the onions. Add the flour and sauté for 3 to 5 minutes, until the flour is light brown in color. Gradually stir in the stock with a wire whisk, taking care that the soup does not become lumpy. Add the cream, pureed peppers, and paprika and simmer for 10 minutes. Season with salt to taste.

Before serving, add the turkey strips and heat gently.

CREAM OF BEET SOUP

YIELD: 4 servings
¾ cup medium prunes, halved and pitted
2 cups light rosé wine
1 pound red beets, tops removed
1 teaspoon cornstarch
3 tablespoons honey
½ cup sour cream
½ teaspoon cinnamon
⅛ teaspoon cloves
Salt

Pour the wine over the prunes and marinate while preparing the other ingredients.

Wash the beets. Boil with water in a saucepan for 15 to 20 minutes. Plunge into cold water, then peel. (Rubber gloves will prevent the beet juice from staining hands.) Puree the beets in a blender or food processor and set aside.

In a large saucepan, bring the puree, prunes, wine and, 1¾ cups water to a boil. Mix the cornstarch with a little cold water, then whisk it into the saucepan. Simmer for about 2 minutes. Stir in the honey and sour cream and season to taste with salt, cinnamon, and cloves. Serve hot or cold.

PUMPKIN AND CHEESE CREAM SOUP

Yield: 4 to 6 servings
3 tablespoons butter
1 pound fresh pumpkin, peeled, seeded, and diced
1 large onion, peeled and finely diced
4 cups vegetable or chicken stock
Pepper
Grated nutmeg
¼ cup Emmenthaler or Gruyère cheese, finely grated

Melt the butter in a frying pan and sauté the diced pumpkin and onion for about 15 minutes. Transfer the pumpkin and onion to a saucepan and add 3 cups of stock; season with pepper and nutmeg. Cook for 20 minutes, or until the pumpkin is soft. Puree the pumpkin soup in a blender or food mill.

Reheat the soup in the saucepan, but do not boil. Add three-quarters of the grated cheese and stir until melted.

To serve, ladle the soup into 4 bowls and garnish with the remaining cheese.

CREAM OF TROUT SOUP WITH MINT

YIELD: 4 servings
2 frozen rainbow trout, about 6 ounces each
2 cups crab stock (see FISH STOCK recipe)
Salt and pepper
2 to 3 sprigs fresh mint
¾ cup dry white wine
2 tablespoons flour
⅔ cup heavy cream

Bring the stock to a rolling boil and place the frozen trout into the boiling stock. Season to taste with salt and pepper.

Wash the mint and remove the leaves. Add the mint stalks (reserving the leaves) and wine to the trout. Simmer over low heat for about 30 minutes. Remove from the heat and strain the stock.

Cool the fish enough to handle it and remove the skin and bones. Puree with ¼ cup of stock in a blender or food processor.

Return the remaining stock to a pan over low heat. Stir the flour with 1 to 2 tablespoons water. Whisk the flour paste into the stock and simmer for 5 minutes. Add the pureed fish.

Set four mint leaves aside and chop the remainder. Stir into the soup together with the heavy cream. Season to taste and pour into soup bowls. Garnish with the remaining mint leaves.

CREAM OF RED LENTIL SOUP

YIELD: 4 servings
1 small onion
1 celery stalk
1 small red pepper
2 small carrots
¾ cup beef cubes
¼ cup coarsely chopped ham
2 tablespoons butter
2 tablespoons tomato puree
Salt and pepper
2 ½ cups meat stock
¾ cup dry red wine
½ pound red lentils
1 cup heavy cream
4 tablespoons sour cherry preserves

Clean, wash, and finely dice the vegetables. Dice the beef and ham. Melt the butter in a 2 quart casserole and sauté the meat. Add the tomato puree and the diced vegetables and simmer for 3 minutes.

Add salt and pepper, stock, wine, and lentils. Simmer over low heat for about 50 minutes.

Puree the soup in a blender or food processor. Add additional water if it is too thick. Season to taste.

Stir the heavy cream and cherry preserves together. Pour the soup into bowls and garnish with a dollop of pink cream.

BRAZIL-NUT CHERVIL CREAM SOUP

YIELD: 4 servings
1 cup shelled Brazil nuts
2 cups milk
2 cups vegetable stock
Salt and pepper
1/8 teaspoon nutmeg
1/4 teaspoon cardamon
1 small bunch fresh chervil
1/2 cup heavy cream
1/8 teaspoon anise seed
2 tablespoons almond liqueur

Remove as much of the brown skin from the nuts as possible. Puree with the milk in a blender or food processor.

In a large saucepan, heat the puree with the stock. Season with salt, pepper, nutmeg, and cardamon.

Rinse the chervil and pat dry with a paper towel. Chop very finely. Whip the cream until it stiffens and stir in the chervil, anise seed, and liqueur. Pour the soup into bowls and place a dollop of cream on each serving.

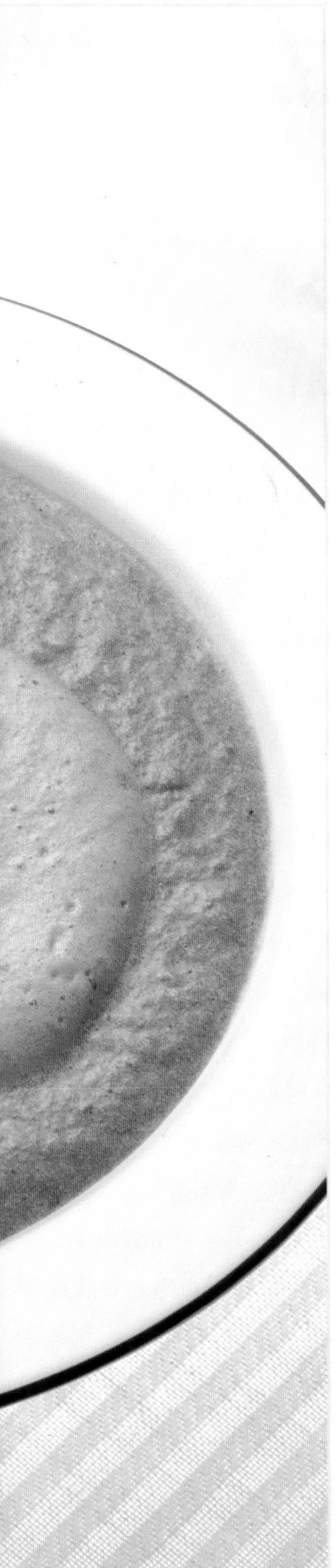

RED CABBAGE SOUP WITH RED WINE

YIELD: 4 to 6 servings
2 tablespoons butter
2 small heads red cabbage, grated
Salt
Cinnamon
Ground cloves
Pepper
1 large apple, peeled and coarsely grated
2 cups vegetable or chicken stock
2 cups dry red wine
2 egg whites, beaten until stiff
2 egg yolks
4 teaspoons cranberry jelly

Melt the butter in a large saucepan and sauté the cabbage for 5 minutes. Season with salt, cinnamon, cloves, and pepper. Add the apple, stock, and red wine and simmer for 1 hour. Puree the soup in a blender or food processor.

Divide the beaten egg whites in half. Mix one half with a ladleful of soup and set aside. Remove the saucepan from the heat and quickly add the other half of the egg whites, stirring constantly. Add the egg yolks, one at a time, and mix thoroughly.

Serve immediately in 4 soup bowls. Garnish with the reserved egg white and cranberry jelly.

PIQUANT APPLE SOUP

Yield: 4 to 6 servings
3 to 5 small onions, peeled, cored and thinly sliced
7 slices thick bacon
1 pound Granny Smith apples, peeled, cored and sliced
2 tablespoons Calvados
3 juniper berries
3 cups chicken stock
Pepper
2 tablespoons flour
1 to 2 tablespoons water

Cut 3 slices of bacon in cubes. Sauté the bacon cubes and the remaining bacon strips in a frying pan until crisp. Drain on paper towels, crumble the cubes, and set aside the 4 strips to use as garnish.

Place the onions in the frying pan and sauté in the bacon fat. Add the apples and continue sautéing for 3 to 4 minutes. Stir in the bacon crumbs, Calvados, juniper berries, and stock; simmer over low heat for 10 to 15 minutes, until the apples are soft but not falling apart. Add pepper to taste and remove the juniper berries.

Mix the flour and water together. Add the flour mixture to the soup, stirring until the soup thickens.

To serve, ladle the soup into 4 bowls and garnish with the reserved strips of bacon.

GRILLED SPINACH SOUP

Yield: 4 servings
1 pound frozen chopped spinach
1 cup water
1 cup milk
1 clove garlic, peeled and finely diced
½ cup whipping cream
Salt
Pepper
4 slices French bread, toasted
1 small onion, peeled and finely diced
8 ounces Mozzarella cheese, cut in thin slices

Put the spinach, water, and milk in a saucepan. Slowly bring to a boil over medium heat. Add the garlic and cream and season with salt and pepper to taste.

Pour the soup into 4 ovenproof soup bowls. Sprinkle the toasted bread slices with onion and cover with cheese. Float the cheese-covered toast on the soup. Place the soup bowls in a preheated broiler and broil until the cheese melts. Serve immediately.

GRATED COCONUT SOUP

Yield: 4 to 6 servings
2 medium fresh coconuts
1 cup chicken stock
½ cup dry white wine
½ cup uncooked vermicelli
2 tablespoons butter
1 clove garlic, peeled and finely chopped
1 to 2 scallions, finely chopped
2 small carrots, peeled and coarsely grated
Salt
Soy sauce
Pepper
1 tablespoon lemon juice
2 teaspoons curry powder
8 ounces fish fillet, cut in small cubes
½ cup whipping cream

Cut the coconuts in half, reserving the milk. Remove the coconut meat with a teaspoon (photograph 1) and cut off the thin brown skin (photograph 2). Reserve the shells. Coarsely grate the coconut meat and set aside.

Combine the wine and stock in a bowl and soak the vermicelli for 15 minutes.

Melt the butter in a saucepan and sauté the garlic, scallions, and carrots. Season with soy sauce, pepper, lemon juice, and 1 teaspoon of curry powder. Add the vermicelli, wine-stock mixture, and reserved coconut milk and bring to a boil. Add the fish cubes (photograph 3).

Cover the outsides of the coconut shells with aluminum foil and fill with soup (photograph 4). Mix the cream with the remaining curry powder and grated coconut and spoon the mixture on top of the soup. Broil until toasted and browned on top. Serve hot.

1

2

3

4

ASPARAGUS AND RICE SOUP

Yield: 4 servings
1 pound asparagus
4 cups water
1 cup long-grain rice
¾ cup salted water
1 bunch fresh chervil
2 cups chicken stock
Salt and pepper
⅛ teaspoon nutmeg
1 teaspoon lemon juice

Peel the asparagus from top to bottom and completely remove the woody sections. Set peelings aside and discard woody sections. Wash the asparagus and cut into 1-inch strips. Bring the salted water to a boil and boil the peelings for 15 minutes. Strain and reserve the water.

Place the asparagus pieces in the reserved water, bring to a boil, and simmer asparagus for 15 minutes.

Bring 2 cups water to a boil and add the rice. Bring the water to a boil again and simmer the rice, covered, for 15 minutes. Drain the rice and rinse with cold water. Drain again.

Carefully rinse the chervil with cold water, pat dry, and finely chop. Melt the butter and sauté the chervil.

Add the chicken stock and bring the mixture to a boil. Add the asparagus, asparagus water, and rice and briefly simmer. Season to taste with salt, pepper, nutmeg, and lemon juice.

LAYERED VEGETABLE SOUP

Yield: 4 to 6 servings
½ pound large carrots, peeled and sliced
1 small bunch celery, thinly sliced
½ pound large potatoes, peeled and sliced
¼ pound boneless smoked pork
¼ pound boneless chicken breast
6 ounces Gouda cheese, coarsely grated
5 cups beef stock
2 medium leeks, thinly sliced
1 bay leaf
Salt and pepper

Preheat the oven to 350° F. Cut the smoked pork and the chicken into ¼ × 1 inch strips.

Break the bay leaf into 3 pieces. Place a layer of potato slices in a 4 quart soufflé dish, crumble ⅓ bay leaf over the potatoes, season with salt, pepper and add ⅓ of the leek and smoked pork.

Make a second layer of carrot slices, ⅓ crumbled bay leaf, salt, pepper, ⅓ leek, and chicken. Make a final layer of celery, leek, salt and pepper, and the stock. Sprinkle the top layer with the cheese.

Tightly seal the dish with a cover or aluminum foil. Bake for 1¾ hours. Remove the cover for the last 15 minutes to brown the cheese.

CORN AND PEPPER SOUP

Yield: 6 to 8 servings
2 7 ounce cans water-packed tuna fish
2 8 ounce cans yellow corn
2 ½ cups vegetable stock
3 tablespoons lemon juice
½ cup dry white wine
1 clove garlic
1 large onion
2 large green peppers
2 tablespoons butter
1 teaspoon paprika
2 tablespoons pepper

In a large saucepan, simmer the tuna fish with the water from the cans, corn, vegetable stock, wine, and lemon juice for 5 minutes over low heat.

Peel and finely dice the garlic and onion. Halve the peppers and remove the seeds and white pith. Slice the peppers into ¼-inch strips.

Sauté the onion, garlic, and pepper strips in the butter until the onion is transparent. Season with paprika.

Stir the sauteéd vegetables into the soup. Season to taste and serve hot.

SEMOLINA AND HORSERADISH SOUP

Yield: 4 servings
4 cups meat stock
½ cup semolina
1 14 ounce fresh horseradish root
Pepper
2 small scallions
½ cup sour cream
4 tablespoons unsweetened applesauce
½ pound pickled tongue

Heat the stock and stir in the semolina.

Peel and finely grate the horseradish. Stir grated horseradish, and pepper, to taste, into the stock. Simmer for 15 minutes.

Clean and wash the scallions and finely chop. Stir the scallions into the stock.

Dice the tongue and reserve a few pieces for garnish. Stir the tongue, sour cream, and applesauce into the stock. Bring to a simmer over low heat.

Remove from heat and pour into soup bowls. Garnish each bowl with a few pieces of diced tongue and greens.

LEMON SOUP WITH ARTICHOKES

Yield: 4 to 6 servings
1 pound boneless chicken breast, cut in bite-sized cubes
½ lemon
Salt
3 peppercorns
2 pimientos
1 medium onion, peeled
4 cups water
1 small can (about 8 ½ ounces) artichoke hearts, drained

Put the chicken, lemon, seasonings, onion, and water in a soup pot and cook over low heat for 2 hours. Strain the broth and place in the refrigerator. When the broth has cooled and the fat has risen to the top, scoop off the fat and reheat the broth. Add the artichoke hearts and cook until heated through.

To serve, ladle the artichoke hearts into 4 warmed soup bowls and pour the broth over them.

CLEAR FISH SOUP

Yield: 8 to 10 servings
1 pound fish heads and bones
3 medium onions, peeled and diced
1 clove garlic, peeled
2 tomatoes, cut in segments
½ bunch parsley
1 sprig fresh thyme
3 peppercorns
1 lemon, halved
Salt
6 cups water
2 flounder fillets, cut in large cubes
¼ cup fresh dill, finely chopped

Put the fish heads and bones, onions, garlic, tomatoes, parsley, thyme, peppercorns, lemon half, salt, and water in a large saucepan. Simmer for 30 minutes, then strain through cheesecloth. If desired, clarify the soup with 1 egg white (see "To Clarify Broth" section in this chapter). Reheat the soup and add salt to taste. Add the fish cubes to

the hot soup and cook over low heat for 3 to 5 minutes.

To serve, cut the remaining lemon half in very thin slices. Garnish the soup with the lemon slices and chopped dill. Serve hot.

ESSENCE OF MUSHROOM SOUP WITH MADEIRA CREAM

Yield: 6 to 8 servings
2 cups sliced mushrooms
4 cups water
1 teaspoon salt
¼ cup Madeira
2 tablespoons soy sauce
¼ cup whipping cream

Place the mushrooms and salt in boiling water in a large saucepan. Reduce the heat to low and simmer for 1½ hours. Drain, reserving the liquid, then squeeze out as much water from the mushrooms as possible. Refrigerate mushrooms for future use.

Return the mushroom liquid to the saucepan and boil until the liquid is reduced to 3 cups. Add half of the Madeira and the soy sauce.

Whip the cream until stiff. Continue to beat the cream while adding the remaining Madeira in a thin stream. To serve, pour the mushroom liquid into 4 soup bowls and serve with the Madeira cream.

ESSENCE OF SHRIMP SOUP WITH PUFF PASTRY

Yield: 4 to 6 servings
4 cups Crab Stock (see Index)
1 pound raw fresh shrimp
3 tablespoons butter
1 2-inch piece lemon peel
2 sheets frozen puff pastry, thawed and cut in half
1 egg, separated

Bring the crab stock to a boil in a large saucepan. Add the shrimp and cook for 5 to 10 minutes, until tender. Take the shrimp from the pan with a slotted spoon and let cool. Remove the meat from the shells and set aside.

Put the shrimp shells in a mortar and crush roughly with the pestle (photograph 1). Melt the butter in a saucepan and cook the shrimp shells for 5 minutes (photograph 2). Add the crab stock and lemon peel and simmer for 10 minutes. Strain the liquid through cheesecloth, then return the soup to the pan and boil until the liquid is reduced to 3 cups. Put the reserved shrimp in 4 ovenproof soup bowls and add the stock; let cool.

Roll out the puff pastry halves and cut out circles a little larger than the diameter of the soup bowls. Brush the edges of the bowls with egg white (photograph 3) and lay the pastry circles over the bowls, pressing firmly against the edges to seal. Brush the pastry with beaten egg yolk (photograph 4).

Bake the pastries in a preheated 425°F oven for 12 minutes, or until the pastry is puffed and brown. Serve immediately.

1

2

3

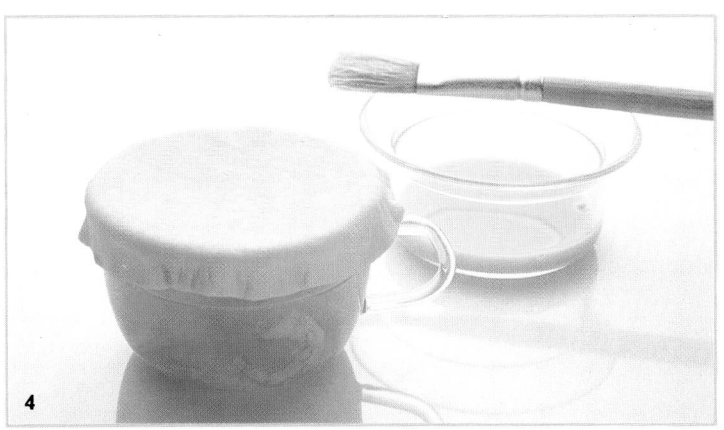
4

OXTAIL SOUP

Yield: 6 to 8 servings
For the soup:
1½ pounds oxtail, in pieces
½ pound veal shank bones
1 large onion
3 large carrots
3 celery stalks
2 tablespoons vegetable oil
4 quarts water
1 cup dry white wine
1 large turnip
1 small bay leaf
1 sprig fresh thyme
1 teaspoon salt
Pepper
1 egg white
Paprika
4 tablespoons sweet red wine
For the spätzle:
¼ cup flour
2 small eggs
Salt
Nutmeg
Vegetable oil for deep-frying

Rinse the oxtail and veal shank in cold water. Clean and wash the vegetables and chop them into ⅛ inch pieces.

Heat the oil and sauté the oxtail, veal, and vegetables for 5 minutes. Pour off any fat and add the water and wine. Peel the turnip and add together with the seasonings except for the paprika.

Simmer over very low heat for 2 to 3 hours. Skim off the foam while cooking. Cool slightly and strain the soup. Reduce to 4 cups by boiling.

Beat the egg white, stir into the soup, and simmer for 1 minute. Strain and season with paprika and red wine. Keep warm while preparing Spätzle.

To make Spätzle: stir the remaining ingredients together to form a runny batter. Heat the vegetable oil to 350°F. Hold a colander over the hot oil and press the spätzle batter through the colander, frying the drippings to a golden brown. Prepare only a small amount at a time, being careful not to splatter the oil.

Drain the spätzle on paper towels. Add to the warm soup and serve.

CELERY CONSOMMÉ WITH DUMPLINGS

Yield: 4 servings
For the broth:
2 bunches celery
1/4 cup celeriac
6 cups water
1 teaspoon salt
1 teaspoon anise seed
1 teaspoon black peppercorns
For the dumplings:
2 eggs
2 tablespoons water
Salt
1/8 teaspoon nutmeg
1/4 cup sifted flour
1 tablespoon grated Parmesan cheese

To make the broth: wash the celery and coarsely chop into 1-inch pieces. Remove some of the young leaves and set aside to use as garnish. Wash and peel the celeriac and cut into 1-inch cubes.

Place the vegetables into a large saucepan with the water, salt, anise seed, and peppercorns. Bring to a boil and continue to simmer over low heat for 1 ½ hours. Cool the soup, then strain. Reduce the broth to 3 cups by boiling and keep warm while preparing the dumplings.

To make the dumplings: beat the eggs and water until very foamy. Quickly stir in the flour and the Parmesan cheese. Place the mixture into a 9 × 3 inch loaf pan lined with baking parchment and bake for 15 minutes in a preheated 350°F oven. Slightly cool the sponge and remove from the pan. Peel away the baking parchment and cool completely.

Cut the sponge into assorted shapes and divide among the serving bowls. Pour in the consommé and garnish with the reserved celery leaves.

CHICKEN CONSOMMÉ WITH PARSLEY DUMPLINGS

Yield: 4 servings
For the broth:
2 cups boneless chicken breast, diced
1 1/4 cups lean ground beef
6 cups meat stock
1 bunch soup greens
1 egg white, beaten
For the dumplings:
4 cups salted water
1 egg, separated
1 teaspoon flour

Simmer the chicken and beef in the meat stock for 2 hours, adding water, if necessary.

Wash the soup greens and add to the stock with the egg white. Bring the stock to a boil again, then reduce heat and simmer for 1 hour. Clarify again with an additional egg white, if necessary.

To make the dumplings: bring the salted water to a boil in a large shallow saucepan. Beat the egg white very stiff and carefully fold in the parsley. Slightly beat the egg yolk and flour together and fold into the egg white.

Drop this mixture into the boiling water by teaspoons. Reduce the heat, cover, and simmer gently for 5 minutes.

Season the consommé with salt and pour into soup bowls. Remove the dumplings with a slotted spoon and place in the soup. Serve immediately.

WEDDING SOUP

Yield: 4 servings
For the soup:
1 pound beef shank and rump bones
1 beef shin bone, about ½ pound
4 beef marrow bones
1 bunch soup greens
1 small onion
6 cups water
½ bay leaf
1 bunch fresh parsley
Salt and pepper
For the marrow balls:
2 tablespoons marrow from the marrow bones
2 tablespoons butter
1 small egg
¼ cup flour
⅛ teaspoon nutmeg
For the dumplings:
1 stale roll
6 tablespoons lukewarm milk
½ small onion
1 teaspoon butter
1 small egg
Salt and pepper
1 teaspoon chopped fresh parsley
For the liver rolls:
¼ cup flour
1 egg
Salt and pepper
⅓ cup milk
¼ pound chicken liver
Sage

Wash the bones and the meat and remove the marrow from the bones (photograph 1). Set aside the marrow for the marrow balls.

Clean the soup greens and peel the onion. Combine the greens, onion, meat, and bones in a large saucepan and cover with water. Add the seasonings and parsley stems. Chop the parsley leaves finely and set aside for garnish.

Bring the soup to a boil, reduce heat, and simmer for 3 hours. After 1½ hours, remove the shin bone, cut off the fat and chop the bone into pieces and set aside. Remove the soup from heat and strain when slightly cooled.

To make the marrow balls: finely dice the marrow and melt with the butter over low heat.

1

2

3

4

5

6

Push this mixture through a sieve and cool. Stir the marrow mixture and egg together until foamy and fold in the flour and seasonings. Form the mixture into 1-inch balls and set aside (photograph 2).

To make the dumplings: cut the roll into thin slices and soak in the milk.

Peel the onion and dice finely. Sauté the onion in the butter for 3 to 4 minutes. Cool slightly. Knead the onion, egg, parsley, salt, pepper, and softened roll to make a firm dough (photograph 3). Form the dumplings into 1-inch balls (photograph 4). Add marrow balls and dumplings to the broth and simmer for about 15 minutes. Add diced meat.

To make the liver rolls: stir the flour, egg, salt, and milk together to form a thin batter. Divide the batter into thirds and fry each third on both sides in a buttered frying pan to make 3 crêpes.

Finely chop the chicken livers and season with salt, pepper, and sage. Spread this mixture on the crêpes (photograph 5).

Roll up the crêpes and cut the rolls into ½-inch thick slices.

Sauté rolls on both sides in 1 tablespoon butter. Divide the hot liver rolls between 4 soup bowls. Add the soup with the meat cubes, marrow balls, and dumplings. Garnish with chopped parsley.

COLD TOMATO AND RADISH SOUP

Yield: 2 to 4 servings

1 pound ripe tomatoes (3 to 5 tomatoes), skinned, seeded, and pureed
3 large red radishes
Salt
Pepper
1 cup whipping cream
2 to 3 tablespoons sherry
1 tablespoon green peppercorns

Put the pureed tomatoes, radishes, salt, pepper, and cream in a blender or food processor and puree until creamy and well blended. Flavor with sherry and peppercorns. Serve chilled.

COLD CREAM OF ONION SOUP

Yield: 4 to 6 servings

1 pound onions, peeled and quartered
4 cups apple cider
Salt
Pepper
1 clove garlic, peeled and crushed
1 small bay leaf
¾ cup whipping cream
½ cup champagne
1 to 2 scallions, cut in thin rings

Place the onions, cider, and seasonings in a saucepan and cook over low heat for 45 minutes. Remove the bay leaf and puree the soup in a blender or food processor. Refrigerate until chilled.

Before serving, add champagne and seasoning to taste to the soup. Whip the cream until it is almost stiff. Pour the soup into 4 bowls and stir in the cream so that a marbled pattern is formed. Sprinkle with the chopped scallions.

ORANGE SOUP WITH PEARL BARLEY

Yield: 4 to 6 servings
4 to 5 oranges
½ cup confectioner's sugar
¼ cup pearl barley
1 sheet frozen puff pastry, thawed
1 teaspoon brown sugar
2 tablespoons orange liqueur
Cinnamon
2 cups strawberries, quartered

Peel one of the oranges in fine strips, being careful to remove the pith from the underside of the peel. Squeeze the juice from all of the oranges and add enough water to make 4 cups of liquid.

Mix the sugar with 1 tablespoon of the juice mixture and melt it in a saucepan over low heat. Add the orange peel and cook until the sugar begins to caramelize. Gradually add the remaining juice. When the caramelized sugar has dissolved, add the pearl barley and cook for 30 minutes, or until tender.

In the meantime, cut the puff pastry in crescent shapes, brush lightly with water, and sprinkle with brown sugar. Bake in a preheated 450°F oven for about 10 minutes.

To serve, flavor the soup with the orange liqueur and cinnamon. Add the strawberries and simmer for 2 minutes. Ladle the soup into 4 bowls and garnish with the pastry crescents.

Tip: If serving the soup cold, do not simmer the strawberries. Blackberries can be substituted for strawberries.

SWEET AVOCADO CREAM SOUP

Yield: 2 to 4 servings
½ vanilla bean
2 small avocados, peeled and seeded
1 cup freshly squeezed orange juice
1 cup dry white wine
1 can (about 7 ounces) lychees
3 to 4 tablespoons honey
½ cup carbonated mineral water

Cut the vanilla bean in half and scrape out the pith. Put the pith in a blender or food processor with the avocado, orange juice, wine, lychees, syrup, and honey; puree to a fine consistency. Refrigerate until chilled.

Before serving, add the mineral water.

CLASSIC CUISINE

A fresh, crisp salad makes a perfect summer supper or festive luncheon. Herbs, fruit, meat, fish, or chicken served with tender lettuce and other attractive, fresh vegetables present infinite opportunities for creating all sorts of salads. The key to making a good salad is for all ingredients to complement each other, from the main elements down to the dressing.

SALADS

2

3

4

5

Several different types of attractive lettuces are shown in photograph 1. Curly endive (or chicory) has tender, feathery leaves and a slightly bitter taste.

Boston lettuce is suitable for a tossed salad.

Escarole is a smooth endive with broad, coarsely indented leaves. It is less bitter than Belgian endive.

Chinese or celery cabbage is about the size of a bunch of celery. Its leaves are firm and crisp, with a flavor somewhere between cabbage and celery.

The lettuce with the curly brownish leaves is called oakleaf lettuce. The type shown here and in photograph 2 is the red oakleaf lettuce. Green oakleaf lettuce is also grown.

Red raddicchio has a bitter but refreshing taste. Iceberg lettuce has crisp, brittle, tightly packed leaves. Iceberg lettuce adds crunch to a salad and does not wilt easily.

Photograph 3 shows the green outer leaves and the light-colored inner leaves of a head of iceberg lettuce.

Chicory (photograph 3) is cultivated without light and does not produce chlorophyll. Chinese cabbage (photograph 3) is also called bok choy. Bean sprouts are shown in photograph 3.

Carrots, kohlrabi, and white and red radishes are common salad vegetables. Cucumbers, red and green peppers, zucchini and tomatoes are also favorite salad staples. Almost every salad tastes better with an onion.

1

2

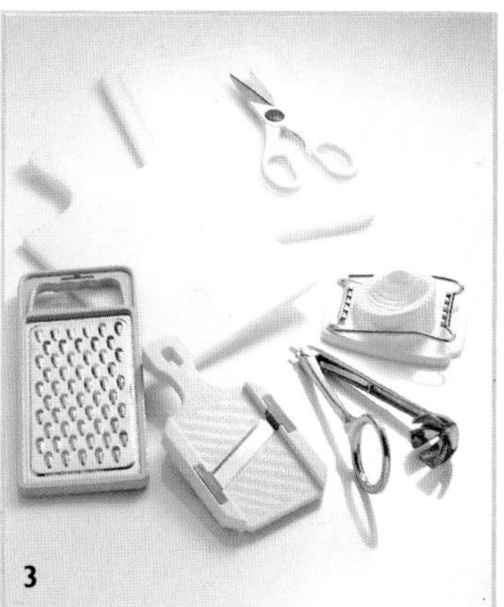

3

4

Each utensil shown in photograph 1 is alongside the vegetable for which it is best suited in salad preparation. These are a chopping knife, serrated knife, vegetable peeler, melon baller, tomato knife, and apple corer.

Photograph 2 shows a salad spinner and other drying accessories.

Photograph 3 shows a selection of graters and slicers. Cutting boards, kitchen scissors, and an egg slicer are all useful additions to a salad utensil collection, and a garlic press is indispensable.

Photograph 4 shows an assortment of salad bowls, cruets, salt and pepper shakers, and a lemon juicer.

SALADS

1. Salad greens and other salad ingredients should always be washed before being cut. Vitamins and minerals are lost from cut vegetables when washed. A trick for cleaning iceberg lettuce is to dip the lettuce in water. Bang the core sharply on a hard surface. Twist out the core so the head falls apart into separate leaves. Dry in a salad spinner.

2. The bitter heart of chicory can be cut out using a pointed knife and slicing from the root end. Another method is to cut ½ inch slices from the root end to loosen the leaves. Chicory can be cut into strips or the leaves coarsely chopped.

3. Raw vegetables are very nutritious. Some prople find raw vegetables difficult to digest whole, so it is advisable to grate raw root and tuber vegetables. Kohlrabi, fennel, carrots, cauliflower, and broccoli florets can be finely or coarsely grated.

4. Leafy salads are best when torn into bite-sized pieces. Endive and chicory can be cut into strips or coarser pieces. Boston lettuce leaves are usually left whole. A serrated knife gives an interesting texture to vegetables. Cucumbers can also be scooped out with a melon baller.

A good salad has absolutely fresh ingredients and an excellent dressing. Various ingredients are used in salad dressings, including herbs, spices, vinegars, oil, cream, yogurt, sour cream or mayonnaise. The quality of the salad dressing ingredients is as important as the composition of the salad.

The basic types of vinegars are distilled white vinegar, cider vinegar , balsamic vinegar, wine vinegar, and herb vinegar.

Distilled white vinegar is a chemical combination with a 40% acetic acid count. Cider vinegar is between 50 and 60% acetic acid content and is very mild. They are best used with mixed fruit and vegetable salads. Wine vinegar, both red and white, has about a 50% acetic acid content. Wine vinegar seasons delicate salads with a more pronounced flavor.

Herb vinegars can be made with any of the vinegars mentioned. Try a favorite combination of herbs to flavor a vinegar, using 3 tablespoons of fresh herb leaves to 4 cups of vinegar. Steep for several weeks in a closed container. Filter and re-bottle in a sterilized container that can be tightly closed.

Fruits and flowers such as raspberries or rose petals are also used to flavor vinegars. To prepare raspberry vinegar, pour 2 quarts of vinegar into a 3- to 4-quart container with a lid. Fill to the top with about 1 quart of fresh, washed raspberries and steep for 8 days. Strain through a fine sieve and re-bottle in a sterilized container with a tight fitting lid. Rose petal vinegar can be made by placing ½ cup clean rose petals in 4 ½ cups red wine vinegar and steeping for 10 days. Strain and re-bottle in a sterilized container with a tight fitting lid.

The best salad oils are virgin pressed olive oil, safflower oil, vegetable oil, or nut flavored oils. A vinegar-oil dressing requires the correct proportion of ingredients: 1 part vinegar and 2 parts oil, seasoned to taste with salt, pepper and other spices. This is a basic vinaigrette dressing.

To make a creamy dressing, use 1 part citrus juice or cider vinegar and 2 parts cream. If sour cream or yogurt is used, the proportions are 5 parts sour cream or yogurt to 1 part citrus juice or cider vinegar, seasoned to taste. Sour cream can be used as a marinade with 1 tablespoon of herb vinegar and seasoned to taste.

Mayonnaise is another salad dressing base. It can be flavored with a variety of sauces such as barbecue sauce, chili sauce, or catsup. Stir in heavy cream whipped to soft peaks, or mix with yogurt. Use 2 parts mayonnaise and 1 part sauce, whipping cream, or yogurt.

1. There are countless salad combinations, and for all it is important that the dressing match the ingredients. Some hearty salad combinations are shown in photograph 1: salad vegetables with cold meat, cheese, shrimp, eggs, olives, and pickles.

2. A teaspoon of mustard makes a tasty addition to a dressing. Extra-hot or strong mustard or mild, sweet mustards are readily available.

3. A liqueur or wine can also give salad dressing a new taste. Lemon or orange juice can replace vinegar for an aromatic, flavorful cream dressing. The acidity of a teaspoon of vinegar or citrus juice improves a dressing made with sour cream, and freshly chopped herbs improve any salad dressing.

4. Salad dressings with a mayonnaise, yogurt, or sour cream base are especially tasty when catsup, soy sauce, or Worcestershire sauce are added. These creamy dressings are ideal for iceberg lettuce and chicory salads, or dips for raw vegetables.

ROMAINE SALAD WITH SALMON

Yield: 4 to 6 servings
1 head Romaine lettuce, torn in bite-sized pieces
4 ounces smoked salmon, cut in julienne strips
1 clove garlic, peeled and crushed
Juice and grated peel of ½ lemon
1 egg yolk
½ teaspoon mustard
¼ teaspoon sugar
Salt
Pepper
½ teaspoon Worcestershire sauce
5 tablespoons walnut oil

Arrange the lettuce on a serving plate and arrange the salmon strips decoratively on top.

Combine the garlic, lemon juice and peel, egg yolk, mustard, sugar, pepper, and Worcestershire sauce. Pour in the oil very slowly, stirring constantly. Sprinkle the dressing on the salad.

RED LEAF LETTUCE AND ORANGE SALAD

Yield: 4 to 6 servings
4 oranges
1 red onion, sliced paper-thin
Salt
1 red leaf lettuce, torn in bite-sized pieces
5 tablespoons olive oil
Pepper
2 tablespoons fresh pumpkin seeds

Peel and slice the oranges, reserving the juice. Sprinkle the onion with salt and let drain for 10 minutes. Combine the oranges, onion, and lettuce in a salad bowl.

Mix the reserved orange juice, oil, and pepper together and toss the dressing with the salad.

Roast the pumpkin seeds in a preheated 300°F oven, stirring frequently. Sprinkle the seeds over the salad and serve.

ENDIVE SALAD WITH ROQUEFORT DRESSING

Yield: 4 to 6 servings
1 large endive, cut in strips
2 tablespoons Roquefort cheese, crumbled
1 tablespoon red wine vinegar
½ teaspoon mustard
4 tablespoons walnut oil
Salt
Pepper
10 shelled walnuts, toasted and chopped

Place the lettuce in a salad bowl.

Combine the cheese, vinegar, mustard, and walnut oil and mix thoroughly. Season with salt and pepper.

Just before serving, pour the dressing over the lettuce and toss. Sprinkle with chopped walnuts.

GREEN SALAD WITH POMEGRANATE

Yield: 4 to 6 servings
Juice of 1 lemon
1 tablespoon sugar
Salt
Pepper
1 teaspoon herb vinegar
¾ cup whipping cream
1 garden lettuce, torn into bite-sized pieces
Seeds from 1 small pomegranate

Combine the lemon juice, sugar, vinegar, salt, and pepper. Pour in the cream in a thin stream, stirring until the dressing is creamy.

Arrange the lettuce on a serving plate and pour the cream dressing on top. Sprinkle with pomegranate seeds.

RED LEAF LETTUCE WITH CHANTERELLE MUSHROOMS

Yield: 4 to 6 servings

3 strips bacon, cut in julienne strips
1 tablespoon butter
1½ cups chanterelle mushrooms, cleaned
1 shallot, peeled and chopped
3 tablespoons sherry vinegar
6 tablespoons walnut oil
Salt
Pepper
1 head red leaf lettuce, torn in bite-sized pieces

Place the bacon in a frying pan and sauté over low heat. Remove from the pan and drain on paper towels. Add the butter to the bacon fat in the frying pan and sauté the mushrooms for 1 minute, stirring constantly. Transfer the mushrooms to a bowl.

To make the dressing, combine the shallot, vinegar, and walnut oil. Season with salt and pepper. Add half of the dressing to the mushrooms and the other half to the lettuce leaves. Arrange the lettuce and mushrooms on salad plates and spread the warm bacon on top.

BOSTON LETTUCE WITH WARM MUSHROOMS

Yield: 4 servings

1 large head Boston lettuce
¼ pound bacon
½ pound mushrooms
2 tablespoons butter
2 tablespoons cider vinegar
Salt and pepper
1 scallion
4 tablespoons hazelnut oil

Clean and wash the lettuce and pat dry with paper towels.

Cut the bacon into ⅛ inch strips and sauté in a frying pan until crisp. Remove the bacon and set aside to use as garnish. Reserve the bacon fat.

Clean, wash, and cut the mushrooms into ⅛ inch slices. Melt the butter in the frying pan with the bacon fat. Saute the mushrooms for 3 minutes. Remove from the frying pan and keep warm.

Mix the vinegar, salt, and pepper together. Skin and chop the scallion and add it to the vinegar dressing. Whisk in the hazelnut oil.

Pour the vinaigrette over the lettuce. Place the salad on 4 serving plates. Garnish with the bacon and warm mushrooms.

MIXED SALAD WITH DANDELIONS

Yield: 4 to 6 servings
1 clove garlic, peeled and crushed
1 shallot, peeled and crushed
3 tablespoons red wine vinegar
1 teaspoon mustard
5 tablespoons walnut oil
Salt
Pepper
1 small radicchio, torn in bite-sized pieces
¾ cup small dandelion leaves
1 medium head chicory
3 strips bacon

Mix the garlic, shallot, mustard, and vinegar together. Slowly pour in the oil, stirring until the dressing is creamy.

Place the bacon in a frying pan and sauté over low heat until crisp. Remove from the pan and drain.

Mix the lettuce and dandelion leaves together and toss with the dressing. Add the hot bacon and 1 tablespoon of the bacon fat. Serve immediately, so the lettuce leaves don't wilt.

AVOCADO AND SPINACH SALAD

Yield: 4 to 6 servings
3 to 6 strips bacon, diced
½ tablespoon lemon juice
1 teaspoon red wine vinegar
Sugar
5 tablespoons olive oil
Salt
Pepper
1 pound spinach
1 ripe avocado, peeled and sliced
1 cup sliced mushrooms

Place the bacon in a frying pan and sauté over low heat until crisp. Remove from the pan and drain on paper towels.

To make the dressing, mix the lemon juice, vinegar, and sugar together. Add the oil, stirring constantly with a wire whisk, and season with salt and pepper.

Wash the spinach well in cold water, then drain; follow this procedure 3 times. Shake the spinach dry and carefully mix it with the avocado, mushrooms, and dressing. Sprinkle with the diced bacon.

Tip: To keep the avocado and mushroom slices from browning, sprinkle with lemon juice as soon as they have been cut.

SPANISH SALAD

Yield: 4 to 6 servings
1 small Spanish onion, peeled and thinly sliced
Salt
1 green-leaf lettuce, torn in bite-sized pieces
2 large tomatoes, sliced
2 tablespoons red wine vinegar
5 tablespoons olive oil

Put the onion slices in a salad bowl and sprinkle with salt. Add the lettuce and tomatoes. Pour the oil and vinegar over the salad and mix well.

CUCUMBER SALAD

Yield: 2 to 4 servings
1 clove garlic, peeled and crushed
1 medium cucumber, peeled and thinly sliced
1 cup sour cream
Salt
Pepper
2 sprigs fresh dill, chopped

Rub the inside of a salad bowl with the garlic, add the cucumber and sour cream and mix well. Season with salt and pepper.

Just before serving, stir the dill into the salad.

SUMMER SALAD

Yield: 4 to 6 servings
4 eggs
12 anchovy fillets
3 to 5 medium tomatoes, quartered and sprinkled with salt
1 cucumber, peeled and sliced
1 medium green pepper, seeded and cut in thin rings
2 scallions, cut in thin rings
1 can (about 8 ounces) large white kidney beans, drained
10 oz. jar black olives
6 tablespoons olive oil
Pepper
Fresh basil leaves, cut in strips

Place the eggs in a saucepan with water to cover. Bring the water slowly to a boil and cook the eggs for 8 minutes. Remove the eggs from the pan and plunge in cold water; shell and cut in eighths.

Rinse the anchovies with cold water, cut in half, and roll up.

Arrange all of the salad ingredients, including the olives, on a large serving plate. Pour the oil over the salad and season with salt and pepper. Sprinkle with basil before serving.

CUCUMBER AND BEAN SPROUT SALAD

Yield: 2 to 4 servings
1 cucumber, cut in julienne strips
1½ teaspoons salt
1½ cups bean sprouts
1 clove garlic, peeled and finely chopped
½ teaspoon fresh ginger, peeled and finely chopped
½ teaspoon lemon pepper
5 tablespoons sesame oil
3 tablespoons rice vinegar.

Sprinkle the cucumber strips with salt and let stand for 30 minutes; dry well.

Put the bean sprouts in a colander and rinse with cold water; drain thoroughly. Mix the cucumber strips and bean sprouts together.

Combine the garlic, ginger, lemon pepper, oil, and vinegar. Pour the dressing over the cucumbers and bean sprouts and mix well.

STRING BEAN SALAD

Yield: 4 to 6 servings
1 pound string beans, broken in pieces
Salt
2 shallots, peeled and diced
2 tablespoons herb vinegar
½ teaspoon mustard
Pepper
¼ teaspoon sugar
6 tablespoons olive oil
1½ cups mushrooms, sliced
2 tablespoons chopped chives

Place the beans in lightly salted boiling water and cook for 15 minutes; drain and place in a bowl.

Mix the vinegar, mustard, pepper, ¼ teaspoon salt, and sugar together. Add the oil slowly, stirring constantly with a wire whisk. Pour the mixture over the beans and marinate for 1 hour.

To serve, add the mushrooms and the chives.

BEAN SPROUT SALAD

Yield: 4 servings
1 cup bean sprouts
1 medium red onion
1 small Bartlett pear
1 bunch fresh chives
¼ pound smoked turkey breast
2 tablespoons white wine vinegar
2 tablespoons dry sherry
Salt
Pepper
6 tablespoons walnut oil
1 tablespoon vegetable oil
2 tablespoons sesame seeds

Rinse the bean sprouts with cold water and drain well. Peel the onion and cut into julienne strips. Wash and core the pear. Cut the pear into julienne strips. Rinse the fresh chives and chop finely. Finely dice the turkey breast.

Mix the white wine vinegar, dry sherry, salt, pepper and walnut oil together to make a dressing. Toss the salad ingredients with the dressing and set aside for 15 minutes.

Heat the vegetable oil in a heavy skillet and stir-fry the sesame seed until they are light brown. To serve, sprinkle the toasted sesame seeds over the salad.

CELERY AND WALNUT SALAD

Yield: 2 to 4 servings
2 stalks celery heart, cut in slices
1 small radicchio, torn in bite-sized pieces
2 medium pears, peeled, cored and cut in julienne strips
20 walnut halves, chopped and toasted
2 tablespoons lemon juice
1 teaspoon herb vinegar
4 tablespoons walnut oil
Salt
Pepper

Mix the celery slices, radicchio, and pears together. Sprinkle the walnuts over the salad.

Combine the lemon juice and vinegar. Gradually add the oil, stirring with a wire whisk until well blended, and season with salt and pepper. Pour the dressing over the salad and toss well.

FENNEL AND ORANGE SALAD

Yield: 2 to 4 servings
2 fennel bulbs, leaves removed and core cut in paper-thin slices
2 oranges, peeled and cut in segments
1 small red onion, peeled and cut in rings
Salt
Pepper
1 tablespoon white wine vinegar
3 tablespoons olive oil
¼ cup pistachio nuts, chopped

Combine the fennel, oranges, and onion rings in a salad bowl.

Stir the salt, pepper, and vinegar together. Add the oil in a steady stream, stirring constantly with a wire whisk. Pour the dressing over the salad and toss.

To serve, sprinkle with chopped pistachio nuts.

SAUERKRAUT SALAD

Yield: 4 to 6 servings
3, ½-inch slices pineapple, skin removed and drained
1 medium apple, cored and diced
1 medium onion, peeled and chopped
1 pound sauerkraut, chopped
1 tablespoon mayonnaise
4 tablespoons whipping cream
1 tablespoon grated horseradish
½ teaspoon sugar
1 tablespoon lemon juice
Salt
Pepper
¼ cup sunflower seeds

Mix all the ingredients together, except the pineapple and sunflower seeds.

Toast the sunflower seeds in a preheated 300°F oven, stirring frequently. To serve, place the salad on a platter. Garnish with the pineapple slices and sprinkle with the sunflower seeds.

CABBAGE SALAD

Yield: 4 to 6 servings
1 large cabbage (about 3 pounds)
Salt
Pepper
¼ teaspoon sugar
2 tablespoons apple cider vinegar
4 tablespoons sunflower oil
¾ cup sour cream
2 tablespoons grated horseradish
2 medium apples, peeled, cored and diced
Fresh pumpkin seeds, for garnish

Add the apples to the dressing as soon as they are diced to prevent discoloration. Remove the outer leaves of the cabbage and set aside. Grate the rest of the cabbage as finely as possible, then blanch in boiling salt water for 1 minute; drain well.

Mix the pepper, sugar, and vinegar together. Add the oil, cream, and horseradish, stirring constantly with a wire whisk. Toss the dressing with the cabbage and apples. Arrange the salad decoratively on the reserved cabbage leaves.

To serve, toast the pumpkin seeds in a 300°F oven, stirring frequently, and sprinkle over the salad.

BEET SALAD WITH MOZZARELLA

Yield: 4 to 6 servings
1 pound fresh beets
2 medium oranges, peeled and cut in segments
1 small red onion, thinly sliced
2 tablespoons balsamic vinegar
Salt
Pepper
1 tablespoon horseradish, freshly grated

5 tablespoons whipping cream
¾ cup Mozzarella cheese, diced
1 small bunch watercress

Place the beets in boiling water in a saucepan and cook for 20 minutes, until tender. Remove the beets from the pan and plunge in cold water, peel and cut in julienne strips. Combine the beets, orange segments, and onion in a bowl.

Blend the balsamic vinegar, salt, pepper, and horseradish together; add the cream after the vinegar and horseradish are well mixed. Toss the dressing with the beets, oranges, and onion.

To serve, sprinkle the salad with the diced cheese and garnish with watercress leaves.

LEEK AND CARROT SALAD

Yield: 4 to 6 servings
1 pound carrots, peeled and grated
3 celery stalks, peeled and grated
1 small leek, cut in small rings
½ cup walnuts, toasted and coarsely chopped
Juice of 1 lemon
1teaspoon honey
Salt
Pepper
½ cup whipping cream
Lettuce leaves

Combine the carrots, celery, leeks, and walnuts in a bowl.

To make the dressing, mix the lemon juice, honey, salt, pepper, and cream together. Toss the carrot mixture with the dressing.

To serve, arrange lettuce leaves on a plate and spoon the salad on top.

MUSHROOM AND ZUCCHINI SALAD

Yield: 4 to 6 servings
1½ cups mushrooms, sliced
1½ cups small zucchini, thinly sliced
1 clove garlic, peeled and crushed
Juice of 1 lemon
½ teaspoon sugar
1 teaspoon Dijon mustard
Pepper
½ cup whipping cream
Salt
Basil leaves, cut in strips

Combine the mushrooms and zucchini in a bowl.

Mix the garlic, lemon juice, sugar, mustard, and pepper together. Add the cream, stirring constantly with a wire whisk, then add salt to taste and the basil strips.

To serve, toss the mushroom-zucchini mixture with the dressing.

ARTICHOKE AND TOMATO SALAD

Yield: 2 to 4 servings
4 small artichokes
1 lemon
Salt
10 to 15 cherry tomatoes, cut in half
1 cup button mushrooms, thinly sliced
1 small red onion, peeled and sliced
1 tablespoon white wine vinegar
1 tablespoon lemon juice
Pepper
Sugar
6 tablespoons olive oil
15 fresh basil leaves, cut in strips

Cut off the stems and about ¼ inch from the top of the artichokes. Immediately rub the cut surfaces with a lemon and place the artichokes in cold lemon water in a saucepan. Add salt and bring the water to a boil; cook for 15 to 20 minutes. Remove from the pan and cut the artichokes in eighths. Arrange on a plate, alternating with the tomato halves to form a circle. Place the mushrooms in the center of the circle and put the onion strips on top of the mushrooms. Sprinkle the basil leaves over the mushrooms and onion.

Mix the vinegar, lemon juice, salt, pepper, and sugar together. Add the oil slowly, stirring constantly with a wire whisk.

To serve, pour the dressing over the salad and sprinkle with basil leaves.

WARM ZUCCHINI AND TOMATO SALAD

Yield: 4 to 6 servings
4 to 6 small zucchini, thinly sliced
Salt
Pepper
Juice of 1 lemon
5 tablespoons olive oil
2 medium tomatoes, peeled, seeded, and cubed
Fresh basil leaves, cut in strips

Bring lightly salted water to a boil in a saucepan and blanch the zucchini for 1 minute. Drain well and sprinkle lightly with salt, pepper, lemon juice, and olive oil. Marinate the zucchini in the dressing for 15 minutes.

To serve, mix the tomatoes and zucchini together. Sprinkle with the basil leaves.

LENTIL SALAD WITH WARM CHICKEN LIVER

Yield: 4 servings
½ cup uncooked lentils
1 medium onion, peeled
2 cloves
½ bay leaf
1 shallot, peeled and chopped
2 tablespoons red wine vinegar
½ teaspoon Dijon mustard
½ clove garlic, peeled and crushed
Salt
Pepper
4 tablespoons walnut oil
1 to 2 heads chicory
3 strips lean smoked bacon, diced
1 pound chicken livers, diced
Parsley

Place the lentils in a bowl and cover with boiling water. Soak overnight, then drain.

Spike the onion with the cloves and bay leaf. Place the onion in lightly salted water in a medium saucepan and bring to a boil. Add the lentils, reduce the heat, and simmer for 45 minutes. Drain the lentils and put in a bowl.

Combine the shallot, vinegar, mustard, garlic, salt, and pepper. Add the oil in a steady stream, stirring with a wire whisk. Pour the dressing over the lentils and let stand for 30 minutes.

Divide the chicory into separate leaves. Cut off the points of the leaves, then cut the lower portion of the leaves in rings. Arrange the leaf points in the shape of a flower on 4 individual plates. Mix the chicory rings with the lentils and put the lentil mixture in the center of the flower.

Slowly sauté the bacon in a frying pan; drain on paper towels. Add the liver to the frying pan and sauté over very high heat until browned.

To serve, arrange the liver and bacon on the lentils. Sprinkle with parsley.

POACHED EGG AND SALMON SALAD

Yield: 4 servings
Juice of ½ lemon
Sugar
Salt
Pepper
1 dash Tabasco sauce
2 tablespoons whipping cream
2 tablespoons sour cream
½ cup water
1 tablespoon herb vinegar
4 eggs
1 head iceberg lettuce, cut in eighths
4 slices smoked salmon
2 sprigs fresh dill

Mix the lemon juice, sugar, salt, pepper, and Tabasco sauce together. Add the whipping and sour cream.

Bring the water and vinegar to a boil in a saucepan. Crack each egg onto a saucer and gently slide, one at a time, into the water; poach the eggs for 3 to 4 minutes and remove with a slotted spoon.

To serve, arrange the lettuce, salmon, and poached eggs on a plate. Top with the dressing, sprinkle with freshly ground pepper, and garnish with dill.

BREAST OF DUCK SALAD

Yield: 4 servings
1 duck breast
1 shallot, peeled and chopped
2 tablespoons balsamic vinegar
4 tablespoons olive oil
Salt
Pepper
1 small head lamb's lettuce
1 small radicchio, cut in strips

Remove the skin from the duck breast and cut the skin in very thin strips. Place the skin in a frying pan, with no fat added, and sauté over medium heat until crisp. Remove from the pan and drain on paper towels; keep warm.

Put the duck breast in the pan and cook in the fat from the skins about 3 minutes on each side. Remove from the pan and wrap in foil.

Mix the shallots, vinegar, oil, and seasonings together. Toss the lamb's lettuce and radicchio with the dressing and arrange on 4 plates. Cut the duck breast in thin slices and arrange on top of the lettuce. Sprinkle the strips of crisp skin over the salad and serve.

SCALLOP SALAD

Yield: 4 servings
2 small heads of chicory, cut in bite-sized pieces
1 small radicchio, torn in bite-sized pieces
½ red pepper, diced
2 tablespoons sherry vinegar
¼ teaspoon Dijon mustard
Salt
Pepper
1 shallot, peeled and chopped
4 tablespoons walnut oil
¾ pound scallops, sliced
2 tablespoons butter
4 to 6 tablespoons dry vermouth

Cut the chicory leaves in bite-sized pieces, reserving several leaves to use as garnishes. Combine the chicory, radicchio, and red pepper.

To make the dressing, mix the vinegar, mustard, salt, pepper, and shallot together. Add the oil slowly, stirring constantly with a whisk.

Melt the butter in a frying pan and sauté the scallops, stirring frequently. Remove the scallops from the pan and add the vermouth. Cook until the liquid is reduced by half.

To serve, toss the salad and dressing together and arrange on individual plates. Place the scallops beside the lettuce. Put 1 teaspoon of the scallop and vermouth liquid on each serving of scallops.

SMOKED SALMON SALAD

Yield: 4 to 6 servings
1 shallot, peeled and chopped
1 tablespoon lemon juice
1 tablespoon red wine vinegar
Salt
Pepper
4 tablespoons walnut oil
2 soft avocados, peeled and cut in ¼- inch-thick slices
1 small head lettuce, cut in strips
8 ounces smoked salmon, cut in strips
1 tablespoon fresh dill, chopped
1 teaspoon red peppercorns

To make the vinaigrette, mix the shallot, lemon juice, vinegar, salt, and pepper together. Add the oil in a steady stream, stirring constantly with a whisk.

Sprinkle the avocado slices with the vinaigrette and arrange in a ring on a serving plate. Toss the lettuce with the vinaigrette and place in the middle of the plate. Put the salmon strips on top of the lettuce. Sprinkle with the dill and red peppercorns.

SQUID SALAD

Yield: 4 to 6 servings
1 pound squid
Salt
2 tablespoons lemon juice
Pepper
1 teaspoon mustard
5 tablespoons olive oil
2 small tomatoes, peeled, seeded, and finely diced
1 small red onion, peeled and cut in rings
3 tablespoons pitted green olives
3 tablespoons black olives
½ cup dried, sliced pepperoni
Fresh basil leaves

Place the squid in boiling salt water in a saucepan and boil for 15 minutes. Drain and let cool before slicing the squid into rings.

To make the dressing, mix the lemon juice, salt, pepper, and mustard together. Add the oil slowly, stirring constantly with a wire whisk. Pour the dressing over the squid and let stand while preparing the rest of the salad.

To serve, carefully add the tomatoes and onion to the squid and dressing. Arrange the salad on plates with the olives, pepperoni, and basil leaves.

SHRIMP SALAD WITH SNOW PEAS

Yield: 4 servings
10 fresh basil leaves
¼ teaspoon salt
1 tablespoon sherry vinegar
Pepper
4 tablespoons olive oil
¾ cup snow peas
1 tablespoon butter
7 ounces shrimp, peeled and deveined
1 head red leaf lettuce

Puree the basil leaves with the salt in a blender or food processor; add the vinegar, pepper, and oil.

Melt the butter in a frying pan and sauté the peas for 1 minute. Add the shrimp and sauté until pink. Season with salt and pepper to taste.

To serve, arrange the lettuce leaves on a serving plate. Place the shrimp and snow peas on top of the lettuce and sprinkle with the dressing.

FRESH SEAFOOD SALAD

Yield: 4 to 6 servings
1 cup salt water
1 onion, peeled and coarsely chopped
¼ cup fresh parsley
1 bay leaf
1 teaspoon white peppercorns
Salt
1 pound fresh squid
½ pound shrimp
8 ounces fresh salmon
1 clove garlic, peeled and crushed
Juice of 1 lemon
1 tablespoon red wine vinegar
Pepper
½ teaspoon mustard
5 tablespoons olive oil

Place the salt water, onion, 5 to 8 sprigs of parsley, bay leaf, and peppercorns in a saucepan and bring to a boil. Add the squid and continue cooking for 5 minutes. Add the shrimp, reduce the heat to low, and simmer for 5 minutes. Remove the squid and shrimp from the pan with a slotted spoon and set aside. Poach the salmon in the remaining liquid for 2 to 4 minutes; drain.

Peel and devein the shrimp, then cut in half lengthwise. Slice the squid in rings. Remove the skin and bones from the salmon and slice in julienne strips. Gently mix the seafood together in a bowl.

To make the dressing, combine the garlic, lemon juice, vinegar, salt, pepper, mustard, and oil. Pour the dressing over the seafood and toss carefully. Cover and let marinate for 2 to 3 hours.

To serve, arrange the seafood salad on individual plates. Chop the remaining parsley and sprinkle over the salad.

ASPARAGUS SALAD

Yield: 4 to 6 servings
1 pound mixed green and white asparagus, peeled and cut in pieces
Salt
1 shallot, peeled and finely chopped
2 tablespoons red wine vinegar
1 tablespoon lemon juice
½ teaspoon sugar
Salt
Pepper
5 tablespoons sunflower oil
2 hard-boiled eggs, coarsely chopped
¼ cup fresh parsley, finely chopped
½ head green leaf lettuce, cut in strips

Blanch the asparagus in boiling salted water for 5 to 8 minutes, or until just tender; drain.

Mix the shallot, vinegar, lemon juice, sugar, salt, and pepper together. Add the oil slowly, stirring constantly with a wire whisk. Pour the dressing over the warm asparagus. Cover and let marinate for 1 to 2 hours. Sprinkle the egg and parsley over the asparagus.

To serve, arrange the lettuce strips on individual plates and place the asparagus salad on the lettuce.

SHRIMP AND RICE SALAD

Yield: 4 to 6 servings
1 cup uncooked long-grain rice
Salt
2 tablespoons mayonnaise
2 tablespoons whipping cream
1 to 2 tablespoons curry powder
2 tablespoons lemon juice
½ teaspoon sugar
¼ teaspoon fresh ginger, grated
Cayenne pepper
1 large apple, peeled, cored and diced
3 slices pineapple, cubed
10 to 15 cooked shrimp, peeled and deveined
3 tablespoons raw pumpkin seeds

Bring 2 cups of water to a boil in a saucepan and add the rice. Reduce the heat to low, cover the pan, and cook for 20 minutes. Let the rice cool.

Combine the mayonnaise, cream, curry powder, lemon juice, sugar, ginger, and cayenne pepper and mix well. Add the apple and pineapple to the rice, then stir in the curry cream. Cover and let stand for 1 to 2 hours.

To serve, add the shrimp to the rice mixture. Toast the pumpkin seeds in a 300°F oven, stirring frequently, and sprinkle over the salad.

PASTA SALAD

Yield: 4 to 6 servings
1 cup spiral pasta
Salt
1 tablespoon olive oil
1 (10-ounce) package frozen peas, cooked
1 small red onion, peeled and diced
1 tablespoon capers
1 (6½-ounce) can tuna fish, drained and flaked
2 small plum tomatoes, seeded and diced
2 tablespoons mayonnaise
½ cup sour cream
1 teaspoon mustard
Juice of ½ orange
Pepper

Cook the pasta in boiling salted water until soft, approximately 8 minutes. Drain, rinse with cold water, and drain again. Add the oil and peas and cool. Mix the onion, capers, tuna fish, and tomatoes with the cold pasta.

To make the dressing, combine the mayonnaise, sour cream, mustard, orange juice, salt, and pepper, mixing thoroughly. Toss the dressing with the salad and let stand for 10 to 15 minutes before serving.

MIXED TURKEY SALAD

Yield: 4 to 6 servings
Juice of 1 lemon
1 tablespoon honey
1 pinch cayenne pepper
2 tablespoons soy sauce
6 tablespoons olive oil
2 small pears, peeled, cored and cubed
3 small carrots, peeled and coarsely grated
1 small Chinese cabbage, cut in fine strips
1 cup smoked turkey breast, cut in julienne strips
2 tablespoons sesame seeds
Butter

Combine the lemon juice, honey, cayenne pepper, soy sauce, and oil, mixing well. Cut the pears in cubes and add immediately to the dressing to prevent discoloration. Add the carrots, cabbage, and turkey.

To serve, toast the sesame seeds in the butter. Fold the warm sesame seeds into the salad and serve immediately.

CHICKEN SALAD

Yield: 4 to 6 servings
1 large chicken breast, cooked, or the equivalent in cold, cooked chicken
1 medium ripe avocado
1 medium tomato
10 black olives
¼ cup fresh parsley
2 tablespoons bleu cheese
Salt and pepper
1 tablespoon cider vinegar
2 tablespoons cashew nuts

Separate the chicken from the bone. Remove the skin and cut the meat into bite-size chunks. Halve the avocado, remove the pit, peel, and dice. Wash the tomato, remove the stalk, and coarsely chop. Pit the olives and cut into eighths. Rinse the parsley and dry. Separate the leaves from the stems and coarsely chop the leaves. Toss chicken, avocado, olives, and parsley and place in serving bowl.

Mash the bleu cheese with a fork. Stir with salt, pepper, olive oil and vinegar. Pour over the salad and lightly toss. Sprinkle with cashew nuts and serve.

COLD VEAL SALAD

Yield: 4 servings
¼ pound string beans, cooked
Salt
1 small red pepper
1 small green pepper
1 bunch red radishes
½ pound button mushrooms
2 tablespoons red wine vinegar
4 tablespoons walnut oil
Pepper
½ pound cold, sliced veal
2 tablespoons butter
Fresh basil leaves to garnish
Red peppercorns, crushed, to garnish

Quarter the red and green peppers. Remove the seeds and white pith. Cut each pepper into ¼ inch strips. Cut the radishes and mushrooms into ⅛ inch slices. Toss string beans, peppers, radishes and mushrooms together in a salad bowl.

Mix the red wine vinegar and walnut oil with a wire whisk. Season to taste with salt and pepper. Pour over the vegetables and marinate

the salad in the refrigerator for 15 minutes.

Arrange slices of veal on each serving plate. Place the salad on the plate and sprinkle each serving with basil leaves and crushed peppercorns.

RED CABBAGE SALAD WITH CHICKEN BREAST

Yield: 4 servings
1 red cabbage, about 1 pound
Salt and pepper
3 tablespoons red wine vinegar
1 teaspoon honey
2 tablespoons lemon juice
2 large boneless chicken breasts, about 1 pound
1 teaspoon butter
10 walnut halves, shelled and coarsely chopped

Remove the outer leaves from the red cabbage. Wash and cut into 1/8 inch strips. Blanch for 1 minute in 4 cups boiling, salted water to which 2 tablespoons red wine vinegar have been added. Remove the cabbage from the water with a slotted spoon and drain well.

Stir together the honey, lemon juice, 1 tablespoon red wine vinegar, and salt and pepper. Toss the dressing with the drained cabbage, and marinate for 1 hour.

Rinse the chicken and pat dry with paper towels. Melt the butter in a heavy skillet and sauté for 3 minutes on each side. Add salt and pepper to taste.

Place a serving of cabbage salad on each plate. Slice the chicken in 1/4 inch slices and arrange several slices next to the cabbage. Sprinkle with walnuts and serve.

WALDORF SALAD

Yield: 4 servings
2 large apples, peeled, cored and cut in julienne strips
3 stalks celery, finely grated
3 slices pineapple, diced
½ cup walnuts, toasted
Juice of ½ lemon
Salt
1 teaspoon sugar
1 teaspoon sugar
Pepper
1 tablespoon mayonnaise
2 tablespoons sour cream

Combine the apples, celery, pineapple, and walnuts in a bowl.

Mix the lemon juice, salt, sugar, and pepper together. Stir in the mayonnaise and sour cream. Toss the dressing with the salad ingredients. Let the salad stand for at least 4 hours before serving, to absorb the flavors.

SLICED BEEF SALAD

Yield: 4 to 6 servings
1 pound cooked roast beef, cut in julienne strips
1 large apple, peeled, cored and cut in julienne strips
2 sweet pickles, cut in julienne strips
1 small red onion, peeled and cut in julienne strips
2 tablespoons capers
1 clove garlic, peeled and crushed
3 tablespoons red wine vinegar
2 teaspoons Dijon mustard
Salt
Pepper
¼ teaspoon sugar
2 dashes Worcestershire sauce
4 tablespoons peanut oil
1 bunch watercress

Combine the roast beef, apple, pickles, onion, and capers in a bowl.

To make the dressing, combine the garlic, vinegar, mustard, salt, pepper, sugar, and Worcestershire sauce and mix well. Add the oil and toss the dressing with the salad ingredients. Let the salad stand for 2 hours to absorb all the flavors.

To serve, arrange the salad on individual plates and garnish with watercress.

HERRING SALAD

Yield: 4 to 6 servings
3 small beets, skinned and diced
2 small boiled potatoes, peeled and diced
2 small apples, peeled, cored and diced
15 sweet pickles
1 cup white herring, diced
1 onion, peeled and chopped
¼ teaspoon salt
1 teaspoon mustard
½ teaspoon sugar
2 tablespoons apple cider vinegar
5 tablespoons whipping cream
Crushed ice
Parsley

Cut off the tops of the beets, leaving 1 inch of stem. Place the beets in a saucepan and half cover with boiling water. Cover the pot and cook until tender, about 1 hour, adding more boiling water if needed. Remove the beets from the pan and cool slightly. Slip off the skins and dice the beets. Mix the beets with the potatoes, apples, pickles, and herring.

Sprinkle the chopped onion with salt and let stand for 10 minutes. Mix the mustard, sugar, and vinegar together, then add the onion. Stir in the cream and toss the mixture with the salad ingredients. Marinate the salad overnight in the refrigerator.

To serve, garnish with a little crushed ice and parsley.

SAUSAGE AND CHEESE SALAD

Yield: 4 to 6 servings

1 cup link sausage, sautéed and cut in julienne strips
½ cup Swiss cheese, cut in julienne strips
2 sweet pickles, cut in julienne strips
¼ cup fresh chives, chopped
4 tablespoons red wine vinegar
½ teaspoon Dijon mustard
Salt
Pepper
4 tablespoons sunflower oil
1 head Bibb lettuce

Mix the sausage, cheese, pickles, and chives together.

To make the dressing, stir the vinegar, mustard, salt, and pepper together. Add the oil in a steady stream, beating constantly with a wire whisk. Toss the dressing with the sausage and cheese.

To serve, arrange the lettuce leaves on individual plates and place the salad on top.

PASTA AND CHEESE SALAD

Yield: 4 to 6 servings

1 cup uncooked colored pasta bows
Salt
1 small red or yellow pepper, diced
½ cup Swiss cheese, diced
1 cup bean sprouts
1 shallot, crushed
3½ ounces Roquefort cheese
½ cup yogurt
1 teaspoon Worcestershire sauce
Pepper
1 tablespoon pistachio nuts, chopped

Cook the pasta in salted water, following the directions on the package. Drain and rinse with cold water; let cool. Mix the pasta with the pepper, cheese, and bean sprouts.

Mix the shallot, cheese, yogurt, Worcestershire sauce, salt, and pepper together in a blender until creamy. Gently toss the sauce with the pasta salad.

Serve the salad on individual plates, sprinkled with chopped pistachio nuts.

EGG SALAD

Yield: 2 to 4 servings

6 hard-boiled eggs, cut in wedges
2 small plum tomatoes, diced
1 tablespoon capers
2 scallions, cut in rings
1 tablespoon vinegar
2 teaspoons Dijon mustard
¼ cup whipping cream
Salt
Sugar
Pepper
Fresh basil leaves

Arrange the eggs, tomatoes, capers, and scallions on a plate. Mix the vinegar, mustard, cream, salt, sugar, and pepper together. Pour the dressing over the salad.

To serve, garnish with basil leaves.

POTATO SALAD

Yield: 4 to 6 servings
1 pound small new potatoes
1 small onion, peeled and diced
½ cup beef or chicken stock
4 tablespoons white vinegar
2 teaspoons sugar
Pepper
Salt
5 to 6 radishes, sliced
½ cup cooked corn kernels
1 to 2 tablespoons grated horseradish
1 tablespoon mayonnaise
½ cup sour cream
2 to 3 tablespoons lemon juice
1 bunch fresh dill, chopped

Boil the potatoes in their jackets for 20 minutes, then peel and slice while still warm.

Put the onion, stock, vinegar, 1 teaspoon of sugar, and pepper in a saucepan and bring to a boil. Season with salt to taste. Pour the liquid over the warm potato slices and mix carefully. Let stand until the potatoes have absorbed all the liquid. Add the radishes and corn to the potatoes.

Mix the horseradish, mayonnaise, cream, lemon juice, and the remaining teaspoon of sugar together; toss with the potato mixture. Just before serving, garnish the salad with dill.

BEET SALAD

Yield: 4 to 6 servings
3 to 6 medium beets
2 celery stalks, diced
4 medium potatoes
1 teaspoon grated horseradish
1 teaspoon honey
3 tablespoons fruit vinegar
Salt
Pepper
5 tablespoons soy sauce
4 tablespoons sour cream
2 cups watercress
1/4 cup raw sunflower seeds

Place the beets, celery, and potatoes in cold water in 3 separate saucepans. Bring each to a boil and cook for at least 20 minutes. Peel the beets and potatoes after cooking; slice the beets in julienne strips and dice the celery and potatoes.

Mix the horseradish, honey, vinegar, salt, and pepper together in a bowl. Add the oil slowly, stirring constantly with a wire whisk. Combine the dressing, beets, celery, and potatoes and marinate for 1 hour.

To serve, garnish with watercress leaves. Toast the sunflower seeds in a 300° F oven, stirring frequently, and sprinkle over the salad.

CLASSIC CUISINE

A fine sauce can enrich almost any dish. This selection of sauces offers tempting ideas for enhancing vegetables, meat, poultry, or desserts.

Stock is a flavored liquid base for sauces, stews or braised dishes. Stocks can be thickened or unthickened. The base of the stock can be veal, beef, poultry, game, vegetables, spices, or fish, which simmer for an extended time. There are three main stocks, light stock, brown stock, and vegetable stock. These stocks are the basis for the following flavorful sauces.

LIGHT STOCK

1 pound veal knuckles
1 pound stewing beef
1 pound chicken parts
4 quarts cold water
1 medium onion
3 stalks celery
2 small carrots
¼ pound mushrooms
1 bay leaf
1 sprig fresh thyme
6 sprigs fresh parsley
4 quarts cold water

Wash and dry meat with paper towels. Peel and quarter onion, wash and trim celery stalks, wash and scrape carrots and wash and slice mushrooms. Place meat, vegetables , bay leaf, thyme, and parsley in a stockpot (photograph 1). Pour in water and bring to a boil (photograph 2). Reduce heat to a simmer immediately and simmer 2½ to 3 hours or until liquid is reduced by half. Strain stock and allow to cool, uncovered. Remaining liquid should be gelatinous (photograph 3).

1

2

3

BROWN MEAT STOCK

2 pounds veal shin and marrow bones
1 pound stewing beef
1 large carrot
2 small onions
¼ cup vegetable oil
2 tablespoons tomato paste
1 clove garlic
3 stalks celery
1 tablespoon white peppercorns
1 bay leaf
1 sprig fresh thyme
3 sprigs parsley
8 cups water

Wash and dry meat with paper towels. Wash and trim vegetables (photograph 4). Dice carrot, onions and garlic.

Heat oil in a large frying pan and brown veal and beef for 5 minutes (photograph 5). Stir in diced vegetables and tomato paste (photograph 6). Lay garlic, celery, peppercorns and herbs on top of meat, pour in water and bring to a boil (photograph 7). Reduce heat and simmer, uncovered, for 2 ½ to 3 hours. Strain stock, cool and refrigerate.

4

5

6

7

1

2

3

4

HOLLANDAISE SAUCE

Yield: About 1½ cups

This classic sauce is traditionally served with vegetables such as asparagus, broccoli, or cauliflower. It is also a delicious complement to sole, turbot, or any broiled fish. Hollandaise sauce can be difficult to make because the mixture must not be allowed to get too hot when cooked over a double boiler.

2 sticks salted butter (½ pound)
3 egg yolks
1 tablespoon water
Salt
White pepper
1 tablespoon lemon juice (photograph 1)

Melt the butter in a saucepan over a very low heat. Remove all foam and water from the butter and allow it to cool. Pour the clarified butter carefully into another container (photograph 2).

Mix the egg yolks and water together in the top of a double boiler. Fill the bottom of the double boiler half full with water. Bring to a boil, add the top part, and cook over low heat, stirring with a wire whisk until the egg is creamy. Stir rapidly until the egg becomes light in color and binds together (photograph 3 from top). Gradually add the butter, pouring slowly in a thin stream. Season with lemon juice, salt, and pepper.

Maltaise Sauce is a variation of Hollandaise sauce. It is made with 2 tablespoons of orange juice instead of lemon juice. Cut orange peel in very fine strips, blanch, and use to garnish the sauce. Maltaise sauce goes well with asparagus and crabs.

To make **Bavarian Sauce** instead of Hollandaise sauce, use crab butter instead of plain butter. At the end of preparing the sauce, fold in 2 tablespoons of whipped cream. Bavarian Sauce is delicious with poached sole, halibut, salmon, and shellfish.

Hollandaise sauce becomes **Chantilly Sauce** when 2 tablespoons of whipped cream are folded into it. Chantilly sauce is served with roast beef, broiled fish, and vegetables such as asparagus, artichokes, and cauliflower.

Béarnaise Sauce is made in a similar manner as Hollandaise sauce. Instead of the water and lemon juice seasonings used in Hollandaise sauce, 2 small chopped shallots, 2 tablespoons of tarragon vinegar, and 3 tablespoons of white wine are used. Boil the mixture until only 2 tablespoons of the liquid remain. Strain the liquid through cheesecloth and stir in 1 teaspoon each of chopped tarragon and chervil. Follow the Hollandaise recipe through the steps in photograph 3, then add the Béarnaise sauce seasonings. Béarnaise sauce is particularly good with grilled fish and meats, especially steak.

BÉCHAMEL SAUCE

Yield: About 3 cups

Béchamel Sauce is one of two sauces in classical cuisine that are bound with flour. The other is Velouté Sauce (photograph right side).

1 tablespoon salted butter
2 small onions, peeled and diced
2 tablespoons flour
1 cup Veal Stock (see Index)
2 cups milk
Salt
White pepper
Grated nutmeg

Melt the butter in a saucepan and sauté the onions until they are soft and transparent. Add the flour and continue cooking, stirring constantly, until the mixture is pale yellow. Mix in the veal stock and milk, stirring rapidly to prevent lumps from forming.

Cook the sauce over low heat for 10 minutes, until the sauce coats the back of a wooden spoon. Season to taste with salt, pepper, and nutmeg.

Béchamel sauce is served with potatoes, cauliflower, broccoli, or poached eggs.

1

2

3

4

VELOUTÉ SAUCE

Yield: About 1½ cups

Basic Velouté Sauce can be turned into a tomato sauce by adding tomato paste. Velouté sauce can also be made into Mornay Sauce by adding 4 tablespoons grated cheese, 1 tablespoon cream, and 1 egg yolk.

1 teaspoon salted butter
1 tablespoon diced onion
1 rounded tablespoon flour
1½ cups beef stock
½ cup whipping cream
Salt
White pepper

Melt the butter in a saucepan and sauté the onion until transparent but not brown. Add the flour and continue cooking until it becomes a light yellow color. Add the beef stock (photograph 1) and simmer on low heat for 10 minutes.

Continue to simmer until the cream is reduced to half its volume and then add it to the sauce, using a whisk (photograph 2).

Finally, strain the liquid through a very fine sieve, return to the saucepan and reheat over low heat. Season to taste with salt and white pepper.

A basic brown sauce can be made from the same ingredients. The only difference is that the onions are sautéed in the hot butter until golden brown; 1½ tablespoons of flour are added and cooked until golden brown, while being stirred constantly.

MAYONNAISE

Yield: About 1¼ cups

Homemade mayonnaise is quite simple to make.

2 egg yolks
Salt
White pepper
2 teaspoons Dijon mustard
1 tablespoon lemon juice or wine vinegar
Sugar
1 cup fine salad oil
Worcestershire sauce

Mix the egg yolks, salt, pepper, mustard,and lemon juice or vinegar together in a ceramic bowl. Add a pinch of sugar and, using a whisk, stir in one direction. Continue mixing until all the seasonings have dissolved completely (photograph 3). Slowly drip the oil into the mixture, stirring constantly (photograph 4). As soon as the mixture begins to bind, start pouring the oil in a thin stream. Continue stirring until the mayonnaise becomes creamy. Add Worcestershire sauce and seasonings to taste.

Mayonnaise becomes a **Remoulade Sauce** with the addition of ½ cup of mayonnaise, 1 small onion, finely diced, 1 small pickle, finely diced, and 1 finely diced anchovy fillet. Also add ¼ cup parsley, 2 sprigs tarragon and chervil, and 2 teaspoons capers, all finely chopped. Season with 1 teaspoon mustard and salt and pepper, to taste.

To make **Andalusian Sauce**, mix together ½ cup of mayonnaise, 1 crushed garlic clove, salt, 1 tablespoon tomato paste, 2 raw tomatoes, pureed, 1 pickle, finely diced, 1 very finely diced tomato, and 1 green pepper.

To make **Curried Mayonnaise**, prepare the recipe for basic mayonnaise, adding an extra pinch of sugar to make the mayonnaise milder. Stir in 2 teaspoons of curry powder.

Paprika Mayonnaise is made by adding a pinch of sugar and 1 tablespoon sweet paprika to the basic mayonnaise recipe.

GRAPE SAUCE

Yield: 6 to 8 servings
1 tablespoon salted butter
1 tablespoon flour
1¾ cups chicken stock
¼ cup dry sherry
Salt
Pepper
Grated nutmeg
2 tablespoons whipping cream
1½ cups seedless green grapes, halved
1 tablespoon parsley, chopped

Melt the butter in a frying pan. Add the flour, stirring constantly, and let the flour brown over medium heat. Remove the pan from the stove and let cool slightly.

Return the pan to the stove, add the chicken stock, and bring to a boil, stirring constantly. Stir in the sherry and simmer for 10 minutes. Season with salt, pepper, and nutmeg; then add the cream.

Add the grapes and heat for 1 to 2 minutes. Sprinkle with parsley.

Serve the grape sauce with poultry.

PEPPER SAUCE

Yield: 4 to 6 servings
2 tablespoons peanut oil
2 small onions, peeled and diced
3 strips bacon, diced
2 tablespoons flour
½ cup dry red wine
1 tablespoon tarragon vinegar
Juice of 2 oranges
4 small tomatoes, peeled and chopped
1 red and 1 green small peppers, seeded and roughly diced
Salt
Pepper
1 tablespoon crushed pimientos

Heat the oil in a frying pan and sauté the onions and bacon until lightly browned. Stir in the flour and continue sautéing until the mixture has browned. Stir in the wine, vinegar, and orange juice.

Add the tomatoes, peppers, salt, pepper, and crushed pimientos to the sauce. Cook for 10 to 15 minutes longer.

Serve with beef.

BEEF SAUCE WITH CARROTS

Yield: 4 to 6 servings
2 tablespoons clarified butter
1 medium onion, peeled and diced
3 medium carrots, cut in small pieces
2 tablespoons flour
⅔ cup beef stock
½ cup dry red wine
¼ cup water
½ cup sliced mushrooms
5 juniper berries, crushed
2 tablespoons whipping cream
Salt
Pepper
1 tablespoon parsley, chopped

Heat the clarified butter in a frying pan and sauté the onions gently until they are transparent. Add the carrots and cook until browned. Sprinkle with the flour and continue cooking until the mixture is a medium brown color. Add the beef stock, wine, and water. Bring the liquid to a boil over medium heat.

Add the mushrooms and crushed juniper berries. Cover the pan and cook for 15 minutes. Remove the lid and cook for an additional 10 minutes, to reduce the liquid. Season with salt and pepper. Serve with beef.

SHRIMP SAUCE

Yield: 4 to 6 servings
15 fresh shrimp, shelled (reserve shells) and deveined
2 tablespoons clarified butter
1 small red onion, peeled and chopped
1 teaspoon flour
1 cup beef stock
2 tablespoons whipping cream
½ teaspoon tomato paste
1 teaspoon fresh watercress or dill, chopped
Salt
White pepper

Melt the clarified butter in a frying pan and sauté the shrimp shells for 10 minutes. Strain the butter through a sieve and reserve the liquid.

Reheat the reserved shrimp butter in a frying pan and lightly sauté the onion, being careful not to burn it. Stir in flour and cook for 3 to 5 minutes before adding the stock. Allow the mixture to simmer for 15 to 20 minutes, and then add the shrimp.

Mix the cream with the tomato paste, and add the mixture to the sauce. Add the watercress or dill and season with salt and pepper before serving.

MUSHROOM CREAM SAUCE

Yield: 4 to 6 servings
3 shallots, peeled and finely chopped
1 cup dried Chinese mushrooms
¼ cup dry white wine
1 cup whipping cream
3 medium fully ripe tomatoes, peeled and chopped
Salt
Pepper
1 sprig fresh thyme

1 teaspoon salted butter
1 teaspoon flour

Mix the shallots, mushrooms, and wine together in a saucepan. Bring the mixture to a boil and reduce the liquid until only 2 tablespoons remain. Add the cream, tomatoes, salt, pepper, and thyme.

With your fingers, work the butter into the flour and form it into a ball. Add the ball of butter to the boiling sauce, stirring until the liquid begins to bind.

This sauce can be served with veal or chicken breasts.

SNAIL SAUCE

Yield: 4 servings
1 tablespoon salted butter
1 celery stalk, chopped
1 leek, white part only, chopped
1 slice ham, cut in julienne strips
2 shallots, peeled and diced
1 clove garlic, peeled and diced
2 teaspoons flour
¼ cup hot veal or chicken stock
¼ cup dry white wine
¼ cup whipping cream
12 canned snails
Salt
Pepper
Celery leaves, for garnish

Melt the butter in a frying pan and sauté the celery, leek, ham, shallots, and garlic gently so that they do not brown, approximately 5 minutes. Sprinkle with flour and continue to cook for 3 to 5 minutes. Add the stock, wine, and cream and cook over low heat for 20 minutes.

Heat the snails in the sauce. Season with salt and pepper and serve garnished with celery leaves.

RAW TOMATO SAUCE

Yield: 4 to 6 servings
4 to 5 ripe tomatoes, medium-size, peeled and chopped
2 tablespoons olive oil
Salt
Pepper
1 tablespoon lemon juice
1 tablespoon fresh basil, finely chopped

Mix the tomatoes with the oil, salt, pepper, and lemon juice. Sprinkle the sauce with basil and let stand for 1 hour before serving.

Serve over spaghetti or add to sautéed veal chops.

PUMPKIN SAUCE

Yield: 4 to 6 servings
2 tablespoons porcini mushrooms
1 pound fresh pumpkin
¼ cup beef stock
2 teaspoons curry powder
Salt
Pepper
½ teaspoon dried oregano

Soak the mushrooms in hot water until softened.

Using a melon baller, scoop some balls out of the pumpkin, then dice the remaining pumpkin flesh.

Heat the beef stock, curry powder, salt, and pepper together in a saucepan. Add the diced pumpkin and sauté until soft. Remove from the pan and puree the mixture in a blender or food processor.

Return the sauce to the pan. Add the mushrooms and pumpkin balls and sauté over low heat for 10 minutes. Add the oregano. Season with salt and pepper before serving.

LEEK CREAM

Yield: 4 to 6 servings
1 tablespoon salted butter
2 small leeks, white parts cut in thin rings
¼ cup dry white wine
1 egg yolk
¼ cup whipping cream
Salt
Pepper
1 teaspoon fresh tarragon, chopped

Melt the butter in a saucepan and sauté the leeks over low heat. Add the wine and cook for 20 minutes. Puree the mixture until smooth in a blender or food processor, then return to the saucepan. Do not boil.

Beat the egg yolk with the cream and add to the warm sauce. Season with salt, pepper, and tarragon.

This sauce goes well with pork or veal.

THREE-COLOR PEPPER PUREE

Yield: 4 to 6 servings
2 small green peppers, halved and seeded
2 small red peppers, halved and seeded
2 small yellow peppers, halved and seeded
1 sprig fresh basil, chopped
1 teaspoon tomato paste
1 pinch saffron
¼ cup chicken stock
Salt
Pepper

Place the pepper halves under the broiler until the skins blister (photograph 1). Put the blackened peppers in paper bags for 5 minutes and then remove the skins (photograph 2). Puree the peppers in a blender or food processor, keeping each color separate.

Add the basil to the green pepper puree; add the tomato paste to the red pepper puree. Dissolve the saffron in 1 tablespoon boiling water and add it to the yellow pepper puree. Pour just enough stock into each of the purees to give them the consistency of lightly whipped cream. Season with salt and pepper.

Pour the sauces into a shallow dish, making sure they do not mix (photograph 3). A spiral pattern can be made by carefully drawing the handle of a spoon through the purees (photograph 4), or the purees can be put in the dish in layers. Serve immediately.

Pepper puree goes best with roast beef or veal.

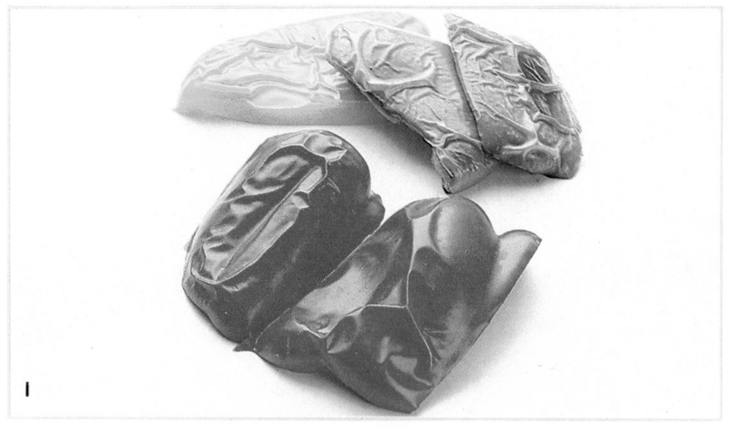
1

2

3

4

5

RADISH PUREE

Yield: 2 to 4 servings
2 bunches radishes
2 tablespoons whipping cream
2 tablespoons low-fat cottage cheese
Salt
White pepper

Wash the radishes, setting aside a few small leaves. Quarter the radishes and puree them in a blender or food processor.

Mix the radish puree, cream, cottage cheese, salt, and pepper together in a bowl. Finely chop the reserved radish leaves and add them to the puree.

Serve with steak.

BASIL FOAM

Yield: 4 servings
1 tablespoon salted butter
1 pound chicken, cut in pieces
1 small onion, peeled and cut in julienne strips
1 teaspoon black peppercorns
1½ cups water
1 cup dry white wine
Salt
1 egg yolk
Pepper
1 tablespoon fresh basil, chopped

Melt the butter in a large frying pan and brown the chicken on all sides. Add the onion, peppercorns, and water. Cover the pan and cook for 45 minutes. Remove the lid for the last 15 minutes of cooking.

Strain the stock through a food mill and transfer to a double boiler.. Add the wine and reduce the liquid to ½ cup. Allow the mixture to cool, then stir in the egg yolk with a whisk. Continue stirring the mixture over a hot, but not boiling, double boiler until the sauce foams. Season with salt and pepper to taste and add the chopped basil.

This sauce goes well with fried chicken.

BURGUNDY SAUCE

Yield: 2 to 4 servings
1 beef marrow bone
1 scallion, white part only, diced
2 small carrots, peeled and cubed
1 celery stalk, cubed
1 cup red Burgundy wine
½ teaspoon reduced rich beef stock
Salt
Pepper
1 pinch thyme
3 teaspoons cold salted butter

Remove the marrow from the bone, dice it, and gently sauté it in a saucepan over medium heat. Remove the diced marrow from the fat and discard.

Sauté the vegetables in the fat until they are a medium brown color. Add the wine and stock. Bring to a boil, over high heat, and reduce the liquid by half. Season with salt, pepper, and thyme. Remove from heat.

Add the butter one piece at a time, swirling the pan to mix. Serve immediately.

Tip: The better the wine, the better the flavor of the sauce.

LEMON AND EGG SAUCE

Yield: 4 servings
4 hard-boiled eggs, shelled
Juice of 2 lemons
½ cup olive oil
½ teaspoon lemon peel, cut in fine strips
Salt
Coarsely ground black pepper

Remove the yolks from the egg and puree them with the lemon juice in a blender or food processor. Gradually add the oil, mixing thoroughly. Stir the lemon peel into the sauce.

Chop the egg whites and add them to the sauce. Season with salt and pepper.

This sauce goes well with roast beef and poultry.

GREEN SAUCE

Yield: 4 to 6 servings
1 bunch mixed fresh herbs (parsley, chives, chervil, watercress, and borage)
1 small onion, peeled and diced
1 gherkin, diced
½ cup sour cream
¼ cup yogurt
2 tablespoons mayonnaise
1 tablespoon lemon juice
1 teaspoon hot mustard
Salt
Pepper

Wash and dry the herbs, removing the stalks; chop the leaves. Mix the herbs, cream, yogurt, mayonnaise, onion, and gherkin together. Season with lemon juice, mustard, salt, and pepper. Refrigerate until ready to use.

BEET SAUCE

Yield: 4 to 6 servings
1 (1-pound) jar sliced beets
1 tablespoon red wine vinegar
½ teaspoon crushed pimiento
¼ teaspoon ground cloves
Salt
Pepper
1 tablespoon parsley, chopped
2 tablespoons sour cream

Drain the beets and puree them in a blender or food processor until smooth. Flavor the beets with the vinegar, pimiento, cloves, salt, and pepper. Sprinkle with parsley.

Just before serving, add the cream in a spiral pattern. Beet sauce goes well with cold roast beef, pork, or turkey.

CAPER REMOULADE

Yield: 4 servings
2 egg yolks, at room temperature
2 tablespoons lemon juice
½ teaspoon mustard
Salt
Pepper
¼ cup peanut oil
3 small gherkins, diced
1 scallion, diced
1 tablespoon parsley, chopped
2 teaspoons capers

Beat the egg yolks with the lemon juice, mustard, salt, and pepper in an electric mixer. Slowly add the oil, mixing continuously. Add the gherkins, scallion, parsley, and capers. Refrigerate until ready to use.

Serve with cold roasts and poultry.

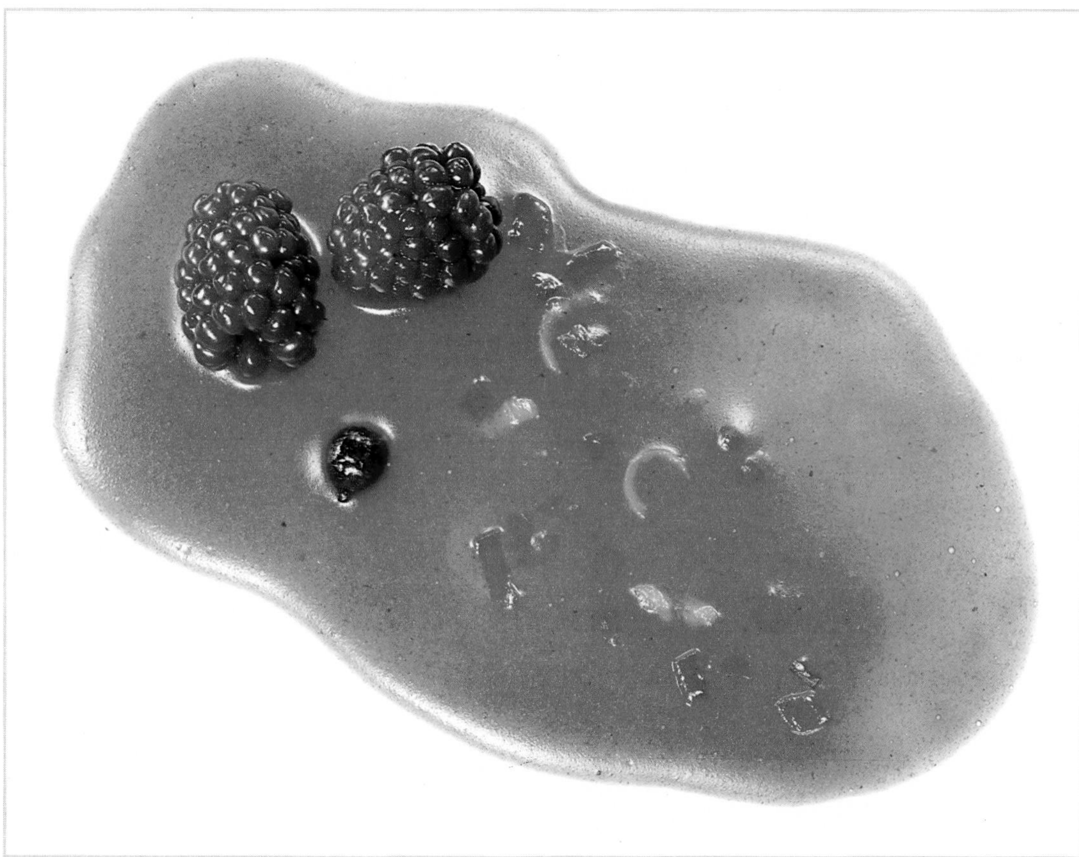

BLACKBERRY SAUCE

Yield: 4 servings
1 tablespoon sweet butter
1 small onion, peeled and chopped
3 tablespoons blackberry jam
1 cup dry red wine
1 pinch crushed pimiento
Salt
Pepper
1 cup fresh blackberries

Melt the butter in a saucepan and brown the onion. Add the jam, stirring until melted, then the wine, pimiento, salt, and pepper.

Just before serving, add the fresh blackberries.

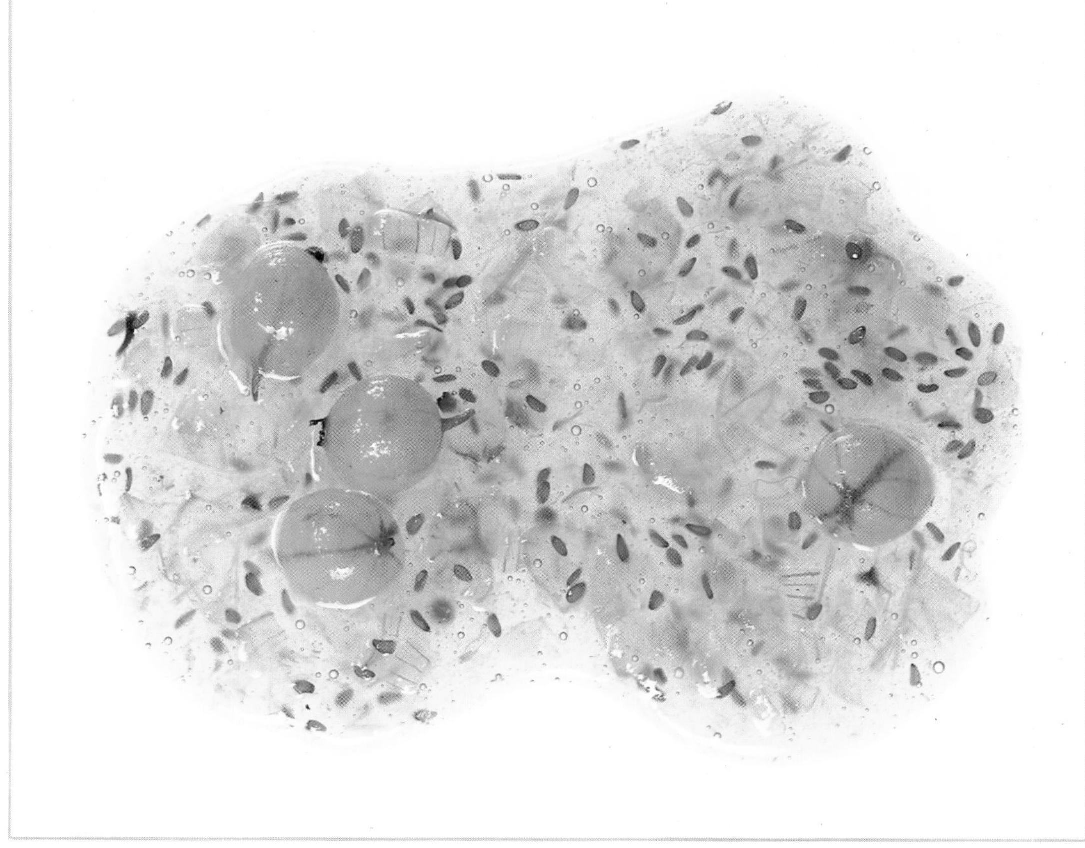

GOOSEBERRY SAUCE

Yield: 4 servings
2 tablespoons sweet butter
1 small onion, peeled and diced
1 tablespoon white wine vinegar
5 tablespoons gooseberry jam
¼ cup dry sherry
1 rounded teaspoon cornstarch
1 teaspoon Worcestershire sauce
Salt

Melt the butter in a saucepan and sauté the onion until light brown. Add the vinegar, jam, and sherry and bring the mixture to a boil.

Mix the cornstarch with 1 teaspoon of cold water. Add the cornstarch mixture, Worcestershire sauce, salt, and pepper to the sauce, stirring until well blended and slightly thickened.

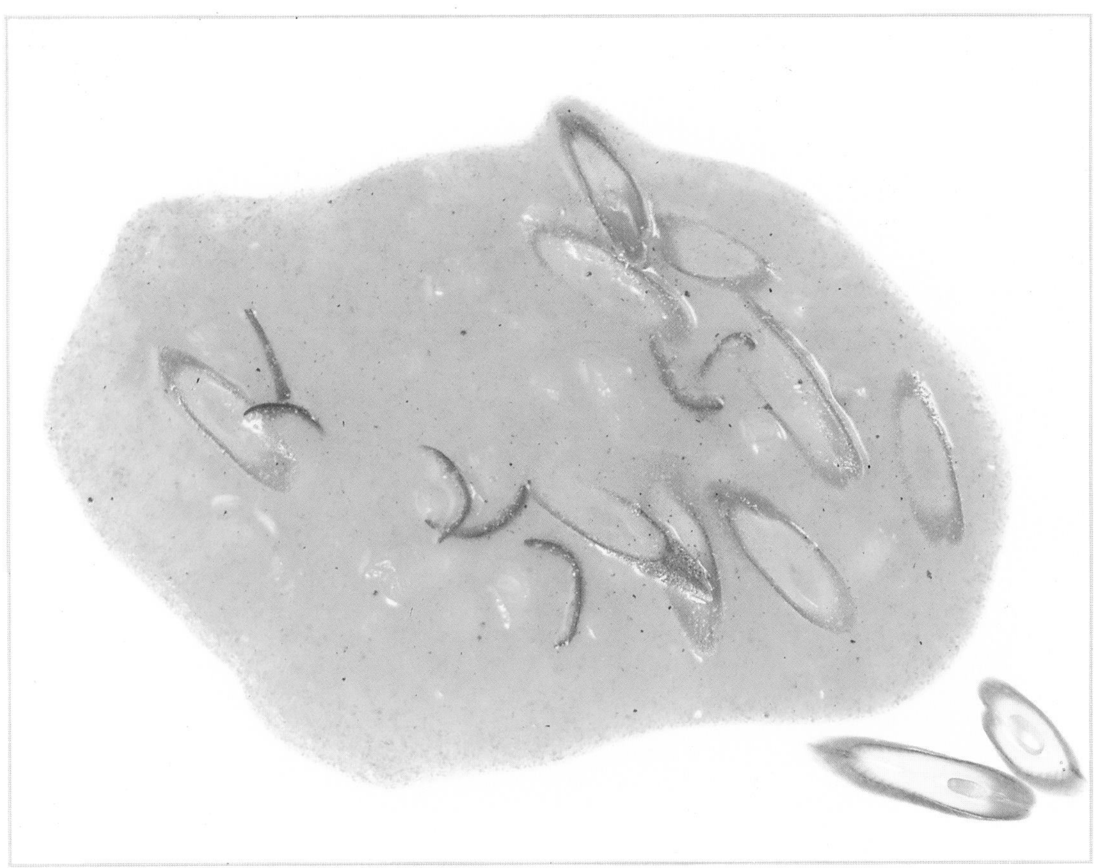

CURRY SAUCE WITH STRING BEANS

Yield: 4 servings
1 tablespoon clarified butter
1 cup string beans, tipped
1 small onion, peeled and diced
1 to 2 teaspoons curry powder
1 cup chicken stock
1 very ripe small banana, mashed
1 medium red pepper, seeded and sliced in strips
Salt
Pepper

Heat the clarified butter in a saucepan and add the string beans and onion. Sprinkle with curry powder and cover with the stock. Cook for 10 minutes.

Add the mashed banana, pepper strips, salt, and pepper.

This sauce is served with chicken, veal, or liver.

TOMATO AND PEPPER SAUCE

Yield: 4 servings
3 to 4 ripe tomatoes, medium size, peeled, seeded, and chopped
1 tablespoon salted butter
¼ cup beef stock
1 small green pepper, seeded and sliced
2 small red peppers, seeded and cut in strips
Salt
Pepper

Sauté the tomatoes in the butter over high heat for 2 to 3 minutes. Add the stock and peppers and cook for 10 minutes more. Season with salt and pepper and serve.

CUMBERLAND SAUCE

Yield: 4 to 6 servings
1 cup fresh currants, crushed
6 tablespoons apple jelly
1 lemon
1 orange
1 teaspoon salted butter
1 small onion, peeled and diced
1 teaspoon mustard seeds, crushed
3 peppercorns, crushed
1 pinch ground ginger
1 tablespoon Worcestershire sauce
Salt
Cayenne pepper

Sprinkle the currants with the apple jelly. Set aside.

Cut a 2-inch strip of peel from the orange and lemon, remove the white pith, and then cut the strips into very fine pieces. Squeeze the fruit, reserving the juice.

Melt the butter in a saucepan and sauté the onion until transparent. Add the reserved citrus juices, currants, mustard seeds, and peppercorns. Flavor the sauce with the ginger, Worcestershire sauce, salt, and cayenne pepper. Bring to a boil and cook for 5 minutes. Stir in the orange and lemon strips. Let the sauce cool before serving.

This sauce goes well with roast beef or steak.

SWEDISH RAISIN SAUCE

Yield: 4 servings
½ cup raisins
¼ cup cognac
2 tablespoons lemon juice
¼ cup port wine
¼ cup beef roasting juices
2 tablespoons brown sugar
4 tablespoons currant jelly
1 teaspoon Worcestershire sauce
Salt
Pepper
Crushed pimiento
Ground cinnamon

Mix the raisins, cognac, and lemon juice together. If necessary, add water until the raisins are completely covered with liquid. Soak for 1 to 2 hours, and then drain.

Combine the raisins, port, roasting juices, and sugar and bring to a boil. Add the currant jelly and flavor with Worcestershire sauce, salt, pepper, crushed pimiento, and ground cinnamon. Bring to a boil again and serve.

PESTO SAUCE

Yield: 4 servings
2 tablespoons pine nuts
4 tablespoons olive oil
¼ cup freshly grated Parmesan cheese
White pepper
2 cups fresh basil, chopped
½ cup parsley, chopped
3 cloves garlic, crushed
1 teaspoon salt

Toast the pine nuts in 1 tablespoon of hot oil. Puree the pine nuts with the remaining oil, cheese, pepper, herbs, and garlic in a blender or food processor until the mixture is smooth and creamy.

CHINESE SAUCE

Yield: 4 servings
¼ cup soy sauce
¼ cup dry white wine
2 tablespoons rice vinegar
1 cup water
3 cloves garlic, crushed
1 pinch ground ginger
1 tablespoon sugar
⅛ teaspoon anise seeds
½ cinnamon stick
5 cloves
1 tablespoon cornstarch
2 tablespoons ketchup
Salt
Pepper

Heat the soy sauce, wine, vinegar, and water in a saucepan. Add the garlic, ginger, sugar, anise seeds, cinnamon, and cloves. Simmer for 30 minutes, then strain the liquid through a sieve.

Mix the cornstarch with 1 tablespoon of cold water. Stir the cornstarch mixture into the sauce, then add the ketchup. Bring the mixture to a boil, stirring constantly until thickened. Season with salt and pepper.

This sauce goes well with fish, pork, and poultry.

TURKISH YOGURT SAUCE

Yield: 4 servings
4 cloves garlic
2 teaspoons salt
1 tablespoon parsley, chopped
2 cups plain yogurt
4 tablespoons sesame seeds

Crush the garlic with the salt to form a smooth paste. Add the yogurt and parsley.

To serve, toast the sesame seeds in a hot oven until golden brown and sprinkle them on the yogurt mixture.

SPANISH OLIVE SAUCE

Yield: 4 servings
5 shallots, peeled
1 tablespoon olive oil
3 strips bacon
1 green leek leaf, cut in strips
1 teaspoon flour
1/4 cup chicken roasting juices
1/4 cup dry sherry
1/4 cup water
1/2 teaspoon thyme
1 bay leaf, crushed
5 pitted green olives, quartered
5 pitted black olives, quartered
Salt
Pepper

Brown the shallots whole on all sides in hot oil. Add the bacon and leek. Sprinkle with the flour and cook until the mixture is light brown.

Add the roasting juices, sherry, water, thyme, and bay leaf. Cook over low heat for 20 minutes.

Add the quartered olives to the sauce and season with salt and pepper to taste.

Serve the sauce with poultry.

TOMATO CREAM DIP

Yield: 4 servings
2 tablespoons tomato paste
½ cup whipping cream
1 small onion, peeled and chopped
1 clove garlic, peeled and crushed
1 tablespoon lemon juice
Salt
Pepper
Cayenne pepper
1 tablespoon diced red pepper

Mix the tomato paste and cream together in a bowl. Add the onion, garlic, lemon juice, salt, pepper, and cayenne pepper.

Before serving, sprinkle with diced red pepper.

GORGONZOLA CREAM DIP

Yield: 4 servings
½ cup Gorgonzola cheese
¾ cup sour cream
Salt
White pepper
2 tablespoons pistachio nuts, chopped

Mix the Gorgonzola cheese with the sour cream. Season with salt and pepper and sprinkle with the chopped pistachio nuts.

Serve with celery, carrot sticks, and crackers.

CHEESE DIP WITH SUNFLOWER SEEDS

Yield: 4 servings
2 cups low-fat ricotta cheese
½ cup milk
1 medium onion, peeled and finely chopped
1 clove garlic, peeled and finely chopped
Salt
Pepper
1 tablespoon peanut oil
3 tablespoons sunflower seeds

Mix the ricotta with the milk. Add the onion and garlic and season with salt and pepper.

Heat the peanut oil in a frying pan. Add the sunflower seeds and roast in the oil until the seeds are medium brown. Stir the seeds into the ricotta mixture.

Serve with raw vegetables or baked potatoes.

GRAPE AND HORSERADISH SAUCE

Yield: 4 servings
¼ cup fresh horseradish, grated
1 tablespoon lemon juice
¼ cup whipping cream
Salt
Pepper
Cayenne pepper
½ cup seedless grapes, cut in half

Combine the horseradish and lemon juice in a bowl.

Whip the cream until stiff and stir into the horseradish mixture. Season with salt, pepper, and cayenne pepper. Add the grapes and serve immediately.

MANGO SAUCE

Yield: 4 servings
1 ripe mango, medium size and peeled
2 tablespoons lemon juice
½ teaspoon chili powder
2 tablespoons pistachio nuts, chopped
¼ cup sour cream
Salt
Pepper

Puree the mango and lemon juice in a blender or food processor. Fold the chili powder, pistachio nuts, and sour cream into the puree. Season with salt and pepper.

Serve with cold meat.

GRAPE CHUTNEY

Yield: 6 servings
¼ cup white wine vinegar
2 cups dry white wine
2 cups brown sugar
3 tablespoons fresh ginger, peeled and cut in small cubes
3 cloves
1 piece cinnamon stick
5 pimientos
1 pound seedless grapes (green, red, or mixed)

Place the vinegar, wine, sugar, and spices in a saucepan and boil for 15 minutes. Add the grapes and cook gently for 10 minutes, not allowing the mixture to return to a boil. Remove the grapes with a slotted spoon and set aside.

Bring the syrup to a boil again for a few minutes. Spoon the grapes into jars and cover with syrup. If it is sealed tightly, the chutney can be stored for several months.

MUSHROOM SAUCE

Yield: 4 servings
2 cups dry red wine
¼ cup red wine vinegar
2 small red onions, peeled and cut in rings
3 cloves garlic, peeled and crushed
1 red pepper, seeded and cut in rings
2 bay leaves
1 tablespoon black pepper
1 sprig fresh thyme
2 teaspoons salt
1 pound small mushrooms, halved

Place the wine, vinegar, onions, garlic, red pepper, and spices in a saucepan and bring to a boil. Add the mushrooms and boil for 10 minutes.

Pour the mixture into jars and cover with foil. Allow the mixture to steep in the refrigerator a few days before serving.

APPLE AND SAGE CHUTNEY

Yield: 4 to 6 servings
1 tablespoon olive oil
1 cup sugar
1 sprig fresh sage
1 pound cooking apples, peeled, cored and diced
3 tablespoons raisins
¾ cup hazelnuts, chopped
1 cup white wine vinegar
1 cup dry white wine
1 small red pepper, seeded and cut in rings
1 teaspoon pimiento, chopped
Salt

Heat the oil in a saucepan. Add the sugar and sage and cook over medium heat until the sugar has caramelized. Stir in the apple, raisins, hazelnuts, vinegar, and wine. Cook over low heat for 20 minutes.

Add the pepper and pimiento to the sauce. Season with salt and serve.

PASSION FRUIT SAUCE

Yield: 4 servings
Juice of 2 oranges
2 tablespoons sugar
2 medium passion fruit, seeded and halved

Heat 1 tablespoon of the orange juice in a saucepan. Add the sugar and cook over medium heat until the sugar is a nut brown color. Add the remaining orange juice and bring to a boil. Add the passion fruit to the sauce and heat.

Serve over ice cream.

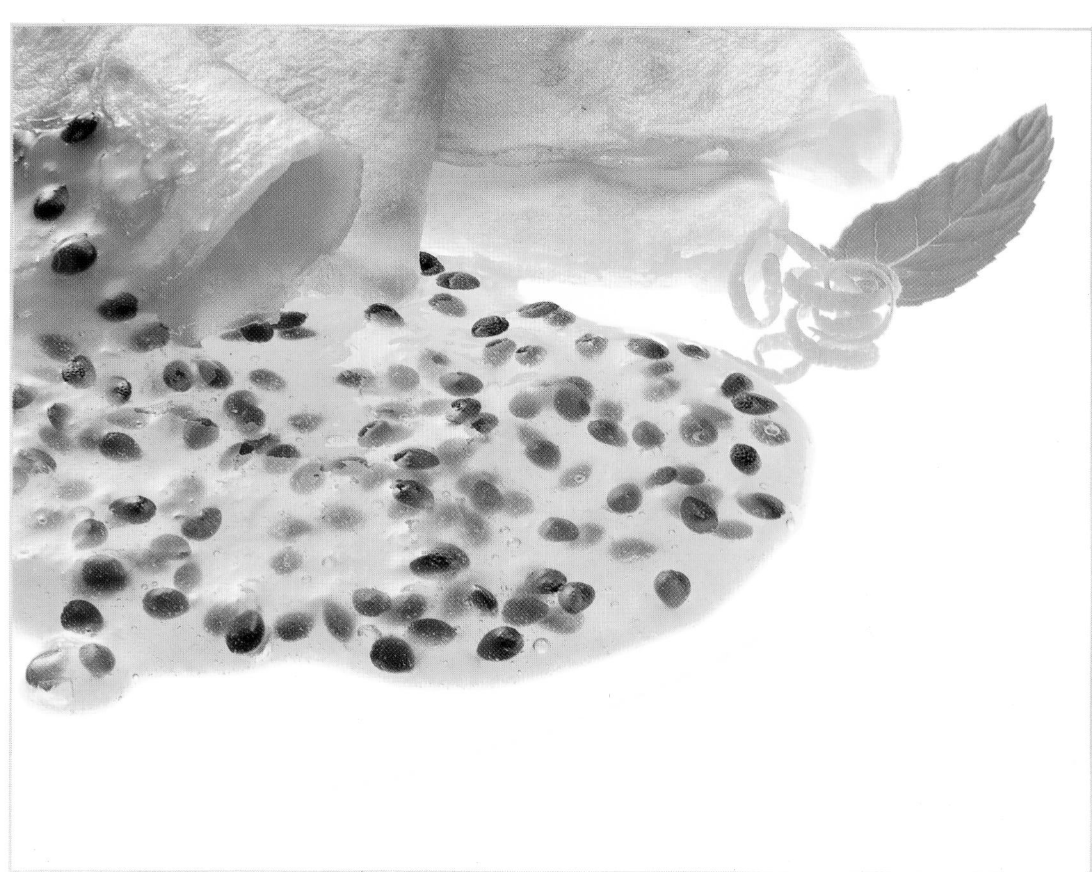

PLUM SAUCE

Yield: 4 servings
1 cup ripe plums
½ cinnamon stick
3 cloves
⅛ teaspoon anise seeds
2 tablespoons brown sugar
2 cups dry red wine
2 teaspoons cornstarch

Place the plums, cinnamon, cloves, anise seeds, brown sugar, and wine in a saucepan and cook over low heat for 15 minutes.

Mix the cornstarch with 2 teaspoons of water and stir the mixture into the sauce until it thickens. Serve over ice cream or poached fruit.

CHOCOLATE SAUCE

Yield: 4 servings
½ cup white grape juice
½ cup whipping cream
1 tablespoon cornstarch
2 tablespoons sugar
2 ounces semisweet chocolate, grated

Place the grape juice and cream in a saucepan and bring to a boil.

Mix the cornstarch with 1 tablespoon of cold water and stir into the grape juice mixture. Stir in the sugar. Add the grated chocolate to the hot sauce and stir until the chocolate melts.

Serve hot over poached fruit.

WINE FOAM SAUCE

Yield: 4 servings
1 egg
3 tablespoons sugar
1 cup sweet white wine
2 tablespoons cherry liqueur

Stir the egg, wine, and sugar together in a double boiler until the sauce is thick and foamy. Flavor with cherry liqueur. Serve with poached fruit.

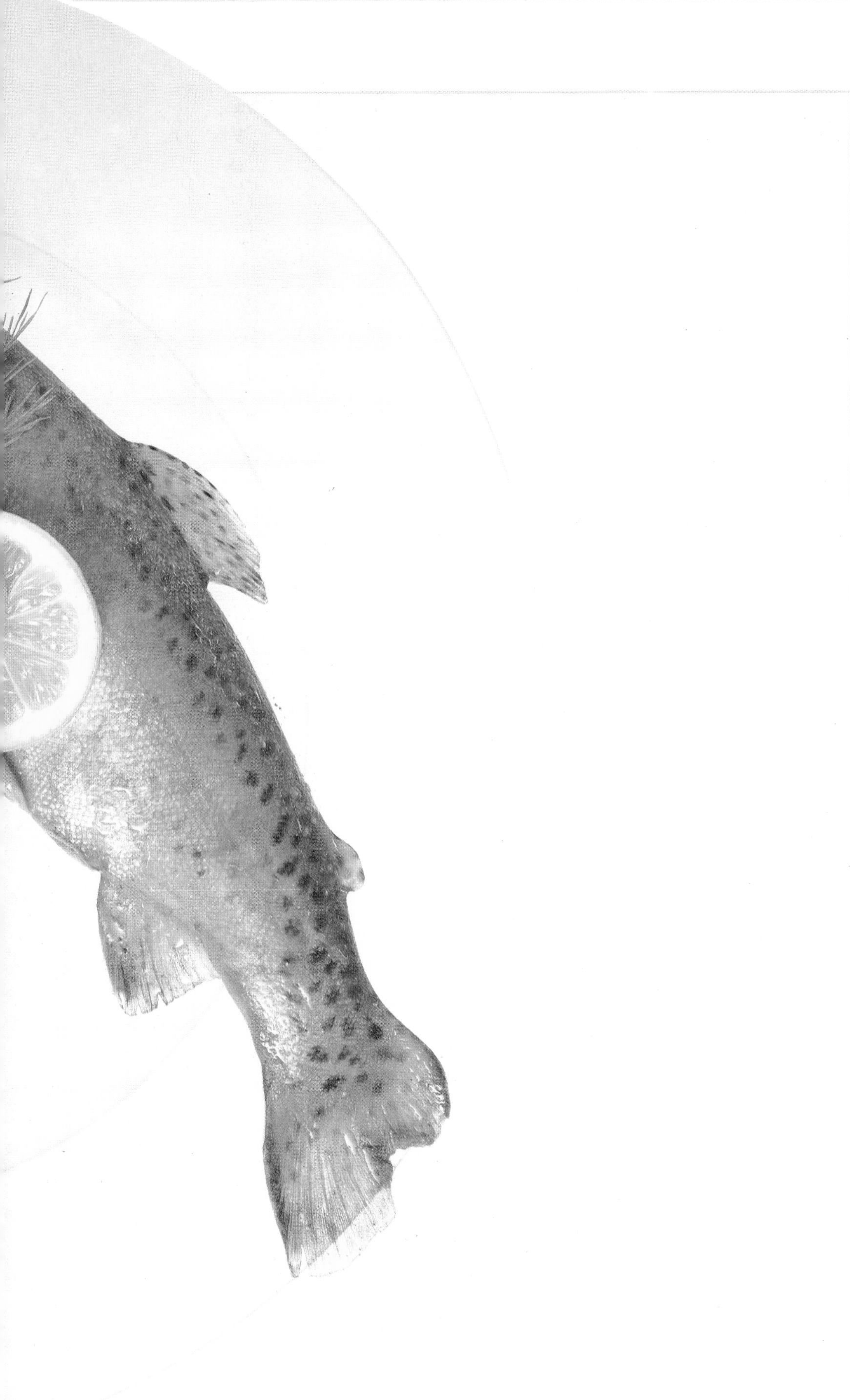

CLASSIC CUISINE

Nothing is better than a fish caught in the morning and cooked before midday. Whether fresh-caught or freshly bought, fresh fish should always be cooked on the same day it is acquired. The fish and shellfish recipes presented here offer an elegant selection of dishes with which to explore the delectable treasures of sea and stream.

TROUT ROLLS WITH BRAISED VEGETABLES

Yield: 6 to 8 servings
8 trout fillets, 6 to 8 ounces each
Lemon juice
Salt
Pepper
1 shallot, peeled and diced
1 sprig fresh thyme, chopped
½ cup fresh chives
½ cup dry white wine
½ cup dry vermouth
2 small tomatoes, skinned and seeded
1 cucumber, seeded and sliced
½ cup heavy cream
1½ tablespoons cold, salted butter

Sprinkle the trout with lemon juice and season with salt and pepper. Roll the fillets into tube shapes and fasten with wooden toothpicks.

Butter a casserole dish and place the shallots, fish, and herbs in the dish. Add the wine and vermouth. Simmer the fish over low heat for 8 to 10 minutes. Remove from the heat and keep warm.

Add the tomatoes, cucumber, and heavy cream to the casserole and boil the liquid until creamy in consistency. Season to taste with salt and pepper. Add the butter a little at a time, stirring with a wooden spoon until each flake is incorporated.

To serve, arrange the fish rolls with the vegetables in the cream sauce.

FILLET OF SOLE IN A PASTRY CRUST

Yield: 4 servings
4 sole fillets, 8 ounces each
Lemon juice
Salt
Pepper
8 sheets frozen puff pastry, thawed
2 egg yolks
2 tablespoons water

Preheat the oven to 325°F.

Sprinkle the sole fillets with lemon juice, salt, and pepper. Arrange the fillets on a buttered baking sheet and bake for 10 minutes. Remove from the oven and keep warm. Turn the oven temperature up to 425°F.

Roll the puff pastry out on a floured bread board. Cut each pastry sheet into the shape of a fish. Place 1 sole fillet on each pastry fish and cover with a second pastry sheet.

Beat the egg yolks with 2 tablespoons of water. Brush the yolks on the edges of the pastry sheets and press them together firmly. Brush the tops of the pastries with egg yolk. Place on a baking sheet that has been rinsed in cold water. Bake for 15 minutes, or until golden brown and crisp.

BROILED SALMON

Yield: 2 to 4 servings
4 salmon slices, 8 ounces each
Salt
Pepper
Lemon juice
4 tomatoes
3 tablespoons herb butter
1 cup watercress

Preheat the broiler.

Season the salmon with salt and pepper and sprinkle with lemon juice. Place the salmon under the boiler and broil for about 5 minutes on each side.

Wash and dry the tomatoes and cut a cross into each one. Season the tomatoes with salt and pepper and broil for 5 minutes.

Serve the salmon and tomatoes with herb butter and watercress.

FILLET OF SALMON JUSTINE

Yield: 4 servings
4 ounces red snapper fillets, finely chopped
1⅓ cups heavy cream
1 egg
Salt
Pepper
4 salmon fillets, 4 to 6 ounces each
2 tomatoes, skinned, seeded, and sliced
1 cucumber, sliced
4 large mushrooms, sliced
2 shallots, finely diced
¾ cup dry white wine
1 bay leaf
1 cup heavy cream

Mix the chopped red snapper fillets to an even consistency with the egg and ⅓ cup of heavy cream. Season with salt and pepper. Spread the red snapper mixture over the salmon fillets. Layer the sliced tomatoes, cucumber, and mushrooms on the salmon.

Butter a casserole dish and sprinkle the diced shallots in the pan. Place the salmon fillets on top of the shallots and add the wine and bay leaf. Poach the fish for 20 minutes over low heat. Remove from the heat and keep warm.

Pour 1 cup of heavy cream into the cooking liquid and boil until the sauce is creamy. Season to taste with salt and pepper and serve with the salmon.

STUFFED CARP

Yield: 4 to 6 servings
1 carp, about 1½ pounds
1 pound red snapper fillets
¼ cup heavy cream
⅓ cup pistachio nuts
2 eggs
½ cup Pernod liqueur
Salt
Freshly ground pepper

Rinse the carp with cold water and pat dry with paper towels. Carefully remove the skin without damaging it, using a small pointed knife. To do this, begin on the belly side toward the back and from there work toward the belly on the other side (photograph 1). There are 2 parts: 1) the head with skin and tail; 2) the flesh and bones (photograph 2). Carefully loosen the flesh from the bones (photograph 3) and mince it in a meat grinder or food processor.

Rinse the red snapper with cold water, pat dry with paper towels, and chop finely. Mix the carp and red snapper with the cream, pistachio nuts, eggs and Pernod (photograph 4). Season with salt and pepper.

Place the stuffing in the carp skin (photograph 5). Wrap the carp twice in aluminum foil and poach it in a water bath at about 200°F for 1½ to 1¾ hours (photograph 6). The carp can be served warm as a main course or as a cold appetizer.

1

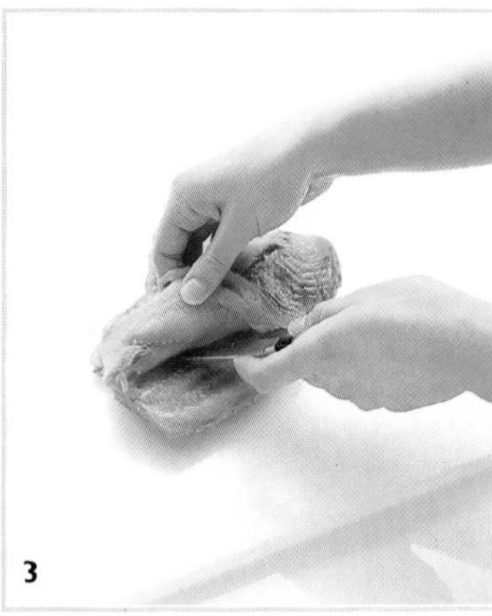
3

4

2

5

6

PERCH IN POPPY SAUCE

Yield: 2 to 4 servings
For the fish:
4 perch fillets, about 6 ounces each
Juice of 1 lemon
Salt
White pepper
1 cup flour
1½ tablespoons salted butter
For the sauce:
½ cup plus 2 tablespoons dry white wine
2 tablespoons ground poppy seeds
3 egg yolks
½ cup salted butter, melted
Juice of ½ lemon

Sprinkle the perch with lemon juice and season with salt and pepper. Dredge each fillet in flour. Melt the butter in a frying pan and sauté the fillets for 5 to 7 minutes. Remove from the pan and keep warm.

Reserve 2 tablespoons of white wine and place the rest in a saucepan. Bring the wine to a boil and pour over the poppy seeds. Beat the egg yolks with the reserved 2 tablespoons of wine in the top of a double boiler until foamy. Add the melted butter in a thin stream, beating until the sauce is creamy. Add the lemon juice. Remove the sauce from the heat and add the poppy seeds. Season to taste with salt and pepper. To serve, pour the sauce over the fish.

HADDOCK IN RIESLING

Yield: 2 to 4 servings
4 haddock fillets, about 6 ounces each
Lemon juice
½ cup cold, salted butter
3 shallots, peeled and diced
1 tablespoon fresh chervil, leaves removed and chopped
3 tablespoons water
¾ cup heavy cream
3 plum tomatoes, skinned, seeded, and cut into strips
1 cup mushrooms, sliced
Salt
Pepper
2 tablespoons sour cream

Sprinkle the haddock fillets with lemon juice. Melt ¼ cup of butter in a large frying pan and sauté the shallots until glazed. Add the fish, wine, chervil, and water. Poach the fillets over medium heat for 10 minutes. Remove the fish from the pan and keep warm.

Add the heavy cream to the fish juices in the pan and bring the liquid to a boil. Add the tomatoes and mushrooms and simmer until heated through. Add the remaining ¼ cup of butter a tablespoon at a time, stirring constantly with a wooden spoon until a creamy sauce forms. Season to taste with salt and pepper. Stir in the sour cream. Pour the sauce over the fish and serve.

RED SNAPPER WITH CHIVE BUTTER

Yield: 2 to 4 servings
4 red snapper fillets, about 6 ounces each
Lemon juice
½ cup cold, salted butter
2 shallots, peeled and finely diced
½ cup fresh chives, cut into rings
½ cup dry white wine
½ cup dry vermouth
Salt
Pepper

Sprinkle the red snapper fillets with lemon juice. Melt 2 tablespoons of butter in a large frying pan and glaze the shallots in it. Stir in the chives. Add the red snapper and then stir in the wine and vermouth. Simmer the fish for 10 to 15 minutes. Remove from the pan and keep warm. Reduce the cooking juices slightly. Add the remaining butter to the sauce a tablespoon at a time, stirring constantly until the sauce thickens. Serve with potatoes.

COD IN BUTTER SAUCE

Yield: 2 to 4 servings
4 cod fillets, 6 to 8 ounces each
Lemon juice
2 carrots, peeled and cut into strips
2 celery stalks, cut into strips
1 medium onion, peeled and cut into strips
1 small leek, cut into strips
3 tablespoons cold, salted butter
Salt
Pepper

Preheat the oven to 325°F.

Sprinkle the cod with lemon juice. Butter a casserole dish. Place the cod and the sliced vegetables in the dish and bake for 20 minutes. Remove the dish from the oven and pour the cooking juices into a saucepan. Keep the fish and vegetables warm.

Reduce the cooking juices to ¼ cup. Add the butter, stirring constantly until the sauce thickens. Season with salt, pepper, and lemon juice to taste.

Pour the sauce over the fish and vegetables and serve with rice or noodles.

1

2

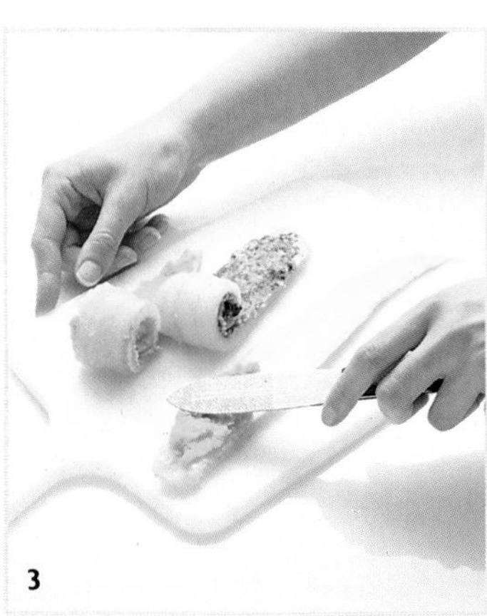
3

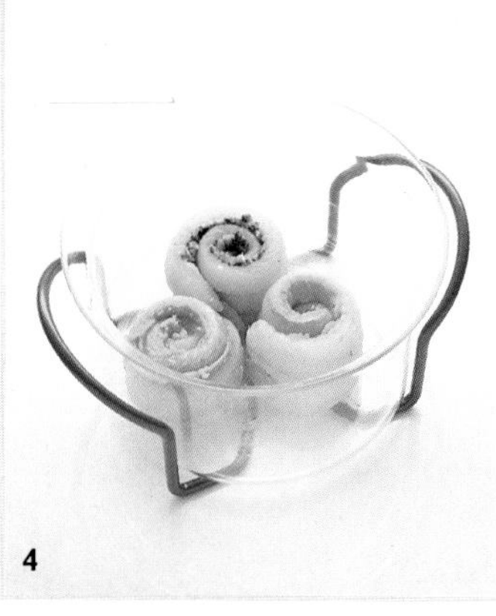
4

SOLE ROLLS IN LEMON SAUCE

Yield: 6 to 8 servings
For the rolls:
12 sole fillets, 2 to 3 ounces each
Salt
Pepper
8 ounces red snapper fillet
¼ cup heavy cream
2 eggs
¼ cup spinach, blanched and chopped
2 tablespoons lobster, crab, or tomato paste
⅛ teaspoon saffron
1 tablespoon salted butter
1 cup dry white wine
For the sauce:
½ cup cold, salted butter
2 shallots, peeled and chopped
¼ cup dry white wine
Juice of 1 lime

Preheat the oven to 325°F.

Season the sole fillets with salt and pepper. Lay the fillets skin side up on a bread board.

Mince the red snapper in a food processor and rub it through a sieve (photograph 1). Mix the red snapper puree with the heavy cream and eggs. Separate the snapper mixture into 3 separate portions. Mix the first portion with spinach; the second with lobster, crab, or tomato paste; and the third with saffron (photograph 2). Spread the 4 sole fillets with each of the mixtures and roll up (photograph 3).

Place the rolls side by side in a buttered soufflé dish (photograph 4). Pour in the wine along the sides of the dish. Cover with foil and bake for 20 minutes.

To make the sauce, melt the butter in a saucepan and sauté the shallots. Add the wine and lime juice and boil over high heat. Add the cold butter to the sauce a tablespoon at a time, stirring constantly until the sauce becomes creamy. Season with salt and pepper. Pour the sauce over the fish and serve with an herbed rice.

SOLE BOWS WITH SNAILS

Yield: 4 to 6 servings

12 sole fillets, 2 to 4 ounces each
Salt
Pepper
1 shallot, peeled and chopped
1 sprig fresh tarragon, leaves removed and finely chopped
1½ tablespoons cold, salted butter
¼ cup dry white wine
1 small bay leaf
¼ cup heavy cream
6 snails (optional)

Make a 1½-inch long slit through the sole fillets. Season with salt and pepper. Butter a small pan with a teaspoon of the butter. Spread the shallot and tarragon on the bottom of the pan and layer the fillets on top. Add the wine and bay leaf. Cover the fillets with parchment paper and poach over low heat for 5 to 10 minutes. Remove the fish and keep warm.

Add the heavy cream and snails to the cooking juices and boil to reduce the liquid slightly. Add the remaining butter a teaspoon at a time, stirring constantly. Pour the sauce over the fish and serve with rice.

HALIBUT WITH TWO MUSTARD SAUCES

Yield: 6 to 8 servings
1½ tablespoons salted butter
1 shallot, peeled and diced
8 slices halibut, 4 ounces each
¼ cup dry white wine
¼ cup dry vermouth
¼ cup heavy cream
1 teaspoon Dijon mustard
1 teaspoon brown mustard
Salt
Pepper

Melt the butter in a saucepan and sauté the shallot until soft. Add the halibut, wine, and vermouth. Simmer over medium heat for 10 to 15 minutes. Remove the fish from the pan and keep warm.

Pour half of the cooking liquid into a second saucepan. Divide the heavy cream between the two pans and bring the liquids in both pans to a boil. Add the Dijon mustard to one pan and the brown mustard to the other. Season both with salt and pepper to taste.

Pour the two sauces over the fish and serve.

MONKFISH IN A SAFFRON SAUCE WITH MORELS

Yield: 2 to 4 servings
⅓ cup dried morel mushrooms
2 shallots, peeled and cut into strips
¼ cup cold, salted butter
4 slices monkfish, 8 ounces each
¼ cup dry white wine
¼ cup dry vermouth
½ cup early peas
2 small carrots, peeled and cut into strips
Salt
Pepper
¼ teaspoon saffron
2 tablespoons heavy cream

Soak the mushrooms in water for 1 to 2 hours. Melt 1 teaspoon of butter in a frying pan and sauté the shallots until soft. Add the fish, wine, vermouth, and ⅓ cup of strained water from the mushrooms. Cook over medium heat for 15 to 20 minutes.

Place the peas and carrots in a saucepan with boiling salt water and simmer for 8 minutes. Drain the vegetables. Remove the fish from the pan and keep warm with the vegetables.

Add the mushrooms to the fish cooking liquid and boil until the liquid has reduced by one-half. Add the remaining butter, stirring constantly until it is incorporated into the sauce. Season with salt, pepper, and saffron. Stir in the heavy cream. Serve the monkfish with the saffron sauce.

MACKEREL IN PINK PEPPER CREAM SAUCE

Yield: 4 servings
8 mackerel fillets, 3 to 4 ounces each
Lemon juice
Salt
1 teaspoon crushed pink peppercorns
6 to 8 tablespoons peanut oil
1 small onion, peeled and diced
1½ tablespoons salted butter
¼ cup dry rosé wine
¼ cup heavy cream

Slice through the skin of the mackerel fillets diagonally 3 times. Sprinkle the fillets with lemon juice and season with salt and pink pepper.

Heat the oil in a frying pan and sauté the fillets on both sides until crisp. Remove the fish from the pan and keep warm.

Melt the butter in the same pan and sauté the onion. Add the wine and heavy cream and bring to a boil. Season with salt and pepper to taste. To serve, pour the sauce over the fish.

1

2

3

4

STUFFED TURBOT

Yield: 6 to 8 servings
For the fish:
8 turbot fillets, about 3 to 4 ounces each, bones removed but reserved for stock
Juice of 1 lemon
Salt
Pepper
For the stuffing:
1 fish fillet, about 8 ounces
2 eggs
¼ cup heavy cream
⅓ cup cooked diced carrots
⅓ cup pistachio nuts
1 teaspoon fresh tarragon leaves
8 cabbage leaves
4 cooked asparagus spears
For the sauce:
¾ cup mayonnaise
2 tablespoons brandy
1 tablespoon fresh sorrel, chopped

Sprinkle the turbot fillets with lemon juice and season with salt and pepper. Set aside.

For the stuffing, pass the fish fillet through a food mill or puree in a food processor. Place the bowl containing the pureed fish in a larger bowl containing ice cubes. Mix in the eggs and cream (photograph 1). Add the carrots, pistachio nuts, and tarragon.

Blanch the cabbage leaves in boiling water. Drain and arrange 2 leaves together on each of 4 buttered pieces of aluminum foil. Place 1 fillet on each pair of cabbage leaves and spread with stuffing ¼ inch thick. Place 1 asparagus spear on each (photograph 2). Spread the 4 remaining fillets with the remaining stuffing, and place them, stuffing side down, on top of the asparagus (photograph 3). Fold the cabbage leaves over the fillets and seal the aluminum foil.

Place the fish bones in a large saucepan with enough water to cover and boil for 15 minutes. Remove the bones and allow the liquid to cool. Put the wrapped fillets in the pan and simmer over very low heat for about 1 hour (photograph 4).

Remove the fillets from the pan, carefully unwrap, and allow them to cool. Cut the turbot into slices and arrange on a serving platter.

For the sauce, combine the mayonnaise, brandy, and sorrel and season with salt and pepper. This dish can be served as a main course or as an appetizer.

FISH BALLS ON SPINACH LEAVES

Yield: 2 to 4 servings
For the fish mixture:
4 ounces red snapper fillet, minced
4 ounces perch fillet, minced
2 eggs
¼ cup heavy cream
Salt
Pepper
Grated nutmeg
For the dough:
¼ cup milk
1 tablespoon salted butter
3 tablespoons flour
2 eggs
For the spinach:
1 tablespoon salted butter
1 clove garlic, peeled and crushed
1 pound spinach leaves, blanched

Mix the minced fish fillets with the eggs and cream. Season with salt, pepper, and nutmeg.

For the dough, bring the milk, butter, and a pinch of salt to a boil in a saucepan. Add the flour all at once, stirring constantly until the mixture forms a ball and comes away from the bottom of the pan. Remove from the heat and immediately stir in 1 egg. Cool slightly, then beat in the remaining egg. Let the dough cool completely.

Combine the dough with the fish mixture and scoop out balls with a spoon. Poach the fish balls in simmering water for 25 minutes.

Melt the butter and sauté the garlic briefly. Add the spinach and sauté for 5 minutes. Season with salt and pepper. Serve the fish balls on the spinach leaves.

FRIED SOLE

Yield: 4 servings
For the fish:
4 sole fillets, 8 ounces each
Lemon juice
Salt
Pepper
2 tablespoons flour
2 eggs
1 cup fine bread crumbs
½ cup vegetable oil
6 tablespoons salted butter
For the herb butter:
½ cup salted butter, softened
4 tablespoons flour
2 egg yolks
2 cups fresh herbs, such as parsley, thyme, dill, marjoram, and basil, finely chopped

Sprinkle the sole fillets with lemon juice. Season with salt and pepper and dust with flour. Beat the eggs well. Dip the fish in the beaten eggs, then dredge in the bread crumbs.

Heat the oil and butter in a frying pan. Add the sole fillets and sauté over medium heat for about 10 minutes. Remove from the pan and keep warm.

Preheat the broiler.

Combine the butter, flour, and egg yolks. Mix the chopped herbs into the butter. Spread the herb butter on the fish and broil briefly.

FRIED FLOUNDER IN RED WINE

Yield: 4 servings
4 flounder fillets, about 6 to 8 ounces each
Lemon juice
Worcestershire sauce
Salt
Pepper
4 tablespoons flour
½ cup vegetable oil
1 cup small mushrooms
4 tablespoons salted butter
8 ounces pearl onions
½ cup dry red wine

Sprinkle the flounder fillets with lemon juice and Worcestershire sauce. Season with salt and pepper and dust with flour. Heat the oil in a frying pan and fry the flounder fillets on both sides for about 7 to 10 minutes. Remove from the pan and keep warm. Pour off the oil. Melt the butter in the same pan and sauté the mushrooms and onions. Add the red wine and boil the mixture until the liquid reduces slightly. Season with salt and pepper. To serve, pour the mushrooms, onions, and red wine sauce over the fish.

BROILED SWORDFISH WITH FENNEL

Yield: 4 to 6 servings
2 large swordfish steaks, about ½ pound each
Lemon juice
Salt
Pepper
2 fennel bulbs, cut into long pieces
4 tablespoons peanut oil
About ¼ cup Pernod liqueur, heated

Preheat the broiler.

Sprinkle the swordfish steaks on both sides with lemon juice and season with salt and pepper. Stuff the swordfish with the fennel and place on a baking sheet. Brush the fish with oil and broil for 15 to 20 minutes.

Arrange the swordfish on a plate, pour on the hot Pernod, and carefully flambé the dish. Serve with parsley potatoes.

POACHED FISH ROLLS

Yield: 8 servings
8 sole fillets, 3 to 4 ounces each
Lemon juice
Salt
Pepper
1 red pepper, seeded and diced
1 green pepper, seeded and diced
½ cup chopped leek
4 shallots, peeled and diced
1 cup fresh dill, chopped
1 tablespoon salted butter
½ cup dry white wine
½ cup dry vermouth
1 bay leaf

Sprinkle the fish fillets with lemon juice and season with salt and pepper.

Combine the vegetables and dill and spread the mixture onto the fish. Roll up the fillets and secure with wooden toothpicks. Place the fish rolls in a large frying pan. Add the butter, wine, vermouth, and bay leaf. Cook over low heat for 7 to 10 minutes.

RED SNAPPER FILLETS WITH WILD RICE CAKES

Yield: 4 to 6 servings
For the fish:
4 red snapper fillets, about 6 to 8 ounces each
Juice of 1 lemon
Salt
Coarsely ground pepper
2 tablespoons butter
For the wild rice cakes:
½ cup wild rice
½ leek, diced
1½ tablespoons salted butter
1 egg
For the sauce:
2 shallots, peeled and diced
1½ tablespoons salted butter
1 tablespoon flour
½ cup dry white wine
2 tablespoons champagne mustard
½ cup heavy cream

Sprinkle the fish fillets with lemon juice. Season with salt and pepper, pressing the pepper into the fish.

Simmer the wild rice in 1-½ cups of boiling water for 35 to 40 minutes. Drain and cool.

Melt the butter in a frying pan and sauté the leeks. Remove the leeks from the pan and let cool.

Melt 2 tablespoons of butter in the frying pan and sauté the fish fillets for 10 to 15 minutes. Remove from the pan and keep warm.

For the sauce, melt 1 tablespoon of the butter and sauté the shallots until glazed. Stir in the flour and cook for 3 to 5 minutes. Add the white wine and bring to a boil, stirring constantly. Reduce the heat and stir in ½ tablespoon of butter, the mustard, and the cream. Season with salt and pepper to taste.

For the wild rice cakes, mix the rice, leek, and egg together. Season with salt and pepper. Melt the remaining butter and, using a spoon, make little mounds of the rice. Place the mounds in the melted butter, press flat, and sauté for 2 minutes on each side.

HADDOCK IN BROWN BUTTER

Yield: 6 to 8 servings
12 haddock fillets, 3½ to 4 ounces each
Salt
Pepper
Worcestershire sauce
4 tablespoons flour
⅓ cup peanut oil
1 small onion, peeled and diced
1 clove garlic, peeled and crushed
3 tablespoons salted butter
2 tablespoons chopped parsley
1 teaspoon capers

Season the haddock with salt, pepper, and Worcestershire sauce, then dust with flour. Heat the oil in a non-stick pan and sauté the fish for 7 to 10 minutes. Remove the fish from the pan and keep warm.

Pour off the oil. Heat the butter in the pan and allow it to lightly brown. Quickly sauté the onion and garlic. Add the parsley and capers and heat well. To serve, pour the caper mixture over the fish fillets.

FLOUNDER FILLETS WITH SHRIMP

Yield: 8 to 10 servings
16 flounder fillets, 2½ to 3 ounces each
Salt
Pepper
3 tablespoons flour
½ cup peanut oil
4 slices toasted bread
6 tablespoons salted butter
1 cup parsley, chopped
20 to 25 small shrimp, shelled and deveined

Season the flounder fillets with salt and pepper and dust with flour. Heat the oil in a non-stick pan and sauté the fillets for 7 to 10 minutes. Remove from the pan and keep warm.

Cut the toast into cubes. Melt the butter in a second pan and brown the bread cubes in it. Stir in the parsley and shrimp. Season to taste with salt and pepper. Simmer for 8 to 10 minutes, or until the shrimp have turned pink. To serve, pour the shrimp mixture over the fish fillets.

SHARK STEAKS IN CAPER BUTTER

Yield: 4 servings
16 anchovy fillets
Salt
Pepper
Worcestershire sauce
Juice of 1 lemon
4 shark steaks, 6 to 8 ounces each
2 tablespoons flour
½ cup peanut oil
6 tablespoons salted butter
2 tablespoons capers

Make a paste with the anchovy fillets, salt, pepper, Worcestershire sauce, and lemon juice. Spread the paste on each side of the shark steaks and dust each steak with flour.

Heat the oil in a frying pan and sauté the steaks for 7 to 10 minutes. Remove from the pan and keep warm. Pour off the oil.

Melt the butter in the pan and stir in the capers. To serve, heat the capers and sprinkle them onto the shark steaks.

WHITE HERRING ASSORTMENT

Yield: 4 to 6 servings
For the white herring tartar:
4 white herring fillets, finely chopped
10 capers, finely chopped
1 pickle, finely chopped
1 shallot, peeled and diced
Freshly ground pepper
For the white herring in chili:
4 white herring fillets, finely diced
2 mild pepperonis, finely diced
4 tablespoons sweet chili sauce
For the white herring with pepper cream:
4 white herring fillets, cut into small cubes
4 tablespoons sour cream
1 teaspoon pickled green peppercorns
For the white herring with chanterelle mushrooms:
4 white herring fillets, diced
1 small (3½- ounce) jar chanterelle mushrooms
2 small pearl onions
2 tablespoons sherry vinegar
Pepper
For the white herring with dill:
4 white herring fillets, diced
½ cup fresh dill, finely chopped
½ cup button mushrooms, sliced
Pepper
1 tablespoon wine vinegar
Plus:
Lettuce leaves
Radicchio leaves
Pickle slices

For the white herring tartar, combine the herring fillets, capers, pickle, and shallot. Season with pepper.

For the white herring in chili, mix the diced fillets and pepperonis with the chili sauce.

For the white herring with pepper cream, mix the fillets with the sour cream and peppercorns.

For the white herring with chanterelles, mix the fillets with the drained chanterelles and pearl onions. Season with vinegar and pepper.

For the white herring with dill, mix the fish, dill, and mushrooms together. Flavor piquantly with pepper and vinegar

Refrigerate the white herring dishes for about 1 hour, then arrange on lettuce leaves and garnish with slices of pickle. Serve with fresh bread and butter.

WHITE HERRING FILLETS WITH CURRY CREAM

Yield: 2 to 4 servings
2 Granny Smith apples, peeled, cored, and sliced
Salt
1 cup heavy cream
2 tablespoons sour cream
1 teaspoon curry powder
Pepper
12 white herring fillets

Poach the apple slices briefly in boiling salt water. Remove the apples from the pan and dry well.

Whip the heavy cream until stiff and mix with the sour cream. Flavor the cream mixture with curry powder, salt, and pepper.

To serve, spread the apple slices onto a plate. Roll up the fish fillets and place them on the apple slices. Pour the curry cream on top.

MARINATED HERRING ROLLS

Yield: 4 to 6 servings
16 herring fillets
2 red onions, peeled and cut into rings
½ cup mild wine vinegar
1 cup medium-dry sherry
3 tablespoons water
3 tablespoons sugar
20 mustard seeds
1 teaspoon white peppercorns
1 teaspoon pimientos
2 bay leaves
4 cloves

Rinse the herring fillets with cold water, roll them up, and fasten the rolls with wooden toothpicks. Layer the herring rolls, onions, and carrots in a jar. Bring the vinegar, sherry, and water to a boil with the sugar and the seasonings, then pour onto the fish while the mixture is hot. Allow the mixture to cool, then store in the refrigerator for about 1 day. Serve with bread and butter.

SARDINES SICILIAN STYLE

Yield: 6 to 8 servings
1 pound fresh sardines
Salt
Pepper
Lemon juice
2 tablespoons flour
½ cup olive oil
1 small onion, peeled and cut into strips
¼ red pepper, seeds removed and cut into strips
¼ green pepper, seeded and cut into strips
5 black olives, quartered
5 green olives, quartered
1 clove garlic, peeled and crushed
1 tablespoon chopped parsley
Oregano

Season the sardines with salt and pepper and sprinkle with lemon juice. Dust with flour. Heat ⅓ cup of olive oil in a frying pan. Add the sardines and sauté for 2 to 5 minutes. Remove from the pan and keep warm.

Put the remaining oil in the pan and cook the onion, peppers, and olives for 3 to 5 minutes. Season with garlic, salt, pepper, parsley, and oregano. Serve the vegetable mixture over the sardines with warm garlic bread.

MUSSEL STEW WITH A PUFF PASTRY HOOD

Yield: 8 to 10 servings
For the mussel stew:
1 pound shelled mussels
½ pound oysters or clams
1 Spanish onion, peeled and cut into strips
3 tablespoons salted butter
2 cups dry white wine
Salt
Freshly ground black pepper
2 carrots, peeled and cut into strips
2 potatoes, peeled and cut into strips
½ leek, peeled and cut into strips
½ cup chopped fennel bulb
Pinch saffron
2 plum tomatoes, skinned, seeded, and diced
12 scallops with roe
For the puff pastry hood:
2 sheets frozen puff pastry, thawed
2 tablespoons flour
2 eggs, separated

Scrub the mussels and other shellfish thoroughly, discarding any open shells. Melt 1 tablespoon of butter in a large saucepan and sauté half of the onion. Add the shellfish, white wine, and 1 cup of water. Cover and boil for 5 minutes. Strain the shellfish through a fine colander and reserve the liquid. Remove the seafood from the shells, discarding any that have not opened.

Melt 2 tablespoons of butter in a saucepan and sauté the remaining onion strips, carrots, potatoes, leek, and fennel. Add the reserved shellfish liquid. Season with salt, pepper, and saffron and boil for 5 minutes.

Pour the soup into 4 large ovenproof soup bowls and let cool. The bowls should only be half to three-quarters full. Add the tomatoes, mussels, oysters or clams, and scallops to the soup.

For the puff pastry hoods, preheat the oven to 400°F. Dust the puff pastry with flour and roll out a little until smooth. Place an empty soup bowl upside down on the pastry and cut around it ½ inch from the edges. Cut out 4 circles. Brush the edges of the soup-filled ovenproof bowls with egg white, lay a circle of pastry on top of each bowl, and press it on firmly around the edges. Carefully brush the surface of the pastry with beaten egg yolk.

Bake for 12 to 15 minutes.

OYSTERS WITH CRAB BUTTER

Yield: 6 to 8 servings
36 oysters
2 shallots, peeled and diced
2 tablespoons salted butter
½ cup dry white wine
½ cup dry vermouth
½ cup heavy cream
1 tablespoon crab butter or paste
Salt
Pepper
12 small round puff pastry shells

Open the oysters and collect the liquid. Bring the oyster liquid to a boil in a saucepan. Add the oysters and briefly blanch them in the boiling liquid. Drain the oysters, reserving the liquid.

Melt the butter in a saucepan and sauté the shallots. Add the reserved oyster liquid, wine, vermouth, and cream. Boil until it is reduced by half. Flavor the sauce with the crab butter, salt, and pepper. Place the oysters into the pastry shells and pour on the sauce.

SCALLOPS AU GRATIN

Yield: 2 to 4 servings
20 scallops
2 shallots, peeled and diced
2 plum tomatoes, skinned, seeded, and diced
1 cup parsley, chopped
4 sprigs fresh marjoram, chopped
Salt
Pepper
3 tablespoons bread crumbs
4 tablespoons salted butter

Preheat the broiler.

Blanch the scallops for about 1 minute in boiling salt water, drain, and place in 4 ovenproof dishes or scallop shells.

Season the scallops with salt and pepper and cover with the diced shallots and tomatoes, herbs, and bread crumbs. Dot with butter and broil for 3 to 5 minutes.

CRAYFISH IN DILL SAUCE

Yield: 2 to 4 servings
24 fresh crayfish
1 bunch soup greens, roughly chopped
½ teaspoon caraway seeds
Salt
½ small cucumber
2 shallots, peeled and diced
1 cup fresh dill, chopped
3 tablespoons salted butter
½ cup dry white wine
½ cup dry vermouth
½ cup heavy cream
Pepper

Scrub the crayfish thoroughly under cold running water. Place the crayfish in a large pot of boiling salt water with the soup greens and caraway seeds and boil for 5 minutes. Remove the crayfish from the water and drain.

Wash the cucumber and cut out small balls. Cook in salt water for about 3 minutes. Melt 2 tablespoons of butter and sauté the shallots. Add the wine and dry vermouth, then the cream and 4 tablespoons of the crayfish liquid. Reduce the mixture by half. Stir in the dill and season with salt and pepper. Slowly incorporate the rest of the butter, stirring constantly.

Remove the crayfish tails from the shells and place them in the sauce together with the cucumber balls. Serve with small buttered potatoes or buttered rice.

LANGOUSTES WITH CHICORY

Yield: 2 to 4 servings
24 langoustes (spiny lobsters), in their shells
1 bunch soup greens, roughly chopped
1 bay leaf
Salt
5 peppercorns
8 small heads of chicory
2 shallots, peeled and diced
3 tablespoons salted butter
1 tablespoon flour
1 cup heavy cream
Grated nutmeg

Scrub the langoustes thoroughly under cold running water. Place the langoustes in a large pot of boiling water with the soup greens, bay leaf, and peppers and boil for 10 minutes. Remove the langoustes from the pan, break off the tails, and keep warm.

Wash the chicory. Remove some of the outer leaves and set aside. Cut the chicory into rough strips. Melt the butter in a saucepan and sauté the shallots. Add the flour and cook for 3 minutes. Add the cream and chicory strips and cook, stirring constantly, for 3 to 5 minutes. Season with salt, pepper, and nutmeg.

To serve, arrange the reserved chicory leaves in a star pattern on a plate, place the vegetables over them, and arrange the langoustes on top.

LOBSTER MEDALLIONS WITH MORELS

Yield: 4 servings
½ cup or 3½ ounces dried whole morels
4 lobster tails, cooked
3 tablespoons cold, salted butter
2 shallots, peeled and diced
1 tablespoon tomato paste
½ cup dry vermouth
½ cup sherry
3 tablespoons brandy
Salt
Pepper
1 teaspoon chopped fresh tarragon leaves
½ cup heavy cream

Soak the morels in ½ cup water for 1½ hours. Remove the lobster tails from the shells. Grind the tails with a mortar and pestle. Melt 1½ tablespoons of butter in a saucepan and sauté the lobster shells. Stir in the shallots and tomato paste and cook together briefly. Add the vermouth, sherry, and brandy; flavor with salt, pepper, and tarragon. Bring to a boil and then strain through a sieve into a second pan. Add the soaked, drained morels and the cream and boil the liquid until it reduces to a thick and creamy consistency. Incorporate the remaining butter into the mixture, stirring constantly.

To serve, cut the lobster meat into medallions and heat in the sauce.

HERBED SHRIMP

Yield: 6 to 8 servings
32 shrimp
½ cup fresh thyme, finely chopped
½ cup fresh marjoram, finely chopped
½ cup fresh basil, finely chopped
4 plum tomatoes, skinned, seeded, and cut into rough cubes
2 onions, peeled and diced
2 cloves garlic, peeled and crushed
4 tablespoons peanut oil
3½ tablespoons salted butter
Salt
Pepper

Rinse the shrimp with cold water and dry well with paper towels.

Heat the oil in a frying pan and sauté the shrimp for about 3 minutes on each side; remove from the pan and keep warm. Pour off the oil and melt the butter. Sauté the onion and garlic. Add the tomatoes. Flavor with the herbs, salt, and pepper. Pour over the shrimp. Serve with fresh bread.

CLASSIC CUISINE

There is nothing quite as satisfying as a juicy steak, a tender herbed veal roast, or a succulent leg of lamb. Hearty appetites appreciate a stuffed pork chop; delicate sweetbreads can be extremely delicious even if complicated to prepare. This chapter covers many different cuts of meat and offers recipes for everything from main course dishes to special Sunday roasts. You'll find enticing ways of preparing beef, veal, pork, and lamb to whet your appetite and inspire many excellent meals.

MEAT

TIPS AND TECHNIQUES FOR COOKING MEAT

Everyone likes their meat done a different way. Who hasn't sat down to dinner and asked for the end slice — or demanded that the steak come off the grill immediately before it turns gray? The cooking times and tips given here accommodate tastes for medium-rare meat. With the exception of pork, which should always be cooked through, beef, veal, and lamb may be grilled, broiled, roasted, or fried to suit all tastes.

Meat is best when prepared on the day it is bought. When that is not possible, it should be kept in the refrigerator, removed from its packing and placed in a china or glass dish covered with a plate. Best storing temperature: 45°F. Pickling or marinating is another method of keeping meat fresh that tenderizes it. An olive oil or vinegar marinade is always improved with fresh herbs. You can also just brush the meat with plenty of olive oil mixed with herbs. Typical marinating time is 24 hours (in the refrigerator). Raw and cooked meat may be frozen and kept for one or two months before using.

Preparing roasting joints and soup meat properly first means trimming. Cut away the skin, sinews, and any surplus fat. Bone splinters are removed by washing. Quickly rinse the meat under cold water and dry with paper towels.

Before roasting, the meat should be seasoned. Rub the surface briskly with salt and pepper. (This technique also applies to seasonings such as paprika and curry powder.) When using herbs, the surface of the meat should be first brushed carefully with oil, and freshly chopped or dried herbs then rubbed into the meat.

Stewing meat should not be washed, but just dabbed with a paper towel. It is important to preserve the nutrient value of meat as well as create a tasty dish. Here are a few basic rules.

Boiling means cooking in liquid. This can be salt water, a mixture of half water and wine, or even vinegar. Sometimes the meat is placed in a saucepan and cold liquid added to cover it, then the liquid is brought to a boil and simmered over low heat until done. Alternatively, meat is put into liquid at a full boil, then the heat reduced and the meat simmers until done. For a concentrated meat stock, boil for as long as possible and keep adding to replace the liquid evaporated. Soup vegetables are cooked with the meat. To serve vegetables with boiled meat, strain the broth after 1½ hours of cooking time and cook fresh vegetables for another 15 minutes in it. Cooking time for 2¼ pounds of meat is about 2 hours.

Braising is a method of cooking which is between boiling and roasting and is more like stewing. A braised joint is a delicious way to prepare meat. Dishes such as sauerbraten, goulash, and stew are often braised. This is a method well suited for tougher cuts of meat. The average braising time is 2 to 3 hours per 2¼ pounds; braised meat is tender and has an excellent flavor. To braise, heat a fair amount of peanut oil in a Dutch oven and brown the meat on all sides. Lightly brown a sliced onion and add other seasonal vegetables. Add a little stock, cover, and braise over low heat. As soon as the liquid has evaporated, add a little more. If you use too much stock, braised meat will end up boiled.

For stovetop "roasting," seasoned meat is put into very hot peanut oil in a Dutch oven and sautéed on all sides. First baste it with the hot oil, later baste now and again with a little of the cooking liquids. After starting the roast, continue to cook at medium heat in a covered Dutch oven and finally brown it uncovered. The meat is done when the juices no longer run out when it is pierced. For cooking times, see Index. Always allow roasts to stand, covered in aluminum foil, for 10 minutes before cutting. Then it can be sliced evenly and the juices do not run out.

Oven Roasting: Preheat the oven to 400°F. Place the seasoned meat in a roasting pan, baste with hot oil or cooking fat, then put into the oven. Gradually add a little stock, and then baste frequently with the cooking juices.

A practical way to make even tough meat tender is to cook it in an earthenware dish. Soak the unglazed dish (and the lid) in water so that the pores absorb the water. Place the seasoned meat in the dish, with or without vegetables, and cover it. Place in a cold oven. As the oven heats to 350°F, steam forms in the dish. The meat cooks in its own juices and becomes particularly tender. You can also braise or boil in an earthenware dish. In roasting, it is best to use a roasting rack so that the meat does not lie in its own juice and prevent it from browning.

Cooking meat in aluminum foil is a similar technique to roasting in an open pan. You must open the foil at the end to brown the roast. There are special roasting foils that help the meat become brown and crisp. These should be used according to the package instructions.

Meat may also be cooked in a puff pastry crust. It must be sautéed and cooled first, before the crust is prepared. This method of cooking is especially good for fillets, joints and boned smoked pork. For quantities, calculate at least ¼ pound of boneless meat and ⅔ pound of meat with bones per portion. Meat lovers, however, are not always satisfied with this measurement. For especially hearty appetites, you'll need about 2¼ pounds of meat with bones and at least 1¾ pounds of boneless meat for 4 portions.

Pressure cookers and pressure frying pans help considerably to save time, energy, and vitamins, and mineral substances are not destroyed in the cooking process.

The principle in pressure cooking is that, in hermetically sealed pressure cookers, the food is cooked in steam under a higher pressure and temperature and in a fraction of the usual cooking time. Tougher cuts of meat, roasts and goulash are juicier and more tender when cooked in a pressure cooker.

Although saving time and energy are valid reasons for using a pressure cooker, another reason is the ability to improve and enhance the flavor of the dish.

A roast or goulash can be prepared amazingly quickly in a pressure cooker: A veal roast of 1 to 1½ pounds is cooked in 14 to 18 minutes, 1 pound of beef goulash needs 20 to 25 minutes, and a beef roast of 1 to 1½ pounds takes 24 to 30 minutes to cook through.

SUCCESSFUL CRISP ROASTS

When sautéing on the stove, briskly rub the meat with salt, spices, or herbs. Sauté in hot oil or in butter, adding vegetables if desired. After the meat has browned on all sides, gradually add 1 cup of water. Cook for about 15 minutes per pound for each 2 pounds of beef; about 30 minutes per pound for pork; about 5 minutes per pound for lamb; and about 30 minutes per pound for veal.

When roasting meat in the oven (which is very practical because it almost cooks itself there), heat the oven to 400°F. Place the meat in the roasting pan, baste it with peanut oil or other cooking fat, and put the pan in the oven. Baste the meat with water or stock, incorporating the roasting juices as well.

Meat can be prepared in an earthenware pottery dish. Soak the dish in water, then place the seasoned meat with any vegetables desired, in it. Cover and place the dish in a cold oven. Bake the meat at 400°F for about 30 minutes. The meat will brown when you remove the lid for 10 minutes at the end of the roasting time. Special roasting bags are available for roasting (photograph at right).

GROUND MEAT AND OFFAL

In photograph 1 are examples of what can be prepared from ground meat. Browned potatoes, fries, kebabs for barbecuing, potatoes wrapped in savoy cabbage, and classic stuffed cabbage are shown.

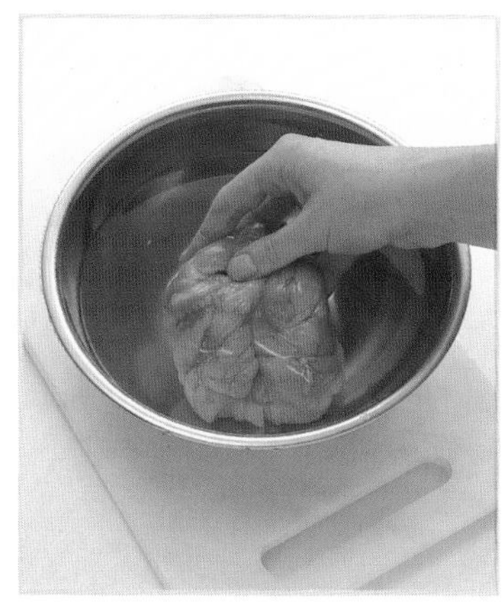

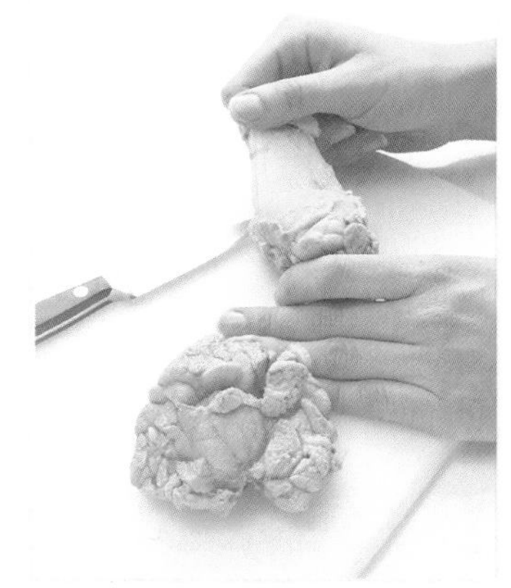

4

In preparing and cooking sweetbreads, it's best to soak the sweetbreads under running cold water until soft. Blanch them in lukewarm water, slowly bringing the liquid to a boil. Strain the water and let the sweetbreads cool completely. Remove the skin from the sweetbreads and any blood vessels that are present. Sweetbreads can be left whole or separated into rosettes. Sweetbreads can be cooked in stock with chopped vegetables, instead of water.

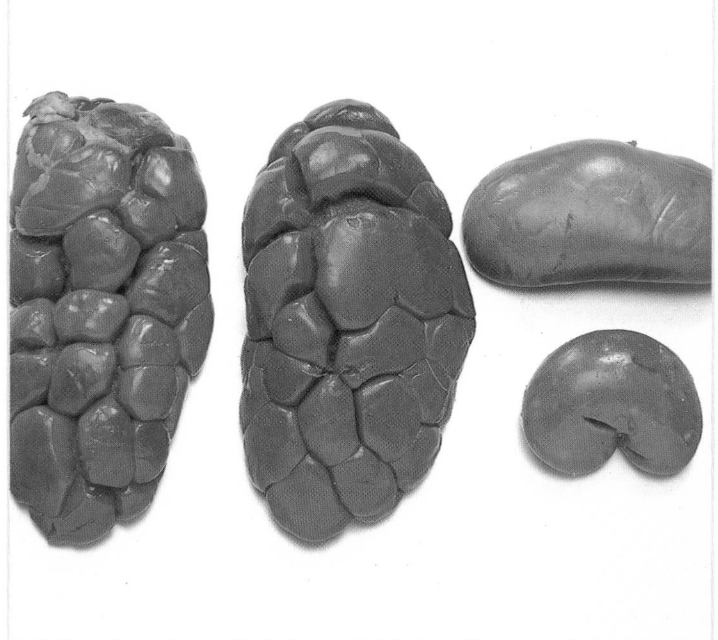

When preparing slices of liver (photograph 5), it is recommended to dredge the slices in flour and then sauté them. This method prevents the protein-rich meat from disintegrating. Liver can be poached without a covering of flour in butter heated to a medium temperature.

Liver is tender and should only be salted after sautéing or frying. It will lose liquid and become tough if salted early. Calf's and lamb's livers need only be cooked for 2 minutes. Beef liver may require 3 to 4 minutes cooking time.

Fine ragoûts or stews can be made from kidneys. Kidneys are also excellent sliced or whole, sautéed or used as a stuffing. For example, lamb's kidney can be quickly poached in butter. From left to right are cow's and calf's kidneys, above a pig's kidney, and below it a lamb's kidney. In preparation, cut each kidney in half lengthwise. Remove the vessels and tough skin. Soak in water for 1 hour before beginning the cooking process.

STUFFED PORK ROLLS

Yield: 6 servings
8 boneless pork loin chops, thinly sliced, 1½ to 2 ounces each
Salt
Pepper
1 clove garlic, peeled and crushed
2 cups spinach
3 tablespoons butter
1 onion, peeled and finely chopped
Grated nutmeg
1 cup raw sausage meat
1 cup mushrooms, sliced
1 cup white wine
1 cup whipping cream
2 tablespoons parsley, chopped

Rinse the pork with cold water and dry well with paper towels. Season with salt and pepper; rub with garlic. Pound the pork with a meat mallet until flattened.

Pick over and wash the spinach. Place the spinach in a saucepan with boiling water and blanch for 1 minute. Immerse the spinach in cold water to cool; squeeze dry.

Melt 2 tablespoons of butter in a saucepan and sauté the onion. Add the spinach and cook for 3 minutes. Season with salt, pepper, and nutmeg. Spread the spinach evenly over the flattened pork. Spread raw sausage meat on top. Roll up the schnitzels and fasten with wooden toothpicks. Season with salt and pepper.

Melt the remaining butter in a large frying pan and sauté the rolls on all sides. Add the mushrooms and cook together briefly. Add wine and cream, and cook for 20 minutes over medium heat. Transfer the rolls to a serving platter and remove the toothpicks; keep the rolls warm.

Bring the sauce to a boil and reduce until creamy. Season to taste with salt and pepper. Stir in the chopped parsley.

To serve, spoon the sauce over the pork rolls.

PORK CHOPS, MUNICH STYLE

Yield: 2 to 4 servings
4 pork chops, 6 to 8 ounces each, with pockets cut in them
½ cup sausage mix
Salt
Pepper
4 tablespoons peanut oil
1 cup brown veal stock (see Index)
16 pearl onions, peeled
½ cup heavy cream
2 tablespoons mustard
2 tablespoons chopped parsley
2 tablespoons butter
2 cups mushrooms, quartered
¼ cup boiled ham, cut in strips

Rinse the chops with cold water and dry well. Stuff the pockets with sausage mix and fasten with toothpicks. Season with salt and pepper. Heat the oil in a large frying pan and sauté the chops for 7 to 10 minutes on each side. Remove from the pan and keep warm.

Heat the veal stock in a saucepan. Add the pearl onions and cook in the veal stock for 15 minutes. Add cream, mustard, salt, pepper, and parsley.

Melt the butter in a large frying pan and sauté the mushrooms for 5 minutes. Add the ham and cook for 3 minutes longer.

To serve, spoon mushrooms and ham over the chops and serve with the sauce.

SMOKED PORK CHOPS ON CURRIED LENTILS

Yield: 2 servings
1½ tablespoons butter
1 medium-sized onion, peeled and sliced
2 apples (Granny Smith), peeled and cut in thin slices
2 tablespoons curry powder
2 tablespoons dry white wine
1 (14-ounce) can lentils
Salt
Pepper

Sugar
4 smoked pork chops

Melt half of the butter in a large saucepan. Sauté the onion and then the apple slices. Dust with curry powder and cook 3 to 5 minutes; add the wine. Strain the lentils and add to the pan. Season with salt, pepper, and sugar to taste.

Rinse the chops and dry well with paper towels. Melt the remaining butter in a large frying pan. Sauté the chops on both sides for about 5 minutes, until golden brown.

To serve, place the lentil mixture on a serving platter and arrange the chops on top.

PORK IN RED PEPPER SAUCE

Yield: 2 to 4 servings
1 cup olive oil
1 pork loin roast, cut in 1½-inch cubes
3 onions, peeled and diced
2 cloves garlic, peeled and diced
3 medium tomatoes, peeled and diced
1 red pepper, diced
1 red chili pepper, finely diced
Salt
1 cup beer
1 bay leaf
1 pinch of ground cumin
1 pinch of oregano
¼ cup parsley, chopped

Heat the oil in a large saucepan and sauté the pork on all sides. Add the onion and garlic and sauté until glazed. Add the tomato, pepper, chili, and beer. Flavor with bay leaf, cumin, and oregano.

Cover the pan and cook for 1 hour over medium heat. Add chopped parsley and serve with rice.

PORK FILLET WITH GREEN PEPPER

Yield: 4 servings
3 tablespoons butter
1½ pounds pork fillet, very thinly sliced
Salt
Freshly ground pepper
2 shallots, peeled and finely diced
2 cups mushrooms, sliced
2 tablespoons brandy
6 tablespoons red wine
1 cup brown veal stock (see Index)
½ cup cream
1 to 2 tablespoons pickled green peppercorns

Melt 1½ tablespoons of butter in a frying pan and briefly sauté the pork on all sides. Season with salt and pepper. Remove the pork from the pan and keep warm.

Melt the remaining butter in the same frying pan and sauté the shallots and mushrooms. Return the pork to the pan and pour the brandy over the pork. Ignite the brandy and flambé until all alcohol is cooked off. Add the wine and veal stock. Bring to a boil and reduce the liquid by half; add the cream. Continue to reduce the sauce until it has thickened.

To serve, stir in the peppercorns and cook for a few minutes.

PORK LOIN WRAPPED IN CABBAGE

Yield: 4 to 6 servings
1½ pounds loin pork fillet
4 tablespoons peanut oil
Salt
Pepper
6 to 8 ounces veal chuck
½ cup sour cream
6 large savoy cabbage leaves
4 tablespoons butter
2 shallots, peeled and finely diced
2 cups mushrooms, chopped
Grated nutmeg
4 tablespoons brandy
1 cup brown veal stock (see Index)
½ cup heavy cream
6 tablespoons dry white wine
¼ cup fresh sage

Preheat the oven to 350°F.

Trim the gristle and sinews from the pork. Rinse the pork with cold water and dry well with paper towels. Heat the oil in a frying pan and sauté the pork on all sides. Season with salt and pepper, remove from the pan, and store in a cold place.

Rinse the veal with cold water and dry well. In a meat grinder, grind the veal finely and mix it with the sour cream. Put the veal mixture in the refrigerator in a covered dish.

Wash the cabbage leaves and blanch in boiling salt water for 2 to 3 minutes. Immediately immerse in ice water to cool, and remove the central rib.

Melt half of the butter and saute the shallots and mushrooms. Mix the sautéed vegetables with the veal mixture and flavor with salt, pepper, nutmeg, and brandy.

Layer the cabbage leaves so that they overlap each other, and spread with the veal stuffing. Place the pork fillet slices on top and then wrap them up in the cabbage leaves. Put the pork rolls in an ovenproof dish and baste with 1½ to 2 tablespoons of melted butter. Bake for 20 minutes.

Remove the pork from the dish and reduce the liquid to a thick sauce, adding the veal stock, cream, and white wine. Flavor the sauce with the chopped sage and serve.

SMOKED SADDLE OF PORK IN PUFF PASTRY

Yield: 4 to 6 servings
3 sheets frozen puff pastry
2 cups frozen spinach
1½ pounds boneless smoked pork
3 tablespoons peanut oil
2 shallots, peeled and diced
1 clove garlic, peeled and diced
2 tablespoons butter
Salt
Pepper
Grated nutmeg
1 egg yolk
2 tablespoons milk

For the sauce:
½ cup brown veal stock (see Index)
½ cup dry red wine
2 tablespoons cold butter
Plus:
Flour

Preheat the oven to 375°F.

Thaw the puff pastry and the spinach. Rinse the pork with cold water and dry well with paper towels. Heat the oil in a large frying pan and sauté the meat until browned (photograph 1); remove from the pan and let cool.

Sauté the shallots and garlic in melted butter in a large saucepan. Squeeze out the spinach thoroughly and add to the pan; cook for 10 minutes. Season with salt, pepper, and nutmeg and layer the spinach on the meat (photograph 2).

Place 2 sheets of dough side by side on a floured work surface and roll them out to join as 1 sheet. Place the cooled meat on this pastry sheet and fold the pastry over it (photograph 3). Press the edges firmly together. Beat the egg yolk together with the milk and brush this on the upper surface of the pastry. Cut decorative shapes out of the remaining pastry and use as garnishes (photograph 4).

Place the meat on a baking sheet that has been rinsed with cold water. Bake for 45 minutes, or until golden brown.

To make the sauce, reduce the veal stock and wine until creamy. Gently swirl in the butter. Serve the meat with the sauce.

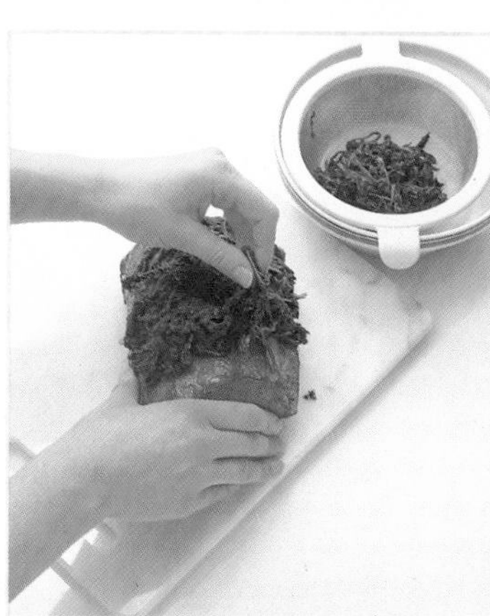

ROAST PORK WITH LEMON GLAZE

Yield: 6 to 8 servings
3 pounds saddle of pork
4 tablespoons fresh rosemary
1 cup dry white wine
½ cup sugar
½ cup lemon juice
3 tablespoons brandy
Salt
Pepper
Plus:
Kitchen string
Peanut oil

Preheat the oven to 425°F.

Rinse the pork with cold water and dry well with paper towels. Cut the pork several times in the direction of the grain and press 3 tablespoons of rosemary into it. Place the pork in a dish. Pour the wine over the pork and add the remaining rosemary. Marinate the meat for about 1-½ hours, turning occasionally.

Remove the meat from the marinade and dry it. Roll the pork into a tight form and tie with kitchen string. Place in a greased roasting pan and place in the oven. After about 15 minutes, reduce the heat to 325°F and roast 30 minutes more, basting frequently with the roasting juices.

Dissolve the sugar in the lemon juice and brandy. Remove the roast from the oven and pour off the roasting juices. Brush the lemon mixture on the pork. Return the pork to the oven and roast for 30 minutes more, brushing frequently with the lemon mixture. Let the cooked meat sit for about 15 minutes before slicing.

SADDLE OF PORK IN BEER SAUCE

Yield: 4 to 6 servings
1½ pounds rib roast, boned, with the bones reserved on the side
Salt
Freshly ground black pepper
1 teaspoon caraway seeds
1 (12-ounce) can beer
1 (12-ounce) can malt beer
2 onions, peeled and diced
1 clove garlic, peeled and diced
2 carrots, peeled and chopped
½ cup celery, chopped
6 tablespoons cold butter

Preheat the oven to 400°F. Rinse the meat with cold water and dry well with paper towels. Season with salt, pepper, and caraway seeds.

Cover the bottom of a roasting pan with the two types of beer and place the meat on top. Add the bones and vegetables. Put the pan in the oven and roast for 50 to 60 minutes. Baste the meat frequently with the beer while it is cooking. Remove the meat from the pan and keep warm.

To make the sauce, remove the bones from the pan and pass the vegetables and roasting juices through a food mill, or puree in a food processor. Gradually beat in the cold butter in flakes until the sauce is thick. Season to taste with salt and pepper.

COLLARED BEEF WITH BASIL

Yield: 4 servings
4 slices beef fillet (6 to 8 ounces each)
Salt
Pepper
1 cup grated celery
1 large bunch fresh basil, finely chopped
4 bay leaves, finely chopped
2 egg yolks
4 slices streaky bacon, finely diced
3 medium-sized onions, peeled and cut in rings
1½ cups beef stock (see Index)
1 cup sour cream
Plus:
Wooden toothpicks

Rinse the beef with cold water and dry well with paper towels. Season with salt and pepper. Mix the celery, herbs, and egg yolks together; season with salt and pepper. Spread this mixture over the beef slices.

Place the bacon in a frying pan and render the fat. Place the bacon, without the fat drippings, onto the mixture. Roll up the beef slices and fasten securely with wooden toothpicks. Season with salt and pepper and sauté in the bacon fat.

Add the onion rings to the beef rolls. Cover the pan and braise for 1 to 1½ hours, gradually adding the meat stock ½ cup at a time. Remove the beef from the pan and keep warm.

Bring the sauce to a boil and reduce until thickened. Puree in a blender or food processor and return to the pan. Add the sour cream and heat through. Do not boil. Serve the sauce with the beef.

BEEF STEW AU GRATIN

Yield: 6 to 8 servings
8 tablespoons olive oil
1 onion, peeled and finely diced
1 clove garlic, peeled and finely diced
1 green pepper, cut in cubes
1 red pepper, cut in cubes
1 large eggplant, peeled and cut in cubes
2 medium zucchini, cut in cubes
2 cups mushrooms, halved
4 medium tomatoes, peeled and chopped
2 tablespoons tomato paste
1 cup sour cream
Salt
Pepper
1½ pounds stewing beef
4 slices processed cheese

Preheat the oven to 475°F.

Heat 4 tablespoons of oil in a large saucepan and sauté the onion, garlic, and peppers. Add the remaining vegetables and cook for about 10 minutes. Stir in the tomato paste and cook briefly. Add the sour cream and season with salt and pepper.

Rinse the beef with cold water and dry well with paper towels. Trim off the hard connective tissues and sinews, and cut the beef into approximately ¾-inch cubes. Heat the remaining olive oil in a frying pan and sauté the beef on all sides. Season with salt and pepper and mix with the vegetables.

Place everything into an ovenproof dish and top with the cheese. Bake for 15 minutes, or until bubbly and browned.

STEAK WITH BURGUNDY FOAM

Yield: 4 servings
4 bottom round steaks (6 to 7 ounces each)
Salt
Freshly ground black pepper
6 large shallots, peeled and diced
¾ cup dry red wine
2 egg yolks
1 tablespoon fresh chervil, chopped
1 tablespoon fresh tarragon, chopped
3 tablespoons cold butter
2 tablespoons whipped cream
Lemon juice
2 tablespoons butter

Preheat the oven to 475°F.

Rinse the steaks with cold water and dry well with paper towels. Season with salt and pepper.

Place the shallots and wine in a saucepan and bring to a boil, cooking until about 3 to 5 tablespoons of liquid remain. Let cool and then add the egg yolk. Beat over medium heat until the sauce thickens. Stir in the herbs and beat in the butter in pieces until the sauce is thick. Flavor with salt, pepper, and lemon juice. Stir in the whipped cream.

Heat the butter in a frying pan and sauté the steaks over high heat on both sides. To serve, spread the Burgundy foam over the steaks and broil briefly.

ROUND STEAKS IN GARLIC CREAM SAUCE

Yield: 4 servings
4 round steaks (7 to 8 ounces each)
3 tablespoons peanut oil
Salt
Freshly ground black pepper
1 tablespoon butter
6 to 8 cloves garlic, peeled
½ cup sour cream
1 pinch of cayenne pepper
¼ cup flat-leaved parsley, chopped coarsely

Rinse the steaks with cold water and dry well with paper towels. Score the fat all around the steaks so that the meat does not curl while it is being sautéed. Heat the oil in a frying pan and sauté the steaks for 2 minutes on each side. Season with salt and pepper. Remove from the pan, place on an inverted plate, and cover with aluminum foil. Let the steaks rest so that their juices can collect.

Melt the butter in a large frying pan and crush the garlic into it. Sauté until the garlic is golden. Stir in the sour cream and heat through. Do not boil. Season with salt, pepper, and cayenne pepper. Add chopped parsley to the sauce.

Place the steaks, and the juices that have escaped, in the frying pan and heat slowly. To serve, arrange the steaks on warmed plates and cover with the sauce.

T-BONE STEAKS WITH A MUSTARD CRUST

Yield: 2 servings
2 T-bone steaks, 1-inch thick
3 tablespoons butter
Salt
Black pepper
3 tablespoons granular hot mustard
1 teaspoon tomato paste
1 tablespoon fine bread crumbs
1 pinch cayenne pepper
Grated lemon peel

Rinse the steaks with cold water and dry well with paper towels. Melt the butter in a frying pan and sauté the steaks over high heat for 2 minutes on each side. Season with

salt and pepper and remove from the pan. Place the steaks side by side in an ovenproof dish.

Mix the mustard, tomato paste, and bread crumbs together. Season with salt, pepper, and cayenne pepper. Add the grated lemon peel. Spread the paste over the steaks.

Broil the steaks for 5 minutes on each side, until a crust has formed. Serve immediately.

STUFFED FILLET STEAKS WITH PEAR FANS

Yield: 4 to 6 servings
4 fillet steaks (7 to 8 ounces each)
1 (3½- ounce) package Roquefort cheese, rind removed and cut in quarters
Black pepper
3 tablespoons butter
Salt
2 ripe pears or 4 canned pear halves, marinated in red wine
Plus:
Wooden toothpicks

Rinse the steaks with cold water and dry well with paper towels. Cut a pocket into each steak. Place a piece of cheese into each pocket and secure with toothpicks. Season on all sides with pepper.

Melt the butter in a large saucepan and sauté the steaks for 2 minutes on each side. Remove from the pan, place on an inverted plate, and cover loosely with aluminum foil to keep them warm. Sprinkle with salt to taste.

Wash the pears and cut in half lengthwise. Remove the cores and stems. Cut each half into slices, but do not cut through the top ½ inch of pear. Apply a little pressure so that the pears will open out to form fans.

To serve, arrange each stuffed steak with a pear fan on a warmed plate.

SIRLOIN STEAKS WITH RED WINE SHALLOTS

Yield: 4 to 6 servings
4 sirloin steaks (6 to 8 ounces each)
3 tablespoons peanut oil
Salt
BLack pepper
1 cup shallots, peeled and quartered
2 tablespoons butter
1 cup dry red wine

Rinse the steaks with cold water and dry well with paper towels. Score the fat around the edges of the steaks so that the meat does not curl when sautéed. Heat the oil in a frying pan. Sauté the steaks for 2 minutes on each side. Season with salt and pepper. Place on an inverted plate and cover loosely with aluminum foil. Let the steaks rest so that their juices can collect.

Melt the butter in a large frying pan and sauté the shallots, turning constantly, until soft but not browned. Add the red wine and reduce until one-third has evaporated. Season to taste with salt and pepper.

Place the steaks, and the escaping juices, in the frying pan and heat briefly. Serve immediately.

BRAISED STEAK IN A BEER SAUCE

Yield: 4 to 6 servings
4 slices beef brisket (6 to 8 ounces each)
5 tablespoons olive oil
3 medium onions, peeled and thinly sliced
Salt
Pepper
2 teaspoons brown sugar
3 tablespoons flour
1½ cups or 1 (12-ounce can) beer
¾ cup beef stock (see Index)
2 bay leaves
2 teaspoons mixed chopped fresh herbs (thyme, oregano, savory)

Preheat the oven to 325°F.

Rinse the meat with cold water and dry well with paper towels.

Heat 3 tablespoons of oil in a large saucepan and sauté the onions over low heat, stirring constantly, until golden brown. Heat the remaining 2 tablespoons of oil in a frying pan and sauté the meat on both sides over high heat. Season with salt and pepper.

Place the meat, and its cooking juices, in the pan with the onions. Add the sugar and stir until dissolved. Add the flour, beer, and stock. Bring the liquids to a boil. Remove from the heat and set aside.

Layer the meat and onions alternately in an ovenproof dish and place a bay leaf on each layer. Sprinkle each layer with herbs. Pour on the liquid, cover the dish, and bake for 2½ to 3 hours.

ROAST BEEF WITH HERBS

Yield: 8 to 10 servings
1 boneless beef roast (about 6 pounds)
Salt
Freshly ground black pepper
1 tablespoon beef marrow
1 clove garlic, peeled and finely diced
4 tablespoons chopped mixed fresh herbs (thyme, rosemary, sage, marjoram)
2 tablespoons fine bread crumbs

Rinse the meat with cold water and dry well with paper towels. Score the surface of the meat and season with salt and pepper. Puree the beef marrow in a food processor and combine with the garlic and herbs. Spread the herb mixture over the beef, cover, and let stand overnight in the refrigerator.

Preheat the oven to 450°F.

Place the meat in a roasting pan and sprinkle with fine bread crumbs. Roast in the oven for 40 minutes.

COUNTRY- STYLE BREAST OF BEEF

Yield: 8 to 10 servings
5 pounds breast of beef (rolled)
2 tablespoons flour
Salt
Pepper
1 tablespoon butter
5 strips bacon, finely diced
6 to 8 medium onions, peeled and diced
4 large carrots, peeled and diced
4 stalks celery, sliced
2 tablespoons brown sugar
1 cup malt beer

Rinse the beef with cold water and dry well with paper towels. Season the flour with the salt and pepper and dredge the meat.

Heat the butter in a Dutch oven and sauté the meat on all sides. Remove from the pan and keep warm. Sauté the bacon until almost done. Add the vegetables to the bacon and sauté for 4 minutes, stirring frequently. Add the sugar and beer. Season with salt and pepper.

Place the meat on the vegetables, cover, and cook over low heat for 2½ hours, turning the meat occasionally. Remove the meat and reduce the liquid slightly. Slice the meat and serve with boiled potatoes and savoy cabbage.

HUNTER'S BEEF STEW

Yield: 4 to 6 servings
1 pound beef chuck roast
½ teaspoon salt
1 pinch of pepper
4 tablespoons peanut oil
2 onions, peeled and chopped
1 pound mushrooms, sliced
½ cup dry red wine
1 cup beef stock (see Index)
3 medium carrots, peeled and sliced
3 medium potatoes, peeled and sliced

Rinse the meat with cold water and dry well with paper towels. Season with salt and pepper.

Heat the oil in a large Dutch oven and brown the meat on all sides over high heat. Add the onions and mushrooms and sauté for 4 minutes. Stir in the red wine, cover, and simmer for 30 minutes.

Add the beef stock and simmer 30 minutes more. Add the carrots and potatoes and simmer for another 30 minutes.

TONGUE IN RED WINE SAUCE

Yield: 4 servings
1 beef tongue (about 2 pounds)
2 onions, peeled
Salt
Pepper
1 bay leaf
3 tablespoons bacon fat
1 carrot, peeled and diced
1 cup celery, diced
1 tablespoon brandy
1 tablespoon tomato paste
1 cup beef stock (see Index)
2 cups dry red wine
3 tablespoons flour

Place the tongue in a large pot and cover with cold water. Cut one onion into rings. Add the onion rings and bay leaf to the tongue, and season with salt and pepper. Bring the water to a boil. Cover the pot and reduce the heat to medium low. Cook for about 45 minutes (photograph 1). Remove the tongue from the pot and immerse in cold water to loosen the skin. Remove the skin (photograph 2).

Chop the remaining onion finely. Melt the bacon fat in a frying pan and sauté the tongue on all sides (photograph 3). Add the chopped onion, carrot, and celery and sauté for 4 minutes. Stir in the brandy and tomato paste, and cook briefly. Transfer everything to a Dutch oven. Add the stock and red wine (photograph 4) and season lightly with salt. Cover and cook over low heat for about 2 hours.

Remove the tongue from the pan and keep warm. Reduce the sauce until thickened and season again with salt and pepper. Mix the flour with 5 tablespoons of cold water and use this to bind the sauce.

Slice the tongue and serve with the sauce.

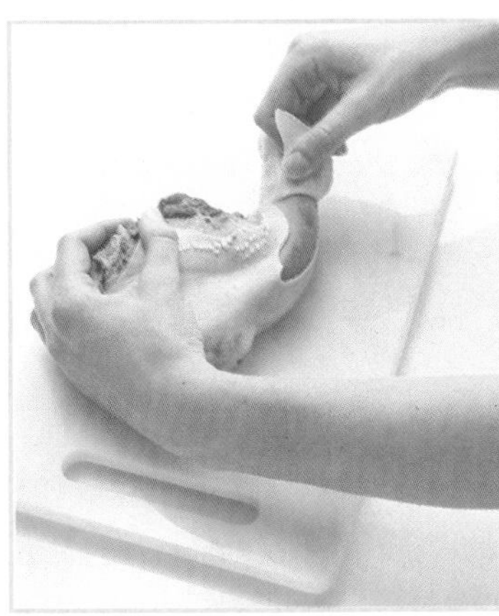

VEAL AND BEEF TONGUE RAGOÛT

Yield: 4 to 6 servings
12 to 16 ounces veal tongue
12 to 16 ounces beef tongue
1 onion, peeled and sliced
1 bay leaf
2 whole cloves
Salt
Freshly ground black pepper
3 tablespoons butter
1 large leek, cut in 2-inch strips
3 medium carrots, peeled and cut in 2-inch strips
½ cup dry white wine
1 cup brown veal stock (see Index)
2 tablespoons mustard
⅓ cup capers

Put both pieces of tongue in a large pot and cover with cold water. Peel and slice the onion and add it to the potato along with the bay leaf and cloves. Bring the water to a boil, then cover and reduce the heat to medium. Boil for 2 hours.

Melt the butter in a medium saucepan and sauté the vegetables for about 5 minutes. Add the wine and stock. Simmer for 15 minutes. Puree the capers in a blender or food processor, and stir into the sauce together with the mustard. Add salt and pepper to taste.

When the tongue has finished cooking, remove from the pot and immerse in cold water to loosen the skin. Remove the skin and cut into bite-sized cubes. Add the tongue to the sauce and heat through.Serve the ragoût with spinach noodles.

VEAL CHOPS PÉRIGORD

Yield: 2 to 4 servings
4 veal chops (6 to 8 ounces each)
Salt
Pepper
2 slices bacon, finely diced
12 shallots, peeled and finely chopped
1 clove garlic, peeled and finely chopped
2 truffles, diced
2 tablespoons fresh chervil, chopped
3 tablespoons peanut oil
⅓ cup Madeira wine
1 cup veal stock (see Index)
2 tablespoons butter

Preheat the oven to 400°F.

Rinse the veal with cold water and dry well with paper towels. Season with salt and pepper. Mix the bacon, shallots, garlic, truffles, and chervil together.

Heat the oil in a frying pan and sauté the chops on both sides. Spread the bacon mixture on the chops and place in a shallow oven-proof dish. Bake for 10 minutes. Remove the chops from the dish and keep warm.

Carefully pour off the cooking fat. Add the Madeira to the dish, then stir in the veal stock. Reduce the liquid to ¼ cup. Gradually swirl in the butter until the sauce thickens.

HERBED VEAL SCALLOPS

Yield: 4 to 6 servings

4 veal scallops (6 ounces each), pounded very thin
Salt
Pepper
3 tablespoons butter
2 tablespoons grated horseradish
2 tablespoons mixed chopped fresh herbs (chives, parsley, chervil, tarragon)
1 to 2 tablespoons bread crumbs
2 egg yolks, beaten

Preheat the oven to 475°F.

Rinse the veal with cold water and dry well with paper towels. Season with salt and pepper.

Cream 2 tablespoons of butter, horseradish, and herbs together. Season with salt and pepper. Stir in the bread crumbs and egg yolks.

Heat the remaining butter in a frying pan and sauté the veal for 2 minutes on each side. Transfer the veal to a shallow, ovenproof dish. Spread the herb mixture on top and bake for about 10 minutes.

VEAL MEDALLIONS IN PORT WINE SAUCE

Yield: 4 servings
1½ pounds veal fillet
Salt
Freshly ground white pepper
2 tablespoons flour
2 tablespoons butter
1 clove garlic, peeled
⅓ cup dry white wine
5 tablespoons white port wine
¼ cup sour cream

Remove the tissues and sinews from the meat, rinse with cold water, and dry well with paper towels. Cut into 8 equal-sized pieces. Season with salt and pepper and dredge in flour.

Melt the butter in a medium saucepan and sauté the garlic. Add the medallions and sauté for 3 minutes on each side. Remove from the pan, cover, and keep warm.

Carefully pour off the fat and remove the garlic. Add the port and white wine to the pan. Reduce the sauce. Stir in the sour cream and heat through. Season with salt and pepper to taste. Arrange the medallions on a plate and serve with the sauce and rice.

LOIN OF VEAL IN SAGE SAUCE

Yield: 6 to 8 servings
2 pounds loin of veal (rolled)
Salt
Pepper
1 clove garlic, peeled and finely chopped
2 tablespoons fresh sage, chopped
3 tablespoons veal fat trimmings
1 medium onion, peeled and diced
1 medium carrot, peeled and diced
2 stalks celery, diced
1 tablespoon tomato paste
5 tablespoons dry white wine
¼ cup heavy cream

Preheat the oven to 400°F.

Rinse the veal with cold water and dry well with paper towels. Season with salt and pepper. Rub the veal with the garlic and 1 tablespoon of chopped sage.

Heat the veal trimmings in a Dutch oven and sauté the meat on all sides over high heat. Add the diced vegetables and sauté them all together for about 4 minutes. Stir in the tomato paste and cook briefly. Add the wine and 1 cup of hot water.

Place the uncovered Dutch oven in the oven and roast for about 1½ hours. Baste frequently with the liquids. Remove the meat from the pan and keep warm.

Pour the sauce through a fine sieve, return to the pan, and reduce the liquid. Add the cream and sage and continue to reduce the liquid until it thickens. Season to taste with salt and pepper.

To serve, cut the meat in slices and cover with the sauce.

VEAL KNUCKLE IN ORANGE SAUCE

Yield: 8 to 10 servings
5 pounds veal knuckle with the bone (in slices about 1½ inches thick)
Salt
Pepper
3 tablespoons flour
2 tablespoons butter
1 medium onion, peeled and finely chopped
1 medium carrot, peeled and finely chopped
1 small leek, cut in fine strips
1 cup meat stock (see Index)
3 oranges
½ cup dry white wine

Rinse the veal slices with cold water and dry well with paper towels. Season with salt and pepper and dredge with flour. Melt the butter in a Dutch oven and sauté the meat on all sides. Add the vegetables and cook gently for about 4 minutes. Add the meat stock, cover, and cook over low heat for 30 minutes.

Wash and dry the oranges and peel thinly. Cut the peel into strips and blanch briefly in boiling water. Add the orange peel to the veal and cook for 1 hour. Remove the meat slices from the pot and keep warm.

Pour the liquid through a sieve, or puree in a blender or food processor. Squeeze the oranges and add the juice and wine to the cooking liquid. Reduce the liquid to half its volume.

To serve, season the sauce with salt and pepper to taste and pour onto the meat.

VEAL WITH SHRIMP

Yield: 2 to 4 servings
1 pound veal fillet or rump steak
Salt
Freshly ground white pepper
12 large shrimp, peeled and deveined
1 medium leek
4 tablespoons butter
1 cup dry sherry
1 cup heavy cream
Worcestershire sauce

Rinse the veal with cold water and dry well with paper towels. Cut into thin slices and season with salt and pepper. Cut the shrimp into 1½-inch pieces and season with pepper.

Clean the leek and remove the green stem. Cut the white part of the leek in half and clean carefully. Cut into 2-inch strips.

Melt half of the butter in a large saucepan. Quickly sauté the shrimp over high heat. Remove from the pan and keep warm. Melt the remaining butter in the pan and sauté the leek for about 4 minutes. Add the sherry and cream and reduce to a thick sauce.

Place the veal and shrimp in the sauce and heat through, but do not boil. Flavor the sauce with Worcestershire sauce, salt, and pepper.

SALTIMBOCCA OF CALF'S LIVER ON RISOTTO

Yield: 4 to 6 servings
For the saltimbocca:
1½ pounds calf's liver
12 fresh sage leaves
8 ounces Parma ham, sliced
5 tablespoons olive oil
Salt
Pepper
For the risotto:
3 tablespoons olive oil
1 medium onion, peeled and finely chopped
1 clove garlic, peeled and finely chopped
1 teaspoon saffron
1½ cups round-grain rice
4 cups boiling meat stock (see Index)
3 tablespoons butter
¼ cup Parmesan cheese
Plus:
12 wooden toothpicks

Preheat the oven to 400°F.

Remove the skin from the liver. Rinse the liver with cold water and dry well with paper towels. Cut into 12 equal-sized slices. Lay 1 sage leaf on each slice of liver. Place a slice of ham on each leaf and fasten securely with toothpicks.

Heat the olive oil in a medium saucepan and sauté the liver over low heat for about 2 minutes on each side. Season with salt and pepper.

To make the risotto, heat the oil in an ovenproof saucepan and sauté the onion and garlic. Stir in the saffron. Add the rice and stock and bring to a boil. Cover and bake in the preheated oven for 15 minutes. Stir in the butter and Parmesan cheese and season with salt and pepper.

Serve the risotto and saltimbocca on 4 individual plates.

CALF'S HEART WITH VEGETABLES

Yield: 4 to 6 servings
1½ pounds calf's heart
Salt
Pepper
5 tablespoons olive oil
4 stalks celery, cut in fine strips
2 medium carrots, peeled and cut in fine strips
2 medium leeks, cut in 2-inch strips
1 small onion, peeled and diced
10 mushrooms, halved
¼ cup fresh chives, finely chopped
⅛ cup parsley, finely chopped
1 cup dry white wine
3 tablespoons whipping cream
10 green peppercorns

Remove the skin and sinews from the heart and quarter it. Rinse with cold water and dry well with paper towels. Season with salt and pepper.

Heat the oil in a medium saucepan and sauté the heart pieces. Add the celery, carrots, leek, and onion and sauté for a few minutes. Stir in the wine, cream, mushrooms, chives, parsley, and peppercorns. Reduce heat to low and simmer for about 1½ hours.

To serve, cut the heart into pieces and arrange on the vegetables.

KIDNEYS IN VERMOUTH SAUCE

Yield: 4 servings

1½ pounds calf's kidneys
Salt
Pepper
5 tablespoons olive oil
2 tablespoons butter
2 shallots, peeled and diced
4 tablespoons dry vermouth
½ cup veal stock or beef stock (see Index)
½ cup heavy cream
2 ripe avocadoes, peeled and diced

Remove the skin and sinews from the kidneys. Rinse with cold water and dry well with paper towels. Season with salt and pepper. Heat the oil in a medium saucepan and sauté the kidneys over low heat for about 10 minutes. They should be pink inside. Remove the kidneys and keep warm. Pour off the fat.

Heat ½ teaspoon of the butter in the pan and sauté the shallots until glazed. Add the vermouth, then the stock and cream. Reduce the liquid. Swirl in the rest of the butter in pieces, until the sauce thickens.

To serve, add the diced avocadoes to the sauce. Season to taste with salt and pepper. Pour the sauce onto a serving plate and add the kidneys.

SWEETBREADS AND CALF'S LIVER ON TRUFFLED LEEKS

Yield: 2 servings
¾ pound sweetbreads
1 medium onion, peeled
1 bay leaf
1 clove
Salt
Pepper
10 to 12 ounces calf's liver, sliced
3 tablespoons flour
3 medium leeks, sliced
3 small truffles, cut in strips
½ cup whipping cream
½ cup chicken stock (see Index)
4 tablespoons truffle juice
4 tablespoons sour cream
6 tablespoons butter

Soak the sweetbreads in several changes of cold water for at least 4 hours. Spike the onion with the bay leaf and the clove.

Blanch the sweetbreads and the onion in boiling salted water and cook for 10 minutes. Remove the sweetbreads and rinse with cold water to cool. Remove the skin from the sweetbreads (photograph 1). Cut into slices and season with salt and pepper.

Rinse the liver with cold water and dry well with paper towels. Dredge the liver and sweetbreads in flour (photograph 2). Mix the cream, stock, and truffle juice together and place in a saucepan. Add the leek and truffles and simmer for about 10 minutes. Add the sour cream and heat through. Do not boil. Season with salt and pepper.

Melt the butter in a frying pan and sauté the sweetbreads and the liver on both sides (photograph 3).

Serve the sweetbreads and liver with boiled potatoes.

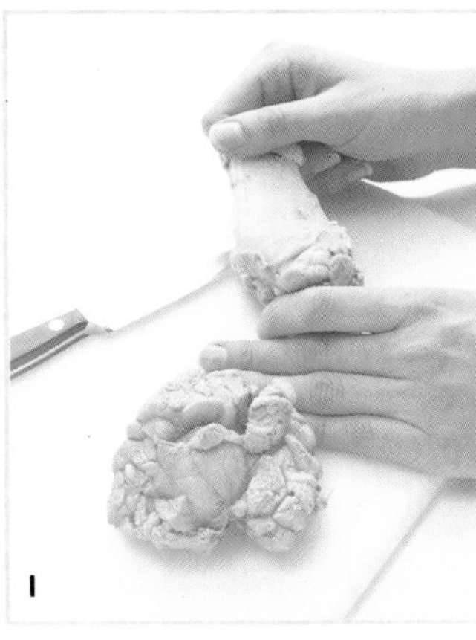
1

2

3

CALF BRAIN FRITTERS

Yield: 4 servings
1¼ pounds calf brains
3 tablespoons butter
5 ounces fresh ham, diced
1 tablespoon flour
¾ cup mushrooms, sliced
2 medium tomatoes, skinned and diced
Salt
Freshly ground white pepper
5 ounces pork fillet
1 egg, beaten
¾ cup cornmeal
2 tablespoons mixed chopped fresh herbs (parsley, chervil, chives)
1 lemon

Remove the skin from the brain. Rinse with cold water and dry between 2 towels. Cut the brains into cubes.

Melt 1 tablespoon of butter in a saucepan and fry the ham. Stir in the flour and sauté briefly. Gradually stir in the milk, taking care that no lumps form. Boil the sauce for about 10 minutes. Let the sauce cool a little and then add the brains, mushrooms, and tomatoes. Season with salt and pepper.

Cut the pork into 4 equal pieces. Divide the brains into 4 portions and put one portion onto the center of each piece of pork. Wrap the pork around the filling.

Dip the fritters first in the beaten egg and then in the cornmeal. Melt the remaining butter and fry the fritters for about 5 minutes on each side. Sprinkle with herbs and serve each portion with a lemon wedge.

SADDLE OF LAMB PICCATA WITH RATATOUILLE

Yield: 4 servings

For the ratatouille:

3 tablespoons olive oil
1 medium onion, peeled and diced
1 clove garlic, peeled and diced
1 red pepper, diced
1 green pepper, diced
1 large eggplant, diced
1 large zucchini, diced
Rosemary
Thyme
Salt
Pepper
2 tomatoes, peeled, seeded, and chopped
1 tablespoon tomato paste

For the piccata:

1 pound boneless saddle of lamb
2 tablespoons flour
2 eggs
1 tablespoon Parmesan cheese
3 tablespoons olive oil

To make the ratatouille, heat the oil in a medium saucepan and sauté the onion, garlic, and peppers. Add the eggplant and zucchini and flavor with rosemary, thyme, salt, and pepper. Sauté for about 20 minutes. Add the tomato and tomato paste.

For the piccata, cut the meat into 1-inch cubes and pound them flat. Season with salt and pepper and dredge in flour. Beat the eggs and stir in the Parmesan cheese. Dip the meat in this mixture. Heat the oil in a frying pan and sauté the meat over low heat until golden on both sides. Serve in four individual portions.

CUBED LAMB WITH ARTICHOKES

Yield: 4 servings
8 shoulder cubes of lamb (3 ounces each)
4 tablespoons Armagnac
½ teaspoon fresh thyme
½ teaspoon fresh sage
1 tablespoon parsley, chopped
8 ounces veal sweetbreads, sliced
1 medium onion, peeled
1 bay leaf
1 clove
Salt
8 small artichokes
Lemon juice
3 tablespoons butter
2 shallots, peeled and chopped
2 tomatoes, peeled, seeded, and finely diced
4 tablespoons dry red wine
8 sauteéd mushroom caps

Marinate the lamb cubes overnight in the refrigerator in a covered dish with half of the Armagnac and the herbs.

Soak the sweetbreads in several changes of cold water for at least 4 hours. Spike the onion with the bay leaf and clove. Place the onion in a medium saucepan with boiling salt water and blanch the sweetbreads for about 10 minutes. Remove the skin.

Wash the artichokes and pluck off the outer leaves. Cut off the upper quarter and the stalk. Rub the cut edges with the lemon juice. Simmer for 30 minutes in salt water. Test for doneness by inserting a knife. If the knife does not hold the vegetable, remove the stringy center from inside with a spoon.

Melt 1 tablespoon of butter in a frying pan and sauté the lamb for about 2 minutes on all sides, until pink. Place the lamb on the artichokes.

Melt 1 tablespoon of butter in the frying pan. Sauté the sweetbreads, then place on the lamb.

For the sauce, melt 1 tablespoon of butter in another pan and sauté the shallots until glazed. Add the remaining Armagnac and wine, then stir in the tomatoes. Bring the sauce to a boil and reduce. Gradually swirl in the remaining butter.

To serve, pour the sauce over the meat and top with the mushroom caps.

LAMB CHOPS WITH POTATO CAPS

Yield: 8 servings
16 lamb chops (2 ounces each)
Salt
Pepper
1 clove garlic, peeled
1 pound potatoes, peeled
3 egg yolks, beaten
2½ tablespoons butter
3 tablespoons olive oil
5 tablespoons dry red wine
1 cup lamb or chicken stock (see Index)

Preheat the broiler.

Rinse the chops with cold water and dry well with paper towels. Season with salt and pepper. Rub the chops with garlic.

Boil the potatoes in salt water for 20 minutes, or until done. Mash while the potatoes are still hot and mix with 2 tablespoons of butter and 2 of the egg yolks.

Heat the oil in a frying pan and sauté the chops for 2 minutes on each side.

Use a pastry bag to pipe the potato puree onto the chops. Brush with the remaining beaten egg yolk. Lay the chops on an ovenproof plate and broil until the potato becomes brown on top.

Carefully pour off the juices from the pan and add the red wine and lamb stock. Reduce the sauce and swirl in the butter in pieces until the sauce thickens. Season to taste with salt and pepper.

To serve, arrange the chops on a plate and pour the sauce around them.

LAMB FILLET IN PUFF PASTRY

Yield: 4 to 6 servings
1¾ pounds lamb fillet
1 pound frozen puff pastry, thawed
3 tablespoons butter
2 shallots, peeled and chopped
2 cups mushrooms, diced
2 tablespoons Madeira wine
1 tablespoon heavy cream
1 tablespoon parsley, chopped
Salt
Pepper
2 egg yolks, beaten
1¾ ounces chicken liver pâté
1 egg, beaten

Preheat the oven to 400°F.

Rinse the lamb with cold water and dry well with paper towels. Cut into 8 slices.

Melt 1 tablespoon of the butter in a medium saucepan and sauté the shallots until glazed. Add the mushrooms and cook until all the liquid has evaporated. Add the Madeira and cream, and reduce again. Stir in the parsley and season with salt and pepper. Let the sauce cool. Stir the egg yolk, and then the pâté, into the mixture.

Season the lamb with salt and pepper. Melt the remaining butter in a frying pan and sauté the lamb. Roll out the sheets of puff pastry to form rectangles large enough to enclose the lamb. Place the lamb on the pastry and spread with the mushroom mixture. Cut the edges of the pastry straight and brush with water. Wrap the lamb in the pastry and press the edges of the pastry firmly together. Prick the pastry several times with a fork to release steam. Brush the egg over the pastry to make a glaze.

Grease a baking sheet and place the pastry on it. Bake for about 20 minutes, until the pastry turns a golden brown. Cool slightly and serve.

LAMB STEW WITH ORIENTAL RICE

Yield: 6 to 8 servings

For the lamb stew:

1½ pounds boneless leg of lamb
2 tablespoons olive oil
2 medium onions, peeled and chopped
1 clove garlic, peeled and chopped
5 tomatoes, peeled and skinned
6 tablespoons brandy
Juice of 2 lemons
1 cup meat stock (see Index)
½ cup dry white wine
1 tablespoon fresh tarragon, chopped
Salt
Pepper
1 lemon, peeled and sliced
1 tablespoon parsley, chopped

For the rice:

8 ounces calf's liver
2 tablespoons olive oil
1 clove garlic, peeled and chopped
1 cup rice
¼ cup raisins
¼ cup almond slivers
¼ cup pine nuts
2 teaspoons ground cinnamon
2 cups meat stock (see Index)

Rinse the lamb with cold water and dry well with paper towels. Cut into 1½-inch cubes. Heat the olive oil in a Dutch oven and sauté the meat on all sides until the juices begin to exit the cubes. Sauté quickly over high heat. Add brandy and lemon juice, and then the onion, garlic, tomato, stock, wine, and tarragon. The lamb should be covered with the liquid, so add more meat stock if necessary. Season with salt and pepper. Cover and simmer for 1½ to 2 hours.

Remove the lamb from the pot. Reduce the sauce to one- third. Return the lamb to the pot and cook for 10 minutes more. Add the lemon slices and parsley.

For the rice, preheat the oven to 400°F. Rinse the liver with cold water and dry well with paper towels.

Dice finely. Heat the oil in an oven-proof saucepan and sauté the liver and garlic. Add the rice, raisins, almonds, pine nuts, and cinnamon and sauté briefly. Add the meat stock and season with salt and pepper. Cover and bake the rice for 20 to 30 minutes.

LAMB WITH OKRA

Yield: 4 servings
1 pound okra
1 lemon
½ pound leg of lamb
3 tablespoons butter
2 medium onions, peeled and chopped
4 tomatoes, peeled, seeded, and diced
Salt
Freshly ground black pepper
1 cup meat stock (see Index)

Wash the okra and remove the stalks. Do not cut in too deeply or the juice with run out. Bring the water and lemon juice to a boil in a pot and cook the okra for about 15 minutes. Remove and drain.

Rinse the lamb with cold water and dry well with paper towels. Cut into ¾- inch cubes. Melt the butter in a medium saucepan and sauté the lamb and onions. Add the tomato and season with salt and pepper. Place the okra on top, cover, and cook for about 45 minutes, gradually adding more meat stock when necessary.

BRAISED SHOULDER OF LAMB

Yield: 4 servings
1 pound shoulder of lamb
2 tablespoons olive oil
1 clove garlic, peeled and chopped
1 sprig fresh thyme
Salt
Pepper
1 stalk celery, cut in pieces
8 tomatoes, peeled, seeded, and diced
2 tablespoons tomato paste
1½ cups meat stock (see Index)

Preheat the oven to 400°F.

Rinse the lamb with cold water and dry well with paper towels. Heat the oil in an ovenproof saucepan and sauté the lamb. Add the garlic and thyme and season with salt and pepper. Mix in the celery and tomato paste. Sauté lightly. Add enough stock to cover the lamb.

Roast the lamb for 1½ hours. Add the tomatoes the last 30 minutes of cooking. Season to taste again.

LAMB FILLET WITH SNAIL SAUCE

Yield: 4 to 6 servings
1½ pounds lamb fillet
3 tablespoons butter
2 medium carrots, peeled and diced
¾ cup celery, diced
1 medium leek, cleaned and diced
4 shallots, peeled and diced
1 tomato, peeled, seeded, and diced
2 tablespoons cognac
4 tablespoons dry sherry
1 cup Brown Veal Stock (see Index)
½ tablespoon fresh chives, chopped
½ tablespoon parsley, chopped
½ tablespoon fresh tarragon, chopped
1 pinch of garlic
24 canned snails, chopped
Salt
Pepper

Rinse the lamb with cold water and dry well with paper towels. Melt 1½ tablespoons of the butter in a saucepan and sauté the vegetables. Ignite the cognac and burn off the alcohol. Then add the cognac, sherry, and veal stock to the pan. Simmer for about 15 minutes. Stir in the herbs.

Heat the remaining butter in another saucepan and sauté the lamb for about 10 minutes, until pink.

To serve, heat the snails in the sauce. Season to taste with salt and pepper. Cut the lamb in slices and arrange on the snail sauce.

SHOULDER OF LAMB WITH CUCUMBER SAUCE

Yield: 4 to 6 servings
2 shoulders of lamb (deboned, rolled, and bound)
Salt
Pepper
¼ cup olive oil
Meat stock (see Index)
3 medium cucumbers, seeded and diced
1 medium onion, peeled and chopped
1 clove garlic, peeled and chopped
½ cup fresh dill, chopped
1 cup sour cream

Preheat the oven to 400°F.

Rinse the meat with cold water and dry well with paper towels. Season with salt and pepper. Heat 3 to 5 tablespoons of olive oil in a Dutch oven and sauté the meat on all sides. Roast for about 1½ hours. Baste frequently with stock.

Season the diced cucumber with salt and pepper to taste. Heat the remaining oil in a saucepan and sauté the onion until glazed. Sauté the cucumber for about 4 minutes and stir in the garlic. Cook for 5 minutes more. Stir the dill into the sauce. Swirl in the sour cream and heat through. Do not boil. Slice the meat and serve with the cucumber sauce.

LEG OF LAMB WITH ROQUEFORT CHEESE SAUCE

Yield: 4 to 6 servings
1½ pounds boneless leg of lamb
1 medium onion, peeled
2 bay leaves
4 cloves
1 bunch soup greens
¾ cup whipping cream
3½ ounces or 1 small package Roquefort cheese
Salt
Pepper

Rinse the lamb with cold water and dry well with paper towels.

Spike the onion with the bay leaf and the cloves. Wash the soup greens. Place the lamb, onion, and soup greens in a pot of boiling salt water and gently cook for about 1½ hours.

Remove 1 cup of the stock and put in another saucepan. Add the cream and reduce. Crumble the cheese into the pan and stir until smooth. The sauce should not boil, or the cheese will break up. Season the sauce with salt and pepper and pour over the lamb.

CLASSIC CUISINE

Whether you're serving chicken, capon, or duck—or perhaps Cornish game hens or a holiday goose, poultry is always a welcome addition to any table. This selection of recipes covers a wide range of dishes and includes a traditional German stuffed goose. The photograph at the left shows tender slices of rare duck breast accompanied by an herbed cream sauce.

CHICKEN WITH PERNOD

Yield: 6 servings
2 chickens, about 2½ pounds each
Salt
Pepper
2 sprigs fresh rosemary
2 sprigs fresh thyme
4 bay leaves
3 tablespoons olive oil
1 tablespoon fennel seeds
4 tablespoons Pernod liqueur
4 cloves garlic, unpeeled
1 pound new potatoes
3 tablespoons cold salted butter

Preheat the oven to 400°F.

Rinse both chickens with cold water and pat dry with paper towels. Rub inside and out with salt and pepper. Place the rosemary, thyme, and bay leaves inside the cavities of the chickens.

Heat the oil in a Dutch oven and sauté the chickens on all sides until golden brown. Sprinkle with fennel seeds and pour on the Pernod. Add the unpeeled garlic to the pan. Scrub the potatoes thoroughly (do not peel) and add to the pan. Cover the Dutch oven and roast the chickens for 50 to 60 minutes.

About 15 minutes before the end of the cooking time, remove the cover and allow the chickens to brown. Remove the chickens and potatoes and keep warm.

Pour the cooking liquids into a saucepan and skim off the fat. Swirl in the cold butter in small pieces until a thick sauce forms. Carve the chickens and serve with the Pernod sauce.

BRAISED CHICKEN

Yield: 4 servings
1 chicken, about 3½ pounds
Salt
Pepper
2 tablespoons salted butter
1 medium onion, peeled and diced
¾ cup dry white wine
2 cups whipping cream
¾ cup sour cream
¼ cup fresh tarragon sprigs, finely chopped

Rinse the chicken with cold water and pat dry with paper towels. Cut the chicken into 8 pieces and season with salt and pepper.

Melt the butter in a large frying pan. Add the chicken pieces and sauté until golden. Add the onion and continue to sauté for 4 to 5 minutes longer. Stir in the wine and then add the cream, sour cream, and tarragon.

Continue to cook the chicken over low heat for about 45 minutes, then remove from the pan and keep warm.

Reduce the sauce until it thickens and season to taste with salt and pepper. To serve, ladle the sauce over the chicken.

CAPON À LA CHIPOLATE

Yield: 8 servings
1 capon, about 6 pounds
Salt
Pepper
8 strips bacon
2 medium onions, peeled and cut into 2-inch cubes
2 medium carrots, peeled and cut into 2-inch cubes
¼ cup celery, cut into large pieces
3 tablespoons salted butter
12 chestnuts, shelled
20 pearl onions
12 cocktail-sized hot dogs

Preheat the oven to 450°F.

Rinse the capon with cold water and pat dry with paper towels. Season inside and out with salt and pepper. Place 4 strips of bacon on top of the breast and secure with kitchen string.

Place the onions, carrots, celery, and butter in a roasting pan. Place the capon on top of the vegetables. Reduce the oven heat to 350°F and roast the capon for 2 hours. Transfer the capon to a serving platter and keep warm. Reserve the roasting juices.

Pass the vegetables through a food mill or puree in a food processor. Cut the remaining bacon into 1-inch strips and sauté until crisp. Remove the bacon from the pan and drain on paper towels. Sauté the chestnuts, pearl onions, and hot dogs in the bacon fat for 8 to 10 minutes. Add the bacon to the pan and stir in the roasting juices. Carve the capon and serve with the sauce.

CHICKEN IN CHEESE SAUCE

Yield: 6 servings
2 chickens, about 2½ pounds each
Salt
Pepper
6 tablespoons salted butter
2 medium onions, peeled and diced
4 cups dry white wine
3 cups whipping cream
2 tablespoons Dijon mustard
½ cup Emmenthaler cheese, grated

Rinse the chickens with cold water and pat dry with paper towels. Cut the chickens into 8 pieces and season with salt and pepper.

Melt the butter in a large frying pan. Add the onions and sauté until transparent. Add the chickens and brown lightly on all sides. Add the wine, then the cream. Stir in the mustard and grated cheese, and simmer for about 30 to 45 minutes. Remove the chickens and keep warm.

Reduce the sauce until it thickens, stirring constantly. Season with salt and pepper to taste. Pour the sauce over the chickens and broil for 5 minutes. Serve with rice.

CHICKEN BREAST WITH LEEKS

Yield: 6 to 8 servings
4 boneless chicken breasts, about ½ pound each
Salt
Pepper
2 leeks, cut into julienne strips
3 tablespoons salted butter
1 large shallot, peeled and diced
1 tablespoon dry vermouth
1 cup dry white wine
½ cup whipping cream
½ cup sour cream
2 tablespoons fresh chives, chopped

Rinse the chicken with cold water and pat dry with paper towels. Sprinkle with salt and pepper.

Blanch the leeks briefly in boiling water and set aside. Melt the butter in a large frying pan and sauté the chicken and shallots until golden brown, about 8 to 10 minutes. Remove the chicken to a serving platter and keep warm. Pour the vermouth and wine into the pan and reduce slightly. Add the cream and sour cream. Simmer, uncovered, until the sauce thickens.

Add the leeks to the sauce and simmer for a few minutes more. Season with salt, pepper, and chives. Serve the chicken with the sauce.

CHICKEN BREASTS WITH BLACKBERRIES

Yield: 6 to 8 servings
4 boneless chicken breasts, about ½ pound each
Salt
Pepper
1½ tablespoons salted butter, melted
1½ cups fresh blackberries
½ cup dry red wine
6 tablespoons sour cream
2 tablespoons cassis liqueur

Preheat the oven to 400°F.

Rinse the chicken with cold water and pat dry with paper towels. Season with salt and pepper; brush with butter. Place in an ovenproof casserole dish and bake for about 10 minutes.

Pick over and rinse the blackberries. Remove the chicken from the dish and keep warm.

Combine the red wine, blackberries, and sour cream in the casserole. Stir well, bring to a gentle boil, and reduce until the sauce thickens. Stir in the cassis and season with salt and pepper. Serve the sauce with the chicken.

CHICKEN WITH CHIVES

Yield: 4 servings

4 boneless chicken breasts, about ½ pound each
4 ounces canned salmon
Salt
Pepper
2 large shallots, peeled and diced
4 tablespoons cold salted butter
¼ cup dry white wine
¼ cup chicken stock
½ cup heavy cream
½ cup chopped fresh chives

Rinse the chicken with cold water and pat dry with paper towels. Carefully cut a pocket into each piece. Cut the salmon into 4 pieces and place in the pockets of the chicken. Close up the pockets with toothpicks or kitchen string, and season with salt and pepper. Melt 2 tablespoons of butter in a large saucepan and sauté the chicken for about 10 minutes over low heat, turning the pieces once. Remove the chicken from the pan and keep warm.

Melt 1 tablespoon of butter in the pan juices. Add the shallots and sauté. Add the wine and chicken stock, bring to a boil, and reduce the sauce to one-third. Add the cream and reduce again. Stir the chives into the sauce, and swirl in the remaining butter, a little at a time. Season the sauce with salt and pepper to taste. Slice the chicken and serve with the sauce.

HERBED CHICKEN BREASTS WITH MUSHROOMS

Yield: 6 to 8 servings
4 boneless chicken breasts, about ½ pound each
Salt
Pepper
3½ tablespoons salted butter
2 cups mushrooms, thinly sliced
1 large shallot, peeled and diced
½ cup sweet white wine
4 tablespoons dry vermouth
1 cup whipping cream
1 fresh sprig chervil, finely chopped

Rinse the chicken with cold water and pat dry with paper towels. Cut the chicken into 1-inch strips, and season with salt and pepper. Melt 1½ tablespoons of butter in a large saucepan and sauté the chicken for 5 to 8 minutes, stirring occasionally. Remove from the pan and keep warm.

Melt the remaining butter in the pan juices. Add the mushrooms and shallot and sauté for about 5 minutes. Add the white wine and vermouth. Boil the sauce until reduced, then add the cream. Reduce the sauce again until it thickens.

Add the chopped fresh chervil to the sauce. Return the chicken to the sauce and heat briefly before serving. Do not boil. Season to taste with salt and pepper.

CHICKEN KEBABS

Yield: 4 servings
1 pound boneless chicken breasts
2 medium onions, peeled and finely chopped
2 cloves garlic, peeled and finely chopped
6 tablespoons melted butter
4 tablespoons soy sauce
2 tablespoons lemon juice
2 teaspoons brown sugar, firmly packed
1 teaspoon dried coriander
Salt
Pepper

Rinse the chicken with cold water and pat dry with paper towels. Cut into bite-sized pieces. Mix the onions and garlic with the remaining ingredients in a large bowl. Add the chicken to the marinade, cover the bowl, and refrigerate for about 7 hours. Stir once or twice to make sure the marinade is evenly distributed.

Put the chicken pieces on skewers. Broil or grill for about 10 minutes, turning to cook evenly on all sides. Serve with rice.

ROSEMARY CHICKEN

Yield: 6 to 8 servings
2 quartered chickens, about 2½ pounds each
Salt
Pepper
2 stalks fresh rosemary, chopped
4 to 6 tablespoons olive oil
1 onion, peeled and finely chopped
1 clove garlic, peeled and finely chopped
1 medium carrot, peeled and diced
¼ cup celery, diced
1 cup dry white wine
½ cup chicken stock
½ cup whipping cream

Preheat the oven to 400°F.

Rinse the chicken with cold water and pat dry with paper towels. Rub with salt, pepper, and 1 tablespoon of rosemary. Heat the olive oil in a Dutch oven. Add the chicken, vegetables, white wine, and stock. Bake, uncovered, for about 45 minutes.

Remove the chicken from the pan; cool briefly. Loosen the meat from the bones and cut into bite-sized pieces.

Strain the sauce and add the cream. Reduce the sauce until it thickens and flavor with the remaining rosemary, salt, and pepper. Pour the sauce over the chicken before serving.

CAPON WITH VEGETABLE SAUCE

Yield: 10 to 12 servings
1 capon, about 6 pounds, cut into 8 pieces and boned
Salt
Pepper
3 tablespoons salted butter
1 medium onion, peeled and diced
1 medium carrot, peeled and cut into bite-sized pieces
1 celery stalk, cut into bite-sized pieces
¼ medium zucchini, cut into bite-sized pieces
1 cup dry white wine
1 cup whipping cream
2 tablespoons fresh tarragon leaves, chopped

Rinse the capon with cold water and pat dry with paper towels. Rub the capon pieces with salt and pepper. Melt the butter in a large saucepan and sauté the capon on all sides for 5 to 7 minutes. Remove from the pan and keep warm. Add the vegetables to the pan and sauté about 5 minutes, then add the wine, cream, and tarragon. Return the capon to the sauce, cover, and simmer for 15 to 20 minutes.

Transfer the capon to a serving dish and keep warm. Puree the sauce in a food processor. Season the sauce with salt and pepper to taste before serving with the capon.

STUFFED TURKEY ROLLS

Yield: 4 servings
4 slices turkey breast, about 4 ounces each
Salt
Pepper
3 teaspoons salted butter
1 medium onion, peeled and diced
2 cups mushrooms, finely chopped
½ cup parsley, finely chopped
4 slices bacon
5 tablespoons dry white wine
2 tablespoons whipping cream

Rinse the turkey with cold water and pat dry with paper towels. Season with salt and pepper.

Melt 1 teaspoon of butter in a saucepan and sauté the onion until glazed. Add the mushrooms and cook until all of the liquid has evaporated. Stir in the parsley and season with salt and pepper.

Spread the mixture over the turkey meat. Roll up the turkey slices and wrap each one in a strip of bacon; fasten them with toothpicks. Melt 2 teaspoons of butter in the saucepan. Sauté the turkey rolls until browned. Add the wine, cover, and cook over low heat for 15 to 20 minutes. Arrange the turkey rolls on a warm serving platter. Remove the toothpicks and cover to keep warm.

Add the cream to the pan juices and boil the sauce until it thickens. Season to taste with salt and pepper and pour over the turkey. Serve immediately.

TURKEY BREAST BLANQUETTE

Yield: 4 servings
1 pound turkey breast fillets
1 medium onion, peeled
1 clove
1 bay leaf
Salt
Pepper
3 tablespoons salted butter
2 tablespoons flour
Grated nutmeg
2 cups assorted, cooked vegetables (e.g., peas, carrots, cauliflower, mushrooms, asparagus)
½ cup whipping cream

Rinse the turkey with cold water and pat dry with paper towels. Cut into 2-inch cubes, then place in a large saucepan. Spike the onion with the clove and bay leaf. Add the onion to the sauce and cover with cold water. Season with salt and pepper. Bring to a boil, reduce the heat, and simmer for about 30 minutes. Skim off any scum that rises to the surface while cooking. Remove the turkey from the pan; remove the onion. Strain the liquid through a fine sieve.

Melt the butter in a medium saucepan, then sauté the flour in it. Measure out ¾ cup of the turkey stock. Gradually stir the stock into the flour, using a whisk and taking care that no lumps form, until the sauce thickens. Flavor the sauce with salt and nutmeg. Add the vegetables and heat the sauce until warm. Finally, stir in the cream and then the turkey.

CHICKEN LIVERS IN PUFF PASTRY

Yield: 4 servings

1 pound chicken livers
3 tablespoons salted butter
2 cups mushrooms, sliced
3 large shallots, peeled and diced
1 cup dry red wine
½ cup whipping cream
4 sprigs fresh marjoram, finely chopped
Salt
Pepper
4 frozen puff pastry cases, thawed

Rinse the liver with cold water and cut into ¾-inch cubes. Allow the cubes to drain.

Melt 1 tablespoon of butter in a large saucepan. Add the livers and sauté for 6 to 8 minutes. Remove the livers from the pan; keep warm. Melt the remaining butter in the pan, and sauté the shallots and mushrooms. Add the wine and cream, and cook the sauce until thick and creamy, about 5 minutes, stirring constantly.

Stir the marjoram into the sauce. Season with salt and pepper. Return the livers to the sauce and heat briefly, but do not boil.

Bake the pastry cases according to the package directions and fill with the chicken livers. Serve immediately.

BREAST OF DUCK WITH QUINCE PRESERVES

Yield: 6 to 8 servings
For the quince preserves:
1 cup quinces, peeled and quartered
2 tablespoons salted butter
¼ cup sugar
Juice of 1 lemon
2 tablespoons dry white wine
For the duck:
4 boneless duck breasts
Salt
Pepper
2 tablespoons salted butter
2 large shallots, peeled and finely chopped
¼ cup dry white wine
4 tablespoons cognac
½ cup whipping cream
½ cup chicken stock
1½ ounces goose liver pâté
2 fresh sage leaves, finely chopped
2 tablespoons port wine

For the quince preserves, remove the cores from the quinces and cut the flesh into pieces. Melt the butter and caramelize the sugar in it. Add the lemon juice, wine, and quinces; cook for about 10 minutes.

Rinse the duck with cold water and pat dry with paper towels. Season with salt and pepper. Melt 1 tablespoon of butter in a large saucepan and sauté the duck breasts on both sides for a total of 10 minutes. Remove from the pan and keep warm.

Melt 1 teaspoon of butter in the saucepan and sauté the shallots in it. Add the white wine and cognac. Stir in the whipping cream and the stock. Boil to reduce the sauce until it begins to thicken. Pass the liver pâté through a sieve or puree in a food processor, then stir into the sauce. Swirl in the remaining butter. Do not allow the liquid to boil again. Add the sage, port wine, salt, and pepper to the sauce. Arrange the duck breasts on plates with the sauce and the preserves.

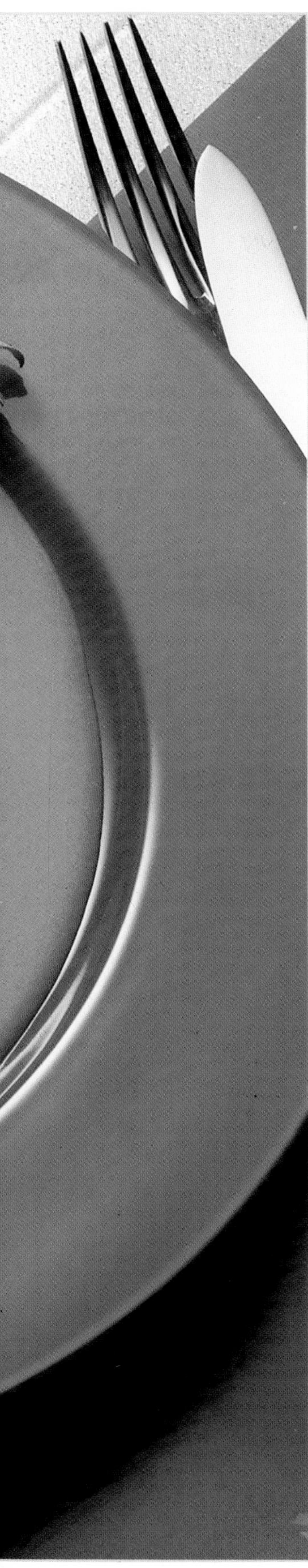

BREAST OF DUCK WITH SHRIMP

Yield: 6 to 8 servings
4 boneless duck breasts
Salt
Pepper
6 tablespoons cold salted butter
12 medium shrimp
2 large shallots, peeled and diced
½ cup dry vermouth
¼ cup whipping cream
¼ cup fresh sorrel, cut into strips
¼ ounce fresh truffles, sliced

Preheat the oven to 400°F.

Rinse the duck with cold water and pat dry with paper towels. Season with salt and pepper, and brush with 1 teaspoon of melted butter. Place in an ovenproof casserole and bake for about 10 minutes. Set aside while preparing the sauce.

Put the shrimp into a pot of boiling salted water and boil for 7 minutes; cool under cold water, then shell.

Melt 1 tablespoon of butter in a saucepan. Add the shallots and sauté until golden. Add the vermouth and reduce the liquid until it thickens. Add the cream and swirl in the remaining butter in pieces.

Add the sorrel and truffles to the sauce; season with salt and pepper. Serve the sauce with the sliced duck breast and shrimp as shown.

DUCK LEGS IN CHERRY SAUCE

Yield: 4 servings
8 boned duck legs, ¼ to ½ pound each
1 teaspoon salted butter
1 large shallot, peeled and finely chopped
½ cup chanterelle mushrooms
1 egg yolk
1 tablespoon parsley, chopped
1 tablespoon fine bread crumbs
Salt
Pepper
1 medium onion, peeled and diced
¼ cup celery, diced
1 medium carrot, peeled and diced
4 tablespoons peanut oil
1 cup cherry juice
3 tablespoons sweet vermouth

Preheat the oven to 400°F.

Rinse the duck legs with cold water and pat dry with paper towels. Melt the butter in a medium saucepan and sauté the shallots and mushrooms until golden. Briskly stir in the egg yolk and add the parsley, bread crumbs, salt, and pepper. Stuff the mixture into the duck legs and fasten together with toothpicks. Season with salt and pepper.

Heat the oil in a Dutch oven, add the duck and vegetables, and bake for about 30 minutes. Pour on the cherry juice and cook for 15 minutes more. Remove the duck from the pan and keep warm.

Puree the sauce in a sieve or food processor and add the vermouth. Reduce the liquid until it thickens. Season with salt and pepper before serving.

STUFFED GOOSE

Yield: 6 to 8 servings
1 goose, about 8 pounds
Salt
Pepper
Fresh marjoram
¼ cup apple brandy
10 ounces boneless chicken breasts, minced
3 ounces calf's liver, minced
1 cup whipping cream
3 ounces goose liver, diced
3 apples
¼ cup shelled chestnuts, diced
3 ounces boiled ham, diced
¼ cup pine nuts
2 medium onions, peeled and coarsely chopped
2 medium celery stalks, coarsely chopped
2 medium carrots, peeled and coarsely chopped

Preheat the oven to 350°F.

Rinse the goose with cold water and pat dry with paper towels. Using a sharp knife, cut the goose open from the back so that the 2 halves of the breast remain joined (photograph 1). Remove the fat and sinews and discard (photograph 2). Rub the inside of the goose with salt, pepper, marjoram, and 2 tablespoons of apple brandy. Let stand for about 1 hour.

Mix the minced chicken and calf's liver with the cream. Wash and quarter 1 apple; remove the core and dice. Combine the goose liver, chestnuts, diced apple, ham, pine nuts, and chicken mixture (photograph 3). Flavor with the remaining apple brandy. Stuff the goose with the mixture (photograph 4). Sew the goose up along the back and lay in a roasting pan (photograph 5).

Wash and core the remaining apples. Place the onions, celery, and carrots in the pan with the goose. Roast the goose, allowing 25 minutes per pound. Remove the goose from the pan and slice (photograph 6). Strain the sauce through a sieve; skim off the fat. Serve the sauce with the goose.

1

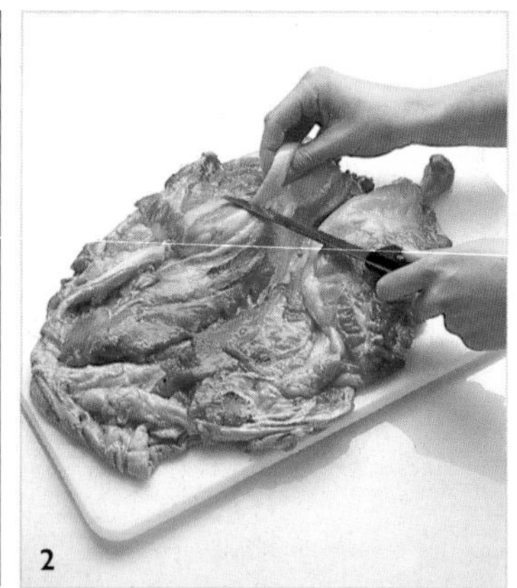
2

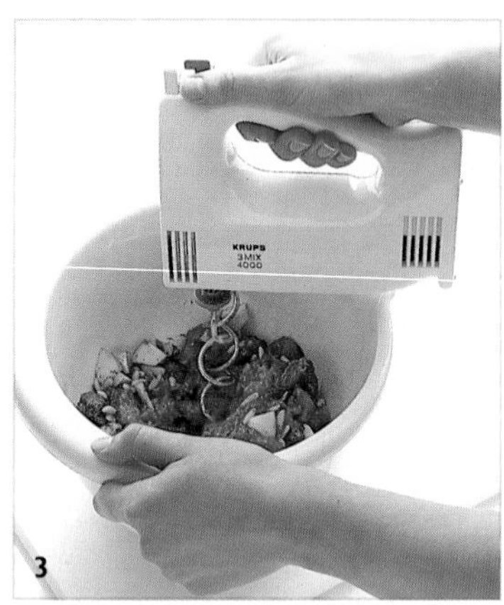
3

FRIED GOOSE LEGS

Yield: 4 servings
4 goose legs, about 1/4 to 1/2 pound each
2 medium onions, peeled and chopped
5 tablespoons sugar
2 bay leaves
1 tablespoon mustard seeds
1 teaspoon salt
1/4 teaspoon ground cinnamon
1 cup white wine vinegar
1/4 cup raisins
2 tablespoons salted butter
2 teaspoons cornstarch
3 tablespoons slivered almonds

Rinse the goose legs with cold water and place in a large saucepan. Add the onions, 4 tablespoons of sugar, bay leaves, mustard seeds, salt, cinnamon, and vinegar. Add cold water to cover. Bring to a boil, cover, reduce to low heat, and simmer for about 2 hours.

Meanwhile, soak the raisins in cold water.

Remove the cooked goose from the stock and pat dry with paper towels. Allow the stock to cool until the fat sets. Heat the butter in a saucepan and sauté the goose legs. Sprinkle with 1/2 tablespoon of sugar and allow to caramelize. Scoop the fat off the stock and add it to the goose. Sprinkle with the remaining sugar and allow to caramelize. Arrange the goose legs on a warm plate.

Measure out 1 cup of stock and place in the saucepan. Mix the cornstarch with a little cold water and add to the stock, stirring until slightly thickened. Add the raisins and almonds, and heat. Pour the sauce over the goose and serve.

ROAST CHICKEN WITH GRAPES

Yield: 6 servings
2 chickens, about 2 ½ pounds each
Salt
Pepper
5 slices bacon
For the champagne cabbage:
2 medium onions, peeled and sliced
1 tablespoon pork drippings
1 pound sauerkraut
½ bottle champagne
For the potato puree:
1 pound potatoes, peeled
1 cup milk
3 tablespoons salted butter
Grated nutmeg
For garnish:
1 cup green seedless grapes

Preheat the oven to 400°F.

Rinse both chickens with cold water and pat dry with paper towels. Rub inside and out with salt and pepper. Fasten the bacon to the tops of the chickens with skewers. Place in a large roasting pan and bake for 50 to 60 minutes.

To make the champagne cabbage, melt the drippings in a large frying pan and sauté the onion until transparent. Add the sauerkraut and champagne. Season to taste with salt and pepper. Cover, and simmer for about 30 minutes.

For the potato puree, cook the potatoes for about 20 minutes in boiling salted water. Mash, adding the milk and butter, and flavor with salt and nutmeg. Using a pastry bag, pipe the puree in a ring around the sides of an oven-proof serving plate. Brown the potato puree under the broiler.

Blanch the grapes and skin them. Add the champagne cabbage to the center of the potato ring and place the roast chickens on top. Garnish with grapes and serve.

CHICKEN BREASTS WITH LENTILS

Yield: 6 to 8 servings
4 boneless chicken breasts, about ½ pound each
Salt
Pepper
1 ½ cups dried lentils
2 stalks celery, diced
½ medium leek, cleaned and diced
1 medium carrot, peeled and diced
6 tablespoons salted butter
¼ cup sour cream
Sherry vinegar
2 tablespoons chopped parsley

Rinse the chicken with cold water and pat dry with paper towels. Cut the chicken into 1-inch strips, and season with salt and pepper. Melt 3 tablespoons of the butter in a large saucepan and sauté the chicken for 5 to 8 minutes, stirring occasionally. Remove from the pan and keep warm.

Melt the remaining butter in the pan juices and glaze the vegetables. Add the lentils and 2 cups of water. Simmer for 25 minutes. Stir in the sour cream, then flavor with the vinegar, pepper, salt, and parsley. Add the cooked chicken and heat through before serving.

BREAST OF DUCK IN APPLE BRANDY

Yield: 6 to 8 servings
4 boneless duck breasts
1 large apple, peeled, cored and diced
2 shallots, peeled and diced
2 tablespoons peanut oil
2 tablespoons salted butter
½ cup dry red wine
½ cup heavy cream
¼ cup apple brandy
Salt
Pepper

In a large frying pan, heat the oil and sauté the duck breasts for 3 minutes on both sides. Remove from the pan and keep warm. Pour off the oil. Melt the butter and sauté the apple and shallots. Add the red wine, and reduce the sauce slightly. Stir in the cream. Flavor with apple brandy and add salt and pepper to taste. Stir in the duck breasts and heat through before serving.

CORNISH GAME HEN WITH CHESTNUT PUREE

Yield: 4 servings
4 Cornish game hens, about 1 pound each
16 grape vine leaves
8 slices bacon
5 tablespoons salted butter
2 medium onions, peeled and diced
2 medium carrots, peeled and diced
Salt
Pepper
1 ½ cups shelled, boiled, sweet chestnuts
¼ cup sour cream
Nutmeg
¼ cup brandy
½ cup white grape juice
½ cup heavy cream

Preheat the oven to 400°F.

Rinse the game hens with cold water and pat dry with paper towels. Rub inside and out with salt and pepper. Fasten the vine leaves and bacon to the tops with skewers. Place the prepared game hens in a large roasting pan.

Melt 3 tablespoons of the butter in a large frying pan and sauté the onions, celery and carrots for about 3 minutes. Add the mixture to the roasting pan. Sprinkle the game hens with salt and pepper and bake for about 45 minutes.

While the game hens are roasting, heat the chestnuts in water and allow them to drain. Mash together with the sour cream, remaining butter, salt, pepper, and nutmeg. Keep warm.

Remove the cooked game hens from the roasting pan, then remove the vine leaves and the bacon. In a saucepan, bring the cooking juices to a boil. Carefully flambé the juices with the brandy. Add the grape juice and heavy cream. Boil until the sauce thickens, then pass the mixture through a sieve. Season with salt and pepper. To serve, arrange the game hens on an attractive platter with the chestnut puree and the sauce.

CLASSIC CUISINE

Vegetables are always at their best when crisp and fresh. The recipes on the following pages include traditional as well as original vegetable dishes to accompany a meal or to be enjoyed on their own. The mixture of crisp green and white asparagus shown here can be served with Hollandaise or Bérnaise sauce.

Dietary experts recommend 1 to 1½ cups of vegetables a day for a healthy diet. However, fresh vegetables must be prepared so that they retain valuable vitamins and minerals. These are some important tips to keep in mind. Prepare fresh vegetables, especially leafy ones such as spinach, on the same day that they are bought. Store them, if necessary, wrapped in aluminum foil in the refrigerator. Never wash vegetables after cutting them into pieces or leave them uncovered, because they will lose vitamins and minerals rather quickly.

Artichokes have been known since antiquity. The flower of this cultivated thorn is one of the more delicate vegetables. It grows on long, strong stalks and has a fleshy flower base on which the petals grow, overlapping like tiles on a roof to form a round or cylindrical shape. The base and the thickened ends of the petals are edible and are considered to be a delicacy.

Artichokes are extremely nutritious because they contain many vitamins, minerals, and healthy carbohydrates that supply needed roughage for a healthy diet.

Asparagus, a popular but relatively expensive stalk vegetable that grows in the ground, is a delectable white or green vegetable. Until recently, asparagus could only be bought from mid-April to late June. Today, however, it may be obtained and enjoyed throughout the year.

Mushrooms have been cultivated for many years. The most popular edible mushrooms are field and oyster mushrooms (photograph above). These mushrooms have a large, wavy cap, are brown in color, and are best suited for braising and frying. Both field and oyster mushrooms are sensitive to pressure and warmth, and should be used quickly after they have been bought, especially oyster mushrooms. Cultivated mushrooms that are substantially bruise-free will keep for a few days in the refrigerator. Mushrooms have a relatively high protein content and are, therefore, quite filling.

Cauliflower and broccoli both belong to the wild cauliflower family. Broccoli forms loose green florets on tender, asparagus-like stalks. Conversely, the cauliflower forms a head with white florets that lie close together.

White cabbage, savoy cabbage, kale, and red cabbage belong to the brassica family, as do Chinese cabbage, kohlrabi, and brussels sprouts (photograph above). Fennel bulbs are leaf stalks that have swollen in layers. The cabbage has one great advantage: thanks to modern storage methods, it can be bought fresh from one harvest to another. Obviously, cabbage that is picked in the morning and is prepared at lunchtime is always more tasty.

The "pointed" cabbage (top right photograph) takes its name from its shape, but is, biologically, a white cabbage. The tender Chinese cabbage can be used in a salad, on its own as a vegetable, or in a stew or Oriental stir-fry. Kohlrabi is available with a white or blue skin.

The onion family includes garlic and leeks, tender spring onions, commonly known as scallions, shallots, white and red onions, and large Spanish onions. All have their own important place in cuisine and are used in countless dishes.

The healthiest way to prepare vegetables is to steam them as briefly as possible so that they remain firm. Here are approximate cooking times in minutes for vegetables that have been cut in pieces:

Artichokes 30
Asparagus 10–20
Beets 30–40
Broccoli 10
Brussels sprouts 15–20
Chinese cabbage 15
"Pointed" cabbage 20–30
Red cabbage 30–40
Savoy cabbage 20–30
White cabbage 30–40
Carrots 15–20
Cauliflower 20
Celery 10–15
Chicory 8–10
Fennel 15
String beans 10–15
Green peas 10
Kale 30–40
Kohlrabi 30–40
Leeks 10–15
Peppers 15
Spinach 5–10
Zucchini 10

VEGETABLES

Carrots and turnips are both root vegetables. Of all the root vegetables, carrots contain the most carotene, which converts to vitamin A in the body. The turnip, on the other hand, contains more vitamin C.

The plump, shiny vegetables shown in the right hand photograph represent the gourd family. Cucumber is mainly used in salads, but is also sometimes stuffed and braised. Zucchini is served in salads and as a cooked vegetable. Also in the gourd family is the mild sweet pepper (capsicum or vegetable paprika), with its high vitamin A and C content. Purple eggplant is also readily available year round.

Celery is cultivated in 3 different forms. The first is celeriac, a popular soup vegetable also used in salads. Stalk celery has a swollen root, but its tender leaf stalks are cooked or served raw in a salad or relish plate. Celery seed is used as a seasoning herb.

Beans and peas are members of the legume family. They can be bought in different degrees of ripeness. String bean varieties are the bush bean, runner bean, and scarlet runner. Broad beans are also well known. Bush and pole beans can also be bought with yellow and red pods, and are called kidney beans. Today, all the varieties are practically free of fibers, which makes "topping and tailing" them a great deal easier. Yellow, white, and red beans (shown in the photograph on the right) are all dried varieties, as are yellow and green dried peas. Shell peas and snow peas also belong to the small green pea family, as do sugar peas, which are used whole. Brown and red lentils (in the photograph on the left) also belong to the legume family and are grown in the United States, South America, France, and Spain.

Artichokes and eggplants, cucumbers and kohlrabi, sweet peppers and celery, and tomatoes and potatoes can all be successfully stuffed. The photographs show how to stuff a sweet pepper. Cut the top off each pepper, remove the seeds and the white pith, then wash in cold water and dry with paper towels. Finally, spoon in the filling.

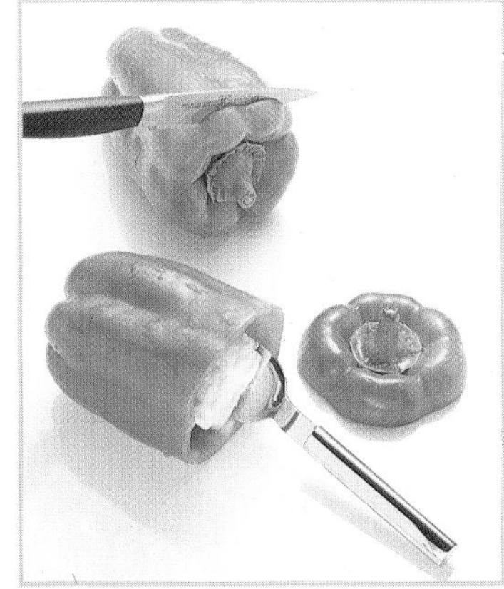

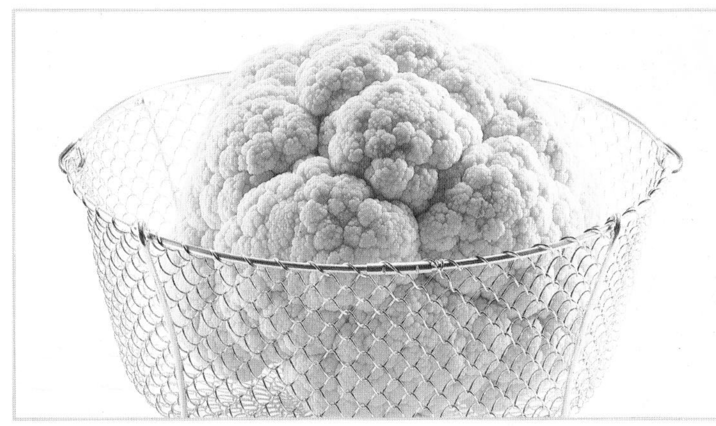

Prepare a chopped meat filling by mixing together 2 slices of bread soaked in water, squeezed out and shredded, with 1 cup of mixed ground meat, 2 teaspoons of diced smoked bacon, 2 chopped onions, 1 egg, and then season with salt, pepper, and paprika. This filling is sufficient for stuffing 4 large sweet peppers, or 8 large tomatoes.

Wire baskets are ideal for cooking vegetables with as little effort as possible. And using a wire basket, vegetables can be steamed in a saucepan so that they have practically no contact with the water. A basket is also useful for deep-frying french fries or bite-sized pieces of vegetable that have been dipped in batter. Wire baskets can also be used to deep-fry in a pressure cooker.

To cook stuffed peppers, heat 4 tablespoons of oil, butter, or margarine in a saucepan and sauté 1 medium onion until transparent. Add the chopped meat mixture and cook until brown. Stuff the peppers with the meat and place them in a Dutch oven. Add 1½ cups of heated chicken stock mixed with 2 tablespoons of tomato puree. Cover and cook for about 30 minutes over medium heat. Thicken the sauce with 1 cup of sour cream. Stuffed tomatoes should be cooked for about 20 minutes.

Cucumbers and kohlrabi are also easy to stuff. Halve and hollow out 4 medium cucumbers or kohlrabi, leaving ½ inch of the flesh within the shell. Reserve the hollowed-out portion of the vegetable, chop into fine pieces, and add to the chopped meat filling before cooking. Preparation and cooking are identical to the method used for stuffed peppers. Cooking time for kohlrabi is about 30 minutes; cooking time for cucumbers is about 20 minutes.

Cook vegetables carefully so that their nutrients and flavor are preserved. To do this, a pressure cooker with two adjustable cooking settings is recommended. One setting is for cooking meat, soups, stews, and braising and the other is for cooking delicate vegetables, such as sugar peas, green beans, brussels sprouts, sweet peppers, and tomatoes. To cook delicate vegetables gently, the vegetables are placed in the inset tray, without coming in contact with the water, and are cooked in the steam. They are cooked at a somewhat higher temperature than usual, but in a fraction of the time. Because of this, the essential vitamins are preserved.

CORN WITH LETTUCE

Yield: 4 servings
6 medium ears of corn
1 tablespoon butter
3 medium onions, peeled and cut in rings
1 teaspoon parsley, chopped
1 sprig fresh thyme
1 teaspoon chopped savory
1 small head lettuce, cut in ¼-inch julienne strips
Salt
Pepper
1 teaspoon sugar
3 teaspoons whipping cream

Remove the husk and silk from the corn and cut the kernels off the cob with a large knife. Melt the butter in a frying pan and sauté the corn and onions. Add the herbs and lettuce. Season with salt, pepper, and sugar. Cook gently over low heat for about 15 minutes.

Carefully fold in the cream, and season again to taste. Remove the thyme before serving.

BAKED SPINACH WITH CHEESE

Yield: 4 servings
4 tablespoons olive oil
1 clove garlic, peeled and cut in half lengthwise
1 pound leaf spinach, washed and thick stems removed
2 to 3 tablespoons pine nuts
½ cup mozzarella cheese, cut in small cubes
5 to 6 teaspoons grated Parmesan cheese
Salt
Pepper

Grease a baking sheet or shallow pan with 2 tablespoons of the olive oil. Rub the pan with the cut surfaces of the garlic. Spread the spinach over the pan, press it down, and sprinkle it with the pine nuts and the remaining oil.

Cover the spinach with the mozzarella cubes and the Parmesan cheese. Season with salt and pepper.

Bake in a preheated 350°F oven for 15 to 20 minutes. Serve immediately.

STUFFED SWISS CHARD

Yield: 4 servings
2 pounds Swiss chard
4 tablespoons butter
1 small onion, peeled and diced
2 tablespoons flour
Salt
Caraway seeds
Pepper
¾ cup feta cheese

Clean and wash the Swiss chard and cut the stalks so that they are even with the bottom of the leaves.

Melt 2 tablespoons butter in a frying pan and sauté the leaves quickly, in batches, until they wilt. Slightly cool the leaves. Cut the stalks into 1-inch pieces Peel and dice the onion. Melt the remaining butter and sauté the stalks with the diced onion.

Sprinkle the flour over the onion mixture and stir in the salt, caraway seeds, and pepper, to taste.

Simmer for 15 minutes, then set aside to cool.

Crumble the feta cheese and stir into the mixture.

Place 1 to 3 teaspoons of the mixture on each Swiss chard leaf. Roll up, folding in the sides before the final roll.

Place the rolls in a greased soufflé dish.

Bake in a preheated 350°F oven for 15 to 20 minutes.

BRAISED ASPARAGUS

Yield: 4 servings
20 white and green asparagus spears
Salt
Sugar
1 tablespoon butter
1 teaspoon lemon juice
For the sauce:
1 teaspoon butter
1 tablespoon flour
1 orange
½ cup whipping cream
1 teaspoon orange liqueur
White pepper

Carefully peel the white asparagus from top to bottom with a vegetable peeler (photograph 1) and cut off the ends. Peel the lower part of the stem of the green asparagus (photograph 2) and cut off the ends.

Put 2 cups of water in a saucepan. Add salt, sugar, butter, and lemon juice and bring to a boil.

Place the asparagus on a steamer tray and place the tray in the saucepan (photograph 3). Cook the asparagus until tender, 8 to 10 minutes. Transfer the asparagus to a warm plate and keep warm.

Measure ½ cup of the asparagus water and set aside.

To make the sauce, knead the butter and flour together and form the dough into small balls, the size of beans. Squeeze the juice from the orange and strain. Put half of the juice, the cream, and the reserved asparagus water in a saucepan and heat gently. Add the flour balls (photograph 4) slowly and boil gently for 5 to 7 minutes, stirring constantly until balls dissolve.

Add the remaining orange juice and the orange liqueur. Season the sauce to taste with salt and white pepper, and serve with the asparagus.

BAKED ARTICHOKES

Yield: 4 servings
4 medium artichokes
Salt
2 teaspoons lemon juice
1 pound ham, cut in small pieces
1 cup sour cream
1 tablespoon parsley, chopped
¼ pound shrimp, shelled and deveined
½ teaspoon lemon rind, grated
Pepper
2 to 3 teaspoons fine bread crumbs
1 tablespoon butter

Cut the stems off the artichokes at the first bud. Rub the artichokes with the lemon juice, then cook for 40 minutes in enough water to cover or until tender. (Artichokes are done when they can be pierced with a knife and the knife can be removed without effort.)

Remove the artichokes, drain, and cut off the ends of the leaves. Bend the artichokes to open them up and remove the "hay" from their bases.

Puree the ham with the sour cream. Add the parsley, shrimp, lemon rind, and pepper to taste.

Stuff each artichoke with some of the ham mixture and sprinkle with fine bread crumbs. Place slivers of butter on top.

Broil the artichokes under a preheated broiler for 15 to 20 minutes. Serve as a side dish or as a light main dish.

BROCCOLI IN WALNUT CREAM

Yield: 4 servings
1 medium bunch broccoli
¼ cup walnut halves
1 tablespoon butter
Salt
Pepper
Grated nutmeg
1 cup dry white wine
1 cup whipping cream
1 pinch ground cloves

Cut the broccoli stalks from the florets. Set the florets aside and cut the stalks into strips about ½-inch wide.

Chop half of the walnuts. Melt the butter in a saucepan and sauté both the chopped and the halved walnuts. Add the broccoli stalks and cook for 2 minutes longer. Season with salt, pepper, and nutmeg.

Add the white wine and cream. Cook for 8 minutes at a rapid simmer.

Carefully add the broccoli florets, placing them downward on the vegetable mixture, and cook for 4 to 5 minutes. Set the florets aside.

To serve, arrange the vegetables on a plate. Add ground cloves to taste, and garnish with the florets.

SPIKED CAULIFLOWER

Yield: 4 servings
1 medium head cauliflower
Salt
1 tablespoon wine vinegar
½ pound garlic salami
2 cups pureed tomatoes
Pepper
1 teaspoon dried basil
½ cup sour cream
2 tablespoons grated Parmesan cheese

Cut a cross deep into the cauliflower stalk. Fill a saucepan with water, add salt and vinegar, and bring to a boil. Add the cauliflower and cook for about 15 minutes (the cauliflower should remain firm).

Cut half of the salami in small slices and the rest in small cubes. Use the small slices to spike the cauliflower by slightly pulling the florets apart with a pointed knife and pushing the salami slices between them.

Season the pureed tomatoes with pepper, salt, and basil. Stir in the diced salami, sour cream, and Parmesan cheese. Pour this sauce into a soufflé dish and place the cauliflower on top.

Bake in preheated 400°F oven for 15 to 20 minutes.

BAY LEAVES AND KOHLRABI IN FOIL

Yield: 6 servings
6 small young kohlrabi
Salt
Pepper
6 small, or 3 large, bay leaves
12 thin strips of bacon

Strip off the kohlrabi leaves and pare the roots. Cut straight down into each kohlrabi from the top, not quite through to the bottom. Sprinkle salt and pepper onto the cut, and push a small, or half of a large, bay leaf into the cut. Wrap each kohlrabi in a strip of bacon, and then wrap individually in foil, with the shiny side inside.

Bake in a 400°F oven for about 1½ hours, depending on size. The kohlrabi is done when a knife inserted comes out clean.

STUFFED RED CABBAGE ROLLS

Yield: 4 to 6 servings
1 medium red cabbage
1 tablespoon butter
3 slices bacon, finely diced
3 slices stale bread, with crust removed and cut in cubes
1 small onion, peeled and finely diced
5 dried apple rings, cut in small pieces
1 cup whipping cream
1 cup dry red wine
Salt
Pepper
Ground cloves
Ground pimiento
Mace
Butter

Remove 8 of the outer leaves of the cabbage, and store the remaining cabbage.

Wash the leaves, then blanch them for about 3 minutes in boiling salted water (photograph 1) until flexible and elastic. Remove and dry the leaves. Score the center rib until the leaves lie flat (photograph) 2).

Melt the butter in a frying pan and render the fat from the bacon. Add the bread cubes and onion; fry until crisp and brown (photograph 3).

Add the apple pieces, cream, and red wine. Remove the mixture from the stove and let stand for 15 minutes. Add seasonings to taste.

Place a small amount of filling on the leaves, and roll them up. Roll a second leaf around each rolled leaf (photograph 4).

Place the stuffed leaves closely together in a greased soufflé dish. Cook in a preheated 350°F oven for 30 minutes.

1

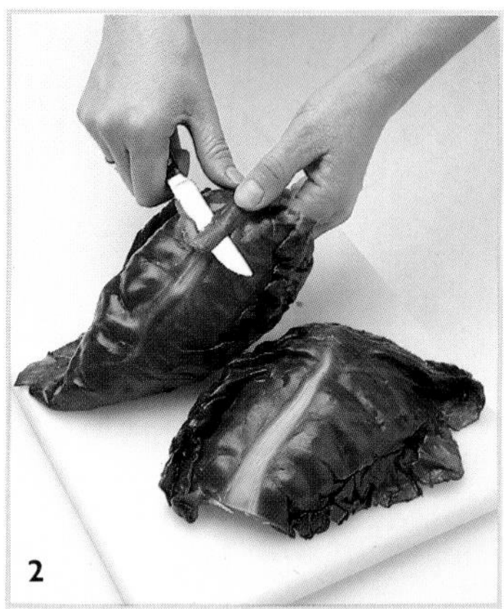
2

3

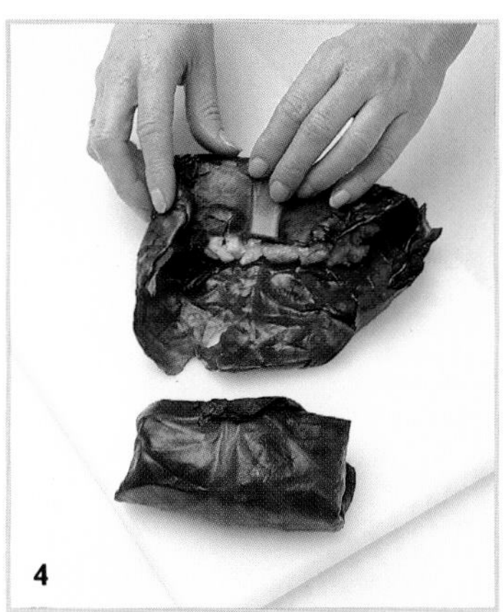
4

SAUERKRAUT DUMPLINGS

Yield: 4 to 6 servings
3 tablespoons pork drippings
½ loaf rye bread, cut in thin slices
5 slices bacon, diced
1 pound sauerkraut, finely chopped
½ cup lukewarm milk
4 eggs
Salt
Pepper
Caraway seeds
1 medium cooked potato, peeled and mashed
Milk
Fine bread crumbs

Melt the drippings in a frying pan and sauté the bread on both sides. Remove from the pan and set aside. Add the bacon and render the fat over low heat. Fry the sauerkraut in the bacon fat for about 10 minutes. Remove from the heat and let cool.

Pour the milk over the bread, add the sauerkraut, and let soak until all the liquid has been absorbed. Knead the sauerkraut mixture together with the eggs and the seasonings. Add the potato. The mixture should be moist but firm (add milk or fine bread crumbs, if necessary).

Form the mixture into 12 small dumplings. Using a slotted spoon, slide the dumplings into boiling salted water, return the water to a boil, and simmer over low heat for 10 to 15 minutes with the lid ajar.

Remove the dumplings with a slotted spoon, drain, and serve hot.

BRUSSELS SPROUTS IN PUMPKIN PUREE

Yield: 4 servings
1 tablespoon butter
1 small pumpkin, about 1 to 3 pounds, peeled, seeded, and cut in large cubes
1 clove garlic, peeled and finely diced
1 small onion, peeled and finely diced
Salt
Pepper
Turmeric
4 tablespoons whipping cream
1 tablespoon mustard
2 cups brussels sprouts

Melt the butter in a saucepan and braise the pumpkin. Add the garlic, onion, and seasonings to taste. Stir in the cream and cook for about 15 minutes or until the pumpkin is soft.

Press the pumpkin mixture through a sieve, add the mustard, and season to taste.

Clean the brussels sprouts and cut a cross in the base of the stems to cook through evenly. Add the brussels sprouts to the pumpkin mixture and cook over low heat for about 15 minutes, until tender. If necessary, add a little more water or cream while cooking.

SWEET AND SOUR CABBAGE

Yield: 4 servings
5 tablespoons sunflower oil
2 small young carrots, grated
4 small tomatoes, sliced
1 cup orange juice
1 tablespoon soy sauce
1 tablespoon honey
1 to 2 tablespoons whole-wheat flour
1 small savoy cabbage

Heat 1 tablespoon of the oil in a saucepan and sauté the carrots and tomatoes. Cook over low heat for about 8 minutes, until the carrots are soft.

Pass the vegetables through a fine sieve or food mill, and stir together with the orange juice, soy sauce, and honey. Return the mixture to the saucepan.

Stir the flour together with 2 to 3 tablespoons of cold water. Add the flour mixture to the vegetable sauce and bring to a boil, stirring constantly. Simmer for about 5 minutes over low heat.

Remove the outer leaves of the cabbage and wash them with warm water. Cut the leaves into ½-inch squares. Divide the cabbage leaves into 4 portions.

Sauté each portion in 1 tablespoon of oil in a frying pan for about 5 minutes over high heat, stirring constantly. Add the cabbage to the sauce and boil for 5 minutes longer. Serve immediately.

SAVOY CABBAGE IN A ROMAN POT

Yield: 4 servings
1 small leek
2 small onions, peeled and diced
1 clove garlic, peeled and diced
1 tablespoon butter
1 cup beef stock
2 tablespoons tomato paste
Black pepper
1 teaspoon dried oregano
1 large savoy cabbage, cut in 8 pieces

Remove the roots and tough green leaves from the leek; wash the white part and cut in julienne strips. Melt the butter in a frying pan and sauté the onions until they are transparent. Add the garlic and leek, pour on the stock, and bring to a gentle boil. Add the tomato paste, pepper, and oregano, and remove from the heat.

Put half the onion mixture into a clay cooking pot that has been soaked in water for at least 10 minutes. Lay the cabbage pieces, heart sides downward, on the onion mixture. Pour the remaining onion mixture over the cabbage. Bake in a preheated 325° to 350°F oven for about 30 minutes.

BRAISED LEEKS

Yield: 2 to 4 servings
4 leeks
1 pound tomatoes, pureed
2 tablespoons gin
1/4 cup grated Parmesan cheese
1 cup ricotta (or cottage cheese)
Salt & Pepper
Butter

Cut off the roots and tough green parts of the leeks to within 4 inches of the white part. Score the sides, wash thoroughly, and drain.

Stir the pureed tomatoes, gin, Parmesan cheese, and ricotta together. Season with salt and pepper. Put the mixture in a shallow, buttered soufflé dish.

Lay the leeks on top of the mixture and place the dish in a preheated 400°F oven. Cook for 45 to 50 minutes.

BRAISED SCALLIONS

Yield: 2 to 4 servings
4 bunches scallions
1 tablespoon butter
½ cup dry white wine
Salt
Pepper
1 teaspoon nutmeg
½ cup whipping cream
½ cup milk
1 to 2 tablespoons flour
2 tablespoons capers
1 egg yolk

Cut the roots and leaves from the scallions, then wash and drain. Melt the butter in a frying pan and briefly sauté the scallion stems. Add the wine and season to taste. Simmer for 20 minutes. Remove the scallions from the pan and keep warm.

Combine the scallion liquid, cream, and milk in a saucepan and bring to a boil. Mix the flour with 2 to 4 tablespoons of cold water. Stir the flour mixture into the boiling sauce, and continue stirring until the sauce thickens. Simmer for about 5 minutes.

Add the capers; let soak for about 2 minutes.

Stir a few spoonfuls of the sauce into the egg yolk. Remove the sauce from the stove and beat in the egg yolk-sauce mixture. Add the scallions, and serve.

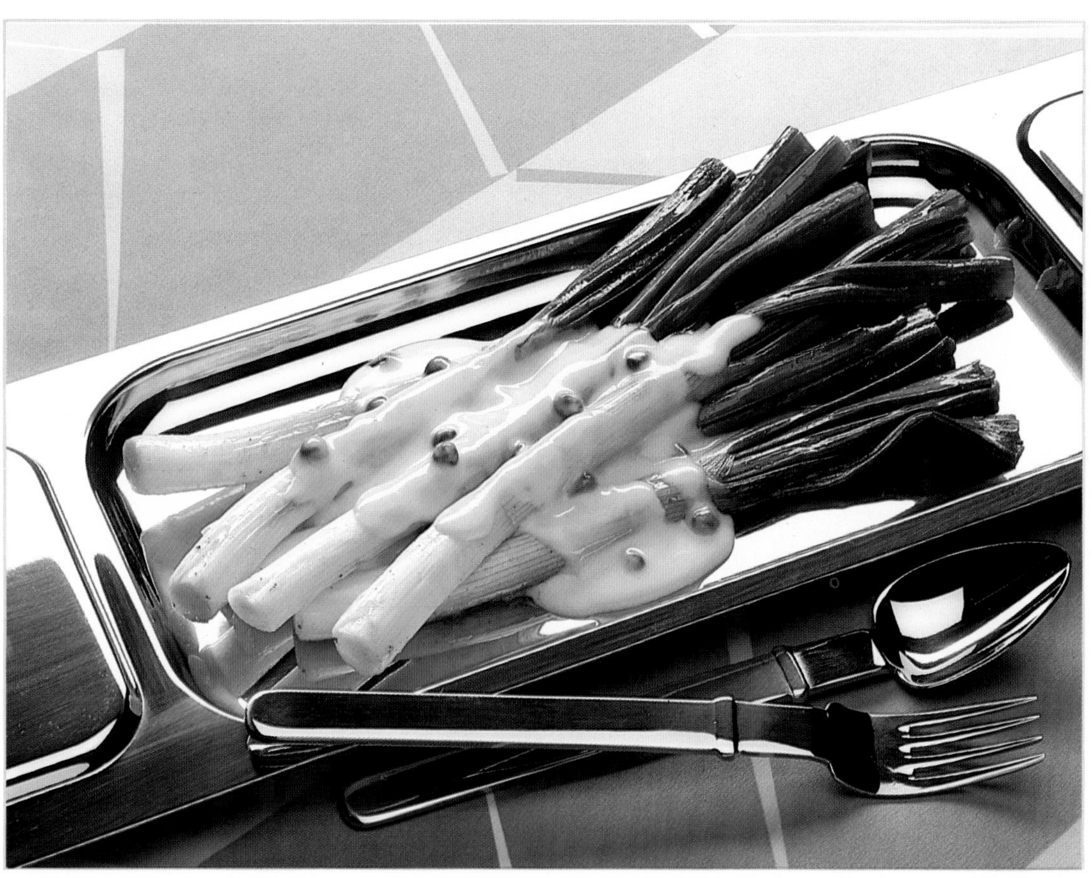

BACON AND ONIONS IN WINE

Yield: 2 to 4 servings
4 medium onions, peeled
Salt
1 tablespoon butter
4 slices bacon, cut in thin strips
Pepper
1 teaspoon caraway seeds
1 bay leaf
½ cup dry white wine
1 teaspoon cornstarch

Blanch the onions for 8 minutes in boiling, salted water. Drain and cut in eighths.

Melt the butter and render the fat from the bacon over low heat. Sauté the onions until transparent in the butter and bacon fat. Add the seasonings and wine; simmer for about 20 minutes. Remove the onions.

Mix the cornstarch with a little cold water, and whisk into the sauce. Add salt to taste, stirring constantly until the sauce thickens. To serve, pour the sauce over the onions.

VEGETABLE MEDLEY

Yield: 4 to 6 servings
4 cups water
1 chicken bouillon cube
20 asparagus spears, cut in pieces
1 pound fresh peas, shelled
1 small cauliflower, cut in florets
1 large kohlrabi, pared and cut in cubes or slices
3 medium carrots, peeled and cut in cubes or slices
1 7-ounce can green peas
3 tablespoons butter
Salt
Pepper
1 bunch parsley leaves, finely chopped

Bring the water and bouillon cube to a boil in a large saucepan; add the cauliflower and cook for 15 minutes. Add the asparagus and fresh peas and cook for an additional 10 minutes; then drain.

Melt 1 tablespoon of the butter and sauté the green peas, kohlrabi, and carrots. Season with salt and pepper and simmer for about 15 minutes, until tender.

To serve, mix the parsley with the remaining butter and the drained vegetables. Stir the parsley into the pea-kohlrabi-carrot mixture.

NUTTY PARSNIPS

Yield: 4 servings
5 large or 8 small parsnips or turnips
2 to 3 tablespoons walnut oil
Salt
Pepper
Grated nutmeg
3 tablespoons chopped walnuts
5 to 6 tablespoons chicken stock
¼ cup whipping cream
1 tablespoon walnut liqueur

Wash the parsnips, remove the roots and greens, and peel. Leave the small parsnips whole and quarter the larger ones from the leaf bases down.

Heat the oil in a saucepan. Sauté the parsnips for 5 minutes, season, and add the nuts. Pour in the chicken stock and simmer for about 30 minutes, or until the parsnips are cooked through.

Add the cream and nut liqueur to taste; bring quickly to a boil. Remove from the heat and serve.

GLAZED CARROTS

Yield: 4 servings
10 small carrots
1 tablespoon butter
Salt
Pepper
3 oranges
1 teaspoon honey
1 tablespoon orange liqueur

Select carrots that are approximately the same size. Scrape the carrots and cut them in pieces that are as long as they are wide. Then cut them into rounds. Melt 1 tablespoon of the butter, sauté the carrots for 5 minutes, and season.

Grate 1 teaspoon of orange rind and squeeze out the juice. Add the orange rind and juice to the carrots. Simmer over low heat for 25 to 30 minutes, or until the carrots are tender. Remove the lid and simmmer until the liquid evaporates.

Add the remaining butter and the honey; stir continuously to glaze the carrots. Place in a serving dish and keep warm.

To serve, peel the 2 remaining oranges and slice them thinly. Heat the oranges in the pan with the liqueur and arrange with the carrots.

WHITE RADISH CURRY

Yield: 4 servings
1 tablespoon butter
1 to 2 tablespoons curry powder
1 teaspoon caraway seeds
Pepper
1 clove garlic, peeled and finely diced
3 small onions, peeled and finely diced
1 tablespoon fresh grated ginger
5 large white radishes, peeled and cut in strips
Salt
Soy sauce
2 medium tomatoes, peeled and cut in small pieces
¼ cup ground cashew nuts
½ cup plain yogurt
1 teaspoon lemon juice
½ cup parsley, chopped

Melt the butter in a casserole dish and gently sauté the curry, caraway seeds, and pepper for 3 minutes. Add the garlic, onions, and ginger and simmer for 5 minutes. Add the radishes, salt, and soy sauce and cook for 15 minutes. Add the tomatoes, nuts, yogurt, and lemon juice and cook for 2 minutes longer.

To serve, spread parsley leaves over the radish curry.

STUFFED TURNIPS

Yield: 4 servings

1 very large turnip, peeled and cut in half horizontally (wash turnip thoroughly and repeatedly in hot water to remove any wax, if turnip appears waxed)
1 clove garlic, peeled and crushed
Salt
Pepper
Ground cinnamon
2 tablespoons butter
2 medium onions, peeled and diced
¾ cup green spiral noodles
¼ cup hazelnuts
¼ cup sour cream
1 tablespoon parsley, chopped
½ cup Brie, without the rind, sliced

Hollow out the turnip halves with a melon baller, leaving a shell about ¼ inch thick. Rub the turnip, inside and out, with garlic, salt, pepper, and cinnamon.

Melt 1 tablespoon of butter in a casserole dish. Add the turnip halves and turnip balls; gently sauté them for about 20 minutes, until almost cooked.

Sauté the onions in the remaining butter until golden. Remove from the pan and let cool.

Cook the noodles in boiling water for about 10 minutes, until tender. Mix the noodles, onions, nuts, sour cream, and parsley together. Season with salt, pepper, and cinnamon. Spoon this mixture into the turnip halves. Lay the Brie slices on top.

Cook in a 400° F oven for about 20 minutes. Add the turnip balls during the last 5 minutes of cooking time. Serve immediately.

FRIED EGGPLANT

2 eggplants (each about 10½ ounces), cut in long slices about ½-inch thick
Salt
¼ cup flour
1 teaspoon dried basil
Pepper
Grated nutmeg
Oil
2 eggs, lightly beaten

Sprinkle the cut surfaces of the eggplants with salt. Layer a few slices over one another, cover with a towel, and place a weight on top. Press the eggplant slices for 2 hours, then thoroughly dry each slice with paper towels.

Mix the flour with the basil and seasonings, and dredge the eggplant slices in the flour.

Heat the oil in a frying pan. Dip the eggplant slices, one at a time, in the beaten eggs and fry them in the oil until golden brown. Drain and serve hot.

Tip: The water must be pressed out of the eggplant slices so they will not absorb fat. It is also important that the oil is at the correct temperature of 325° to 350° F. At this temperature small bubbles will form on the handle of a wooden spoon dipped in hot fat.

BUTTER TOMATOES WITH AVOCADO

Yield: 4 servings
1 tablespoon butter
2 shallots, peeled and finely diced
1 clove garlic, peeled and finely diced
5 medium tomatoes, peeled, seeded, and cut in ½-inch cubes
Salt
Pepper
2 small avocados, peeled and cut in small cubes
4 to 5 basil leaves

Melt the butter in a frying pan. Sauté the shallots for 3 to 5 minutes. Add the garlic and tomatoes, season, and cook for 3 to 4 minutes over low heat.

Add the avocado cubes to the tomatoes. Cook until heated through and season to taste. Garnish with basil leaves.

POTATO AND PEPPER CURRY

Yield: 4 to 6 servings
20 small potatoes, peeled
5 tablespoons sunflower oil
3 medium yellow and 3 medium green peppers, seeded and cut in cubes
2 onions, peeled and diced
1 teaspoon coriander seeds
12 black peppercorns
½ teaspoon caraway seeds
2 tablespoons chopped almonds
½ teaspoon cardamon
1 grated nutmeg
1 clove garlic, peeled and crushed
1 teaspoon salt
1 cup plain yogurt
2 tablespoons chopped parsley

Pierce the potatoes with a fork and sauté them in 3 tablespoons of oil, turning them frequently, for 15 minutes, or until brown. Set aside.

Heat 1 tablespoon of oil in a saucepan and sauté the peppers for about 2 minutes. Remove from the pan and set aside.

Heat another tablespoon of oil in the pan and sauté the coriander, pepper, caraway seeds, almonds, cardamon, and nutmeg. Add the onions and sauté for 5 minutes, until transparent. Add the garlic, salt, and 5 tablespoons of water. Simmer for 10 minutes, gradually stirring in the yogurt.

Add the potatoes and peppers. Simmer for 10 minutes. Stir in the parsley, and serve.

SAUTÉED RED PEPPERS WITH LEEKS

Yield: 4 servings
2 to 3 tablespoons corn oil
2 small red peppers, seeded and cut in small pieces or strips
2 small leeks, cut in slanted slices
3 small zucchini, cut in thin strips
1 cup bean sprouts, rinsed and drained
1 clove garlic, peeled and crushed
Pepper
1 tablespoon lemon juice
Soy sauce

Heat the oil in a large frying pan or wok. Add the vegetables and sauté, stirring constantly.

Add the garlic and seasoning to the vegetables. Sauté over high heat until the vegetables are cooked but still crisp. Keep the cooking temperature high so no juices form.

Add seasoning to taste and serve hot.

PUMPKIN WITH ALFALFA PUREE

Yield: 4 servings
1 tablespoon butter
1 large pumpkin, 3 to 4 pounds, peeled, seeded, and diced
Salt
1 egg
1 teaspoon apple cider vinegar
1 teaspoon honey
1 tablespoon dried currants
3 tablespoons cornstarch
Cinnamon
Grated nutmeg
Pepper
Soy sauce
4 to 5 tablespoons sunflower oil
For the puree:
1 tablespoon chopped walnuts
1 tablespoon chopped Brazil nuts
1 tablespoon chopped pecans
1 cup buttermilk
3 tablespoons alfalfa sprouts

Peel the pumpkin; remove the seeds and membrane, and dice. Melt the butter in a frying pan and sauté the diced pumpkin. Season with ½ teaspoon of salt. Cook for about 25 minutes, until cooked through.

Mash the pumpkin and mix it with the egg, apple cider vinegar, honey, currants, and cornstarch. Add the spices to taste, and let stand for about 30 minutes; then form into several small, flat loaves.

Heat the oil in a frying pan and fry the "loaves" on both sides. Drain on paper towels.

To make the puree, roast the nuts and puree them with the buttermilk. Heat the mixture and stir in the alfalfa. Add salt and pepper to taste. Serve the puree hot with the pumpkin loaves.

PUMPKIN IN SHERRY SAUCE

Yield:4 servings
1 tablespoon butter
¼ cup raw shelled pumpkin seeds
3 small onions, peeled and sliced
1 small pumpkin (about 1 pound), peeled, seeded, and cut in ½-inch cubes
Salt
Pepper
Grated nutmeg
½ cup sherry
3 dried figs, finely diced
½ teaspoon lemon rind, grated
½ cup whipping cream
Worcestershire sauce to taste
1 teaspoon cornstarch

Melt the butter in a frying pan and roast the pumpkin seeds. Add the onions and pumpkin cubes; season to taste.

Add the sherry, figs, and lemon rind, and simmer for about 20 minutes. Add the cream and Worcestershire sauce to taste.

Dissolve the cornstarch in a small amount of water and mix until it is a smooth paste. Whisk this into the mixture in the frying pan, stirring constantly and bring mixture to a boil. Remove from the heat immediately, and serve.

ZUCCHINI PUDDING

Yield: 4 to 6 servings
¼ cup flour
3 eggs, separated
1 cup whipping cream
Salt
Pepper
1 teaspoon dried basil
1 tablespoon butter
10 small zucchini, coarsely grated
Butter
Flour for dusting

Stir ¼ cup of flour together with the egg yolks, cream, and seasonings. Let stand for at least 1 hour.

Melt the butter in a frying pan and sauté the zucchini for 3 to 4 minutes, stirring continuously. Drain on paper towels, season lightly, then incorporate into the batter.

Whip the egg whites until stiff and fold into the zucchini batter. Put the batter in a greased mold that has been dusted with flour. Place the mold in ¾ inch of hot water and bake in a 350°F oven for 50 to 60 minutes. Let stand for about 5 minutes, then turn out of the mold.

Note: If a ring mold is used, cover it with aluminum foil before placing it in the water bath.

BOUILLON PEAS WITH CUCUMBER

Yield: 2 to 4 servings
1 cup chicken bouillon
1 pound fresh green peas, shelled (or 1 box frozen peas or extra small canned peas)
1 small cucumber, peeled and cut in ¼-inch cubes
1 tablespoon butter
2 to 3 sprigs mint
Salt
Pepper
1 to 2 teaspoons cornstarch

Bring the bouillon to a boil in a saucepan; add the fresh peas and cook for about 10 minutes (about 5 minutes for frozen peas and 1 minute for canned peas).

Add the cucumber cubes halfway through the cooking time. Add the butter and 1 tablespoon of chopped mint; season with salt and pepper.

Simmer the liquid until it has been reduced by ⅔. Add a small amount of water to the cornstarch and mix to a smooth paste. Whisk the cornstarch paste into the cucumber mixture, stirring constantly, and bring to a boil. Add seasoning to taste, sprinkle with mint leaves, and serve immediately.

RED LENTIL PUREE

Yield: 4 servings
1 teaspoon butter
12 small onions, peeled and finely diced
1 clove garlic, peeled and finely diced
3 ounces ham, cut in small cubes
1 (10½ ounce) can lentils
2 cups red dry wine
¼ cup sour cream
Pepper
Salt
3 tablespoons tomato paste
½ teaspoon dried basil
3 eggs
3 strips fatty bacon, finely diced
Butter

Melt the butter in a frying pan and sauté the onions until transparent. Add the garlic, ham, lentils, red wine, sour cream, pepper, salt, tomato paste, and basil. Simmer for about 30 minutes, until soft. Puree this mixture, season, and let cool.

Beat the eggs and slowly incorporate them into the lentil cream. Pour the lentil puree into a greased, 2-quart soufflé dish. Sprinkle with the bacon and cook in a preheated 325°F oven for 40 minutes.

Tip: If dried lentils are used, rehydrate the lentils by placing in a pot of water. Bring the water and lentils to a boil and turn off the heat. Let the lentils sit in cooling water for 2 to 3 hours. Then proceed as above.

BEAN PUFFS WITH CHEESE

Yield: 4 servimgs
l pound fresh green beans
Salt
1 teaspoon chopped rosemary
8 thin slices cheese
4 sheets frozen puff pastry
1 egg yolk

Boil the beans for about 10 minutes in salted water (they should still be firm and crisp). Drain and cool quickly. Divide the beans in 8 equal sections, sprinkle with a pinch of rosemary, and wrap each portion in a slice of cheese.

Thaw the puff pastry, cut each sheet in half, and roll the halves out large enough to wrap each bean section. Wrap the beans, then firmly press the edges of the pastry together. If desired, decorate the tops with pieces of leftover pastry. Brush with beaten egg yolk.

Bake in a preheated 375°F oven for 20 minutes.

DEEP-FRIED CHICORY

Yield: 4 servings
8 small heads chicory
¾ cup goat cheese
1 tablespoon butter
Pepper
2 to 3 tablespoons lemon juice
¼ cup flour
1 to 2 eggs
¼ cup fine bread crumbs
¼ cup grated Parmesan cheese
Oil for frying

Wash the chicory and drain well. Cut out the bitter, wedge-shaped part of the stalks from the bottom upward.

Knead the goat cheese with the butter; season with pepper. Press this mixture firmly into the cut chicories.

Sprinkle the chicories with the lemon juice. Dredge in flour, then in the beaten egg, and finally in a mixture of fine bread crumbs and Parmesan cheese. Press in this mixture firmly.

Deep-fry for about 8 minutes in hot fat at 325°F until golden. Drain and serve hot.

BAKED CELERY

Yield: 2 to 4 servings
2 small white celery stalks
¼ cup roquefort cheese
1 tablespoon soft butter
Salt
1 clove garlic, peeled and crushed

Wash the celery and remove the ribs from the base. Remove the strings and cut off the leaves; cut the long stems in half.

Knead the roquefort, butter, salt, and garlic together until creamy, and fill the celery ribs. Chop the celery leaves, then sprinkle them on top of the cheese spread.

Wrap each stick in a piece of aluminum foil, shiny side on the inside, and seal well. Bake in a preheated 350°F oven for 30 to 40 minutes.

APPLES AND MUSHROOMS

Yield: 2 to 4 servings
1 pound mushrooms
½ tablespoon butter
1 small onion, peeled and finely diced
1 small apple, peeled and coarsely grated
3 tablespoons cider
Salt
Pepper
Worcestershire sauce
3 tablespoons sour cream

Clean the mushrooms, remove the stems from the caps, and slice the stems. Cut the caps into quarters or eighths, according to size.

Melt the butter in a frying pan and saute the onion for 3 minutes. Add the mushroom stems and caps, grated apple, and the cider. Season with salt and pepper to taste. Simmer for 5 minutes on medium-high heat.

Reduce the heat and add Worcestershire sauce and sour cream to taste. Serve immediately.

FRIED MUSHROOMS

Yield: 2 servings
8 large mushrooms
¼ cup flour
1 tablespoon grated Parmesan cheese
1 egg
½ cup dry white wine
Salt
Pepper
Grated nutmeg
1 teaspoon dried parsley
1 tablespoon butter
1 tablespoon oil

Clean the mushrooms, dry them well, and dust them with flour.

Mix the remaining flour, Parmesan cheese, egg, wine, seasonings, and parsley to make a thick batter. Let stand for 15 minutes.

Heat the butter and oil in a frying pan until hot. Thickly coat the mushrooms with batter. Sauté the mushrooms, a few at a time, over high heat until crispy brown on both sides, being careful not to burn them.

Drain on paper towels and serve hot.

POTATOES, PASTA, AND RICE

CLASSIC CUISINE

Potatoes, pasta, and rice are essential accompaniments to a meal and have a prominent place on almost every menu. They can be prepared in many appetizing ways, such as the spaghetti with cream sauce and caviar shown here.

Potatoes are full of nutrients. They are 80 percent water, but contain 14.8 percent carbohydrate in the form of starch, 2.5 percent roughage, and 2 percent protein. This protein is biologically one of the most valuable of the plant proteins. Potatoes also contain potassium, calcium, phosphorus, iron, vitamins B1, B2, C, and niacin.

Potatoes are not as fattening as some believe. On the average, one small peeled potato has only 66 calories. However, they are frequently served with butter and sour cream.

Potatoes are divided into two categories: thick-skinned and thin-skinned (left photograph).

Some potatoes are more suitable for special dishes than others.

Thin-skinned potatoes, better known as new potatoes, have a waxy texture and can be boiled or steamed. They are good for making potato salad.

Thick-skinned potatoes, better known as Russet or Idaho potatoes, have a mealy texture. They are also suitable for potato salad and are used for baked potatoes and deep-fried dishes. They are also indispensible for potato soups, puree, and potato dumplings.

To make jacket potatoes: Thoroughly wash and brush the potatoes. Start off in the same manner as for boiled potatoes, but after the water comes to a boil, reduce the heat and simmer for 25 to 30 minutes until the potatoes are tender. Drain and return to the pan. Steam off any remaining moisture over low heat for 2 minutes. Peel the potatoes and serve.

To make baked potatoes carefully scrub the potato skins under running water and pierce all over with a fork.

Wrap the potatoes firmly and smoothly in aluminum foil. Place on a baking sheet and bake on the middle rack of a preheated 400°F oven for 1 hour, adding 10 minutes for very large potatoes. Carefully fold back the foil and cut a cross in the thickest part of the potato with a knife.

Using potholders, squeeze the potatoes with both hands so they break open. Add a little butter or hollow out slightly and add a filling such as herb butter, sour cream, or plain yogurt mixed with a teaspoon of fresh chives.

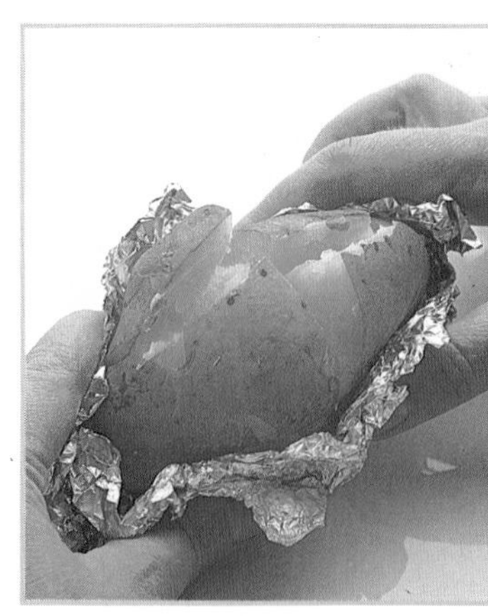

Potatoes can be prepared in more ways than any other vegetable. Some of the most popular potato dishes are fried, including the potato nests, chips, crisps, and matchstick potatoes shown here (photograph left). For successful fried potatoes, the potatoes should be dried carefully after being cut and should be fried until golden in hot oil. An electric deep-fat fryer is helpful in bringing the oil to the correct temperature.

To test the oil temperature in a frying pan, dip a wooden spoon into the oil. If light bubbles form on the spoon, the oil is at the correct temperature for frying. There are special baskets available for making potato nests.

Boiled potatoes are cooked in the following manner: Place peeled potatoes in a saucepan with a little cold salt water. Bring to a boil and simmer, covered, over low heat for 20 minutes, until tender. Drain and return to the pan. Steam off any remaining moisture over very low heat for 2 minutes, shaking from time to time. If the potatoes will not be served immediately, cover loosely with a clean dish cloth with the saucepan lid on top; the potatoes will remain dry.

Ingredients for potato dough: 1½ pounds cooked potatoes, 1 tablespoon butter, 2 egg yolks, 3 tablespoons flour, salt, grated nutmeg. For dredging: 2 eggs, 1 cup fine bread crumbs. Mash the hot potatoes and stir in the butter. Cool slightly. Add the egg yolk, flour. Add salt and nutmeg to taste.

Form the potato dough into rolls about 1¼ inches in diameter, and cut into portions. Shape into balls or croquettes. Roll the balls in almond flakes, if desired. Fry in hot oil until golden brown and drain on paper towels. Makes 6 servings.

Duchess Potatoes: Mash 2 pounds of freshly boiled, peeled potatoes. Add 4 tablespoons of butter and nutmeg and salt to taste. Carefully stir in 5 egg yolks and beat until creamy. Put the mixture in a pastry bag, and using a jagged tip, pipe out small rosettes onto a greased baking sheet. Brush with beaten egg yolk. Bake in a preheated 425°F oven for 10 minutes, until golden. Makes 6 servings.

POTATO DUMPLINGS

Yield: 8 to 10 servings

Potato dumplings are madefrom raw or cooked potatoes, or a mixture of both. The mixture is held together with eggs or semolina, bread soaked in water, fine bread crumbs, or flour.

Dumplings are seasoned with salt, pepper, and nutmeg, and sometimes roasted with onion and bacon cubes. They can be filled with toasted white bread cubes. In general, potato dumplings should be light, with a slightly dry consistency. It is very important to test cook- one dumpling before cooking all the others.

Important: never cook dumplings in rapidly boiling water or they will disintegrate. The correct method is to place the dumplings in boiling water, then turn down the heat immediately and simmer until cooked. The following recipe is an example of half and half potato dumplings, which make a delicious accompaniment to a roast:

3 pounds potatoes, peeled
Salt
½ cup flour
2 eggs
2 slices white bread
1 tablespoon butter

Place half the potatoes in a large bowl. Cover with water and set aside. Boil the rest of the potatoes in salt water; drain, then steam off any remaining moisture in an uncovered saucepan for 2 minutes over very low heat. Mash the cooked potatoes and let cool.

Grate the raw potatoes into a bowl (photograph 1). Squeeze out the liquid and work into a dough with the mashed potatoes, flour, and eggs. Season with salt.

Fry the cubed white bread in hot butter until golden. Form the dough into small, flat rounds (photograph 2). Place 3 or 4 bread cubes in the center of each round and roll into balls. Cook for 20 minutes in lightly simmering salt water.

PASTA

There is an enormous variety of pasta and egg noodles available. Since noodles are relatively neutral in flavor, they can be used in soups, as side dishes, and in soufflés and gratins. They are also available colored with vegetable concentrates, such as spinach and carrots (large photograph).

Pasta is prepared from semolina or flour (durum wheat), with or without eggs, but always without a rising agent. Here is a recipe for homemade pasta:

2¼ cups flour
3 to 4 eggs
1 tablespoon salt
4 to 6 tablespoons water

Sift the flour into a bowl. Make a hollow in the center and add the eggs (photograph 1). Stir with a whisk (photograph 2).

Dissolve the salt in 4 tablespoons of water and add to the dough. Knead briskly until a smooth silky dough forms. If the dough is too stiff, add another 2 tablespoons of water. Wrap the dough in a cloth and let stand for 30 minutes.

Roll the dough out on a floured surface until very thin. Cut into strips or put through a pasta machine (photograph 3). Let the dough dry out slightly. To cook, bring 4 quarts of water with 1 tablespoon of vegetable oil to a rolling boil. Gradually push the pasta into the water, without breaking the strands, until it softens and bends. Stir gently occasionally so the pasta does not stick together. Cook for 10 minutes after the water begins rapidly boiling again. Makes 6 servings.

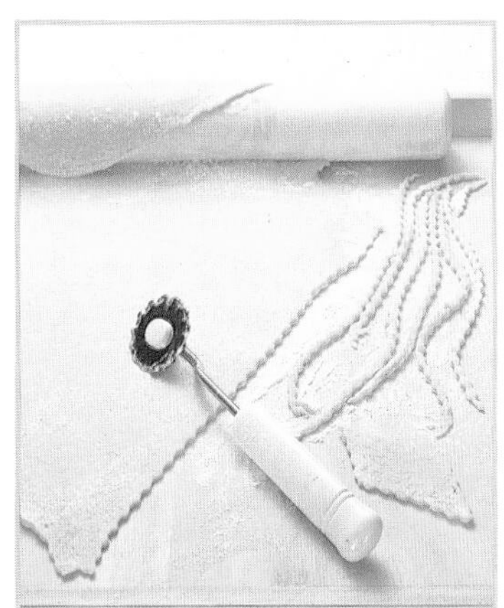

RICE

Rice is the daily foodstuff for approximately 1 million people on the earth, as it has been for several thousand years. There are 3 basic types of rice:

Long-grain rice cooks up with dry white grains. **Round-grain rice** is a short-grained, soft-cooking rice.

Soft-cooking, medium-grain rice is popularly used for Risotto. These basic types (large photograph) are now differentiated according to their commercial processing, as described below:

Brown rice. The husks are removed from the grains, but they still contain the silver outer covering, which is rich in fat and all the essential vitamins and minerals.

White rice. This is a polished rice without a silver outer covering. It is milled to remove the hull, germ, and most of the bran and is long-lasting.

Parboiled rice. Important vital substances are added to the grains by means of a special pressure treatment. The rice grains remain dry and separate when cooked.

Quick-boiling rice. This is a commercial rice that is precooked and dried, and is ready to serve in 5 minutes.

Wild rice. Wild rice (front photograph) has dark, almost black, long grains, and so can be easily distinguished from cultivated rice. It has a slightly nutty flavor and takes at least 40 minutes to cook. It is considered to be something of a delicacy.
Rice is frequently overcooked, which causes it to become mushy and sticky. Correctly cooked rice is firm and the grains are separate and dry, but cooked through.

Rice pudding (photograph 1) and other sweet dishes are made from round-grain rice. To make rice pudding, boil 1 cup of round-grain rice in 1½ cups milk, 2 tablespoons sugar, salt, and a little vanilla extract. Cook the rice in a covered saucepan over a very gentle heat for 30 to 35 minutes. Serve with cinnamon sugar. Makes 2 to 4 servings.

1

2

3

Risotto (photograph 2) can be made from medium-grain or long-grain rice. Sauté 1 cup of rice and 1 chopped onion in 4 tablespoons of butter or oil until the onion is transparent. Add 2 cups of chicken stock and salt, and bring to a boil. Cover the saucepan and cook 20 minutes for long-grain rice, at least 30 minutes for medium-grain. Add herbs or cooked vegetables according to taste. Makes 4 servings.

Boiled rice (photograph 4): Bring 2 cups of water and 1 teaspoon of salt to a boil in a large saucepan. Add 1 cup of long-grain rice and boil gently, uncovered, for 15 to 20 minutes; drain (photograph 5). This rice can be fried in a pan with diced onion (photograph 2), and seasoned with curry or paprika, or mixed with vegetables such as corn or cooked strips of sweet pepper and diced tomato.

To make another kind of rice dish, sauté ground meat and chopped onion in oil. Finely chop sweet peppers and tomatoes, add to the meat mixture, and continue sautéing. Add boiled rice and seasonings. Makes 4 servings.

Steeped rice (photograph 6) is made in the following way: Bring 2 cups of water and 1 teaspoon of salt to a boil. Add 1 cup of long-grain rice and stir. Cover the pan and steep over low heat for about 20 minutes, until all the water has been absorbed. Makes 2 to 4 servings. The basic rule of thumb is to use 1 part rice to 2 parts water.

Steeped rice can be made into little balls in greased cups or into a rice ring in a greased mold (photograph 3). It can be served with chopped parsley and 1 tablespoon of butter.

For rice dishes served with meat and vegetables, allow ¼ cup to ½ cup of rice per portion.

For rice side dishes, allow ¼ cup rice per portion.

For soups, 3 to 5 tablespoons of rice per portion are sufficient.

Important Rice Tips: Rice can be cooked in meat stock for savory dishes, or in a mixture of half water and half tomato juice flavored with Worcestershire or soy sauce.

To make an especially savory curried rice: Gently sauté 1 chopped onion in butter. Add 1 teaspoon curry powder and cook gently. Add water and rice and bring to a boil. Reduce the heat and cook, covered, for 20 minutes.

Sweet rice dishes can be cooked in fruit juices.

Always time rice carefully so it remains separate and firm.

Rice increases three-fold in volume when cooked. Therefore, 1 cup of dry rice becomes 3 cups of cooked rice.

Cooked rice can be covered and stored for 4 days in the refrigerator. It can also be frozen. Reheat or defrost rice in a strainer over steam.

LYONS POTATOES

Yield: 6 servings
1 1/2 pounds potatoes
3 onions, peeled and diced
2 tablespoons butter
1/4 cup parsley, finely chopped
Salt
Pepper
Juice of 1 or 2 lemons (optional)

Place the potatoes in boiling water to cover and cook for 20 minutes. Drain, peel, and cut into finger-sized sticks.

Melt half the butter in a frying pan and gently sauté the onions until golden. Melt the remaining butter in a second pan and sauté the potatoes over low heat for 10 minutes.

To serve, add the parsley and onions to the potatoes; season with salt and pepper. If desired, pour the lemon juice over the potatoes and shake to mix well.

ROSEMARY POTATOES

Yield: 8 servings
2¼ pounds small, fairly long potatoes, peeled
4 cloves garlic, peeled and sliced
1 tablespoon fresh rosemary
4 tablespoons olive oil
1 teaspoon butter
5 shallots,peeled
Salt
Pepper

Place the potatoes in boiling water to cover and cook for 15 minutes. Drain, cool, and cut into quarters lengthwise. Season with the garlic and rosemary.

Heat the olive oil and butter in a frying pan and add the shallots and potatoes. Fry the potatoes until crisp, turning occasionally; season with salt and pepper.

RÖSTI OR GRATED FRIED POTATOES

Yield: 6 servings
1½ pounds potatoes, cooked the previous day and refrigerated overnight
1 teaspoon salt
Pepper
1 tablespoon clarified butter

Peel the potatoes, grate coarsely, and season with salt and pepper. Melt the clarified butter in a frying pan. Add the potatoes, spreading them out and pressing flat. Cover with a flat plate; there should almost be no space between the plate and the potato.

Fry the potatoes over very low heat until golden, about 15 minutes. Very carefully, turn the potatoes over and sauté for 15 minutes longer. Add a little more butter to the pan, if necessary

POTATO PANCAKES

Yield: 8 servings
2¼ pounds potatoes, peeled
1 small onion, peeled
4 eggs
1 teaspoon salt
2 tablespoons flour
Oil for frying

Finely grate the potatoes and onion; drain well. Combine the eggs, salt, flour, potatoes, and onion.

Heat the oil in a non-stick pan. Spoon in the batter and immediately press it flat. Fry on both sides over medium heat until the edges are crisp and brown. Remove from the pan and serve with apple puree and blueberry preserves.

For a more savory flavor, add 3 tablespoons of finely chopped ham, cheese, or herbs into the potato batter.

POTATO CRÊPES WITH CAVIAR

Yield: 4 servings
1 pound potatoes
5 eggs
1 tablespoon flour
1¾ cups sour cream
½ shallot, peeled and crushed
Salt
Pepper
Grated peel of ½ lemon
1 tablespoon clarified butter
4½ ounces salmon caviar

Place the potatoes in boiling water to cover and cook for 20 minutes; drain. Cool the potatoes a little, then peel and grate finely.

Stir the potatoes together with the eggs, flour, 1 cup of sour cream, and the shallot. Season with salt, pepper, and lemon peel.

Melt the butter in a frying pan. Adding a spoonful of the potato mixture at a time, sauté until golden. Keep warm in the oven.

To serve, garnish each potato crêpe with 1 teaspoon of sour cream, caviar, and a little dill.

SCALLOPED POTATOES

Yield: 6 servings
Butter for greasing
2 onions, peeled and finely diced
1¾ pounds potatoes, peeled and thinly sliced
⅔ cup grated Emmenthaler or Gruyère cheese
Pepper
1 clove garlic, peeled and crushed
¼ cup milk
¼ cup whipping cream
Grated nutmeg
½ teaspoon salt
Butter for greasing

Grease 1 large or 4 small gratin molds with butter. Divide the onions into the 4 molds. Place an overlapping layer of potatoes on the onions and sprinkle with the grated cheese and pepper. Lay the rest of the potato slices on top.

Combine the garlic, milk, cream, nutmeg, and salt. Pour the liquid over the potatoes. Bake in a preheated 425°F oven for 45 minutes.

MASHED POTATOES

Yield: 6 to 8 servings
2¼ pounds potatoes, peeled and cut in small pieces
1 teaspoon salt
½ cup milk
Butter
Grated nutmeg

Place the potatoes in boiling water to cover and cook for 25 minutes. Drain, then mash or puree the potatoes.

Gently bring the milk to a boil in a saucepan; remove from the heat and stir gradually into the potato mixture. Add the butter, salt, and nutmeg to taste.

Tip: If desired, stir 4 tablespoons of grated cheese into the potato puree before serving or sauté 2 strips of bacon and 1 small diced onion and sprinkle over the puree.

POTATO AND LEEK DUMPLINGS

Yield: 4 servings
2 leeks, cut into thin rings
1 pound potatoes, peeled
3 small eggs
1½ teaspoons salt
Pepper

Fill a large saucepan with water, salt lightly and bring to a boil. Add the leeks and blanch for 10 to 15 minutes; drain, reserving the water. Squeeze the leeks dry and puree in a food processor.

Bring the reserved leek water to a boil in the saucepan; add the potatoes and boil for about 20 minutes, or until tender. Drain and mash the potatoes. Knead together the leek puree, mashed potatoes, eggs, salt, and pepper together until a stiff dough is formed. Form the dough into egg-sized dumplings.

Fill a large saucepan with salted water and bring to a boil. Add the dumplings, reduce the heat to low, and cook gently for 15 minutes.

HEAVEN AND EARTH

Yield: 6 servings
1½ pounds potatoes, peeled and cut in small pieces
3 apples, peeled, cored, and cut in small pieces
1 tablespoon sugar
1 teaspoon butter
Salt
Pepper
2 slices bacon, diced
2 onions, peeled and cut in rings

Place the potatoes in boiling salted water to cover and cook for about 15 minutes, until tender. Drain, reserving the water, and mash the potatoes.

Put the apple pieces and sugar in another saucepan, cover, and cook over medium heat until the apples are soft. Add the mashed potatoes and butter. If the puree is too thick, add a little more potato water. Season with salt and pepper.

In a frying pan, render the fat from the bacon and gently sauté the onion in it for 3 minutes. Add both the onion and the bacon to the potato puree.

RAW POTATO DUMPLINGS

Yield: 8 to 10 servings
2 cups milk
Salt
½ cup semolina flour
2¼ pounds potatoes, peeled, grated and drained

Bring the milk and ½ teaspoon salt to a boil in a saucepan. Stir in the semolina and bring to a boil again. Remove the pan from the heat and let the semolina steep for about 30 minutes.

Add the potatoes to the semolina, mix until blended and salt to taste. Form the dough into a roll about 1½ inches thick. Cut into small pieces, about 1¼ inches wide, and shape into balls. Drop the balls into lightly salted boiling water, reduce the heat to low, and cook until the dumplings rise to the surface.

VEGETABLE NOODLES

Yield: 4 servings
¼ pound ribbon noodles
6 cups water
Salt
1 thin leek
1 tablespoon butter
2 tablespoons olive oil
1 small carrot, peeled and cut in fine strips
2 small, thin, firm zucchini, cut in fine strips
¼ cup freshly grated Parmesan cheese

Place the ribbon noodles in boiling salt water and cook for 8 to 10 minutes; drain.

In the meantime, cut the light, tender part of the leek into fine strips. Heat the butter and oil in a frying pan and gently sauté the carrot, zucchini, and leek strips for 4 minutes, turning constantly.

To serve, add the drained noodles to the vegetables and mix well. Sprinkle with the Parmesan cheese.

TAGLIATELLE WITH SMOKED SALMON

Yield: 6 to 8 servings
1 tablespoon butter
2 shallots, peeled and finely chopped
1 tablespoon butter
1 cup dry white wine
1 cup whipping cream
Salt
Pepper
¼ pound tagliatelle
1 tablespoon oil
8½ ounces smoked, mild salmon, cut in strips
3 sprigs basil leaves, cut in strips

Melt the butter in a frying pan and sauté the shallots until softened. Add the white wine and boil until the liquid is reduced by half. Stir in the cream and season with salt and pepper to taste.

Cook the tagliatelle in 2 quarts of boiling salted water. Add the oil and boil the pasta for 8 to 10 minutes, until cooked but still firm. Drain the pasta and add to the sauce.

To serve, heap the pasta on a warm plate. Spread the salmon over the pasta and garnish with basil leaves.

Tip: To save time, stir whipping cream into the pasta instead of preparing the sauce and sprinkle with trout caviar.

SPAGHETTI WITH ROQUEFORT

Yield: 6 to 8 servings
½ pound spaghetti
Salt
1 tablespoon oil
¾ cup Roquefort cheese
½ cup whipping cream
Pepper
2 tablespoons shelled sunflower seeds

Cook the spaghetti in 2 quarts of boiling salt water and add the oil. Boil for about 8 minutes, until the noodles are cooked but still firm; drain.

Using a food processor, puree the Roquefort with the cream and season with pepper. Mix with the spaghetti and let steep for 1 minute.

Roast the sunflower seeds in a dry pan. Serve the spaghetti on warmed plates sprinkled with the roasted seeds.

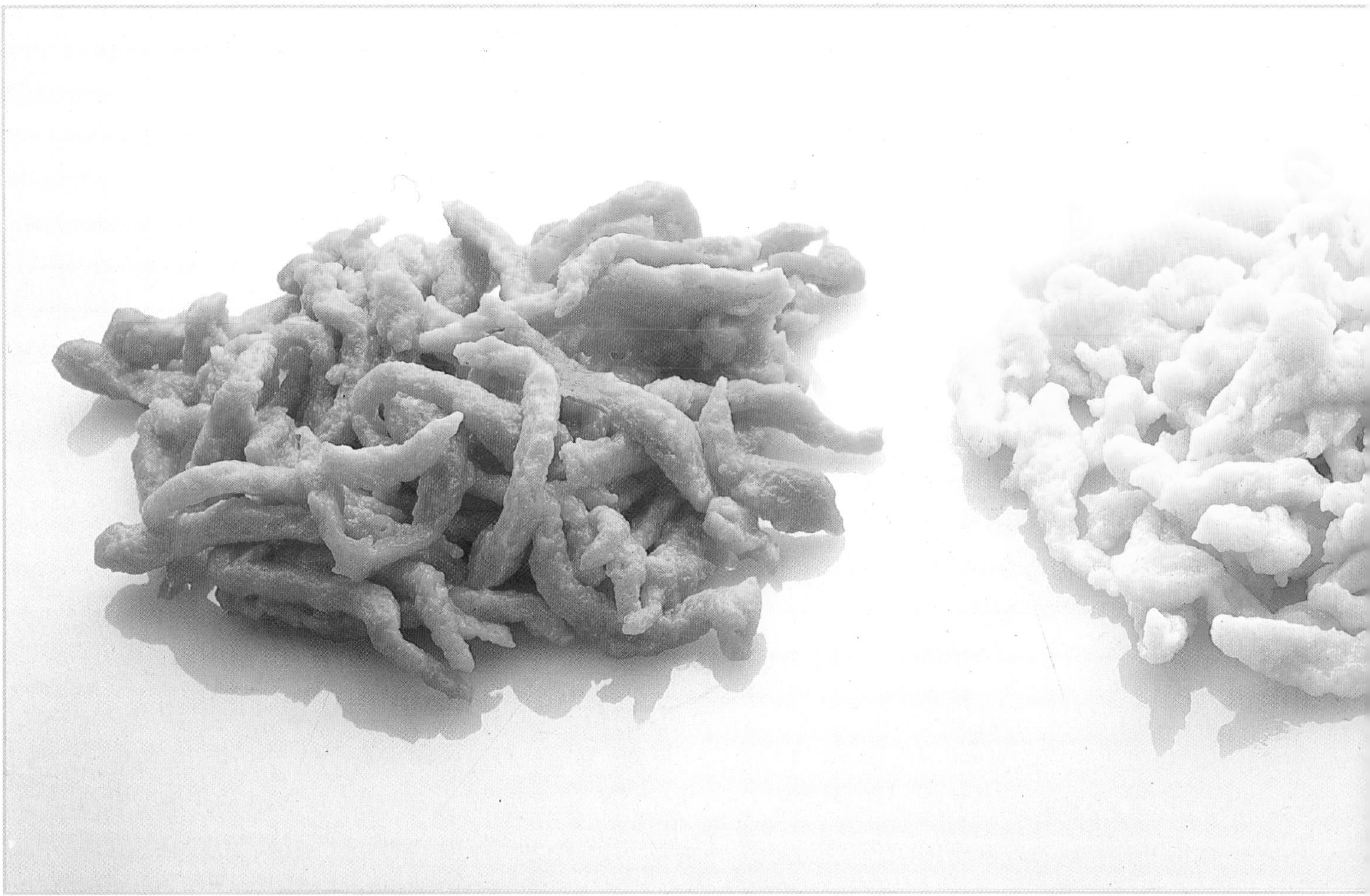

SPÄTZLE

Yield: 2 to 4 servings
1 cup flour, sifted
2 small eggs
1 teaspoon salt
4 tablespoons sour cream
5 tablespoons water
Butter for tossing

Combine the flour, eggs, salt, sour cream, and water in a mixing bowl. Beat vigorously until the dough is smooth. Set aside for 30 minutes.

Press the dough through a special spätzle press or grate it in portions directly into boiling, salted water (photograph left). When the dough is cooked, it will float to the surface. Scoop it out immediately with a slotted spoon, rinse with warm water, and drain well. Toss in melted butter.

Tip: For green spätzle, stir in ½ cup of chopped parsley; for red spätzle, stir in 2 tablespoons of tomato paste.

FRIED SPÄTZLE

Yield: 2 to 4 servings
1 cup flour
2 small eggs
1 teaspoon salt
4 tablespoons sour cream
5 tablespoons water
1½ tablespoons butter
2 eggs
Salt
Pepper
Parmesan cheese

Prepare the spätzle following the directions in the previous recipe. Drain well.

Melt the butter in a frying pan and sauté the spätzle until golden brown. To serve, sprinkle with freshly grated Parmesan cheese.

FISH DUMPLINGS

Yield: 4 to 6 servings
For the pasta dough:
1½ cups flour
4 eggs
3 tablespoons cooking oil
1 teaspoon salt
For the fish stuffing:
1 tablespoon butter
7 ounces sole or flounder fillets, cut in small pieces
5½ ounces shrimp, shelled and deveined
3½ ounces mussels, drained
1 cup dry white wine
½ cup whipping cream
Salt
1 tablespoon olive oil
Fresh basil leaves

Knead the flour, eggs, oil, and salt together to make a smooth dough; cover and set aside for 2 hours. Roll out the dough thinly on a floured breadboard and cut it into eight 6-inch squares. Spread the dough squares on a lightly floured pastry cloth; cover with a slightly damp cloth to keep from drying out.

To make the stuffing, melt the butter in a frying pan and gently fry the fish, shrimp, and mussels until the shrimp become pink; remove from the pan and set aside. Add the white wine to the pan juices and boil until most of the liquid evaporates. Stir in the cream and add salt to taste. Return the fish, shrimp, and mussels to the pan and keep warm.

Cook the pieces of dough in boiling salted water. Add oil, boil for 2 minutes, and remove from the water with a slotted spoon. Drain. Divide fish stuffing into 8 equal portions. Place on portion in the center of each piece of pastry. Fold up the edges and garnish with basil. Serve at once.

FILLED PASTA ROLLS

Yield: 6 to 8 servings
For the pasta dough:
1¼ cups flour
3 eggs
2 tablespoons olive oil
1 teaspoon salt
For the filling:
1 pound tomatoes, skinned and cut in small pieces
5½ ounces mozzarella cheese, diced
¼ cup parsley, finely chopped
¼ cup fresh basil, finely chopped
2 cloves garlic, peeled and crushed
Grated peel of ¼ lemon
¾ cup sour cream
½ cup freshly grated Parmesan cheese
Pepper
Salt
1 cup whipping cream
2½ ounces tomato paste
Sweet paprika
3 tablespoons softened butter

Prepare the pasta dough following the instructions in the previous recipe. Roll out the dough on a floured pastry cloth to 2 large rectangles, about 12½ by 10 inches each. Brush with sour cream and sprinkle with Parmesan cheese.

Combine all the ingredients for the filling and spread over the rectangles. Sprinkle with salt and pepper. Using the cloth to help, roll up the dough and refrigerate, still wrapped in the cloth, for 1½ hours. Cut the rolls into ¾-inch-thick slices.

Stir the cream and tomato paste together and season with paprika, salt, and pepper to taste. Pour into 1 or 2 shallow soufflé dishes. Lay the dough slices on top of the sauce and brush with butter. Bake in a preheated 425°F oven for 20 to 25 minutes.

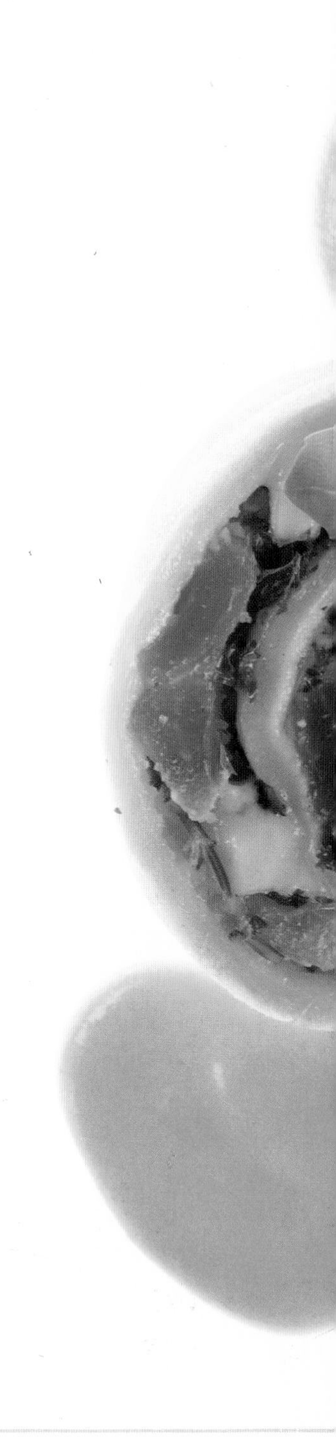

CANNELONI

Yield: 4 to 6 servings
For the filling:
$2\frac{1}{4}$ cups spinach
$1\frac{1}{4}$ cups ricotta cheese
$\frac{1}{4}$ cup freshly grated Parmesan cheese
Salt
Pepper
Grated nutmeg
For the Béchamel sauce:
1 tablespoon butter
1 tablespoon flour
$1\frac{1}{4}$ cups milk
$1\frac{1}{4}$ cups cooked cannelloni
Butter

Wash the spinach and place, still dripping, in a saucepan. Cover and steam until the water evaporates. Drain the spinach, press out the remaining moisture, and chop coarsely. Combine the ricotta and Parmesan cheese with the spinach and season with salt, pepper, and nutmeg.

To make the Béchamel sauce, melt the butter in a frying pan and cook the flour, stirring constantly, until the flour is light yellow. Gradually stir in the milk and season with salt, pepper, and nutmeg.

Fill the cannelloni with the spinach mixture and lay side by side in a shallow, greased soufflé dish. Pour on the sauce and sprinkle with Parmesan cheese. Bake for 40 minutes in a preheated 400°F oven.

Tip: To make homemade cannelloni, prepare the dough as in Fish Dumplings (see Index). Roll the dough out thinly and cut into 6-inch squares. Place 1 tablespoon of the filling in the center of each square and roll the dough into a tube. Place in a baking dish with the seam underneath. Cottage cheese can be substituted for ricotta.

RAVIOLI

Yield: 6 to 8 servings
For the pasta dough:
1¼ cups flour
3 eggs
2 tablespoons oil
1 teaspoon salt
For the filling:
1 tablespoon butter
1 clove garlic, peeled and finely chopped
1 shallot, peeled and finely chopped
1 tablespoon fine bread crumbs
3 tablespoons freshly grated Parmesan cheese
1 egg
2 tablespoons sour cream
Salt
Pepper
Grated nutmeg
Flour for rolling out
Freshly grated Parmesan cheese
3 tablespoons melted butter

Prepare the dough following the instructions in Fish Dumplings (see Index). Divide the dough in half. On a floured breadboard, roll out the dough as thinly as possible in 2, equal-sized, oblong shapes.

To make the filling, melt the butter in a frying pan and gently sauté the garlic and shallots until transparent. Transfer to a bowl and let cool. Stir in the bread crumbs, Parmesan cheese, egg, and sour cream (photograph 1). Season with salt, pepper, and nutmeg.

On 1 of the dough sheets, place teaspoons of the filling at equal distances from one another (photograph 2). Using a brush and a little beaten egg white, paint finger-wide lines as straight as possible between the heaps of filling. Cover with the second dough oblong (photograph 3). Press the sheets of dough together in the spaces between the fillings. Cut the ravioli apart with a knife or cutting wheel (photograph 4). Press the edges firmly together. Leave the ravioli on a floured pastry cloth until they are ready to be cooked.

To cook, fill a large pot with salted water and bring to a boil. Add the ravioli, reduce the heat to low, and cook for 3 to 4 minutes. Drain and arrange in deep plates. Sprinkle with melted butter and Parmesan cheese. Serve with tomato sauce, creamed mushroom sauce, or a cheese Béchamel sauce.

TORTELLINI

Yield: 6 to 8 servings
For the pasta dough:
1½ cups flour
4 eggs
3 tablespoons cooking oil
1 teaspoon salt
For the filling:
¼ cup pistachio nuts, finely chopped
3½ ounces mortadella (summer sausage), finely chopped
3½ ounces boiled ham, finely chopped
1 egg
2 tablespoons cottage cheese
Salt
Pepper
Grated nutmeg
4 cups chicken stock
For the sauce:
1 large tomato, skinned and diced
1 clove garlic, peeled and chopped
1 teaspoon butter
1 cup whipping cream
2 sprigs fresh basil, cut in strips
Freshly grated Parmesan cheese

Prepare the dough following the instructions in Fish Dumplings (see Index). Roll out the dough as thinly as possible on a floured breadboard and cut in 1½-inch circles.

To make the filling, combine the pistachio nuts, mortadella, ham, egg, and cottage cheese. Season to taste with salt, pepper, and nutmeg. Place 1 teaspoon of the filling in the center of each dough circle. Brush the edges of the circles with water, fold over to make half moons, and press the edges firmly together. Set aside on a floured cloth.

Bring the stock to a boil in a saucepan and cook the tortellini over low heat for 8 to 10 minutes; remove from the pan and drain.

To make the sauce, melt the butter in a small saucepan and gently sauté the tomato, garlic, and pepper for 1 minute. Add the cream and salt to taste; pour immediately over the tortellini. Add the basil and Parmesan cheese and serve.

RICE WITH JULIENNED VEGETABLES

Yield: 2 to 4 servings
1 tablespoon butter
1 tablespoon oil
1 medium carrot, peeled and cut in julienne strips
1 celery stalk, cut in julienne strips
1 leek, cut in julienne slices
1 small onion, peeled and chopped
1 tablespoon butter
¾ cup uncooked rice
1 cup dry white wine
2 cups vegetable stock
5½ ounces bean sprouts
½ cup goat cheese, finely crumbled

Heat the butter and the oil in a saucepan and sauté the vegetables gently for about 5 minutes. Add the rice and sauté briefly. Pour in the wine and stock and simmer, uncovered, for 30 minutes. During the last 3 minutes of cooking, add the bean sprouts. To serve, sprinkle the grated cheese over the hot rice.

RED AND GREEN RISOTTO

Yield: 6 to 8 servings
7 tablespoons oil
1 medium onion, peeled and chopped
1 clove garlic, peeled and chopped
1½ cups uncooked long-grain rice
4 cups beef stock
5½ ounces fresh shelled peas
1 pound spinach, cooked briefly and drained
3 tablespoons water
2 tablespoons butter
1 medium tomato, skinned and diced
1 medium red sweet pepper, finely diced
3 tablespoons oil
¼ cup grated Parmesan cheese

Heat the oil in a saucepan and sauté the onion and garlic until transparent. Add the rice and sauté briefly.

Ladle 1 cup of stock into the rice mixture. Gradually add the rest of the stock and simmer for 20 minutes. The rice should be tender, but not sticky.

To make the green rice, gently cook the peas in 3 tablespoons of water and 1 teaspoon of butter for 5 minutes. Puree the spinach and half of the cooked peas together in a food processor. Mix the puree and the remaining peas with half the rice.

To make the red rice, heat the remaining oil in a frying pan and gently sauté the tomatoes and peppers until soft. Combine with the remaining rice.

To serve, toss the remaining butter and the Parmesan cheese in both types of rice. In a serving dish, form a ring with the green rice and place the red rice in the center.

FENNEL WITH WILD RICE

Yield: 2 servings
4 small fennels
Salt
½ cup uncooked wild rice
½ cup uncooked long-grain rice
1 tablespoon butter
1 shallot, peeled and diced
2 tablespoons sherry
Pepper
1 to 2 tablespoons toasted pistachio nuts

Clean the fennel and simmer in salted water for 20 to 30 minutes. Remove from the pan and slice in half; scoop out and dice the flesh. Set aside the fennel halves and the diced flesh.

In another saucepan, cook the wild rice in boiling water for 10 minutes. Add the long- grain rice and boil for 20 minutes longer. Drain the rice.

Melt the butter in a frying pan and gently sauté the diced fennel and shallot. Add the rice and season with sherry, salt, pepper, and the green parts of the fennel.

To serve, pile the rice mixture in the hollowed-out fennel halves. Sprinkle with the pistachio nuts.

FRIED RICE

Yield: 4 servings
1 cup uncooked long-grain rice
8 tablespoons oil
3 to 4 strips bacon, finely diced
1 cup smoked chicken breast fillet, cut into small strips
2 small carrots, cut into small strips
1 onion, peeled and diced
1½ cups white cabbage, cut in small pieces
2 eggs
Salt
Pepper
8 tablespoons oil
½ pound cooked shrimp, shelled and deveined
2 to 4 tablespoons soy sauce

Cook the rice in boiling water for about 20 minutes, until all the liquid is absorbed.

Heat 2 tablespoons of oil in a large frying pan and sauté the bacon; remove from the pan and set aside. Heat 2 more tablespoons of oil in the pan and sauté the chicken and vegetables; remove from the pan and set aside.

Season the eggs with salt and pepper and pour into the pan; cook very gently to make a paper-thin omelette. Cut the omelette in strips.

Heat the remaining oil in the pan and add the shrimp, rice, half the omelette, the vegetables, and soy sauce. Sauté, stirring constantly, until heated through. Serve with the remaining omelette.

LAMB PILAF

Yield: 4 to 6 servings
1½ cups yogurt
2 tablespoons ground fennel
1½ pounds lean lamb (from the leg joint), cut in small cubes
1 cup uncooked long- grain rice
2 tablespoons clarified butter
2 teaspoons ground cardamon
1 cinnamon stick
2 bay leaves
4 cups chicken stock
Salt
½ cup fresh spinach, roughly chopped
2 tablespoons pine nuts
3 small tomatoes, sliced
Lemon slices

Stir the yogurt and fennel together and spread over the meat. Cover and marinate overnight in the refrigerator.

Cover the rice with cold water and soak for 1 hour; drain.

Melt 1 tablespoon of clarified butter in a Dutch oven. Add the rice, cardamon, cinnamon stick, and bay leaves. Sauté for 5 to 6 minutes, until the rice is transparent.

Drain the meat, allowing the yogurt marinade to drip on the rice. Add enough stock to cover the rice to a depth of about ¼ inch. Bring to a boil and stir in the salt and spinach. Cover and cook in a preheated 400°F oven for 15 minutes.

Melt the remaining clarified butter in a saucepan and brown the meat on all sides. Add the rice and cook together for about 10 minutes.

To serve, roast the pine nuts in a frying pan until light brown. Sprinkle the pilaf with pine nuts and garnish with tomato and lemon slices.

RICE BALLS

Yield: 6 to 8 servings
1 teaspoon butter
2 small onions, peeled and finely chopped
3 to 4 strips bacon, finely diced
1 pound cooked rice or risotto
3 tablespoons freshly grated Parmesan cheese
2 small eggs
Grated nutmeg
½ cup mozzarella cheese, diced
Fine bread crumbs
Oil or vegetable fat for deep-frying

Melt the butter in a saucepan and sauté the onion and bacon until the onion is transparent, stirring constantly. Add the cooked rice.

Transfer the rice mixture to a bowl. Add the Parmesan cheese, beaten egg, and nutmeg to taste, mixing well. Scoop out 1 tablespoon of the rice, press a hollow in it, and insert a piece of mozzarella. Add another tablespoon of the rice mixture and roll into a ball. Make the rest of the balls in the same manner.

Dredge the rice balls in the fine bread crumbs and deep-fry in hot oil (about 300° F) until golden. Drain and serve.

SHRIMP AND WILD RICE PILAF

Yield: 2 servings
½ cup uncooked wild rice
1 tablespoon butter
4 small onions, peeled and diced
¾ cup mushrooms, sliced
2 eggs
1 tablespoon sherry
1 tablespoon soy sauce
½ pound cooked shrimp, peeled and deveined
¼ cup parsley, finely chopped
¼ cup fresh dill, finely chopped

Cook the wild rice in 1 cup of boiling water for 3 minutes. Remove from the heat and steep for about 1 hour; drain.

Melt the butter in a large pan and sauté the onion until transparent. Add the mushrooms and sauté quickly, stirring constantly. Stir in the rice.

Beat the egg, sherry, and soy sauce together. Press a hollow in the rice and pour in the egg mixture. Slowly stir from the inside outward. Fold in the shrimp and chopped herbs and heat through.

NASI GORENG

Yield: 4 to 6 servings
1 cup uncooked long-grain rice
Salt
1 cup lean pork, cut in small cubes
1 clove garlic, peeled and chopped
3 small onions, peeled and chopped
5 tablespoons olive oil
2 to 4 tablespoons soy sauce
Tabasco
Lettuce leaves
1 scallion, cut in fine strips

Cook the rice in 1 cup of boiling water until tender.

Heat the oil in a large frying pan and sauté the garlic and scallion until transparent; remove from the pan and set aside. Brown the pork in the same frying pan. Add the rice and soy sauce and sauté, stirring frequently, until the rice is evenly browned. Add the cooked garlic and scallion; add salt and Tabasco sauce to taste.

To serve, arrange the Nasi Goreng on the lettuce leaves and garnish with scallion strips.

CHICKEN PAELLA

Yield: 6 to 8 servings
1 (2½- pound) chicken, cut in 12 pieces
Salt
Pepper
4 medium onions, peeled and diced
2 medium green peppers, cut in fairly large pieces
1 cup mushrooms, sliced
4 medium tomatoes, skinned and cut in quarters
½ cup parsley, chopped
1 clove garlic, peeled and sliced
4 tablespoons olive oil
Salt
2 pinches saffron
2 cups chicken stock
1 cup uncooked long- grain rice
½ cup shelled fresh peas

Heat the oil in a large frying pan or paella pan. Fry the chicken pieces on all sides over high heat and season lightly with salt and pepper. Remove from the pan and set aside.

Gently sauté the onions and peppers in the pan juices until the onions are transparent. Add the mushrooms, parsley, and garlic and sauté for 5 minutes. Add the tomatoes. Mix the saffron with a little of the stock and add to the vegetables with the rice, chicken pieces, and peas.

In a saucepan, bring the chicken stock to a boil. Pour the stock over the paella and cook, covered, over low heat for 30 to 45 minutes.

CLASSIC CUISINE

From breakfasts to dinners and from soups through desserts, eggs appear in an incredible number of different dishes. Souffles, sauces mayonnaise, binding for stuffings, batter coatings, and all-purpose garnishes for hot and cold foods are only a few of the basic uses for eggs. Egg whites alone make fluffy meringues, cakes, or gleaming glazes for pastry. After reading this chapter you'll agree that there is nothing quite like an egg.

EGGS

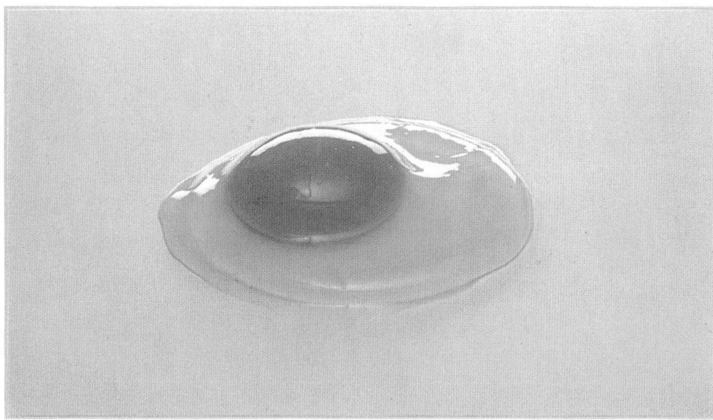

To prepare fried eggs, break the egg open, let it slide into hot butter in a frying pan, and let it set over low heat. Fry until the edges are golden, salting only the white of the egg.

The omelette is one of the classic egg dishes (photograph right). The basic rule for an omelette is that it must be made from very fresh eggs. To make an expert omelette, beat 2 to 3 eggs per portion, salt lightly, and pour the eggs into hot butter in a medium-sized omelette pan. Lightly push the eggs toward the edges as they set. The upper surface should remain creamy. Fry for 3 minutes, then fold over, first adding a filling if desired.

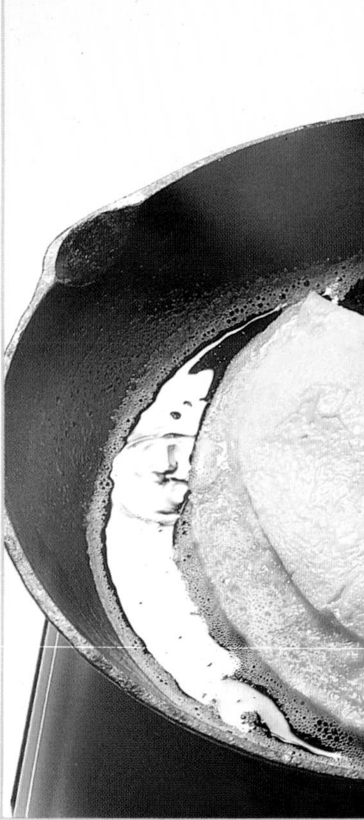

Poached eggs are usually served in savory sauces. The egg is broken open and slid into simmering, lightly salted water mixed with a dash of vinegar. As the egg goes under the water, the egg white coagulates. Simmer for 3 to 4 minutes, then remove the egg with a slotted spoon.

When making stiffly beaten egg whites, remember that the firmer the egg white is, the better it can be whipped. As it is being beaten, the egg white absorbs air, and small bubbles are formed. The fresher the egg is, the more voluminous the egg white will be. It does not matter whether it is beaten with a whisk, a hand-operated mixer, or an electric mixer.

Preparing eggs is basically simple but it's important to pay attention to a couple of things. For instance, the time needed to boil an egg depends on the degree of hardness desired. On the average, 3 to 4 minutes of boiling time is needed to make a soft-boiled egg, 5 to 6 minutes to make a medium hard-boiled egg, and 10 minutes to make a hard-boiled egg. Add at least a minute to the cooking times for large eggs. When the eggs have finished cooking, plunge them immediately in cold water so they do not continue to cook in their own heat.

When scrambling eggs, beat only until the white and the yolk have combined. Pour the eggs into a frying pan and cook in hot butter over low heat. Let the eggs set, pushing them with a spatula from the outside edge of the pan to the center. Scrambled eggs that have been stirred instead of pushed develop a crumbly, rather hard texture.

Eggs are indispensible for coating and deep-frying. Coating meat and fish pieces before deep-frying helps seal in their juices. First, the meat or fish is tossed in flour, then dipped in beaten, slightly salted egg, and finally dipped in fine bread crumbs.

A soufflé is also a delicious egg dish. Savory soufflés can serve as an appetizer or main dish, while sweet soufflés make light and elegant desserts.

CHEESE SOUFFLÉ

Yield: 4 servings
Ingredients (photograph 1)
Softened butter
Fine bread crumbs
7 egg whites
4 egg yolks
1 cup finely grated cheese
Pepper
Grated nutmeg

Grease the bottoms and lower sides of 4 small soufflé dishes with butter, and dust with fine bread crumbs. Beat the egg whites to a stiff but still elastic foam (photograph 2). They must not be firm enough to cut or the soufflé will not be a success.

Beat the egg yolks and fold into the egg whites. Fold in the cheese (photograph 3) and add seasoning to taste. Divide the mixture among the soufflé dishes; bake on a baking sheet in the center of a preheated 350°F oven for 40 minutes.

Another method for making cheese soufflé is to sauté 3 tablespoons of flour in 3 tablespoons butter for 3 to 5 minutes. Add 1 cup of hot milk, and bring to a boil, stirring, until creamy and thick. Remove from the heat. Stir in 4 egg yolks and 1 cup grated cheese. Fold in 6 beaten egg whites. Add seasoning to taste. Bake as in the previous instructions. Serve immediately.

Never open the oven door while a soufflé is baking. Soufflés are very delicate and will immediately fall.

EGG CROQUETTES

Yield: 2 servings
2 tablespoons butter
4 tablespoons flour
1 cup milk
Salt
Pepper
Grated nutmeg
Lemon juice
6 eggs
3 tablespoons grated cheese
6 tablespoons fine bread crumbs
6 tablespoons clarified butter

EGGS WITH VEGETABLES

Yield: 2 servings
3 tablespoons butter
2 small cucumbers, peeled, seeded, and thinly sliced
⅔ cup sour cream
Salt
White pepper
Worcestershire sauce
Lemon juice
3 eggs
2 bunches fresh dill, chopped

Heat the butter in a frying pan and gently sauté the cucumber slices for 3 minutes. Stir in the sour cream; season with salt, pepper, Worcestershire sauce, and lemon juice. Cover and simmer over low heat for 10 minutes.

Put the eggs in a saucepan and cover with cold water. Slowly bring the water to a boil and boil the eggs for 5 minutes. Remove from the pan and chill. Shell the eggs, then slice in half lengthwise.

To serve, sprinkle the chopped dill on the cucumbers. Arrange on a platter and place the eggs on top.

In a small saucepan, melt the butter over low heat. Add 2 tablespoons of flour and blend over low heat for 3 to 5 minutes, stirring constantly. Gradually add the milk. Heat the milk just to the boiling point, still stirring constantly, until the sauce thickens. Add salt, pepper, and a little nutmeg to taste. Cool completely.

Put 4 eggs in a saucepan and cover with cold water. Slowly bring the water to a boil and boil the eggs for 10 minutes. Plunge the eggs in cold water and allow to cool.

Shell and finely chop the eggs; mix with the grated cheese and sauce. Form the mixture into small rolls. Coat the rolls first in flour, then in 2 beaten eggs, and finally in fine bread crumbs.

Melt the clarified butter in a frying pan and sauté the croquettes over medium heat until golden. Remove from the pan and serve immediately.

INDIAN EGG CURRY

Yield: 4 servings

8 eggs
3 tablespoons clarified butter
2 large onions, peeled and cut in thin rings
3 cloves garlic, peeled and crushed
1 tablespoon curry powder
½ teaspoon cumin
1 pinch ground cardamon
1 pinch ground coriander
Salt
Pepper
3 tablespoons tomato paste
1 large can (about 30 ounces) peeled plum tomatoes
½ cup parsley, chopped

Put the eggs in a saucepan and cover with cold water. Slowly bring the water to a boil and cook the eggs for 10 minutes. Plunge the eggs in cold water; shell and cut in quarters.

Heat the clarified butter in a frying pan. Gently sauté the onion until softened; remove from the pan and keep warm. Add the garlic and spices to the frying pan and cook gently. Stir in the tomato paste and sauté briefly. Add the tomatoes with their juice. Simmer over low heat for 30 minutes, or until the sauce is creamy.

To serve, arrange the onions on a plate. Pour the sauce over the onions and place the egg quarters on top. Sprinkle with parsley.

EGGS IN ASPIC WITH CHERVIL

Yield: 4 to 6 servings
6 eggs
1 bunch fresh chervil leaves
2½ packages unflavored gelatin
1 cup oxtail soup or beef stock
Salt
Pepper
¼ cup dry sherry
White wine vinegar, to taste

Put the eggs in a saucepan and cover with cold water. Slowly bring the water to a boil and cook the eggs for 10 minutes. Plunge the eggs in cold water and let cool; shell and slice them.

Strain the oxtail soup or beef stock into a saucepan; add ¾ cup water and bring to a boil. Add salt, pepper, sherry, and vinegar to taste.

Soak the gelatin in cold water for 10 minutes, then dissolve it in the soup, stirring constantly.

Cover the bottom of a dish or rectangular mold with ⅛-inch layer of soup and refrigerate until set. Arrange a layer of sliced eggs and chervil on the aspic (photograph 1) and cover with another layer of soup (photograph 2). Refrigerate until set again, and then repeat the process until all ingredients have been used. The final layer should be soup. Refrigerate overnight.

To serve, dip the mold briefly in hot water and turn the aspic out on a plate (photograph 3).

STUFFED EGGS

Yield: 4 servings
8 eggs
4 tablespoons hot mustard
Salt
Pepper
Cayenne pepper
Worcestershire sauce
2 bunches of watercress

Place the eggs in a saucepan and cover with cold water. Slowly bring to a boil and cook the eggs for 10 minutes. Plunge the eggs in cold water; shell and slice in half lengthwise. Carefully remove the yolks.

Mix the salt, pepper, cayenne pepper, and Worcestershire sauce together. Spoon a little of this mixture into each egg half and place the yolk on top, rounded side up.

To serve, arrange the eggs on a platter or round plate. Garnish with watercress.

POACHED EGGS ON TOMATOES

Yield: 4 servings
2 tablespoons butter
1 medium onion, peeled and finely chopped
2 cloves garlic, peeled and crushed
2½ pounds ripe tomatoes, skinned, seeded, and cut in eighths
Salt
Pepper
1 bunch scallions, cut in thin rings
2½ cups water
⅓ cup white wine vinegar
8 eggs

Melt the butter in a frying pan and sauté the onion until softened. Add the garlic and sauté briefly. Stir in the tomatoes, salt, and pepper; cook gently over medium heat for 3 minutes.

Bring the water and white wine vinegar to a boil in a medium saucepan. Break each egg, one at a time, into a soup ladle and slide it gently into the water. Reduce the heat to a simmer and poach for 4 minutes. Remove the eggs carefully with a slotted spoon and drain.

To serve, mix the scallions with the tomatoes and add white wine vinegar to taste. On a platter, form a ring with the tomato mixture. Arrange the poached eggs in the middle.

BEEF BROTH WITH EGGS

Yield: 4 servings
4 tablespoons white wine vinegar
1-½ cups water
Salt
4 eggs
1½ cups beef stock
1 bunch fresh chives, chopped

Combine the vinegar, water, and a pinch of salt in a saucepan and bring to a boil. Break the eggs, one at a time, into a soup ladle and slide it gently into the water. Reduce the heat to a simmer and poach for 3 minutes. Carefully remove the eggs from the water with a slotted spoon and arrange on 4 soup plates.

To serve, bring the meat stock to a boil, then pour it over the eggs. Sprinkle the soup with chives.

POACHED EGGS ON LETTUCE

Yield: 4 servings
5 rashers bacon, cut in thin strips
1 clove garlic, peeled and crushed
2 cups oyster mushrooms, sliced
Pepper
7 tablespoons white wine vinegar
1½ cups water
Salt
4 eggs
1 head romaine lettuce

Sauté the bacon until crisp. Add the garlic and mushrooms and sauté for 3 minutes in the bacon fat. Season with pepper; add 3 tablespoons of white wine vinegar.

Bring the water, remaining white wine vinegar, and salt to a boil in a medium saucepan. Break the eggs into a soup ladle, one at a time, and slide it gently into the water. Reduce the heat to a simmer and poach for 4 minutes. Carefully remove the eggs from the water with a slotted spoon.

To serve, arrange the lettuce on 4 plates. Spoon the mushrooms onto the lettuce and place an egg on top. Serve immediately.

EGGS IN BEEF BROTH

Yield: 4 servings
2 eggs
4 tablespoons milk
Salt
Pepper
Grated nutmeg
1 bunch fresh chives, chopped
1½ cups beef stock
Butter

In a bowl, mix the eggs with the milk, salt, pepper, and nutmeg. Divide the mixture in half and stir the chives into one half.

Grease 2 small ovenproof bowls and pour half the egg mixture into each. Cover with foil. Place the bowls in a pan filled with enough hot water to come halfway up the sides of the bowls. Cook over medium heat for 30 minutes. Remove the egg from the bowls and cut in cubes or diamonds.

Place the egg in 4 soup plates. Bring the beef stock to a boil, pour it over the egg, and serve immediately.

CHINESE EGG DROP SOUP

Yield: 2 servings
3 eggs
1 tablespoon soy sauce
1 teaspoon sesame oil
White pepper
1½ cups chicken stock
¼ cup boiled ham, cut in fine strips
1 scallion, cut in thin rings
1 tablespoon chopped parsley

Mix the eggs with the soy sauce and sesame oil; add pepper to taste. Bring the chicken stock to a boil in a saucepan. Strain the egg mixture into the stock. The soup should not reboil or the egg whites will curdle.

Add the ham and scallion rings and cook in the hot soup for a few minutes. Sprinkle with parsley before serving.

ZUCCHINI AND MUSHROOM QUICHE

Yield: 6 to 8 servings
For the dough:
4 tablespoons cold butter
1 cup flour, sifted
1 egg
2 tablespoons water
Salt
For the filling:
4 tablespoons butter
1¼ pounds small zucchini, thinly sliced
1¼ pounds mushrooms, sliced
4 cloves garlic, peeled and crushed
Pepper
Cayenne pepper
1 teaspoon oregano
1 cup whipping cream
5 egg yolks
Grated nutmeg
Butter

To make the dough, combine the flour, butter, eggs, water, and salt in a large bowl; knead quickly until smooth. Wrap the dough in waxed paper and refrigerate for 1 hour.

To make the filling, melt the butter in a frying pan and sauté half of the zucchini and mushrooms for 4 to 5 minutes. Remove from the pan and sauté the other half for 4 to 5 minutes. Mix the zucchini, mushrooms, and garlic together; season with salt, pepper, cayenne pepper, and oregano.

Roll out the dough on a floured breadboard until ⅛-inch thick. Line a greased, 10-inch quiche pan with the dough, making sure the dough comes about 1½ inches up the sides of the pan. Prick the bottom of the dough several times with a fork. Spread the vegetables evenly over the dough.

Beat the cream and egg yolks together; season with nutmeg, salt, and pepper. Pour the cream mixture over the vegetables and bake in a preheated 425°F oven for 40 to 50 minutes.

EGGS IN TOMATO NESTS

Yield: 4 servings
4 large ripe tomatoes
Salt
Pepper
¼ cup fresh basil leaves
4 eggs
2 teaspoons white wine vinegar
1 tablespoon olive oil

Slice off the tops of the tomatoes and scoop out the flesh. Season the insides of the tomato shells with salt and pepper. Puree the tomato flesh and tops in a food processor or a food mill.

Put a basil leaf in each tomato shell. Place the tomato shells in an ovenproof dish and break an egg into each one. Bake in a preheated 350°F oven for 20 minutes, or until the eggs have set.

Cut the remaining basil in strips and stir into the tomato puree. Add the white wine vinegar, olive oil, and salt and pepper to taste.

To serve, place the tomato shells on 4 plates and spoon some sauce over each.

GARLIC SCRAMBLED EGGS ON POTATO PANCAKES

Yield: 8 servings

- 8 potato pancakes (See index for POTATO PANCAKES)
- 3 tablespoons butter
- 6 cloves garlic, peeled and crushed
- 8 eggs
- 3 tablespoons whipping cream
- Salt
- Pepper
- Grated nutmeg
- 2 bunches parsley, finely chopped

Prepare the potato pancakes (see index for POTATO PANCAKES); keep warm.

Melt the butter in a large frying pan and sauté the garlic gently. Whisk the eggs with the cream, salt, pepper, and nutmeg. Pour the egg mixture into the frying pan and cook over low heat until set, constantly loosening it from the pan with a spatula. The eggs should be light and loose.

Spoon the eggs on the potato pancakes. Sprinkle with parsley and serve immediately.

SHRIMP-FLAVORED SCRAMBLED EGGS ON BLACK BREAD

Yield: 4 servings
8 eggs
4 tablespoons whipping cream
Salt
Pepper
Worcestershire sauce
6 tablespoons butter
10½ ounces shrimp, cooked, shelled and deveined
4 slices dark black bread
¼ cup fresh dill, finely chopped

Beat the eggs with the cream, salt, pepper, and Worcestershire sauce. Melt 1 tablespoon butter in a frying pan; pour in ¼ of the egg mixture and cook over low heat until set. As soon as the eggs begin to set, add ¼ of the shrimp, stirring so the mixture doesn't stick. Remove from the pan and keep warm while preparing the 3 other portions of egg and shrimp.

To serve, spread the remaining butter on the bread and place the scrambled eggs and shrimp on top. Sprinkle with dill.

LYONS OMELETTE

Yield: 4 servings
4 tablespoons clarified butter
10½ ounces sausage, skin removed and thinly sliced
8 eggs
4 tablespoons whipping cream
Salt
Pepper
Grated nutmeg
½ cup fresh chives, chopped

Melt the clarified butter in a frying pan and brown the sausage slices on both sides.

Beat the eggs with the cream, salt, pepper, and nutmeg. Stir in the chives. Slowly pour the egg mixture over the sausage slices and cook over low heat until set, constantly shaking the pan to prevent sticking.

When the bottom has set, slide the omelette onto a saucepan lid; flip it over into the pan and cook the other side. To serve, quarter the sausage omelette and arrange on 4 plates.

PANCAKE PIE WITH CAULIFLOWER

Yield: 6 to 8 servings
For the pancakes:
3 eggs
¾ cup flour
1 cup milk
Salt
Pepper
4 tablespoons clarified butter
.
For the filling:
2 tablespoons clarified butter
1 small onion, peeled and finely diced
1 clove garlic, peeled and finely chopped
1½ cups ground beef
3 tablespoons tomato paste
1 small can (about 16 ounces) skinned plum tomatoes
5 tablespoons dry red wine
1 teaspoon oregano
1 bay leaf
Cayenne pepper
1 cauliflower (about 1-½ pounds), broken into florets
For the Béchamel sauce:
1 tablespoon butter
1 tablespoon flour
1¼ cups milk, heated
9 ounces freshly grated Emmenthaler cheese
Grated nutmeg

To make the pancakes, combine in a bowl the eggs, flour, milk, salt, and pepper; set aside for at least 30 minutes. Melt the clarified butter in an omelette pan. Pour in ¼ cup batter and cook until bubbles form and the edges are set; flip over and briefly cook the other side. Make 6 to 8 pancakes in this manner and keep warm.

To make the filling, melt the clarified butter in a large saucepan and gently sauté the onion and garlic until softened. Add the ground beef and cook until crumbly. Add the tomato paste, tomatoes and juice, and red wine. Season to taste with salt, pepper, oregano, bay leaf, and cayenne pepper. Boil, uncovered, until creamy, then simmer for 30 minutes.

While the filling is cooking, boil the cauliflower in salt water for 6 to 8 minutes, until just tender; drain. Add to the meat sauce and season to taste; remove the bay leaf.

To make the Béchamel sauce, melt the butter in a frying pan; add the flour and stir until golden. Gradually add the heated milk and mix well. Heat the sauce for 15 minutes, letting it bubble gently; stir in the cheese. Season with salt, pepper, and nutmeg.

Lay 1 pancake in a round, greased ovenproof dish; spread a little of the cauliflower filling over it, then a little of the Béchamel sauce. Cover with another pancake and continue the layers until all the ingredients have been used. Spread Béchamel sauce over the top pancake and bake for 15 to 20 minutes in a preheated 400°F oven.

APPLE PANCAKES WITH CINNAMON SAUCE

Yield: 4 servings
For the pancakes:
½ cup flour
1 cup milk
1 tablespoon sugar
2 eggs
3 tablespoons melted butter
4 tablespoons clarified butter
2 apples (Granny Smith), peeled, cored and thinly sliced
For the sauce:
1 cup sour cream
1 teaspoon cinnamon
2 tablespoons apple brandy
1 tablespoon sugar

In a medium bowl, mix the flour, milk, sugar, and eggs together to form a thick batter. Stir in the melted butter, cover, and set aside for at least 20 minutes.

Heat 1 tablespoon of clarified butter in a large frying pan and gently sauté a quarter of the apple slices until almost soft. Pour a quarter of the batter over the apples and let set, shaking the pan so the pancake does not stick. Turn the pancake over and sauté until cooked. Make 4 pancakes in this manner; keep warm.

To make the sauce, mix the sour cream with the cinnamon, apple brandy, and sugar until creamy. Before serving, pour the sauce over the pancakes.

CHOCOLATE SOUFFLÉ WITH PINEAPPLE

Yield: 4 servings
8½ ounces stale cornbread
1 cup pineapple juice
3 tablespoons almond liqueur
3 ounces milk chocolate, melted
2 tablespoons softened butter
¼ cup sugar
Salt
3 eggs, separated
4 slices canned pineapple

Slice the cornbread and dry in a toaster oven on the lowest setting; crumble finely. Slightly warm the pineapple juice and add to the bread crumbs; set aside for about 30 minutes. Add the almond liqueur and melted chocolate.

In a separate bowl, cream the butter, sugar, and salt together; gradually add the egg yolks and fold in the bread-crumb mixture (photograph 1). Beat the egg whites until stiff and fold into the mixture (photograph 2).

Grease 4, 3½-inch ovenproof dishes and dust with sugar (photograph 3). Place a slice of pineapple in the bottom of each dish and add the soufflé mixture (photograph 4). Bake in a preheated 425°F oven for 15 minutes. Serve immediately.

Tip: Also try baking the mixture in a large soufflé dish and serve with fresh pineapple slices. The baking time will be 5 minutes longer.

1

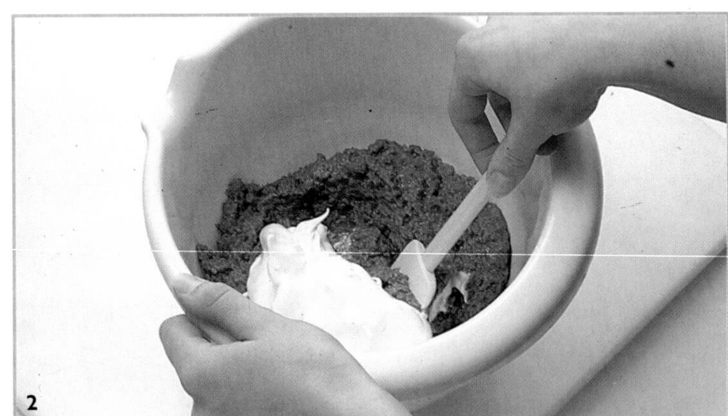
2

3

4

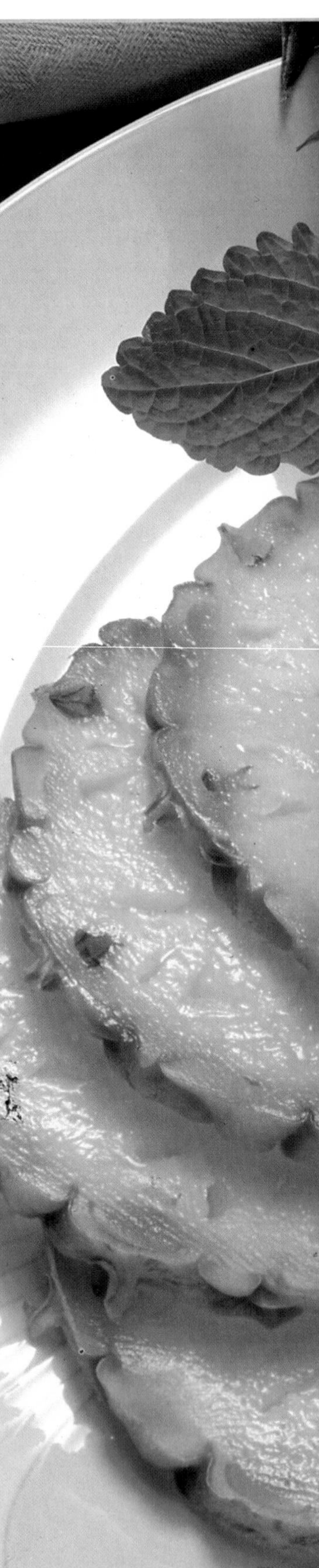

PUMPKIN SOUFFLÉ IN AN ORANGE SHELL

Yield: 4 servings
1½ tablespoons butter
14 ounces peeled, fresh pumpkin, coarsely diced
3 tablespoons sugar
1 tablespoon orange liqueur
½ teaspoon cinnamon
Salt
1 pinch grated orange rind
2 eggs, separated
2 large oranges
2 tablespoons almond flakes

Melt 1 teaspoon of butter in a frying pan and gently sauté the pumpkin. Stir in the sugar, cover, and simmer for 30 minutes. After 30 minutes, remove the lid and let the liquid evaporate over high heat, being careful not to burn the pumpkin. Puree in a food processor or food mill and let cool.

Mix the pumpkin puree together with the remaining butter, orange liqueur, cinnamon, salt, orange peel, and egg yolk.

Wash the oranges, halve them, and remove the fruit, discarding the membranes. Cut the fruit into small pieces. Replace the fruit in the orange shells. Beat the egg white until very stiff and fold into the pumpkin mixture. Spoon some pumpkin into each orange half. Sprinkle with almond flakes.

Place the orange halves on a baking sheet and bake in a preheated 400°F oven for 20 minutes. Serve immediately.

CHEESE SOUFFLÉ

Yield: 4 servings
1 tablespoon butter
1 tablespoon flour
1 cup milk
Salt
Pepper
Grated nutmeg
Grated lemon peel
4 ounces grated Gouda cheese
4 eggs, separated

Melt the butter in a frying pan. Add the flour and cook, stirring, over low heat for 3 to 5 minutes. Whisk in the milk, taking care that no lumps form. Bring the mixture to a boil; remove from the heat and let cool. Season with salt, pepper, nutmeg, and lemon peel.

Add the cheese and gradually stir in the egg yolks. Beat the egg whites until stiff and fold into the mixture. Pour into 4 greased soufflé dishes. Bake in a preheated 425°F oven for 15 minutes.

CARROT SOUFFLÉ

Yield: 4 to 6 servings
1 tablespoon butter
6 to 8 medium carrots, peeled and sliced
½ teaspoon salt
Cinnamon
Grated nutmeg
Pepper
½ cup shelled almonds
4 eggs, separated
¼ cup sour cream

Melt the butter in a frying pan and sauté the carrots. Add the salt, cinnamon, nutmeg, and pepper. Cover and cook over low heat for 20 minutes. Uncover and let any pan liquids evaporate over high heat, being careul not to burn the carrots.

Fill a small saucepan with water. Add the almonds and bring to a boil. Drain the nuts, then plunge them into cold water and remove the skins. Puree the carrots and almonds together in a food processor or food mill.

Beat the egg yolks until creamy; stir in the sour cream and carrot-almond puree. Beat the egg whites until stiff and fold into the mixture.

Pour the mixture into a greased soufflé dish and bake in a preheated 425°F oven for 20 minutes. Serve immediately.

PARSLEY SOUFFLÉ

Yield: 4 to 6 servings
1 cup whipping cream
1 cup milk
¼ cup cream cheese
3 tablespoons flour
Salt
Pepper
Worcestershire sauce
4 eggs, separated yolks
½ cup parsley, finely chopped

Gently heat the milk and cream in a saucepan. Add the flour and stir over low heat for 3 to 5 minutes. Remove from the heat, add the cream cheese, and beat for 2 minutes with an electric mixer. Season with salt, pepper, and Worcestershire sauce and fold in the egg yolks and chopped parsley. Beat the egg whites until stiff and fold into the yolk mixture.

Place in a greased soufflé dish and bake in a preheated 425°F oven for 20 minutes.

HAM SOUFFLÉ

Yield: 4 to 6 servings
12 prunes
6 tablespoons Madeira wine
½ cup whipping cream
1 to 2 slices of white bread, crust removed
1 cup boiled ham, diced
4 eggs, separated
Pepper
Fresh ginger

Soak the prunes in the Madeira for 3 hours; drain, reserving the Madeira.

Gently heat the cream in a small saucepan; remove from the heat. Soak the bread in the cream and sprinkle with the reserved Madeira. Puree the bread, ham, and egg yolks together in a food processor. Season with the pepper and ginger. Beat the egg whites until stiff and fold in.

Divide the prunes among 4 small, greased soufflé dishes and cover with the puree. Tap the dishes to prevent air bubbles from forming. Bake in a preheated 425°F oven for 15 minutes. Serve immediately.

CLASSIC CUISINE

The attractive soufflé shown here includes baked zucchini, carrots, and potatoes, and is topped with melted cheese that has been lightly broiled. It may be served as a main course along with a salad, or as a delicate accompaniment to a heartier meal. Soufflé recipes are plentiful throughout international cuisine because a soufflé can be made from so many different combinations of ingredients. Soufflés can be prepared from garden vegetables, potatoes, meat, poultry, fish, eggs, pasta, or rice. Most soufflés are bound with cheese or cheese sauce, heavy cream or sour cream beaten with eggs, and are baked or broiled. After you have made a few of the soufflés in this chapter, you'll find an abundance of ideas and inspiration for creating tempting recipes of your own.

SOUFFLÉS

SAVORY OR SWEET SOUFFLÉS

Soufflés are made up of layers of a variety of different, but complementary, ingredients. A delicious savory soufflé can be assembled by layering ham, slices of tomato, wedges of hard-boiled egg, and a top layer of cooked broad noodles. Cream (or milk) beaten with egg and seasoned with salt, pepper, and a dash of mace is poured over the ingredients after these have been layered in an oven-proof soufflé dish. The finished noodle soufflé

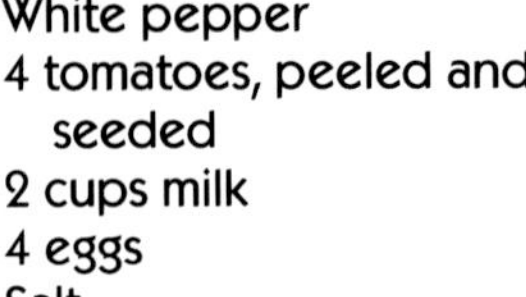

emerges from the oven when it is golden brown.

Sweet soufflés are prepared from butter, sugar, and egg yolks, and are often mixed with milk, cooked rice, and fresh fruit. Dessert soufflés may be served with fruit sauces, vanilla custard, or a rich chocolate sauce. Here is an introductory recipe for a savory ground meat and vegetable soufflé:

Ground Meat and Vegetable Soufflé:

1 medium cauliflower, blanched
Salt
1 teaspoon grated nutmeg
3 slices white bread, soaked in milk
1 cup mixed ground meat (beef, pork, veal)
1 medium onion, chopped
1 egg
White pepper
4 tomatoes, peeled and seeded
2 cups milk
4 eggs
Salt
1 tablespoon butter

Preheat the oven to 400°F.

Blanch the cauliflower for 10 minutes in boiling, salted water seasoned with ½ teaspoon of nutmeg. Drain the cauliflower well. Squeeze the bread and mix it with the ground meats, onion, and egg. Add salt and pepper to taste (photograph 1).

Butter an ovenproof soufflé dish. Layer the meat mixture in the soufflé dish. Place the cauliflower on top of the meat and lay the tomatoes on top. Press lightly into the meat mixture. Salt the tomatoes (photograph 2). With a whisk, beat the eggs and milk together. Season with salt and ½ teaspoon of nutmeg. Pour the egg and milk over the cauliflower (photograph 3). Dot with butter on top (photograph 4). Place the soufflé on the bottom rack in the oven and bake for 40 to 50 minutes, until golden brown. Do not open the oven door while the souffle is cooking or it will fall.

Essential cooking tip for soufflés: When preparing a soufflé, be sure not to open the oven door—even just a crack—until the soufflé is done. Cold air from the kitchen will cause the soufflé to fall and, although it will taste just as good, it will not be very attractive. This advice is particularly important for sweet soufflés, or those made mostly of eggs and other light ingredients. A glass-doored oven is very useful for checking up on a soufflé without ruining it.

Soufflé dishes must be ovenproof to withstand the heat from an electric or gas oven. These can be made of china, ceramic, glass, cast-iron, or glazed earthenware. Since the soufflé is always served from the same dish it is baked in, the dish should be attractive enough to be presented at the table.

The large soufflé dishes shown in photograph 1 are made of enamelled cast-iron and glass (front). These are designed for serving four people. A soufflé dish with a pyrex cover can be used in both a freezer and an oven (bring the dish and contents to room temperature before placing in the oven). Square, oval, and rectangular dishes are best for broiled soufflés or Duchess potatoes. Individual soufflé dishes make an attractive way of presenting a special dessert.

The topping on a soufflé can add extra flavor to an already delicious dish. Here are three suggestions for preparing a soufflé with a particularly attractive, tasty crust:

1. Sprinkle the top of the soufflé heavily with grated cheese and dot with butter before baking.

2. Sprinkle the top of the soufflé with fine bread crumbs mixed with grated cheese and dot with butter (see photograph 2).

3. Mix fine bread crumbs with ground or chopped nuts (walnuts or hazelnuts) and sprinkle onto the top of a sweet soufflé. Dot with butter before baking.

On the average, the baking time for a soufflé is 40 to 60 minutes in a preheated oven at 400°F or 425°F. Always place the soufflé on the lowest or middle rack of the oven.

Béchamel and Mornay sauces are two popular ways to bind a savory soufflé together.

BÉCHAMEL SAUCE

Yield: About 3 cups
1 tablespoon butter
2 onions, peeled and diced
2 tablespoons flour
1 cup Veal Stock (see Index)
2 cups milk
Salt
White pepper
Grated nutmeg

Melt the butter in a saucepan. Add the onions and sauté until soft and transparent. Add the flour and continue cooking, stirring constantly, until the mixture is pale yellow. Mix in the veal stock and milk, stirring rapidly to prevent lumps from forming.

Cook the sauce over low heat for 10 minutes, until the sauce can coat the back of a wooden spoon. Season to taste with salt, pepper, and nutmeg.

When mixed with cheese, Béchamel Sauce becomes Mornay Sauce (photographs 3 and 4), which can also be called a cheese Béchamel Sauce.

ZUCCHINI AND NOODLE SOUFFLÉ

Yield: 4 servings
1 cup Gorgonzola cheese
½ cup ground hazelnuts
¾ cup heavy cream
1 cup Ricotta cheese
Pepper
2 tablespoons brandy
Salt
2 cups spinach noodles, precooked and cooled
5 to 6 small zucchini, grated
½ cup fresh basil, chopped
3 tablespoons fine bread crumbs
1 tablespoon salted butter

Preheat the oven to 425°F.

Mix the Gorgonzola, nuts, cream, Ricotta, pepper, and brandy together in a bowl until creamy. Season with salt to taste.

Layer a third of the noodles, zucchini, basil, and cream mixture in a buttered soufflé dish. Repeat this layering procedure twice. Sprinkle the top layer of cream with the bread crumbs and dot with butter. Bake for 50 minutes, or until golden brown. Serve hot.

Rice Soufflé

Yield: 4 servings
1½ cups rice
2 cups chicken stock
1 clove garlic, crushed
1 bay leaf
4 peppercorns
¼ cup raisins
1 cup sour cream
½ cup heavy cream
½ teaspoon ground cinnamon
⅛ teaspoon paprika
10 small pickles, very thinly sliced
8 ounces smoked pork, cut in strips
Sour cream, for garnish

Preheat the oven to 425°F.

Place the rice and chicken stock in a saucepan and bring to a boil. Add the garlic, bay leaf and peppercorns. Cover and cook over low heat for 20 to 30 minutes. Remove the peppercorns, bay leaf and garlic. Mix the raisins into the rice.

Combine the sour cream and heavy cream and flavor with cinnamon and paprika.

Place a quarter of the rice mixture into a buttered soufflé dish. Layer a third of the pickles, pork, and cream mixture on top. Repeat this process 2 more times. The final layer should be rice.

Bake for 50 minutes. Serve the soufflé hot, garnished with cold sour cream.

COUSCOUS SOUFFLÉ

Yield: 4 servings
2 cups chicken stock
1 cup couscous
2½ tablespoons salted butter
2 boneless chicken breasts, cubed (about 14 ounces)
4 tablespoons tomato paste
1 tablespoon soy sauce
Pepper
1 cup heavy cream
1 pound spinach, cleaned, blanched and drained

Preheat the oven to 400°F.

Pour half of the boiling chicken stock on the couscous and soak for 10 minutes.

Melt 1 tablespoon of butter in a saucepan. Add the chicken and sauté. Add the tomato paste, soy sauce, and pepper. Pour in the remaining stock and the cream. Simmer for 3 minutes. Add salt to taste.

Layer the ingredients in a buttered soufflé dish in the following order: couscous, spinach, chicken, and sauce. The final layer should be couscous. Dot the top with 1 tablespoon of butter and bake for 40 minutes. Serve immediately.

NOODLE AND LEEK SOUFFLÉ

Yield: 4 to 6 servings
4 to 5 leeks, cut into rings
1½ tablespoons salted butter
½ cup dry white wine
Salt
1 cup milk
½ cup sour cream
¾ cup Gorgonzola cheese
1 tablespoon cornstarch
1 to 2 tablespoons water
Pepper
3 cups egg noodles, precooked and cooled

Preheat the oven to 400°F.

Clean and thoroughly wash the leeks. Cut them into rings ¼ inch wide. Melt the butter in a saucepan. Add the leeks and sauté until softened. Add wine and salt to taste and simmer for 3 minutes. Remove the pan from the heat. Transfer the leeks to a bowl and set aside. Add the milk and sour cream to the cooking liquid. Crumble the Gorgonzola cheese into the liquid and stir until the cheese melts.

Dissolve the cornstarch in 1 or 2 tablespoons of water. Add the cornstarch mixture to the cheese sauce, stirring constantly until the sauce has thickened. Season with pepper.

Place half of the noodles in a buttered soufflé dish. Add a layer of leeks and cheese sauce. Put the remaining half of the noodles on top. Bake for 25 minutes and serve hot.

CORN SOUFFLÉ

Yield: 6 servings
2 cans yellow corn (net weight 12 ounces)
1½ tablespoons salted butter
1 tablespoon flour
1 cup milk
1 teaspoon sweet paprika
Salt
Pepper
2 teaspoons lemon juice
3 medium tomatoes, peeled and sliced
4 hard-boiled eggs, shelled and chopped
1 cup Mozzarella cheese, grated

Preheat the oven to 400°F.

Drain the liquid from the cans of corn and reserve it. Melt the butter in a saucepan. Add the flour and heat together until the mixture turns light yellow. Remove the pan from the stove and immediately add the milk and reserved corn liquid. Bring the mixture to a boil and boil for 5 minutes, whisking constantly. Season with paprika, salt, pepper, and lemon juice.

Layer a third of the corn, tomato, egg, sauce, and Mozzarella side by side in a buttered soufflé dish. Continue creating layers until all of the ingredients have been used up. Bake for 45 minutes and serve hot.

ITALIAN BREAD SOUFFLÉ

Yield: 6 servings
½ cup olive oil
2 cloves garlic, peeled and crushed
5 slices firm white bread, cubed
1 cup tomato juice
2 eggplants, cut in 4 slices lengthwise
1 tablespoon salt
4 eggs, separated
1½ tablespoons grated Parmesan cheese
10 black olives, pitted and cut in quarters
6 tablespoons bread crumbs, toasted

Preheat the oven to 400°F.

Heat ¼ cup of the oil in a saucepan. Add the garlic and bread cubes and lightly sauté for 5 minutes. Remove the pan from the heat and pour the tomato juice over the bread. Set aside to soak for 15 minutes.

Sprinkle the cut surfaces of the eggplant with salt. Fit the eggplants back together again and place a weight on top. Press the slices firmly together after 30 minutes. Pat the juice and salt off the eggplants with paper towels. Cut the slices into cubes.

Heat ¼ cup of olive oil in a frying pan. Add the eggplant and sauté for 10 minutes, or until browned. Remove from the pan and drain.

Mix the soaked bread, eggplant, egg yolks, Parmesan cheese and olives together. In a separate bowl, beat the egg whites until stiff. Gently fold the egg whites into the eggplant mixture. Put the mixture into a buttered soufflé dish and sprinkle with bread crumbs. Bake for 50 minutes and serve hot.

SAVOY CABBAGE SOUFFLÉ

Yield: 6 servings
1 clove garlic, finely chopped
1½ tablespoons salted butter, softened
5 slices rye bread, toasted
1 small savoy cabbage, about 1 pound
10 strips bacon
2 medium onions, peeled and diced
½ cup grated cheese
1 package onion soup mix
3 cups hot water

Mix the garlic with the butter and spread on the slices of bread. Remove the outer leaves and the stalk from the cabbage. Blanch the cabbage leaves in boiling salted water for 3 minutes. Immediately plunge the leaves in cold water and drain.

Cut 4 strips of bacon into small pieces. Place the bacon pieces in a frying pan and cook over low heat to render the fat. Add the onions and sauté until brown.

Place 2 or 3 bread slices, buttered side down, in a buttered soufflé dish. Sprinkle the bacon and onion mixture over the bread. Add a layer of cheese, then a layer of cabbage leaves. Repeat this layering process until all of the ingredients are used.

Prepare the onion soup mix with 3 cups of hot water. Pour the soup over the soufflé. Bake for 45 minutes and serve hot.

SEMOLINA PANCAKES WITH CREAM

Yield: 6 to 8 servings
1 cup chicken stock
1 cup milk
2 cloves garlic, peeled and crushed
2 sprigs fresh basil, finely chopped
Salt
Pepper
Grated nutmeg
1 cup semolina flour
½ cup Parmesan cheese, grated
3½ ounces feta cheese, grated
1 cup heavy cream

Preheat the oven to 425°F.

Mix the stock, milk, garlic, and basil together in a saucepan. Season with salt, pepper, and nutmeg. Stir in the semolina and bring to a boil. Reduce the heat to low and simmer for 15 minutes.

Pour the mixture into a greased loaf pan and smooth the top evenly. Refrigerate until chilled, then cut into slices. Place the slices in a greased soufflé dish so that they overlap. Mix the cheeses and sprinkle over the semolina slices. Bake the pancakes for 15 to 20 minutes.

Heat the cream in a saucepan. Pour the cream over the pancakes and serve immediately.

POTATO AND CARROT GRATIN

Yield: 6 to 8 servings

1 pound potatoes, peeled and sliced very thinly
1 pound carrots, peeled and sliced very thinly
2 cups milk
½ cup heavy cream
Salt
Pepper
½ teaspoon grated nutmeg
½ cup ground almonds
¼ cup fresh marjoram, chopped

Preheat the oven to 400°F.

Butter a shallow soufflé dish. Layer the potatoes and carrots in the dish so that they overlap and form an attractive pattern.

Mix the milk and cream together and season with salt, pepper, and nutmeg. Stir in the almonds and marjoram. Pour the cream mixture over the vegetables until they are just covered. Bake for 1 hour and serve hot.

MEATBALL, POTATO, AND BRUSSELS SPROUT GRATIN

Yield: 6 to 8 servings
2 tablespoons salted butter
1 pound brussels sprouts
1 pound new potatoes, peeled and cut to the size of the sprouts
1 pound ground beef
3/4 cup low-fat ricotta cheese
1 egg
1 medium onion, peeled and diced
1 clove garlic, chopped
Salt
Pepper
1 tablespoon curry powder
2 cups sour cream
1/4 cup milk

Preheat the oven to 400°F.

Melt the butter in a large saucepan. Add the sprouts and potatoes and sauté over low heat for 15 to 20 minutes, stirring frequently.

Combine the ground beef, cheese, egg, diced onion, and half of the garlic. Season with salt and pepper and roll into balls the same size as the sprouts.

Stir the remaining garlic and curry powder into the sour cream, then add the milk. Place the potatoes, brussels sprouts, and meatballs together in a shallow, buttered soufflé dish, creating a colorful pattern. Pour the milk mixture on top and bake for 1 hour.

KOHLRABI AND CARROT SOUFFLÉ

Yield: 4 to 6 servings
1 pound carrots, peeled and thinly sliced
1 pound kohlrabi, peeled and thinly sliced
Soy sauce
Pepper
1 medium leek, cleaned and cut into thin strips
2 cloves garlic, diced
1 cup low-fat cottage cheese
1/2 cup heavy cream
3 tablespoons chopped parsley
10 tablespoons sesame seeds, toasted
1/2 teaspoon salt
1 cup milk

Preheat the oven to 400°F.

Sprinkle the carrots and kohlrabi with soy sauce and pepper. Mix the leek, garlic, cottage cheese, cream, parsley, 6 tablespoons of sesame seeds, salt, and pepper together.

Place half of the carrots and kohlrabi in a buttered soufflé dish and sprinkle with half of the cheese mixture. Repeat this procedure and gently pour the milk on top. Sprinkle the remaining sesame seeds over the soufflé. Bake for 1 hour, 15 minutes and serve hot.

ONION GRATIN

YIELD: 4 servings
2 cups vegetable stock
1 cup kasha or buckwheat groats
4 slices bacon
1 pound small white onions
1/2 cup tomato puree
1 sprig fresh basil
1/8 teaspoon salt
1/4 teaspoon freshly ground black pepper

Bring the vegetable stock to a boil and pour over the kasha or buckwheat groats. Set aside for 15 minutes to soak.

Preheat the oven to 375°F.

Grease an ovenproof soufflé dish and spread the soaked kasha or buckwheat groats evenly over the bottom of the dish.

Dice the bacon strips finely and fry until crisp. Remove from the pan with a slotted spoon and discard.

Peel and halve the onions. Sauté the onion halves in the bacon fat for about 2 minutes.

Place the onions, cut side down, on the kasha or buckwheat groats in the casserole dish.

Finely chop the fresh basil sprig. Season the tomato puree with the salt, freshly ground black pepper and chopped, fresh basil. Pour the seasoned tomato puree over the onions.

Bake for 45 minutes and serve hot.

NUT CRÊPES WITH RADICCHIO FILLING

Yield: 4 to 6 servings
For the crêpes:
3 eggs
½ cup flour, sifted
½ teaspoon salt
¾ cup milk
3 tablespoons chopped walnuts
Water
For the sauce:
2 tablespoons salted butter
3 tablespoons flour
1 cup milk
1 cup chicken stock
¼ cup heavy cream
¼ cup sour cream
3 tablespoons currant jelly
3 tablespoons chopped walnuts
For the filling:
2 heads radicchio, cleaned and separated

Preheat the oven to 400°F.

To make the crêpes, mix the eggs and flour together. Add salt, then gradually incorporate the milk. Stir in the walnuts (photograph 1). Set aside for 30 minutes. Lighten the mixture, if necessary, with a dash of water.

Preheat a crêpe pan and make 8 thin crêpes (photograph 2). Remove the crêpes from the pan and wrap in plastic wrap, so that they do not dry out.

To make the sauce, melt the butter in a saucepan. Add the flour and sauté for 4 minutes, or until the flour turns light yellow. Remove from the stove and gradually add the milk, stirring constantly with a wire whisk. When the milk has been fully incorporated, add the stock and simmer for 5 minutes. Add the creams, port wine, jelly, and walnuts.

Remove the whole leaves from the radicchios. Blanch the radicchio leaves in boiling, salted water for 1 minute. Cover the crêpes with the radicchios. Pour 1 small ladleful of sauce over the crêpes (photograph 3). Roll up the crêpes and place in a shallow, buttered soufflé dish (photograph 4). Pour the remaining sauce over the crêpes and bake for 40 minutes.

Chicory or firm endive lettuce can be substituted for radicchio.

PANCAKES AU GRATIN

Yield: 4 to 6 servings
1 cup flour, sifted
3 eggs
1¼ cups milk
½ teaspoon salt
10 tablespoons vegetable oil
1 cup Ricotta cheese
1 cup low-fat cottage cheese
½ cup ground hazelnuts
Pepper
2 Granny Smith apples, peeled and finely grated
¾ cup fresh sorrel, chopped
3 tablespoons grated Emmenthaler cheese

Preheat the oven to 400°F.

Mix the flour, eggs, milk, and salt to make a thick, runny batter. Heat the oil in a pan and make 6 pancakes. Stir the Ricotta, cottage cheese, and hazelnuts together. Season with pepper. Fold the grated apples into the cottage cheese mixture.

Place the first pancake in a buttered soufflé dish and spread one-sixth of the cheese mixture over it. Top with sorrel leaves. Repeat this process until the last pancake has been spread with the cheese mixture. Sprinkle the grated cheese on top. Bake for 40 minutes and serve hot.

ALMOND TOAST SOUFFLÉ

Yield: 4 to 6 servings
1/4 cup marzipan
9 slices packaged almond toast
2 cups milk
2 ripe bananas
3 to 4 tablespoons orange liqueur
1 (14-ounce) can apricots, drained
2 egg whites
1/4 cup confectioners' sugar

Preheat the oven to 400°F.

Spread the marzipan on the almond toast. Puree the milk, bananas, and orange liqueur in a blender or food processor. Alternately layer the toasts and apricots in a buttered soufflé dish. The top layer should be apricots. Gently pour the banana milk on top. Bake for 40 minutes.

Beat the egg white until stiff and gradually whip in the confectioners' sugar. About 10 minutes before the end of the cooking time, pipe the egg white onto the soufflé and continue to bake until the meringue mixture begins to turn a light brown. Serve immediately.

GRAPE SOUFFLÉ

Yield: 4 to 6 servings
3½ ounces white chocolate
¾ cup heavy cream
3½ ounces apricot liqueur
1 egg
¾ pound seedless grapes, halved
½ cup apricot jam
1½ cups broad egg noodles, cooked and cooled
3 tablespoons slivered almonds
1 tablespoon salted butter

Preheat the oven to 325°F.

Combine the chocolate and the cream in the top of a double boiler. Simmer until the chocolate has melted. Stir in the apricot liqueur and allow the mixture to cool. Beat in the egg.

Mix the grapes and jam together. Place one-third of the noodles in a buttered soufflé dish and spread one-third of the sauce and one-half of the grapes on top. Repeat this until all the ingredients have been layered in the dish. The last layer should be the sauce. Sprinkle almond slivers on top and dot with butter. Bake for 40 minutes and serve hot.

Raisins soaked in rum for 2 hours can be substituted for fresh grapes.

DATE SOUFFLÉ

Yield: 4 to 6 servings
¾ cup dry white wine
¼ cup honey
2 teaspoons vanilla extract
¼ cup rolled oats
3 eggs, separated
⅛ teaspoon salt
2 tablespoons salted butter, softened
14 ounces dried dates, halved and pitted
3 tablespoons rose water
3 egg whites
¼ cup slivered almonds
¾ cup heavy cream
¼ cup candied rose leaves

Preheat the oven to 400°F.

Stir the wine and honey together in a saucepan and bring to a boil. Add the vanilla and rolled oats. Cover and cook over low heat for about 15 minutes. Remove from the heat and set aside to cool.

Cream the egg yolks, salt, and softened butter together. Add to the oat mixture, stirring constantly. Sprinkle the dates with rose water and place in a buttered soufflé dish.

Beat the egg whites until stiff and fold into the oat mixture. Spread the oat mixture over the dates. Sprinkle with slivered almonds and bake for about 35 minutes.

Whip the cream until slightly stiff and spoon into a bowl. Garnish with rose leaves and serve separately with the soufflé.

APPLE AND POTATO SOUFFLÉ

Yield: 4 to 6 servings
1 pound potatoes, boiled and peeled
1 pound Granny Smith apples peeled, cored and pre-baked
½ cup sugar
3 to 4 tablespoons apple liqueur
¼ cup dried fruit, chopped
½ cup raisins
1 teaspoon ground cinnamon
⅛ teaspoon mace
4 eggs, separated

Preheat the oven to 400°F.

Mash the potatoes and apples together using a potato masher. Place the sugar in a saucepan. Over high heat, caramelize the sugar by adding 1 to 2 tablespoons of water and bringing the mixture to a rapid boil. Continue to boil the sugar until the color of the liquid becomes a light nut brown. Immediately add the apple and potato mixture and sauté until all of the water has evaporated. Add the apple liqueur and remove from the stove. Fold the dried fruit, raisins, and spices into the mixture. Allow the mixture to cool, then beat in the egg yolks.

In a separate bowl, beat the egg whites until they form stiff peaks, and then gently fold them into the cooled mixture using a rubber spatula.

Carefully turn the batter into a prepared soufflé dish and bake for 40 minutes.

ROCK ALMOND SOUFFLÉ

Yield: 4 to 6 servings
1 cup confectioners' sugar, plus a little for sprinkling
1 cup slivered almonds
3 tablespoons salted butter
½ cup round-grain rice
3 cups milk
½ teaspoon saffron
Salt
2 tablespoons honey
¼ cup Amaretto
4 eggs, separated

Preheat the oven to 400°F.

Melt one-third of the sugar in a saucepan, stirring constantly (photograph 1). Gradually add the remaining sugar. Caramelize the sugar by adding 2 to 3 tablespoons of water to the mixture and boiling over high heat until the liquid become light brown. Immediately remove the pan from the stove and add the almonds. Add the butter as the mixture cools slightly (photograph 2).

Place the rice in another saucepan and cover with boiling water. Add the milk, honey, saffron, and salt, and bring the mixture to a boil. Reduce the heat to low, cover, and simmer for about 30 minutes. Remove from the stove and add the remaining butter and Amaretto. Allow the mixture to cool a little, then beat in the egg yolks. Crumble the almond mixture into a fine powder and stir into the rice mixture.

In a separate bowl, beat the egg whites until they form stiff peaks. Gently fold the egg whites into the batter using a rubber spatula. Carefully turn the mixture into a buttered soufflé dish.

Bake for 35 minutes. To serve, sprinkle the hot soufflé with confectioners' sugar.

BANANA SOUFFLÉ

Yield: 4 to 6 servings
2 cups cottage cheese
½ cup grated coconut
2 tablespoons flour
¾ cup confectioners' sugar
3 eggs, separated
4 very ripe bananas, peeled and halved lengthwise.
3 tablespoons salted butter

Preheat the oven to 400°F.

Mix the cottage cheese with the coconut and the flour. Using a whisk or an electric mixer, beat the confectioners' sugar and the egg yolk until foamy and fold into the cottage cheese mixture. Pour the mixture into a shallow buttered soufflé dish. Place banana halves on top and dot with butter. Bake for 35 minutes and serve immediately.

CLASSIC CUISINE

Desserts come in many enticing sizes and shapes, and among the most attractive is the sabayon, the elegant cream dish shown here. This tempting selection of desserts includes recipes for many other luscious creams and also offers suggestions for preparing fanciful ice cream dishes.

ENGLISH CREAM

Yield: 4–6
6 eggs, separated
¼ cup sugar
Salt
2 cups milk
2 teaspoons vanilla extract

English Cream is a vanilla sauce used as a basis for numerous cream desserts as well as for ice cream.

Place the egg yolks, sugar and a pinch of salt into a mixing bowl. Beat with an electric mixer on low setting (photograph top left). It is important that the sugar dissolve completely, but the mixture must not become too foamy.

Meanwhile, bring the milk and vanilla to a boil in a saucepan. Gradually stir in the egg yolk mixture, a little at a time. Turn the custard into the top of a double boiler set over boiling water, stirring constantly. Continue to heat the custard until it binds and, when tested, is creamy and coats the back of a wooden spoon (middle photograph).

When the custard is done, place the pan in a bowl filled with ice water (bottom photograph) to stop the cooking process. Strain it through a fine sieve and allow to cool, stirring occasionally. This is the basis for Bavarian cream.

CHOCOLATES AND NUTS
Each item shown in the photograph is an important ingredient in garnishing and flavoring desserts.

Cocoa comes from cocoa beans. After being shelled and fermented, roasted cocoa beans are ground and pressed to produce cocoa butter and cocoa powder.

Chocolate is made with cocoa powder, butter, sugar, and spices, and can have milk or cream added. Milk chocolate, bittersweet chocolate, and white chocolate are differentiated according to the proportion of cocoa powder and milk used in preparation. The more cocoa butter chocolate contains, the firmer it is.

Marzipan is a blend of ground almonds and sugar.

Nuts may be whole, roasted, chopped, ground, or flaked. Hazelnuts, walnuts, and almonds are most commonly used in desserts, although pistachio nuts are also popular. Before using nuts that have a "skin," roast them and rub the skin off with a slightly dampened towel.

SUGAR
Sugar is made from sugar cane or sugar beets; the method of extraction is the same for both. Both are ground, and the juice extracted, purified, and thickened to a syrup from which sugar crystals come. This is raw sugar. White sugar is produced from raw sugar by washing and refining it.

Confectioners' sugar is finely ground refined sugar. It is used for icings, meringues, and glazes because it dissolves quickly.

Brown sugar can be either raw cane sugar or raw sugar beet sugar.

Granulated sugar is large-crystal sugar produced from refined sugar.

Sugar cubes are made from dampened refined sugar pressed into cubes.

Candy sugar consists of large sugar crystals from a refined sugar solution. Brown candy sugar is colored with caramel or other food colorings.

CRÈME CARAMEL

Yield: 6–8
½ cup sugar
1 tablespoon water
½ teaspoon lemon juice
3 eggs
3 egg yolks
2 teaspoons vanilla extract
1 cup warm milk
1 cup warm heavy cream

Crème caramel has always been part of the classic dessert cuisine. It is a sweet egg cream with an additional coating of caramelized sugar. Here is a recipe for crème caramel:

Place ¼ cup of the sugar in a saucepan, add just enough water to cover, and heat slowly. As soon as the sugar begins to melt, stir continously until it has dissolved completely. Add the water and lemon juice. The mixture should rest to a light brown color (photograph above). Then remove it from the heat, and immediately pour into a smooth-sided ovenproof bowl so that the whole dish is fully lined with a layer of caramel (center photograph).

In another bowl, vigorously beat the eggs, egg yolks, remaining sugar, and vanilla with a wire whisk. Do not beat it to a foamy consistency. Gradually stir in the warm milk and cream; then pour the mixture into the bowl with the caramel. Heat water in a deep pan until it is almost boiling; place the dish in the water (photograph below). The water must come at least halfway up the sides of the dish. Place the dish, in the water bath, in the center of a preheated 350°F oven, for 50 to 60 minutes or until it sets.

Remove from the oven, allow to cool, and then cool thoroughly in the refrigerator. To serve, loosen the edges with a sharp knife, and carefully turn the crème caramel onto a plate. Crème caramel can also be prepared in 6 small timbale molds in a water bath, and cooked at 400°F for 20 minutes.

CARAMELIZED SUGAR

Oeufs à la Neige or floating islands, a dessert of heavenly sweetness, is often served with meringue covered with a web of caramelized sugar threads.

Caramel syrup adds flavor to any dessert. A caramel syrup may also be used to cook fruit, to glaze nuts, or to prepare cream desserts. Caramel sugar is called light, medium, or dark, depending on its use. Texture and color depend upon the proportion of water to sugar used and the length of cooking time. Lighter syrups (for fruits and sauces) are made by boiling 1 cup sugar and 2 cups water for 1 minute. The heavier the syrup is to be, the less water is used. For caramel and caramel threads, 1 cup sugar and ¼ cup water are used. The syrup is boiled until it is a light brown, and is drawn into threads as it cools (center photograph).

Oeufs à la Neige is made in the following way: Caramelize ¼ cup sugar, add 2 cups milk and 2 teaspoons vanilla extract, and bring to a boil. Stir continuously for 15 minutes. Whip 4 egg whites with ¼ cup sugar and 1 teaspoon lemon juice until stiff. Cut out small balls with a teaspoon, and slide them onto the caramel cream (photograph top left). Bake in a covered ovenproof dish in a 300°F oven for 8 minutes. Remove the meringues, and put them the refrigerator. Mix 4 egg yolks and 6 tablespoons of milk together. Gradually stir in the hot caramel cream over low heat; do not boil. Allow to cool. To serve, divide among deep plates, and gently set the "snowballs" on top of the caramel cream. Boil ½ cup sugar and 1 to 2 tablespoons of water together to make a caramel that pulls into threads as it cools (center photograph). Remove from the stove. Using a tablespoon, carefully and gradually spoon the caramel over the snowballs, 1 portion at a time, so that they are covered with caramel threads (photograph below left). Serves 4 to 6.

GARNISHING

Desserts can be decorated so that they are a treat for the eye as well as for the palate. Chocolate leaves can be made in the following way: Melt a fine grade of bittersweet chocolate slowly in a double boiler. Pull freshly picked, washed, and dried leaves through the melted chocolate. Allow the chocolate leaves to harden, and gently remove the real leaf. Melted chocolate can also be poured into small molds to make an edible dish that can be filled with ice cream.

Sugar garnishes are available in every color of the rainbow, along with sugar pearls, glittering silver dragees, and tiny sugar flowers.

CUSTARDS AND OTHER CREAM DESSERTS

Custard is the basis of many cream desserts. Bavarian Cream is one example of a cream based on custard. Here is a basic recipe: First prepare a custard, using the English Cream recipe at the beginning of the chapter, then dissolve 1½ tablespoons gelatin in ¼ cup cold water and gently fold this mixture in the hot custard. Allow it to cool in the refrigerator until it begins to thicken, but is not yet set. To be safe, stir it from time to time. Finally, fold in 2 cups of stiffly whipped cream. Turn the mixture into a mold that has been either greased, or rinsed out with cold water. Allow the cream to set in the refrigerator, and then turn it out onto a plate just before serving.

Technically, every cream that has been beaten with a wire whisk or electric mixer has been whipped. Here whipped cream means custard that is whisked over a double boiler. The volume is doubled and the cream becomes light through the stirring and the heat. The proper method is to heat water in the bottom of a double boiler to the boiling point, then reduce to a gentle simmer. In the top of the double boiler, the cream is stirred with a wire whisk, spreading the heat evenly throughout. Typical whipped cream dishes such as Zabaglione (see Index) can be prepared this way.

Blancmange is a sweet or salty dish cooked in a covered mold that has been placed in a water bath. It is eaten warm, and can be made of batter or from an egg mixture. A typical blancmange mold is shown in the second photograph from the top. Since blancmange is always removed from the mold, the mold must be greased and dusted with fine bread crumbs first; the lid of the mold should also be greased and dusted with bread crumbs because a blancmange mixture usually rises.

ICE CREAM, SORBETS, PARFAITS, AND GRANITA

Ice cream comes in almost every flavor imaginable. Many people also enjoy making their own ice cream; for those who often do so, it is worthwhile to own an ice cream machine (second photograph from the bottom). It is still possible to make ice cream without an ice cream machine. The ice cream mixture is placed in a container in the freezer, and is stirred once every 30 minutes.

Parfaits are made with layers of ice cream and gelatin-stiffened whipped cream. They are not stirred as they freeze, so the colorful layering is intact. Parfaits are served in clear glasses or cut into slices.

Sorbet is an ice made from fruit juice or puree, champagne, or even wine. It must be stirred often as it freezes so that it remains light. Sorbet works especially well in an ice cream machine.

Granita is made by freezing slightly sweetened liquid such as juice, wine, or champagne. The ice is then scraped out of the container with a wooden paddle or pastry scraper and looks like crushed ice shavings.

ICE CREAM BOMBES

An ice cream bombe always looks impressive. Ice cream is spread in a bombe mold in layers. Fruit, nuts, chocolate, candies, or candied fruit can be placed between the layers of ice cream. When making the bombe, take care that each layer is frozen hard before the next layer is added, because melting layers will run together. To prevent the bombe from melting, it is best to stand the mold in a dish of ice cubes (bottom photograph) while each layer is added. If you do not have a special bombe mold, a smooth-sided bowl does just as well. To make a simple bombe, layer several kinds of ice cream on a plate.

NECTARINES IN RASPBERRY SAUCE

Yield: 4 servings
3½-ounces marzipan
Green food coloring
1 cup raspberries, picked over
2 to 3 tablespoons raspberry liqueur
¼ cup sugar
4 ripe nectarines, washed and sliced
Confectioner's sugar for garnish

Knead the marzipan with the food coloring, and form into small leaves. Puree the raspberries in a blender or food processor. Strain the puree through a fine sieve, stir in the raspberry liqueur and sugar, and spoon the mixture into 4 deep plates.

Arrange the nectarine slices on the raspberry puree in the shape of a flower. Garnish with marzipan leaves and dust with confectioners' sugar.

YELLOW PLUM TARTLETS

Yield: 6 servings
1½ tablespoons butter
¼ cup uncooked oatmeal
¼ cup sugar
½ cup heavy cream
1 pound, 2 ounces yellow plums, washed and pitted
½ cup apricot nectar
1 tablespoon cornstarch
½ cup Ricotta cheese
Whipped cream

Preheat the oven to 400°F. Melt the butter in a frying pan, and brown the oatmeal in it briefly. Stir in the sugar until it is caramelized. Gradually add the cream, and bring to a boil. Add the cornstarch and cook until the mixture firms.

Line 6 small brioche molds with aluminum foil, and spoon the oatmeal mixture into them. Press the mixture against the walls of the molds with a spoon to form the tart shells. Bake in the center of the oven for about 15 minutes, then allow to cool.

Wash the plums and remove their stones. In a large saucepan, bring the plums to a boil with the apricot nectar. Simmer gently for about 10 minutes, and then cool. Fill the tartlets with a layer of Ricotta cheese and then spoon on the plum mixture. Garnish with rosettes of whipped cream.

CANTALOUPE WITH NOUGAT CREAM

Yield: 4 servings

¼ cup nut nougat
2 cups milk
1 package vanilla pudding mix
1 tablespoon brandy
1 ripe cantaloupe melon, quartered and seeded
4 tablespoons toasted hazelnuts
Sweetened whipped cream for garnish

Grind the nougat to a coarse powder using a food processor or blender. In a saucepan combine the milk, pudding mix, and brandy, and prepare the pudding according to the package directions. When the pudding begins to firm, divide it in equal portions among 4 deep plates and let set in the refrigerator. Just before serving, place a slice of melon on top of each dish of pudding, sprinkle with hazelnuts, and garnish with a dollop of whipped cream.

AMBROSIA

Yield: 6–8 servings
2 pounds fresh cherries
¼ cup sugar
1 teaspoon vanilla extract
1 cup cornbread, crumbled
3 tablespoons cherry liqueur
1¾ ounces semisweet chocolate
1 cup heavy cream
2 tablespoons superfine sugar
1 cup sour cream
Grated chocolate for garnish

Wash, halve, and pit the cherries, and remove their stems, reserving the juice. Bring the cherries, sugar, and vanilla to a boil in a saucepan. Puree the mixture through a food mill or food processor, and measure out 2 cups of the juice.

Pour the warm juice over the bread, and let it stand until completely absorbed. Add the cherry liqueur. Grate the chocolate, and add it to the bread mixture.

Whip the cream with the sugar and sour cream until it is stiff. Spoon the cherries, bread mixture, and whipped cream into a glass dish in alternate layers, finishing with a layer of cream on top. Sprinkle with grated chocolate, and refrigerate until serving.

STRAWBERRY SURPRISE

Yield: 4 servings
2½ pounds strawberries, washed and hulled
1 lemon
¾ cup sugar
3 tablespoons cornstarch
½ cup raspberries, picked over
For the whipped cream:
1 cup heavy cream
1 teaspoon vanilla extract
2 tablespoons sugar

Set a quarter of the strawberries to one side, and bring the rest to boil in 4 cups of water. Drain over a dampened, tightly spread cheesecloth, and collect the juice. Squeeze out the fruit pulp after it has cooled. Add enough water to make 2 cups of juice.

Wash the lemon, and peel it thinly. Add the peel and the sugar to the juice, and bring it to a boil. Slowly add the cornstarch, stirring constantly, and bring to a boil again. Simmer for about 20 minutes, then remove the lemon peel.

Add the raspberries to the boiled strawberry mixture, together with the strawberries that were set aside, and boil for 1 more minute.

Whip the cream until it is stiff, gradually adding vanilla and sugar. Serve with the lukewarm or cold strawberry surprise.

SUMMER COMPOTE

Yield: 4–6 servings
1 pound sour cherries
1 pound apricots
1 cup grape juice
1 tablespoon cornstarch
⅓ cup ground almonds
1 egg white
¼ cup confectioners' sugar

Preheat the oven to 450°F. Wash the fruit, and remove the stems and pits. Quarter the apricots. Heat the grape juice in a large saucepan; mix the cornstarch with water, and stir it into the juice. Bring to a boil, add the fruit, and simmer for 5 minutes. Tuen the mixture into an ovenproof dish.

Beat the egg white until it is stiff, then beat in the confectioners' sugar. Fold in the almonds, and spread the meringue over the compote. Bake for 5 minutes.

RHUBARB JELLY

Yield: 6–8 servings
1½ pounds rhubarb, leaves removed
6 tablespoons sugar
1 package unflavored gelatin
½ cup cottage cheese
2 egg whites
1 teaspoon vanilla extract
2 tablespoons sugar

Wash the rhubarb, being careful to remove the leaves as they are poisonous, if eaten. Cut the rhubarb stalks into small pieces. In a saucepan, combine the rhubarb with 4 tablespoons sugar and ½ cup water. Bring to a boil, reduce heat, and simmer for about 20 minutes. Drain the rhubarb in a colander, reserving the juice, and puree in a food processor. Measure out 1 cup of the rhubarb juice and stir in the gelatin, then refrigerate. Stir the cottage cheese and the rhubarb puree together, and refrigerate.

Beat the egg whites until they are stiff. Still continuing to beat the egg whites, stir in the cold rhubarb mixture one spoonful at a time. Add sugar and vanilla to taste, and spread the mixture on top of the jelly. Refrigerate until serving.

MINT JELLY WITH MELON BALLS

Yield: 4 servings
½ cup fresh mint leaves, washed
3 tablespoons honey
Cardamon
2 packages unflavored gelatin
½ ripe honeydew melon
2 tablespoons lemon juice

In a saucepan, cover the mint leaves with 2 cups of boiling water. Allow to soak for 10 minutes, then strain through a fine sieve, reserving the leaves. Flavor the liquid with honey and cardamon.

Dissolve the gelatin in hot tea according to package directions.

Cut balls out of the melon with a melon baller. Add the melon balls to the tea together with the lemon juice and the reserved mint leaves, and pour into 4 gelatin molds. Refrigerate for 6 hours, and then turn out of the molds before serving. Serve with Wine-Foam Sauce (see Index).

CITRUS FRUIT WITH CUSTARD

Yield: 4 servings
1 cup heavy cream
1 to 2 tablespoons sugar
2 pieces candied ginger in syrup
1¼ packages unflavored gelatin
½ cup orange juice
¼ cup Brazil nuts, coarsely chopped
2 oranges
2 tangerines
Candied orange peel for garnish

Beat the cream until it is stiff, and stir in 1 tablespoon sugar and 1 teaspoon ginger syrup. Dissolve the gelatin in the orange juice, and fold it into the cream. Add sugar to taste.

Chop the ginger finely, and fold it into the cream with the nuts. Spoon the custard into 4 fluted pudding molds, and refrigerate for about 6 hours.

Peel the oranges and cut them into slices. Peel the tangerines, and divide them into segments, removing the white pith and seeds.

Arrange the fruit on 4 plates, turn the custards out onto the fruit, and garnish with orange peel.

WINE GELATIN WITH ROSES AND FRUIT

Yield: 4 servings
1 8-ounce can lychee nuts
1 cup rose water
1 cup sweet white wine
2 packages unflavored gelatin
20 fresh rose leaves
1 8-ounce can cherries

Drain the lychees, and reserve the syrup. Measure out 1 cup of lychee syrup, and mix with half the rose water and half the wine. Dissolve 1 package of gelatin in 3 tablespoons hot lychee liquid (photograph 1). Stir this into the remaining liquid. Rinse out 1 (4-cup) mold with cold water. Pour in the lychee liquid to a height of 2 inches and refrigerate.

Cut 6 lychees into segments. As soon as the liquid in the mold has set, pour in the rest of the gelatin liquid. Arrange the lychee segments and half the rose petals in it (photograph 2), and refrigerate.

Drain the cherries, and reserve the juice. Measure out ½ cup of cherry juice, and mix with the remaining rose water and the wine. Dissolve the remaining package of gelatin in 3 tablespoons of the cherry-wine-rose mixture over low heat. Stir together with the remaining liquid. Add ½ cup of cherries and 10 rose petals to the cherry liquid.

When the lychee gelatin has set, gently pour the cherry mixture over the back of a spoon onto the lychee gelatin, using the back of a spoon. Refrigerate for about 6 hours. To serve, dip the mold briefly in hot water, and turn out the gelatin (photograph 3).

1

2

3

RICE PUDDING

Yield: 4–6 servings
2 cups milk
1 teaspoon sugar
1 teaspoon vanilla extract
1 cup short-grain rice
2 packages unflavored gelatin
2 tablespoons cherry liqueur
1½ cups heavy cream
1½ packages cherry-flavored gelatin
1 cup sweet white wine
½ cup rosé wine

Preheat the oven to 350°F. Bring the milk, ¼ cup sugar, and the vanilla extract to a boil in a Dutch oven. Cover the Dutch oven and bake the rice for 40 minutes. Heat the cherry liqueur, and dissolve 1¼ packages of the unflavored gelatin in it. Fold this into the cooked rice, and refrigerate.

Whip half the cream until it is stiff, and fold it into the rice. Dissolve the remaining unflavored gelatin in 2 tablespoons of hot white wine, and stir it into the remaining white wine with ¼ cup sugar until the sugar has dissolved. Turn this into a rice pudding mold, and refrigerate. Repeat this process with the cherry gelatin and the rosé wine plus ¼ cup sugar.

When the light-colored gelatin has set, add the rice cream to the mold and press down lightly. Layer the cherry gelatin on top, and refrigerate until it has set. Turn the rice pudding out of the mold after 6 hours.

BLACKBERRY FOAM

Yield: 4 servings
¾ cup sweet red wine
1 cup apple juice
¼ cup sugar
1 cinnamon stick
½ cup cornstarch
4 egg whites
1½ cups blackberries, picked over

In a large saucepan, bring the red wine, ⅔ of the apple juice, the sugar, and the cinnamon stick to a boil. Stir the cornstarch together with the remaining apple juice, then mix it into the boiling wine mixture. Bring the liquid to a boil again. Beat the egg whites until stiff, and fold them into the wine cream. Bring the liquid to a boil again.

Set aside ¼ cup of berries and stir the rest into the foam. Refrigerate until serving, then garnish with the fresh, reserved blackberries.

GRAPEFRUIT WITH MARSALA GELATIN

Yield: 4 servings
2 grapefruit
1 cup Marsala wine
2½ tablespoons sugar
½ package unflavored gelatin
4 teaspoons maple syrup

Halve the grapefruit, remove the fruit and the white pith between the segments, collecting the juice. Reserve the shells of the grapefruit. Add enough Marsala to the juice to make 1¼ cups of liquid. Dissolve the sugar in the grapefruit juice mixture. Add 2 tablespoons of water to the gelatin, then dissolve over low heat in 3 tablespoons of grapefruit liquid. Stir in the remaining grapefruit liquid, pour into a mold, and refrigerate for 6 hours. Clean the inside of the grapefruit halves.

Cut the gelatin into bite-size pieces and spoon into the grapefruit halves. Add grapefruit sections, and 1 teaspoon of maple syrup to each one.

CHOCOLATE MOUSSE

Yield: 6–8 servings
3½ ounces milk chocolate
3½ ounces bittersweet chocolate
3 eggs, separated
4 tablespoons confectioners' sugar
1 cup heavy cream
Grated chocolate for garnish

Melt the chocolate in the top of a double boiler. Using a wire whisk, beat the egg yolks and 2 tablespoons of confectioners' sugar until they form a light-colored cream. Fold in the melted chocolate evenly with a whisk. With the whisk, beat the egg whites with the remaining confectioners' sugar until they are very stiff; fold them into the chocolate cream.

Whip the cream until it is stiff, and fold into the mixture. Place the mousse in the refrigerator to set for 3 hours. Garnish with grated chocolate and whipped cream.

ZABAGLIONE

Yield: 4–6 servings
4 egg yolks
¼ cup sugar
½ cup Marsala or port wine

In the top of a double boiler, beat the sugar and egg yolks together. Once the mixture becomes foamy or thick, beat Marsala into the mixture. Refrigerate.

CRÈME CARAMEL

Yield: 6 servings
¾ cup sugar
½ teaspoon lemon juice
1 cup milk
1 cup heavy cream
3 eggs
3 egg yolks
2 teaspoons vanilla extract
¼ cup sugar

Preheat the oven to 325°F. Heat the sugar with 1 tablespoon water and the lemon juice, stirring constantly, until the sugar dissolves and becomes nut brown. Pour the hot caramel into a warmed mold with smooth sides, and swirl it around until the caramel has covered the whole mold.

Warm the milk and the cream; stir in the eggs, the egg yolks, and the vanilla. Pour the mixture into the mold. Heat water in a saucepan until it is almost boiling, then place the caramel mold in it and simmer for 10 minutes. To finish, bake for about 50 minutes. Allow the caramel to cool before it is turned out onto a decorative serving platter.

MARQUISE ALICE

Yield: 4–6 servings
4 egg yolks
¾ cup sugar
1½ cups milk
½ package unflavored gelatin
¼ cup apricot jam
2 egg whites
½ cup heavy cream

In the top of a double boiler, beat ¼ cup sugar and the egg yolks until foamy; add the milk and stir over heat until the mixture thickens. Soften the gelatin in 1 tablespoon cold water, then dissolve it in the hot cream. Strain the jam through a sieve, and stir 3 tablespoons of it into the cream. Pour this into a shallow mold, and place it in the refrigerator for 6 hours. Remove the mixture from the mold.

Beat the egg whites and the remaining sugar until stiff. Gradually beat in the heavy cream, and layer this mixture onto the egg yolk cream. Using a pastry bag, pipe the remaining jam in spirals onto the whipped cream. Serve immediately.

MOCHA SPONGE

Yield: 6–8 servings
2 tablespoons instant mocha coffee powder
3 eggs, separated
3 tablespoons honey
½ pound Ricotta cheese
1 thin sponge cake
1 tablespoon cocoa powder

In a saucepan, bring the mocha powder and ¾ cup of water to a boil, then allow it to cool.

Whip the egg yolks and the honey until foamy, and stir in the Ricotta. Beat the egg whites until stiff, then stir them into the cream. Spoon a third of this mixture into a shallow dish. Arrange a thin layer of sponge cake on top, and sprinkle with the mocha cream. Dust the cake with a little cocoa powder over the cake, and cover with the remaining cream. Refrigerate before serving. To serve, dust each portion with cocoa powder.

CHARLOTTE ROUSSE

Yield: 6 servings
2 cups milk
1 teaspoon vanilla extract
4 egg yolks
½ cup sugar
1½ packages unflavored gelatin
2 tablespoons orange juice
1 8- to 10-ounce can apricots
15 ladyfingers
3 tablespoons apricot liqueur
2 cups heavy cream

Combine the milk and vanilla in a saucepan and bring to a boil. Beat the egg yolk and sugar until foamy; gradually add the hot milk. Mix the gelatin with 2 tablespoons cold water. Mix the gelatin with the orange juice, and stir over low heat until the gelatin is dissolved. Allow to cool, and then add it to the cream. Allow the mixture to cool.

Drain the apricots and puree them in a food processor. Line a smooth-sided charlotte rousse mold with ladyfingers, and sprinkle with apricot liqueur.

Fold the heavy cream into the egg mixture, and put aside 3 tablespoons for garnishing. Spoon one third of the mixture into the mold, and spread with half of the apricot puree. Repeat this procedure, and top with the last third of the cream. Let set in the refrigerator for 24 hours. To serve, remove from the charlotte rousse mold, and garnish with whipped cream.

MARZIPAN TIMBALE WITH MIXED BERRIES

Yield: 6 servings
1 cup blanched, ground almonds
Red food coloring
8 ounces marzipan
1 1/4 packages unflavored gelatin
5 tablespoons almond liqueur
4 tablespoons sugar
1 cup sour cream
1 pound mixed fresh berries (raspberries, blackberries, and blueberries)
2 cups heavy cream

Knead the almonds and a few drops red food coloring with the marzipan mix on a work surface dusted with confectioners' sugar. Place this mixture between sheets of plastic wrap, and roll out a very thin layer. (photograph 1). Line a dome-shaped dish with the sheet of marzipan (photograph 2). Trim the edges, knead the cut-off marzipan, and roll it out to fit the base of the dish.

Soften the gelatin in 2 tablespoons of cold water for about 10 minutes. Dissolve the gelatin mixture in the almond liqueur over low heat. Stir in 3 tablespoons of sugar; allow to cool. Stir in the sour cream, and cool in the refrigerator.

Pick over the berries. Stir three-quarters of the berries into the sour cream mixture. Whip half the heavy cream until stiff, and fold it into the sour cream mixture. Spoon into the marzipan-lined mold and cover with the marzipan "lid" (photograph 3). Place in the refrigerator overnight.

To serve, carefully turn the timbale out onto a plate. Whip the remaining cream with 1 tablespoon of sugar until stiff, and use it for garnishing the timbale (photograph 4). Decorate with the remaining berries.

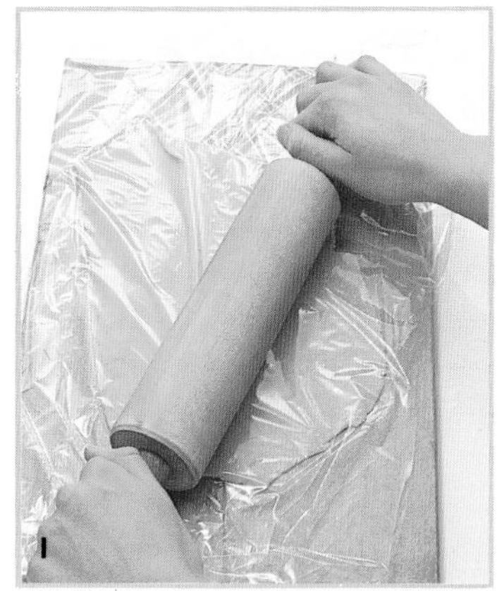
1

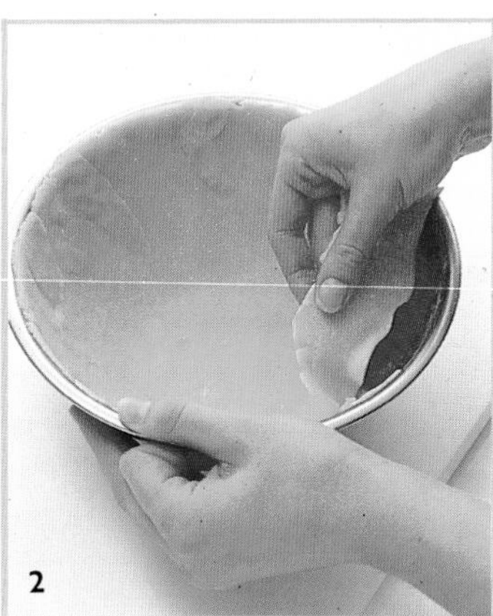
2

3

4

ORANGE BLOSSOM BAVAROISE

Yield: 4–6 servings
3 eggs, separated
3 tablespoons honey
1 cup milk
1¼ packages unflavored gelatin
½ cup orange blossom water
6 tablespoons sugar
1 teaspoon vanilla extract
1 cup heavy cream
Fruit or herb blossoms for garnishing

Beat the egg yolk and the honey together until foamy. Heat the milk in the top of a double boiler, and add the egg-yolk mixture to it. Stir until the mixture thickens. Soften the gelatin in 2 tablespoons cold water for about 10 minutes. Dissolve the gelatin mixture in the hot cream, and stir in the orange blossom water. Leave the mixture in the refrigerator until the cream begins to set.

Beat the egg whites until they are stiff. Beat in the sugar and the vanilla extract, and gently fold the mixture into the cream. Whip the heavy cream until stiff, and fold it into the cream mixture. Turn into a serving dish and refrigerate. Garnish with fruit or herb blossoms.

CHOCOLATE PARFAIT

Yield: 6 servings
For the parfait:
4 ounces milk chocolate
2 ounces bittersweet chocolate
5 egg yolks
4 tablespoons apricot liqueur
1 cup heavy cream
For the sauce:
1 16-ounce can apricot halves
1 tablespoon apricot liqueur
1 cup heavy cream
1 teaspoon vanilla extract

Combine 2 ounces of the milk chocolate with the dark chocolate, and stir until melted in the top of a double boiler. Remove from heat. Cream the chocolate and the egg yolks together with a wire whisk. Stir in the apricot liqueur and allow the mixture to cool. Whip 1 cup of heavy cream until stiff. Chop the remaining milk chocolate into small pieces, and fold it into the chocolate mixture together with the whipped cream. Turn the mixture into a container, and freeze.

Drain the apricots and puree them in a food processor. Stir in the apricot liqueur. Whip 1 cup of heavy cream and the vanilla together, and divide evenly among 6 parfait dishes. Do the same with the apricot puree.

Scoop out chocolate parfait balls, with an ice-cream scoop, and place in the parfait glasses. Garnish with chocolate flakes and apricot pieces.

DOUBLE MELON SORBET

Yield: 6 servings
For the honeydew sorbet:
¼ ripe honeydew melon
¾ cup sugar
1 tablespoon honey
3 tablespoons almond liqueur
⅛ teaspoon ground ginger
For the watermelon sorbet:
1 slice watermelon
¼ cup sugar
3 tablespoons Crème de Cassis liqueur
⅛ teaspoon ground cinnamon
For the sauce:
½ cup sour cream
2 tablespoons lemon juice
1 teaspoon grated lemon peel
Plus:
5 kiwis
10 chocolate cookie rolls

Cut the honeydew melon away from the rind and remove the seeds. Puree in a food processor with ¼ cup sugar, honey, almond

liqueur, and ginger. Turn into a freezer container, then freeze.

Cut the watermelon away from the rind and remove the seeds. Puree with the sugar, cassis liqueur, and cinnamon. Turn the puree into a freezer container, and freeze. To prevent ice crystals from forming, beat the mixture with a whisk every 20 minutes.

Peel the kiwis, cut into slices, and arrange on 6 plates.

Stir the sour cream with the lemon juice, lemon peel, and 3 tablespoons of sugar, and divide evenly among the 6 plates. Spoon portions of both sorbets onto each plate, using an ice-cream scoop. Serve with chocolate cookies.

RED CURRANT GRANITA

Yield: 4 servings
2 cups red currants
½ cup water
1 teaspoon vanilla extract
5 tablespoons honey
1¾ cups sweet white wine

Pick over the currants, and wash them. Reserve ¼ cup for garnishing. Boil the berries with the water and vanilla for about 10 minutes. Drain the berries, reserving the liquid. Sweeten the liquid with honey, and strain it through a dampened muslin cheesecloth to clarify. Freeze in a shallow, flexible mold.

When the ice is hard, scrape it off in flakes with a wooden spoon, or crush it in an ice crusher. Spoon it into 4 glasses. Add white wine, and garnish with the reserved red currants.

THREE-LAYER ICE BOMBE

Yield: 4–6 servings
For the apple and pistachio ice cream:
2 apples
¼ cup chopped pistachio nuts
2 egg yolks
¼ cup sugar
2 tablespoons honey
2 drops green food coloring
1⅔ cups heavy cream
For the raspberry and almond ice cream:
¾ cup raspberries, picked over
1 egg yolk
2 tablespoons sugar
1 tablespoon almond liqueur
¼ cup ground almonds
½ cup heavy cream
For the marzipan center:
1 egg yolk
1½ tablespoons sugar
3 ounces marzipan
1 tablespoon sweet sherry
½ cup heavy cream
Plus:
Heavy cream
¼ cup raspberries
Marzipan leaves

Preheat the oven to 400°F. Wrap the apples in foil, and bake for 30 minutes. Allow the apples to cool, remove the skin, and puree in a food processor. Mix the pistachio nuts into the puree. Beat the 2 egg yolks, sugar, and honey until foamy, and tint with the green food coloring. Beat 1⅔ cups heavy cream until it is stiff, and mix together with the apple puree and the egg mixture. Turn the mixture into a freezer container and freeze.

To make the raspberry ice cream, puree the raspberries and strain out the seeds. Beat 1 egg yolk and the sugar together until foamy. Stir in the almond liqueur and the almonds, and add this mixture to the raspberries. Beat ½ cup heavy cream until stiff, and fold into the marzipan mixture. Freeze in an ice cream bombe mold.

Layer the apple and pistachio ice cream into the frozen mold, and press it against the sides with a spoon. Freeze again. After 30 minutes, add the raspberry and almond ice cream, pressing it against the apple ice cream with a spoon. Freeze again for 30 minutes.

Fill the mold with the marzipan ice cream, and freeze for 2 hours. Dip the mold in hot water to loosen the bombe. Turn it out, and place the ice cream in the freezer again. Garnish with whipped cream, rasp-

ICE CREAM CONFECTIONERY WITH DATES AND FIGS

Yield: 4 servings
3 heaping tablespoons slivered almonds, toasted
⅔ cup mixed candied fruit
¼ cup sugar
½ cup rose water
3 tablespoons honey
3 egg whites
1 cup heavy cream
12 fresh dates
3 figs
Chocolate ice cream glaze for garnish

Finely chop the candied fruit. In the top of a double boiler, gently heat the sugar and the rose water to make a thickish syrup; stir in the honey. Beat the egg white until stiff, and gradually beat in the boiling hot syrup. Continue to beat it in a double boiler until it is stiff and hard. Mix it with the warm almonds and the candied fruit. Whip the heavy cream until it is very stiff, and fold it into the mixture. Pour into a rectangular mold, and freeze it. When it is frozen through, dip the mold in hot water.

Cut the ice cream first into slices and then into sticks, and then allow it to freeze again.

Peel the dates, halve them, and remove the pits. Halve the figs. Put the chocolate ice cream glaze into a bowl and dip the ice cream sticks in it to cover them halfway. To serve, arrange the ice cream sticks on a plate with the fruit.

CASSATA

Yield: 8 servings
1 quart cherry ice cream
2 tablespoons cherry liqueur
1 quart almond and caramel ice cream
2 tablespoons whole almonds
⅓ cup cherries
1 quart vanilla ice cream
Heavy cream for garnish

Place an ice cream mold in the freezer for 1 hour. Stir the liqueur into the cherry ice cream, and press it into the sides of the mold, using a spatula to spread evenly and smoothly. Place in the freezer for about 30 minutes.

Mix the almonds into the almond ice cream, and press into the layer of cherry ice cream. Freeze for about 30 minutes.

Pit and chop the cherries, reserving some whole cherries for garnishing. Mix the cherries with the vanilla ice cream, and layer the ice cream into the mold. Smooth it, and place in the freezer for 1 hour. To serve, dip the mold in hot water, and remove the ice cream. Garnish with whipped cream and cherries before serving.

CLASSIC CUISINE

This tempting selection of international dishes presents recipes that best characterize the cooking traditions of their respective countries and that have also become well-known in international cuisine. Ratatouille, photographed here, originates in southern France.

RATATOUILLE

Yield: 4 to 6 servings

2 large Spanish onions, peeled and thinly sliced
2 cloves garlic, peeled and thinly sliced
4 small plum tomatoes, peeled, seeded, and diced
4 zucchini, cut in large cubes
2 medium eggplants, peeled and cut in large cubes
3 red peppers, cored, seeded, and cut in large cubes
3 green peppers, cored, seeded, and cut in large cubes
2 cups olive oil
Salt
Pepper
1 bunch fresh thyme, finely chopped

Heat the olive oil in a frying pan. Sauté the vegetables for 3 minutes in the hot oil; season with salt, pepper, and thyme to taste. Simmer for 15 to 20 minutes.

Serve hot or cold, as a side dish or main course.

LEG OF LAMB PROVENÇAL

Yield: 4 servings

1 boneless leg of lamb (about 1¾ pounds)
Salt
Pepper
1 bunch fresh rosemary, finely chopped
1 bunch fresh basil, finely chopped
1 bunch fresh thyme, finely chopped
2 cloves garlic, peeled and finely chopped
4 to 5 tablespoons olive oil

Remove the skin and sinews from the lamb. Season it with salt, pepper, herbs, and garlic.

Preheat the oven to 325°F. Heat the olive oil in a roasting pan. Add the lamb and roast it covered for 30 to 40 minutes, or until its juices run clear.

DUCK À L'ORANGE

Yield: 4 servings
1 (2-to 2½-pound) duck
Salt
Pepper
1 tablespoon peanut oil
3 oranges
1 cup Basic Stock (see Index)
2 tablespoons orange liqueur
1 sprig fresh thyme, finely chopped
Sugar

Preheat the oven to 400°F.

Season the duck, inside and out, with salt and pepper. Heat the oil in a roasting pan. Add the duck and roast it covered, breast side down, for about 1 hour, or until its juices run clear. Remove from the pan and keep warm.

Cut paper-thin strips from the oranges. Quarter the oranges and remove the pulp, collecting the juice.

Combine the basic stock, orange juice, orange pulp, orange peel strips, and liqueur. Cook until the liquid has been reduced by one-third. Add thyme, salt, pepper, and sugar to taste. Carve the duck and serve with the sauce on the side.

1

2

3

4

BOUILLABAISE

Yield: 4 to 6 servings
8 ounces red snapper
8 ounces monk fish
8 ounces fresh sardines
10 to 15 shrimp
2 bay leaves
1 onion, peeled and cut in rings
1 fennel bulb
2 tomatoes
4 shallots, peeled
2 cloves garlic, peeled
2 to 3 tablespoons olive oil
4 tablespoons dry vermouth
4 tablespoons Pernod
Salt
Pepper

Rinse the fish with cold water and cut out the fillets (photograph 1). Put the bones and heads to one side to use for the stock. Cut the fillets in pieces.

Place the shrimp, bay leaves, and onion rings in boiling water for 3 minutes (photograph 2). Remove the shells from the shrimp, but reserve them.

Bring the fish heads, bones, and shrimp shells to a boil in 8 cups of water; boil until the liquid has been reduced by one-half. Strain the stock through a piece of cheesecloth.

Dice the fennel bulb, tomatoes, shallots, and garlic (photograph 3). Heat the olive oil and gently sauté the vegetables (photograph 4). Add the fish and shrimp (photograph 5). Stir in the fish stock, vermouth, and Pernod; season to taste with salt and pepper. Simmer gently for about 5 minutes before serving.

5

6

COQ AU VIN

Yield: 6 servings
2 chickens (2 pounds each), quartered
Salt
Pepper
2 tablespoons flour
3 tablespoons peanut oil
4 tablespoons butter
¾ cup button mushrooms, sliced
1 cup pearl onions
1 cup dry red wine
1 bay leaf
1 sprig fresh thyme, chopped
1 ⅓ cups heavy cream

Season the chicken with salt and pepper, and dust with flour. Heat the oil in a large frying pan and sauté the chicken pieces on all sides. Remove them from the pan and pour off the fat.

Melt 1½ tablespoons of the butter in the pan. Sauté the mushrooms and pearl onions gently in the butter. Add the red wine and bring to a boil.

Return the chicken pieces to the pan. Add the bay leaf, thyme, and cream. Simmer gently over very low heat for 30 to 35 minutes. Remove the chicken pieces and keep warm.

Allow the sauce to cool slightly. Add the rest of the butter to the sauce a little at a time; swirl until the butter has melted completely. Season to taste with salt and pepper. Place the chicken on a serving platter and cover with sauce.

OSSO BUCCO

Yield: 4 servings
½ cup olive oil
4 slices calf's tail with bone
1 tablespoon butter
1 carrot, cut in lengthwise strips
1 stick celery, cut in lengthwise strips
1 small leek, cut in rings
1 onion, peeled and diced
¼ cup dry white wine
4 cups meat stock
3 small plum tomatoes, skinned, seeded, and diced
1 bunch parsley, finely chopped
1 clove garlic, peeled and diced
½ teaspoon grated lemon peel
Salt
Pepper

Heat the olive oil in a frying pan and brown the meat on all sides.

Melt the butter in a roasting pan. Gently cook the carrot, celery, leek, and onion in the butter. Stir in the white wine and bring the mixture to a boil. Add the meat, meat juices, stock, and tomatoes to the vegetables.

Bake the meat, covered, in a preheated 350°F oven for 1½ hours. Just before the meat has finished cooking, add the parsley, garlic, and lemon peel. Season to taste with salt and pepper before serving.

MINESTRONE

Yield: 4 servings
3 tablespoons olive oil
1 small cauliflower, separated into florets
2 small heads broccoli, separated into florets
4 carrots, peeled and sliced
2 stalks celery, diced
1 large Spanish onion, peeled and cut in strips
1 leek, cut into rings
3 small plum tomatoes, skinned, seeded, and cut in eighths
1 clove garlic, peeled
4 cups beef stock
Salt
Pepper

Heat the olive oil in a frying pan and gently sauté the vegetables. Stir in the garlic and stock.

Simmer gently over medium heat for about 20 minutes. Season to taste with salt and pepper before serving.

SALTIMBOCCA

Yield: 6 to 8 servings
8 veal scallops
8 sage fresh leaves
8 slices Parma ham, folded in half
Salt
Pepper
1 to 2 tablespoons flour
3 tablespoons olive oil
2 cups Basic Stock (see Index)
2 tablespoons dry vermouth

Lay the veal scallops side by side on a platter. Place a sage leaf and a folded ham slice on each scallop and fasten them with toothpicks.

Heat the oil and sauté the scallops for 2 to 3 minutes on each side. Remove the scallops from the pan and keep warm.

Pour off the fat from the pan juices. Add the stock and vermouth to the pan juices and bring to a boil. If necessary, add more seasoning to the sauce. Serve the veal scallops with the sauce.

POLLO AL DIABOLO

Yield: 4 to 6 servings
2 (2 pounds each) chickens
2 tablespoons hot mustard
Salt
Pepper
Cayenne pepper
1 sprig fresh rosemary, finely chopped
3 tablespoons olive oil

Cut the chickens open along the backbone (photograph 1), using a pair of poultry shears. Remove the backbones (photograph 2), but leave on the legs and wings. With a mallet, lightly pound the chickens flat (photograph 3). Season them with salt, pepper, cayenne pepper, and rosemary.

Heat the oil in a large frying pan and sauté the chickens, skin side down. Continue to sauté the chickens for 10 to 15 minutes, turning them once. Serve hot.

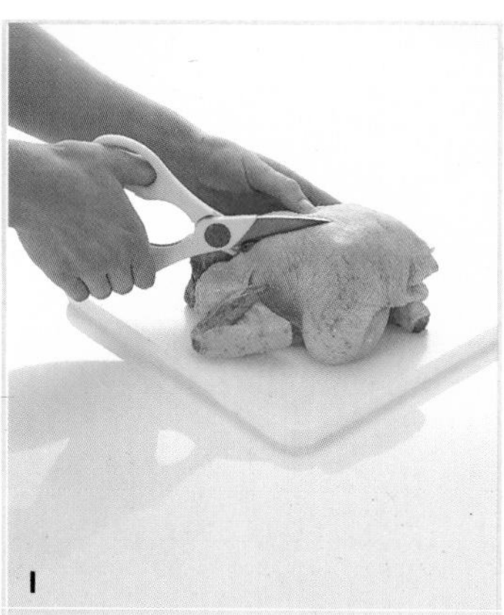

1

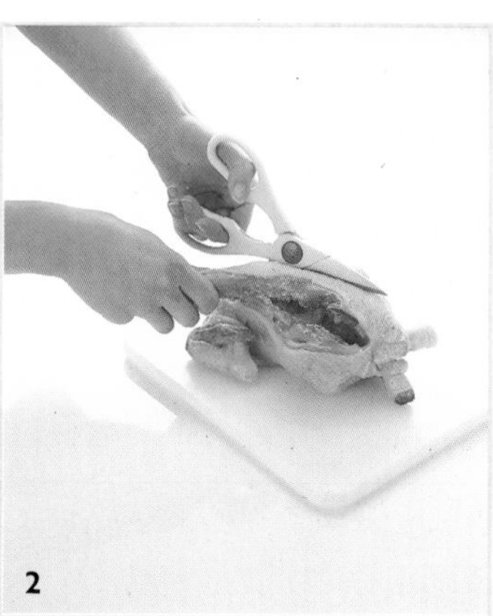

2

3

RABBIT IN OLIVE SAUCE

Yield: 4 to 6 servings
1 3-pound rabbit, cut in 8 pieces
Salt
Pepper
4 tablespoons olive oil
2 carrots, peeled and cut in small pieces
¼ cup celery, cut in small pieces
2 medium onions, peeled and diced
2 tomatoes, skinned, seeded, and cut in large pieces
30 pitted black olives, quartered
2 cups dry white wine
2 cups chicken stock
1 sprig fresh rosemary, finely chopped
1 cup sour cream

Heat the oil in a large frying pan. Brown the rabbit pieces on all sides. Add the vegetables and sauté them for 3 minutes. Stir in the white wine, olive quarters, stock, and rosemary. Simmer the rabbit and vegetables over a very low heat for about 1 hour, or until tender. Remove the rabbit from the pan and keep warm.

Puree the sauce in a blender or food processor. Stir in the sour cream and heat the sauce until it thickens. If necessary, add seasoning to taste. Arrange the rabbit on a serving platter and serve with the sauce on the side.

ZARZUELA

Yield: 4 servings
2 pounds mussels
4 squid
3 tablespoons olive oil
2 shallots, peeled and finely diced
2 cloves garlic, peeled and finely diced
¼ cup parsley, finely chopped
3 small plum tomatoes, skinned, seeded, and diced
8 shrimp, shelled and deveined
½ pound haddock fillet, diced
2 tablespoons sherry
Lemon juice
Salt
Pepper
16 green olives

Thoroughly scrub the mussels in cold water (photograph 1). Place them in 4 cups of boiling water and cook for 3 to 4 minutes, or until the shells open. Remove the mussels from the shells, discaring any that have not opened, and set aside the cooking liquid.

Rinse the squid and cut them in rings (photograph 2).

Heat the oil and gently sauté the shallots, garlic, parsley, and tomatoes for 3 minutes. Add the mussels, squid, shrimp, and fish. Stir in the reserved cooking liquid from the mussels, being careful not to add the sand remaining in the bottom of the pan. Season with sherry, lemon juice, salt, and pepper (photograph 3). Add the olives and simmer for 10 to 15 minutes (photograph 4). Serve the Zarzuela in an attractive casserole dish.

1

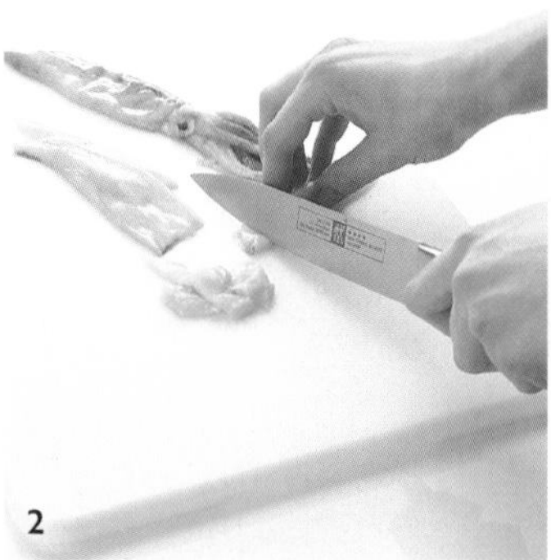
2

3

4

PORK WITH MUSSELS

Yield: 4 to 6 servings
2 pounds mussels
4 tablespoons dry vermouth
4 tablespoons olive oil
2 red peppers, diced
1 onion, peeled and finely diced
3 cloves garlic, peeled and finely diced
1 pound pork, cut into ¼-inch strips
Salt
Pepper

Scrub the mussels thoroughly in cold water. Bring 2 cups of water and the vermouth to a boil; cook the mussels until the shells open, approximately 3 minutes. Remove the mussels from their shells, discarding any that have not opened, and reserve the cooking liquid.

Heat the oil in a frying pan and sauté the pork over high heat. Remove the pork and keep warm.

Heat the remaining oil and gently sauté the peppers, onion, and garlic for 3 minutes. Add the mussel liquid, being careful not to add the sand remaining in the bottom of the pan. Boil the mixture for 5 minutes. Add the pork and mussels and simmer until they are heated through. Do not allow the mixture to continue to boil, or the mussels will toughen. Season to taste with salt and pepper before serving.

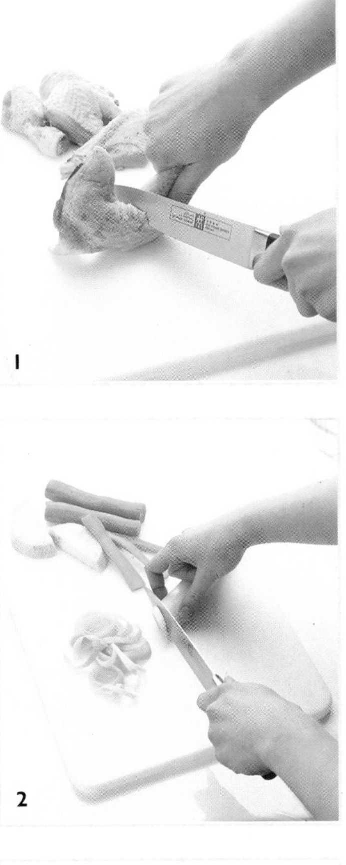

1

2

3

4

CHICKEN ON A RACK OF VEGETABLES

Yield: 6 servings
1 (2½ pound) chicken, cut in 8 pieces
Salt
Pepper
1 leek, cut in rings
1 onion, peeled and diced
1 carrot, peeled and cut in small cubes
½ cup celery, cut in small cubes
2 tablespoons butter
2 tablespoons chopped parsley
½ cup chicken stock
2 egg yolks

Season the chicken with salt and pepper.

Melt the butter in a Dutch oven, and spread the vegetables and the parsley over it. Place the chicken pieces on top (photograph 3); add the chicken stock. Cover the pot, keeping the lid slightly ajar. Allow the mixture to simmer over low heat for 1 hour.

Remove the chicken from the pan. Pour the egg yolks into the sauce in a thin stream, stirring constantly to thicken the sauce (photograph 4). Add the chicken and serve immediately.

BREAST OF BEEF WITH VEGETABLES

Yield: 4 to 6 servings
4 cups beef stock
1½ pounds breast of beef
2 pounds carrots, peeled and cut in small pieces
1 pound onions, peeled and chopped
2 pounds potatoes, peeled and cut in small pieces
2 tablespoons butter
Salt
Pepper

Pour the stock into a large Dutch oven. Add the meat and simmer over very low heat for 1 hour. Add the carrots and onions; cook for another 20 minutes. Remove the meat from the stock and keep warm.

Pour the carrots, onions, and stock through a sieve; reserve the stock.

Place the potatoes in the stock; cook for 15 to 20 minutes, or until tender. Strain the potatoes and again reserve the stock.

Mash the potatoes, onions, and carrots, stirring in the butter and reserved stock to make a creamy puree. Heat the puree and season to taste with salt and pepper. Slice the meat, arrange on the puree, and serve.

1

2

3

4

ROAST BEEF WITH YORKSHIRE PUDDING

Yield: 4 servings
For the roast beef:
2 pounds round roast of beef
Salt
Coarsely ground black pepper
3 tablespoons peanut oil
For the Yorkshire pudding:
1 cup flour
3 egg yolks
1 cup milk
6 ounces beef kidney fat
3 egg whites, beaten until stiff
White pepper

Preheat the oven to 350°F.

Season the beef with salt and pepper (photograph 1). Heat the oil in a roasting pan and brown the beef in it. Put the beef in the oven and roast for 30 to 45 minutes.

To make the Yorkshire pudding, sift the flour into a bowl. Add the egg yolks and milk (photograph 2). Melt the kidney fat, add it to the mixture, and stir until a smooth batter is formed. Fold the egg whites into the batter. Season with salt and pepper. Pour the batter into ¼ cup molds (photograph 3). Place the molds in the oven for 30 to 40 minutes. Carefully loosen the puddings from the molds with a knife (photograph 4) and turn them out. Place the meat on a serving platter and arrange the Yorkshire puddings around the meat and serve immediately.

IRISH STEW

Yield: 6 servings
12 potatoes, peeled
4 onions, peeled and cut in rings
2½ pounds lamb, cut in pieces
Salt
Freshly ground black pepper
1 sprig fresh thyme, finely chopped
Salt

Cut 4 of the potatoes in slices and cut the rest in quarters. Layer the potato slices in a baking dish. Add half of the onion rings and the meat. Season with salt, pepper, and thyme. Add the remaining onions and potatoes in the pan; season with salt. Pour on 2 cups of water.

Cover the pan with aluminum foil and place a lid on top. Cook in a preheated 350°F oven for about 2½ hours.

The potato slices will disintegrate during the cooking process and thicken the stock. If necessary, add salt to taste.

1

2

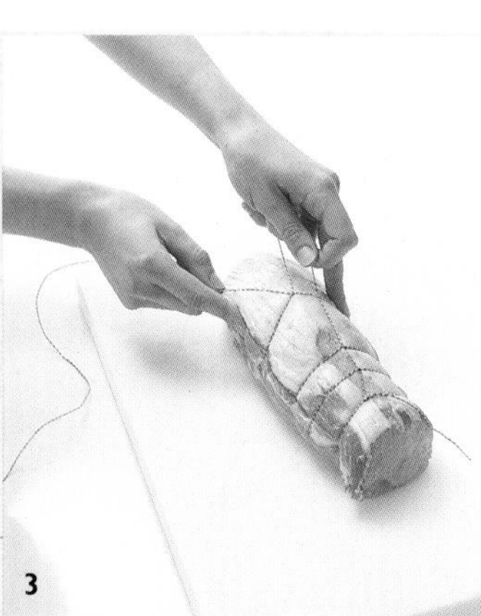

3

4

SADDLE OF PORK WITH PRUNES

Yield: 4 to 6 servings
30 pitted prunes
2 pounds boneless saddle of pork
Salt
Pepper
2 teaspoons ground ginger
2 tablespoons butter
2 cups chicken stock
¼ cup whipping cream

Soak the prunes in cold water for about 1 hour, then drain.

Cut a long slit in the pork (photograph 1); stuff the prunes into the slit (photograph 2). Tie the meat with kitchen string (photograph 3). Rub salt, pepper, and ginger into the meat.

Preheat the oven to 350°F. Melt the butter in a roasting pan and brown the meat on all sides (photograph 4). Add the stock, cover, and place in the oven for 1 hour. Baste with the stock repeatedly throughout the cooking time.

Remove the string from the meat. Let the meat cool for 10 minutes, then slice and keep warm.

Pour the cream into the cooking juices. Bring the liquid to a boil; season with salt, pepper, and ginger. To serve, pour the sauce over the meat.

SHRIMP IN DILL SAUCE

Yield: 4 servings
4 cups Fish Stock (see Index)
1 carrot, peeled and cut in cubes
¼ leek, cut into rings
2 bunches fresh dill, coarsely chopped
6 crushed peppercorns
Lemon juice
1 bay leaf
Salt
20 shrimp, peeled and deveined

Combine the fish stock, vegetables, dill, peppercorns, lemon juice, bay leaf, and salt in a saucepan. Bring to a boil, then add the shrimp. Boil for 5 minutes. Remove the shrimp from the pan. Serve with French bread and butter.

PEARS, BEANS, AND BACON

Yield: 4 to 6 servings
1 pound bacon
½ teaspoon black peppercorns
1 pound string beans, broken into 1½-to 2-inch pieces
4 pears, peeled, cored and quartered
Salt
1 tablespoon cornstarch
Pepper
1 tablespoon chopped parsley

Bring 2 cups of water to a boil in a saucepan. Add the bacon and peppercorns; simmer over medium heat for 30 minutes. Pour in more water as it evaporates. Add the beans, pears, and salt to taste; cook for 25 to 30 minutes longer. Remove the bacon, beans, and pears and reserve the stock. Cut the bacon in slices and arrange it in a warm dish with the pears and beans.

Mix the cornstarch with 1 tablespoon cold water; stir it into the reserved stock. Season with pepper.

To serve, pour the stock into serving dishes. Spoon some bacon, beans, and pears into each dish. Sprinkle with parsley.

SMOKED PORK WITH PICKLED CABBAGE

Yield: 4 to 6 servings
1 pound smoked pork
2 tablespoons pork drippings
1 medium onion, peeled and diced
1 pound sauerkraut
1 apple, peeled, cored, and diced
12 juniper berries, tied in a cheesecloth bag
1 cup dry white wine
½ cup meat stock
1 pound bacon
2 tablespoons cherry liqueur
4 pork sausages

In a saucepan, boil the smoked pork in 4 cups of water for about 1 hour.

Melt the drippings in a frying pan and sauté the onion until transparent. Add the sauerkraut and continue sautéing for 5 minutes. Add the apple, juniper berries, white wine, stock, bacon, and cherry liqueur; simmer for 40 minutes. Put the sausages in the pan and simmer for 25 minutes more.

Place the sauerkraut in a dish. Remove the juniper berries.

To serve, slice the pork and the bacon and arrange on the sauerkraut with the sausages.

SAUERBRATEN

Yield: 4 to 6 servings
2 pounds lean beef
1 medium carrot, peeled and coarsely chopped
2 celery stalks, coarsely chopped
1 small bunch parsley, coarsely chopped
1 medium onion, peeled and coarsely chopped
1 cup white wine vinegar
3 slices bacon, diced
1/4 cup seedless raisins
3 tablespoons crumbled honey cake
1 bay leaf
3 level tablespoons flour
Salt
Pepper

For the marinade, bring 2 cups of water, the vinegar, and vegetables to a boil in a saucepan. Let the mixture cool, then pour it over the meat. Marinate the meat in the refrigerator for 3 to 4 days, turning it daily.

Set the meat aside and strain the marinade through a sieve.

Sauté the bacon lightly to render the fat. Brown the meat on all sides in the bacon fat. Pour off the fat. Combine 1½ cups of the marinade and ½ cup of water. Pour ¼ cup of this mixture over the meat. Braise the meat for about 1½ hours, adding more liquid gradually. Add the raisins, honey cake, and bay leaf; and braise for another hour.

Remove the meat and slice it.

Stir the flour together with 4 tablespoons of cold water; add it to the pan liquids and stir until thickened. Season to taste with salt, pepper, and sugar.

1

2

3

SADDLE OF VENISON

Yield: 6 to 8 servings
1 (2½-pound) saddle of venison
3 tablespoons peanut oil
1 large onion, peeled and diced
1 celery stalk, cut in cubes
1 large carrot, peeled and cut in cubes
5 crushed juniper berries
Salt
Pepper
2 large pears
¾ cup sweet white wine
Juice of 1 lemon
¾ cup dry red wine
1½ cups whipping cream
½ cup cranberry preserves

Remove the skin and sinews from the venison (photograph 1). Heat the oil in a roasting pan and brown the meat on all sides. Add the diced vegetables, juniper berries, salt, and pepper. Bake in a preheated 400°F oven for 45 minutes. Remove the meat from the pan and keep warm. Drain the vegetables, reserving the roasting juices.

Wash and halve the pears, and remove the cores (photograph 2). Gently poach the pears in the white wine and lemon juice for about 10 minutes.

Combine the red wine and the reserved roasting juices; bring to a boil. Puree the vegetables in a food processor and add them to the liquid. Stir in the cream and 2 tablespoons of cranberry preserves; continue boiling until the liquid thickens.

Strain the sauce through a fine sieve (photograph 3). Season again with salt and pepper to taste.

To serve, carve the venison and arrange on a platter. Fill the pear halves with cranberry preserves and arrange around the meat. Serve the sauce separately.

STUFFED BREAST OF VEAL

Yield: 6 to 8 servings
5 slices toasted bread
¼ cup milk
2 large onions, peeled, 1 of them diced
1 tablespoon butter
1 pound sausage meat
2 tablespoons chopped parsley
2 eggs
Salt
Pepper
Grated nutmeg
1 (4-to 4½-pound) breast of veal, with a pocket cut in it
2 tablespoons sausage drippings
2 celery stalks, diced
1 large carrot, peeled and diced

Remove the crusts from the bread, cut it into cubes, and pour hot milk over them.

In a frying pan, melt the butter and sauté the diced onion until transparent.

Mix the bread, onion, sausage meat, parsley, and eggs together. Season with salt, pepper, and nutmeg.

Season the veal with salt and pepper. Spoon the stuffing into the pocket in the veal; sew it closed with kitchen string. Heat the sausage drippings in a roasting pan and sauté the veal on all sides. Add the remaining onion, celery, and carrot. Then place the pan in a preheated 400°F oven. After 5 minutes add ¼ cup of hot water. Roast for about 2 hours, adding a total of 2 cups of hot water, ¼ cup at a time, about every 15 minutes. Remove the veal from the pan and keep warm.

Boil the sauce until it thickens. Pour it through a fine sieve and season again with salt and pepper to taste.

To serve, remove the twine from the breast, cut the meat in slices, and arrange these on the sauce.

OLD-FASHIONED GERMAN POTATO SOUP

Yield: 6 servings
3 tablespoons butter
2 celery stalks, diced
3 large carrots, peeled and diced
1½ pounds potatoes, peeled and diced
4 cups meat stock
2 onions, peeled
1 bay leaf
1 clove
1 leek, cut in rings
¼ cup sour cream
Salt
Pepper
Marjoram
Grated nutmeg
2½ cups chanterelle mushrooms
2 tablespoons chopped fresh herbs (chervil, chives, flat-leaved parsley)

In a large soup pot, melt 1 tablespoon of the butter and gently sauté the celery and carrots for 3 minutes. Add the potatoes and meat stock. Spike 1 onion with the bay leaf and clove. Add it to the pot, cover, and boil for about 20 minutes. Add the leek rings and simmer for 10 minutes. Remove the spiked onion.

Remove a third of the potatoes from the pot and puree them. Stir in the cream into the puree, then add the puree to the soup. Season with salt, pepper, marjoram, and nutmeg.

Finely dice the remaining onion. Gently sauté it for 3 minutes in the remaining butter. Add the mushrooms and sauté for 5 minutes longer. Add the mushroom mixture to the soup. Simmer for 5 minutes, until heated through. Sprinkle with the herbs just before serving.

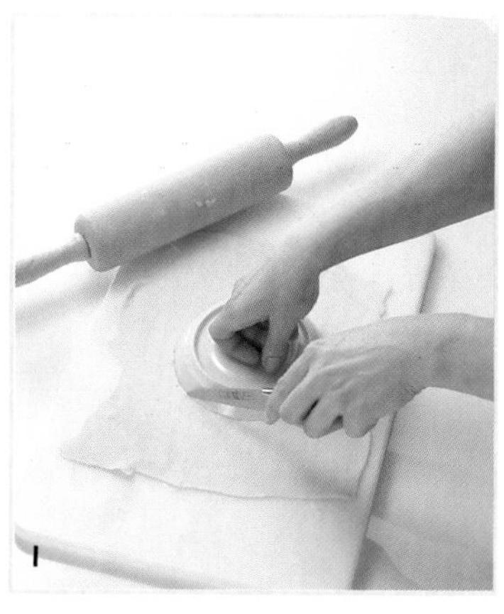
1

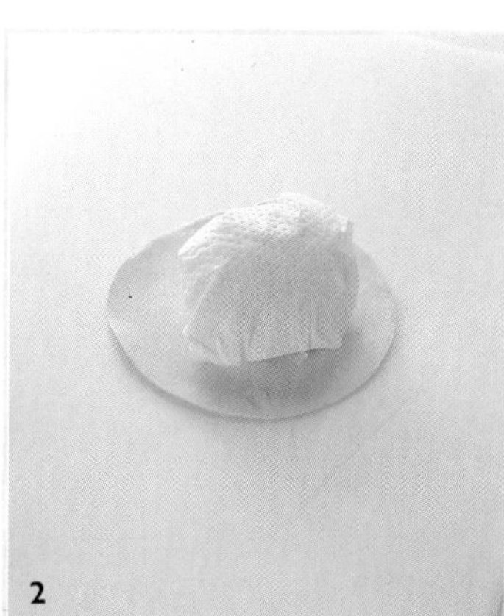
2

3

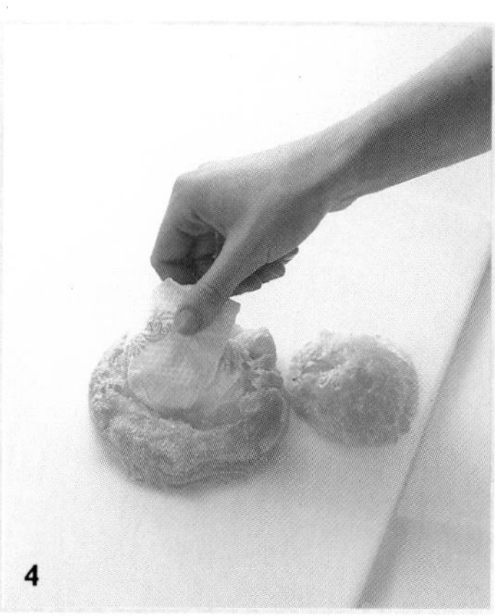
4

VOL AU VENT

Yield: 4 servings
For the pastry shells:
1 pound frozen puff pastry
1 egg, beaten
For the filling:
1 pound lean veal
4 cups water, salted
1 onion, peeled and spiked with 1 bay leaf and 2 cloves
2½ cups sliced mushrooms
1 tablespoon butter
1 (10-ounce) box frozen peas
¾ cup asparagus tips, cooked and coarsely chopped
5 tablespoons whipping cream
Salt
White pepper
Lemon juice
1 tablespoon flour

Place the veal in a pan with 4 cups of water. Add the onion and simmer for 1¼ hours.

Lay the sheets of pastry side by side and allow to thaw. Roll out half of the pastry to a thickness of 1½ to 3 inches. Lay a 10-inch plate on the pastry and cut around it (photograph 1). Cut out a second circle (diameter 10½ inches). Crumple paper towels into a ball and place on the smaller pastry circle (photograph 2).

Brush the edge of the smaller circle with a little beaten egg. Cover the paper towel ball with the second pastry circle (photograph 3) and press the edges together well. Brush the upper surface of the pastry with beaten egg. Place it on a baking pan that has been rinsed with cold water.

Make a second pastry shell from the remaining pastry and place it on the baking pan. Bake in a preheated 400°F oven for about 15 minutes.

In the meantime, remove the veal from the stock and dice it finely. Reserve the stock.

Melt the butter in a frying pan and gently sauté the mushrooms and peas for 3 to 5 minutes. Add the meat and asparagus tips. Mix the flour and 1 tablespoon of cold water together. Add 3 cups of the hot stock and bring to a boil. Pour in the cream and season to taste with salt, pepper, and lemon juice. Add the meat and vegetables and bring to a boil again for 3 to 5 minutes.

Slice the tops off the baked pastry shells and carefully remove the paper towel ball (photograph 4). Fill both shells with the veal mixture and serve at once.

AUSTRIAN POT ROAST

Yield: 6 to 8 servings

For the meat:
- 2 large carrots, peeled and diced
- 4 sprigs parsley
- 4 celery stalks, diced
- 2 onions, peeled, 1 diced and 1 halved
- 1 leek, cut in rings
- 1 bay leaf
- 1 tablespoon peppercorns
- Salt
- 2 pounds beef shoulder

For the sauce:
- 1 slice stale bread
- 1 teaspoon white wine vinegar
- 3 hard-boiled egg yolks
- 2 egg yolks
- 8 tablespoons cooking oil
- Sugar
- White wine vinegar
- Pepper
- 4 tablespoons chopped fresh chives

Place the carrots, parsley, celery, diced onion, leek, bay leaf, and peppercorns in a saucepan. Cover with water. Season with salt and cook over low heat for 10 minutes.

Brown the cut edge of the onion halves in a frying pan. Add to the stock with the meat. Cover and simmer gently for 3 to 4 hours; do not allow to boil.

In the meantime, cut the crusts from the bread, then cut the bread in pieces. Pour ½ cup of water and the white wine vinegar over the bread. Soak for about 30 minutes, then squeeze dry.

Sieve the hard-boiled egg yolks and stir into the bread; sieve again. Stir this mixture together with the egg yolks until foamy. Whisk in the oil, 1 drop at a time. Season the sauce with salt, pepper, white wine vinegar, and sugar. Fold in the chives.

To serve, remove the meat from the stock and cut in slices. Arrange the meat and vegetables in a bowl with a little stock. Serve the sauce separately.

STUFFED VEAL SCALLOPS

Yield: 8 servings
1 cup sliced mushrooms
¾ pound ground veal
8 3½-ounce veal scallops
Salt
Pepper
8 strips bacon
4 tablespoons peanut oil
1 cup Veal Stock (see Index)
¾ cup dry white wine
1 cup whipping cream

Mix the mushrooms with the ground veal. Season with salt and pepper.

Pound the veal scallops lightly to flatten them. Spread the mushroom mixture over the scallops, then roll up and secure each roll with a toothpick. Lard each roll by pulling 1 strip of bacon through each roll with a larding needle.

Heat the oil in a frying pan; sauté the veal rolls on all sides. Add the veal stock and white wine. Braise the rolls for about 40 minutes. Remove from the pan and keep warm.

Pour the cream into the stock and boil until thickened. Add salt and pepper to taste. To serve, pour the sauce over the rolls.

AUSTRIAN DICED PORK

Yield: 8 servings
3 tablespoons peanut oil
2 pounds pork, cut in 1½-inch cubes
2 celery stalks, cut into ¼-inch julienne pieces
4 large carrots, peeled and cut into ¼-inch julienne pieces
2 large onions, peeled and sliced
Salt
6 peppercorns
1 sprig fresh thyme
4 tablespoons white wine vinegar
4 cups beef stock
1 pound potatoes, peeled and cubed
2 tablespoons butter
¼ cup grated horseradish
4 tablespoons bread crumbs

Heat the oil in a saucepan and brown the meat on all sides. Add the vegetables and sauté them for 5 minutes. Season with salt, peppercorns, and thyme. Add the vinegar and beef stock; simmer for 40 minutes. Add the potatoes and simmer for 25 minutes longer.

Melt the butter in a frying pan and sauté the horseradish and bread crumbs. Before serving, pour the horseradish mixture over the pork, or serve it separately.

ROAST BEEF WITH MUSTARD SAUCE

Yield: 6 to 8 servings
2½ pounds rump roast beef
¼ cup pork drippings
1 large onion, peeled and diced
2 large carrots, peeled and cut in strips
2 celery stalks, cut in strips
1 medium leek, cut in rings
1 bay leaf
1 teaspoon salt
½ teaspoon pepper
2 tablespoons butter
Juice of ½ lemon
1 tablespoon mustard
1 cup sour cream
1 tablespoon chopped parsley

Brown the beef on all sides in the pork drippings. Remove the meat from the pan. Sauté the onion and half of the other vegetables in the fat for 3 minutes. Add 1¼ cups of water, the bay leaf, salt, and pepper. Return the beef to the pan. Cover and simmer over low heat for 40 minutes. Remove the cooked meat from the pan and keep warm. Reserve the stock.

Melt the butter and gently sauté the remaining vegetables for 15 minutes. Combine the reserved stock and all of the vegetables. Puree in a blender or food processor. Stir in the lemon juice, mustard, and sour cream.

Add the beef to the sauce and simmer gently, but do not allow it to boil.

To serve, cut the meat in slices and arrange on the sauce. Sprinkle with parsley.

SAVORY STEW

Yield: 8 servings
5 tablespoons peanut oil
5 strips bacon, cut in small cubes
1½ pounds beef, cut in 1½-inch cubes
1½ pounds pork, cut in 1½-inch cubes
2 cups beef stock
4 medium green peppers, seeded, cored, and diced
2 large plum tomatoes, diced
2 large Spanish onions, peeled and diced
¼ cup parsley, chopped
2 tablespoons sweet paprika
Caraway seeds
Salt
Pepper

Heat the oil in a saucepan. Very slowly sauté the bacon. Add the beef and pork and brown on all sides. Pour in 1 cup of the stock; simmer for 30 minutes.

Add the vegetables, parsley, and the remaining stock. Season with paprika, caraway seeds, salt, and pepper. Cook gently for about 1½ hours over low heat. If necessary, add more water. Before serving, add more salt and pepper to taste.

PORK SHOULDER WITH PEPPERS

Yield: 6 to 8 servings
2 pounds pork shoulder, cut in 1½-inch cubes
¼ cup drippings
3 medium onions, peeled and cut in rings
1 large green pepper, seeded, cored, and diced
1 large yellow pepper, seeded, cored, and diced
3 large plum tomatoes, skinned and cut in strips
1 clove garlic, peeled and finely chopped
3 tablespoons tomato paste
2 tablespoons sweet paprika
1 tablespoon vinegar
1 teaspoon ground caraway seeds
Salt
Pepper

Brown the pork in the drippings, a little at a time. Sauté the onions and peppers with the meat for a few minutes.

Stir in the tomatoes and tomato paste; simmer for 2 minutes. Add the paprika, vinegar, and ½ cup of hot water. Season with garlic, ground caraway seeds, salt, and pepper. Simmer for another hour. If necessary, add more liquid to maintain a smooth consistency.

HOT BORSCH

Yield: 6 to 8 servings
3 tablespoons peanut oil
½ pound stewing beef, cut in small cubes
4 cups chicken stock
2 smoked minced-pork sausages, sliced
2 large fresh beets, cut in strips
1 leek, cut in strips
2 celery stalks, cut in strips
1 3-pound white cabbage, cut in strips
1 large plum tomato, cut in strips
1 large Spanish onion, cut in strips
2 tablespoons chopped fresh parsley
1 bay leaf
Salt
Pepper
1 cup sour cream

Heat the oil in a frying pan. Brown the beef cubes on all sides. Add the chicken stock and simmer for 45 minutes. Add the sausage slices, vegetables, parsley, and bay leaf; season with salt and pepper. Cook for 30 minutes. Serve with sour cream.

CABBAGE PASTRY

Yield: 4 to 6 servings
For the pastry:
1 cup flour
1 tablespoon yeast
1 pinch sugar
¼ cup lukewarm water
½ teaspoon salt
4 tablespoons peanut oil
1 egg yolk
For the filling:
1 pound white cabbage, cut into ½-inch strips
Salt
1 large Spanish onion, peeled and cut in strips
¼ cup fresh dill, finely chopped
1 bunch parsley, finely chopped
Pepper
2 hard-boiled eggs, finely chopped
2½ tablespoons melted butter

Prepare a Yeast Dough from the pastry ingredients (see Index). Allow it to rise for about 30 minutes.

Blanch the cabbage in boiling salted water for 3 to 5 minutes. Drain and mix with the herbs and onion. Season with salt and pepper.

Roll out the dough to a rectangle and place the cabbage mixture on it. Sprinkle with the chopped egg and melted butter. Fold over and seal the pastry. Place on a greased baking tray and brush with egg yolk. Bake in a preheated 325°F oven for 40 minutes. Cut in slices and serve.

POLISH CARP

Yield: 4 to 6 servings
1 large Spanish onion, peeled and cut into rings
4 ounces gingerbread, diced
1 cup dry red wine
2 cups beer
2 tablespoons chopped parsley
1 bay leaf
2 cloves
Thyme
Salt
Pepper
2 pounds carp fillet, cut into 1-inch slices
2 tablespoons sugar
Vinegar
2 tablespoons raisins
2 tablespoons chopped almonds

Combine the onion, gingerbread, wine, beer, parsley, and seasonings in a saucepan and bring to a boil. Add the carp and simmer for 20 to 30 minutes. Remove the fish from the pan and strain the liquid through a sieve.

Caramelize the sugar in 1 tablespoon of water; add to the sauce. Add vinegar to taste; stir in the raisins and almonds. Serve the sauce with the fish.

PORK AND SAUSAGE STEW

Yield: 6 to 8 servings
10 strips bacon, finely diced
1 pound pork, cut in 1½-inch cubes
½ pound sausages, sliced
1 large red pepper, cored, seeded, and cubed
1 large Spanish onion, peeled and finely diced
1 3-pound white cabbage, cut into ½-inch strips
2 tablespoons tomato paste
1 bay leaf
Salt
Pepper
Caraway seeds
Marjoram
2 cups meat stock
¼ cup mushrooms, sliced
1 cup sour cream

Render the fat from the bacon in a Dutch oven. Sauté the pork and sausages in the bacon fat for 5 minutes. Add the pepper, onion, mushrooms, and cabbage and sauté for 3 minutes. Stir in the tomato paste and bay leaf. Season with salt, pepper, caraway seeds, and marjoram. Add the meat stock and cook for 40 minutes over medium heat.

Just before serving, stir in sour cream and heat, but do not allow the stew to boil.

LAMB AND VEGETABLE KEBABS

Yield: 6 to 8 servings
1 pound lamb shoulder, cut in bite-sized pieces
1 large red pepper, seeded, cored, and cut in large pieces
1 large green pepper, seeded, cored, and cut in large pieces
1 large Spanish onion, peeled and cut in eighths
1 ear of corn on the cob, cut into ¼-inch slices
1 large zucchini, cut into ¼-inch slices
8 strips bacon
Sweet paprika
¼ cup sunflower oil
Salt
Freshly ground black pepper

Alternate the meat and vegetables on 4 skewers. Dust with paprika. Place the kebabs in a dish and pour oil over them. Refrigerate for 1 to 2 hours.

In a frying pan, saute the kebabs over medium heat for about 20 minutes, turning them to brown on all sides. Season with salt and pepper before serving.

SHOULDER OF LAMB WITH EGGPLANT

Yield: 4 to 6 servings
4 medium red peppers, seeded, cored, and diced
4 medium green peppers, seeded, cored, and diced
2 large carrots, peeled and diced
2 large onions, peeled and finely chopped
2 cloves garlic, peeled and finely chopped
2 large plum tomatoes, skinned, seeded, and diced
1 cup okra, cut in slices
2 medium eggplants, peeled and cut in slices
Salt
Pepper
Sweet paprika
1 shoulder of lamb (rolled and tied)
5 tablespoons sunflower oil

Mix the vegetables and garlic together; season with salt, pepper, and paprika.

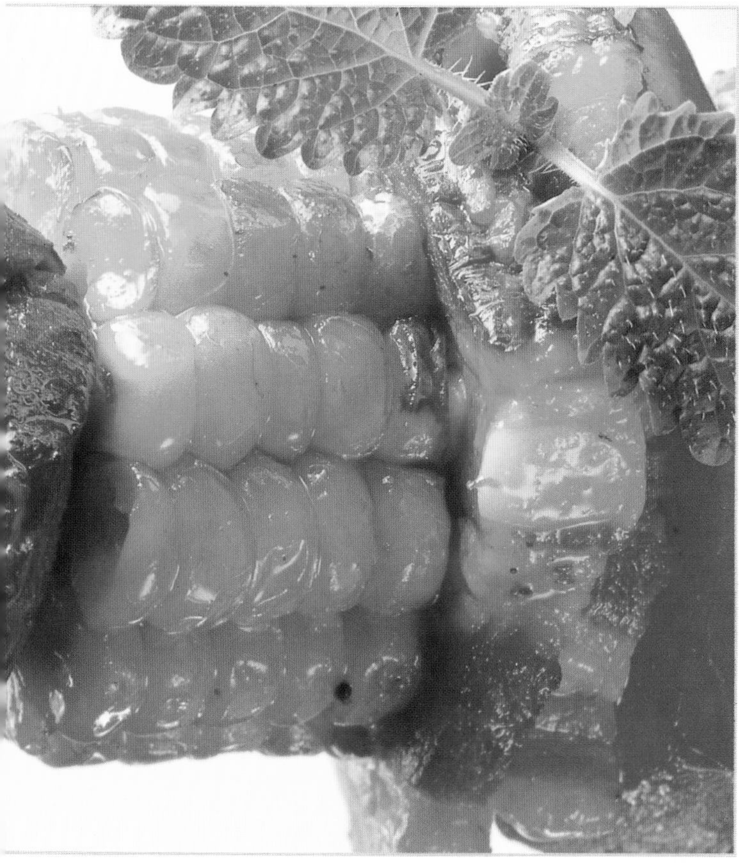

BOSNIAN MEAT AND POTATO STEW

Yield: 4 to 6 servings
1 pound stewing beef, cut in 1½-inch cubes
1 pound lamb shoulder, cut in 1½-inch cubes
5 small carrots, peeled and diced
4 celery stalks, diced
¼ cup parsley, finely chopped
1 pound potatoes, peeled and diced
5 medium onions, peeled and diced
1 whole garlic bulb, peeled and crushed
1 3-pound white cabbage, diced
1 large green pepper, seeded, cored, and diced
½ pound string beans, diced
3 small plum tomatoes, skinned, seeded, and diced
3 cloves
2 bay leaves, broken in pieces
Salt
Pepper
1 teaspoon sweet paprika
3 tablespoons tomato paste
2 cups white wine
4 tablespoons olive oil

Soak a clay cooking pot in water. Put the vegetables and meat in the dish in alternate layers, seasoning each layer with the cloves, bay leaves, salt, pepper, and paprika. The top layer should consist of vegetables.

Add the tomato paste, wine, and olive oil. Add enough water to cover completely. Bake in a preheated 325°F oven for 2½ to 3 hours.

Put the vegetables in an ovenproof dish and put the meat on top. Pour the oil over the meat and vegetables. Roast in a 325°F oven for about 1½ hours.

GROUND MEAT ROLLS

Yield: 6 to 8 servings
2 pounds ground meat (1 pound beef, 1 pound pork)
2 eggs
Salt
Pepper
Sweet paprika
¼ cup peanut oil
1 large Spanish onion, peeled and diced
1 large red pepper, seeded, cored, and cut in rings
1 large green pepper, seeded, cored, and cut in rings

Mix the ground meat with the eggs. Season with salt, pepper, and paprika to taste. Roll the mixture into finger-sized lengths.

In a frying pan, heat the oil and sauté the rolls for 5 minutes. To serve, arrange the meat rolls on a plate with the onion rings and pepper slices.

LAMB WITH SPINACH AND LEMON SAUCE

Yield: 4 to 6 servings
3 tablespoons butter
1½ pounds lean lamb, cut in small cubes
2 onions, peeled and finely chopped
Salt
Pepper
1 cup beef stock
1 pound fresh spinach, washed and stemmed
3 egg yolks
Juice of 1 lemon

Melt half of the butter in a large saucepan; sauté the onion until transparent. Then sauté the lamb over high heat for 5 minutes. Season with salt and pepper. Add half of the stock and cook over medium heat for 45 minutes, adding more water if necessary.

Bring the remaining stock to a boil, add the spinach, and simmer about 5 minutes. Drain the spinach, reserving the liquid. Chop the spinach coarsely and spread it over the cooked meat. Dot with the remaining butter and reheat the casserole.

Beat the egg yolks until foamy. Heat the reserved spinach liquid and carefully whisk it into the egg yolk. Add the lemon juice and salt to taste. Pour the sauce over the spinach. Warm in a preheated 400°F oven for 2 to 3 minutes.

CINNAMON CHICKEN

Yield: 4 to 6 servings
1 (2½-pound) chicken, cut in 8 pieces
Salt
Pepper
3 tablespoons butter
2 medium red onions, peeled and sliced
1 cup chicken stock
1 teaspoon ground cinnamon
2 cloves garlic, peeled and rubbed with salt
8 small skinned tomatoes, seeded and cut in slices
2 cups dry white wine
1 tablespoon tomato paste
4 celery stalks, thinly sliced
2 tablespoons chopped parsley
½ pound broad noodles
½ pound fine noodles
2 tablespoons grated cheese

Season the chicken pieces with salt and pepper. Heat the butter in a large frying pan and brown the chicken on all sides. Add the onions and stock; simmer for 45 minutes. Sprinkle with cinnamon.

Bring the garlic, wine, and tomatoes to a boil in a saucepan; stir in the tomato paste and celery. Season with salt and pepper and boil 15 minutes. Add the parsley.

Boil the noodles in salt water in another saucepan for 10 minutes, rinse with cold water, and drain.

To serve, mix the noodles with half of the cheese and place on a serving dish. Arrange the chicken on the bed of noodles. Pour the sauce on top of the chicken and sprinkle with the remaining cheese.

MOUSSAKA

Yield: 6 to 8 servings
1 large eggplant, peeled and cut into slices
Salt
5 tablespoons olive oil
3 tablespoons butter
2 large onions, peeled and diced
1½ pounds ground lamb or beef
Cinnamon
Pepper
4 large tomatoes, skinned and cut in small pieces
3 tablespoons chopped parsley
1 teaspoon oregano
½ cup meat stock
6 tablespoons grated Parmesan cheese
¼ cup flour
1 cup milk
3 egg yolks

Sprinkle the eggplant with salt; set aside for 30 minutes to let it drain. Thoroughly wipe the salt off the eggplant slices.

Heat the oil in a frying pan. Sauté the eggplant until lightly browned; remove from the pan and set aside.

Melt 2 more tablespoons of butter and sauté the onions until transparent. Add the meat; season with salt, pepper, and cinnamon to taste, mixing well. Stir in the tomatoes, parsley, and oregano. Add the stock and simmer for 20 minutes.

In another saucepan, melt the remaining butter over low heat. Add the flour and sauté over low heat for 3 to 5 minutes. Gradually stir in the milk. Cook the mixture for 5 minutes, stirring constantly, until thickened and smooth; season with salt and pepper. Remove from the heat and stir in the egg yolk.

Grease an ovenproof dish; spoon in half of the meat mixture. Cover with half of the eggplant slices and sprinkle with 3 tablespoons of cheese. Add the remaining meat and eggplant slices, and 3 tablespoons of cheese. Pour the sauce over this and sprinkle with cheese.

Bake in a preheated 325°F oven for 45 minutes.

LAMB STEW WITH OKRA

Yield: 4 to 6 servings
1 ½ pounds boneless leg of lamb, cut in 1 ½-inch cubes
2 large Spanish onions, peeled and cut in eighths
4 medium plum tomatoes, cut in eighths
¼ cup fresh parsley, finely chopped
5 tablespoons olive oil
3 cups chicken stock
1 cup okra, stalks cut out
2 cloves garlic, peeled and crushed
Salt
Pepper

Heat the oil in a frying pan and brown the lamb on all sides. Add the onions and tomatoes and sauté for 10 minutes. Add the parsley and chicken stock; reduce the heat and simmer for 4 minutes. Add the okra and garlic and simmer for 15 to 20 minutes longer. Season with salt and pepper to taste before serving.

STUFFED VEGETABLES

Yield: 8 servings
2 large eggplants, diced
2 large zucchini
1 large Spanish onion, peeled and finely chopped
2 cloves garlic, peeled and finely chopped
2 large plum tomatoes, skinned, seeded, and cubed
1½ pounds ground lamb
2 eggs
1 tablespoon chopped fresh mint
Salt
Pepper
3½ ounces goat cheese

Cut the eggplants and zucchini in half horizontally and scoop out the flesh, leaving a ¼ inch thick shell.

Mix the diced vegetables, onion, garlic, eggs, and ground lamb together. Season with salt and pepper. Put the lamb mixture into the scooped-out vegetables. Place the stuffed vegetables in a greased soufflé dish. Cook in a preheated 325°F oven for 30 to 40 minutes.

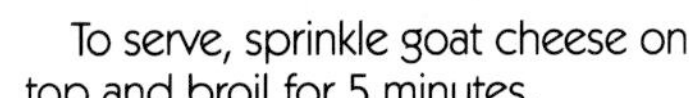

To serve, sprinkle goat cheese on top and broil for 5 minutes.

LAMB MEAT BALLS

Yield: 6 servings
2 large eggplants
¼ cup fresh mint, finely chopped
¼ cup raisins, finely chopped
¼ cup pine nuts, finely chopped
1½ pounds ground lamb
2 eggs
Salt
Pepper
1 cup olive oil
Juice of 1 lemon

Place the whole eggplants in an ovenproof dish and bake in a preheated 350°F oven for 30 minutes, then set aside to cool.

Meanwhile, mix the mint, raisins, and pine nuts with the ground lamb. Add the eggs, salt, and pepper. Form into small balls.

Heat 1 cup of olive oil in a frying pan. Sauté the meat balls for 5 to 10 minutes.

Halve the eggplants and scoop out the flesh. Puree it in a food processor with the oil and lemon juice. Season the eggplant puree with salt and serve it with the lamb balls.

TURKISH PILAF

Yield: 4 to 6 servings
4 boneless chicken breasts, cut into 2-inch pieces
1 large Spanish onion, peeled and diced
2 medium red peppers, seeded, cored, and diced
4 tablespoons olive oil
1 cup uncooked rice
¼ cup raisins
2 cups chicken stock
Pinch saffron
Ground ginger
Salt
Pepper

Heat the olive oil in a frying pan. Sauté the chicken pieces, skin side down, until lightly browned. Add the onion and peppers; continue sautéing until the onions are transparent. Stir in the rice, raisins, and stock. Season with saffron, ginger, salt, and pepper.

Simmer over low heat for 30 minutes until the rice is cooked.

PEKING DUCK

Yield: 6 to 8 servings
For the duck:
1 (3-pound) whole duck
Salt
3 tablespoons molasses or honey
1 teaspoon ground ginger
For the sauce:
2 tablespoons sesame oil
4 tablespoons sweet soy bean paste
4 tablespoons sugar
8 small leeks, cut in 2½-inch long pieces

Rub the inside of the duck with salt. Using a drinking straw, blow air between the skin and the flesh, until the duck is almost one and a half times bigger. Tie the neck cavity closed by wrapping kitchen twine around the neck several times.

Bring ½ cup of water to a boil and dissolve the molasses or honey in it. Stir in 2 teaspoons of salt and the ginger powder. Brush the duck evenly with this liquid. Hang the duck by a cord around its neck in a cool, airy place for 10 to 24 hours.

Preheat the oven to 400°F. Fill a roasting pan halfway with warm water; lay the duck on a wire rack over the pan. Roast the duck for 45 minutes. Reduce the heat to 350°F, turn the duck over, and roast for 45 minutes longer. Toward the end of the cooking time, turn the heat up to 400°F so the skin becomes crisp and golden brown.

For the sauce, heat the sesame oil in a saucepan. Mix 2 tablespoons of water with the soy bean paste and sugar; add to the hot oil, taking care to avoid being spattered. Cook, stirring continuously, until the sauce has thickened. (Instead of this sauce, ready-made Hoisin sauce can be used.)

Make several cuts in one end of each leek piece, then soak in ice water. This causes the cut ends to bend outward to form a decorative brush.

To serve Peking duck, cut the skin off the duck in small, even pieces, using a sharp knife. Cut the meat from the bones, then cut it at an angle into fine strips. Use the leek brushes to brush the sauce onto the skin and meat. Serve with small, paper-thin Chinese pancakes.

FIVE-COLOR RICE

Yield: 4 to 6 servings
7 dried black Chinese mushrooms
1 cup uncooked rice
1 cup frozen peas
Salt
2 eggs, lightly beaten
½ cup peanut oil
3 ounces pork fillet, cut in small cubes
3 ounces ham, cut in small pieces
10 shrimp, shelled and deveined
1 tablespoon light soy sauce
1 medium onion, peeled and finely diced
Pepper

Soak the mushrooms for at least 1 hour, or until soft. Bring 1 cup of water to a boil, add the rice, and simmer for 20 minutes. Gently cook the peas in salt water to cover for 5 minutes; drain and keep warm.

Heat 1 tablespoon of oil in a pan. Scramble the eggs, then set aside, keeping them warm

Heat 2 tablespoons of oil in a wok and sauté the mushrooms. Add the pork and continue cooking for 3 minutes. Add the ham and cook for 2 minutes longer. Place the shrimp in the wok and sauté for 1 minute. Season with soy sauce. Remove the ingredients and keep warm.

Heat 4 tablespoons of oil in the wok and sauté the onion until transparent. Add the rice, peas, scrambled eggs, pork, mushrooms, ham, and shrimp. Season with salt and pepper to taste.

SUSHI

Yield: 4 servings

6 ounces very fresh prime fillet of red tuna
8 ounces very fresh halibut fillet, skinned
6 ounces very fresh squid, body only, skinned and cleaned
3 2 × 2½-inch pieces nori
4 tablespoons wasabi powder
1 ounce Beluga caviar

Cut the tuna fillet into 1-inch thick pieces and arrange 3 pieces on each serving plate. Slice a ½-inch wide strip from the halibut fillet and roll into a circular shape for the middle of each serving plate. Slice the remaining halibut fillet thinly and arrange 6 slices on each serving plate.

Lay a single thickness of squid flat on a cutting board. Cut a 2 × 2½-inch piece from the squid. Place a nori sheet, shiny side down, on a bamboo rolling mat, with the mat strips crosswise. Place a slice of squid on the nori. Bring front edge of the mat and nori up and over, using the mat to roll the nori and squid into a cylinder. Press firmly and hold about 10 seconds to seal. Unroll the mat to release the roll and place the roll on cutting board. Using a moistened, very sharp knife, cut the roll into 3 equal slices with a single downward cutting motion. Repeat this process until all the nori sheets are used. Place 3 squid rolls on each serving plate.

Mix the wasabi powder with enough water to make a thick paste; cover and let stand 10 minutes. Arrange wasabi cones on each plate.

Place a small spoonful of caviar on each serving plate and garnish with celery leaves, lime slices, and carrot slices before serving. Serve with soy sauce.

CURRIED SHOULDER OF LAMB

Yield: 4 to 6 servings
2 tablespoons clarified butter
1 medium onion, peeled and finely chopped
2 cloves garlic, peeled and finely chopped
1 teaspoon chili powder
2 teaspoons pepper
2 teaspoons ground coriander
1 teaspoon cumin
1 teaspoon turmeric
3 small ripe tomatoes, quartered
1½ pounds boneless shoulder of lamb, cut in 1-inch cubes
Juice of 1 lemon
Salt
1 cup meat stock
2 teaspoons garam masala*

Heat the butter in a large pan and sauté the onion and garlic. Add the chili, pepper, coriander, cumin, turmeric, and tomatoes. When the tomatoes are cooked, add the meat cubes. Sprinkle with lemon juice and salt.

Heat the stock and add it to the meat; cook over medium heat for 45 minutes, stirring occasionally. Add the garam masala; simmer for 10 minutes.

To serve, garnish with cherry tomato halves and fresh mint leaves.

*Garam masala is a mixture of Indian spices. It can be bought in specialty stores.

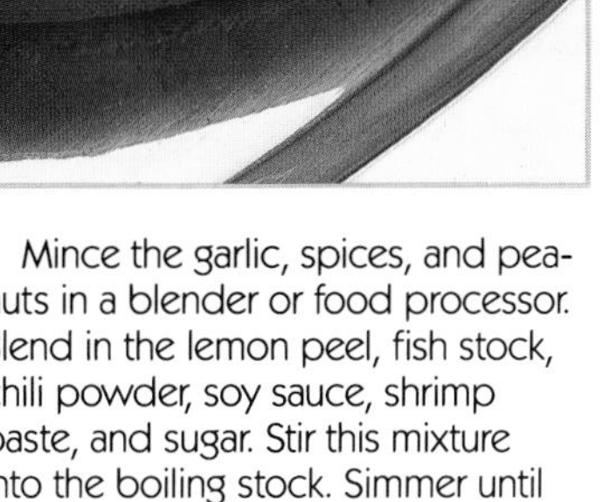

CHICKEN IN COCONUT SAUCE

Yield: 6 servings
1 (2-pound) chicken
2½ cups coconut milk
Salt
5 cloves garlic, peeled
1 tablespoon caraway seeds
1 tablespoon ground coriander
4 peppercorns
1 tablespoon roasted peanuts
1 teaspoon grated lemon peel
2 teaspoons fish stock
2 teaspoons chili powder
2 tablespoons dark soy sauce
1 tablespoon shrimp paste
1 teaspoon sugar

Place the chicken in a saucepan with the coconut milk. Cover the pan and simmer for 1 hour. Remove the chicken from the pan; separate the meat from the bones; set aside, keeping warm.

Boil the liquid until it has reduced by half.

Mince the garlic, spices, and peanuts in a blender or food processor. Blend in the lemon peel, fish stock, chili powder, soy sauce, shrimp paste, and sugar. Stir this mixture into the boiling stock. Simmer until thickened, add salt to taste.

To serve, arrange the chicken on a plate; pour the sauce over it.

BAMI GORENG SAUTÉ

Yield: 4 to 6 servings
3 cups egg noodles
Salt
3 tablespoons peanut oil
1 small onion, peeled and finely chopped
2 cloves garlic, peeled and finely chopped
1 celery stalk, cut in small pieces
8 ounces chicken breast or pork fillet, cut in ½-inch cubes
15 shrimp, shelled, deveined and cut in small pieces
2 tablespoons light soy sauce
Pepper

Cook the noodles in salted water for 8 to 10 minutes, or until they are slightly al dente; drain.

Heat the oil in a frying pan and sauté the onions, garlic, and celery. Add the chicken or pork and the shrimp. Cook over low heat until shrimp become pink. Add the cooked noodles and stir well. Season the mixture with soy sauce and pepper to taste.

BARBECUED PORK RIBS

Yield: 4 to 6 servings
5 pounds pork ribs
2 medium onions, peeled and finely chopped
2 cloves garlic, peeled and finely chopped
⅔ cup corn oil
¼ cup tomato paste
4 to 6 tablespoons rice vinegar
1 teaspoon salt
1 teaspoon basil
1 teaspoon thyme
1 teaspoon mustard
½ teaspoon Tabasco sauce
1 cup beef stock
½ cup honey
4 tablespoons Worcestershire sauce

Heat the oil in a frying pan and sauté the onion and garlic until transparent. Stir in the tomato paste, vinegar, seasonings, stock, honey, and Worcestershire sauce. Boil for 10 minutes, stirring constantly.

Place the ribs on a rack in an ovenproof pan. Brush them with the sauce. Cook in a preheated 350°F oven for 1 hour.

JAMBALAYA

Yield: 4 to 6 servings
2 (2-pound) chickens, quartered
Salt
Pepper
Pinch paprika
4 tablespoons peanut oil
1 cup uncooked rice
2 medium red peppers, seeded, diced and cored
2 medium green peppers, seeded, diced and cored
2 shallots, peeled and finely chopped
3 ounces ham, diced
3 tablespoons butter

Season the chickens with salt, pepper, and paprika; brush with oil. Place on a baking sheet in a preheated 425°F oven. Roast for 40 to 45 minutes, brushing occasionally with oil. Remove the cooked chicken meat from the bones.

Bring 2 cups of lightly salted water to a boil; add the rice and simmer for 20 minutes.

Melt the butter in a frying pan and sauté the peppers, shallots, and ham. Add the cooked chicken and rice, and sauté until the mixture is heated through. Season with salt and pepper before serving.

ROAST TURKEY

Yield: 6 to 8 servings
1 (10-pound) turkey
Salt
Pepper
5 tablespoons peanut oil
4 small tomatoes
2 large Granny Smith apples, cut in slices
2 cups small mushrooms, sliced
3 tablespoons butter
12 asparagus tips
1 tablespoon chopped tarragon
¼ cup dry white wine
¾ cup whipping cream

Season the turkey with salt and pepper, and brush with oil. Place in a roasting pan, cover, and roast in a preheated 325°F oven for 2½ to 3 hours, brushing frequently with oil.

Cut a cross in the tomatoes and sprinkle with pepper. Cook the tomatoes with the turkey for the last 10 minutes.

Remove the cooked turkey from the pan and pour off the fat. Heat 1 tablespoon of butter in the roasting pan and sauté the apple in it. Add the asparagus and continue sautéing until heated. Set the apple and the asparagus aside, keeping warm.

Cook the mushrooms and tarragon in the butter. Add the wine and bring to a boil. Add the cream and continue boiling; stir until the sauce thickens. Season with salt and pepper.

To serve, arrange the mushrooms, tomatoes, apples, and asparagus around the turkey.

GLAZED HAM

Yield: 6 servings
1 (2½-pound) salted, smoked ham
Pepper
¼ cup peanut oil
1 (8-ounce) can pineapple slices
15 cloves
1 tablespoon confectioner's sugar

Season the ham with pepper. Heat the oil in a large saucepan and brown the ham on all sides.

Drain the pineapple slices and fasten them to the ham with toothpicks. Insert the cloves into the meat, distributing them evenly.

Roast in a preheated 425°F oven for 1 hour. To serve, sprinkle with confectioner's sugar; broil for 3 to 5 minutes to glaze.

ROAST BEEF WITH BEANS

Yield: 4 to 6 servings

1 (2½-pound) rump roast beef
2 cloves garlic, peeled and finely chopped
2 tablespoons sweet chili sauce
Salt
Pepper
1 medium onion, peeled and diced
2 tablespoons butter
1 10½-ounce can red kidney beans

Mix the garlic with the chili sauce, salt, and pepper. Spread the mixture on the beef and marinate for 1 hour.

Place the roast, with the layer of fat uppermost, on a greased rack in a roasting pan. Sprinkle the rack with water. Place in a preheated 425°F oven for 40 minutes, turning occasionally. Remove the meat and wrap it in aluminum foil; let stand for 10 minutes.

Melt the butter in a frying pan and sauté the onion until transparent. Add the beans and sauté for 5 minutes; season with salt and pepper. Serve the beans with the meat.

TORTILLAS

Yield: 4 to 6 servings

For the batter
1½ cups cornmeal
1½ cups flour
2 eggs
2 cups milk
Salt
Peanut oil
For the filling:
2 avocados, peeled and mashed
25 shrimp, shelled, deveined and cooked
Juice of ½ lemon
2 tablespoons chopped parsley
Pepper
Egg white

Sift the cornmeal and flour together; stir in the eggs, milk, and salt until a smooth batter is formed. Pour 2 tablespoons of batter on a nonstick frying pan. Cook for about 1 minute on each side. Set the tortillas on paper towels to drain.

For the filling: Mix the avocados with the shrimp, lemon juice, parsley, salt, and pepper.

Fill each tortilla by spooning the filling on half of each flat cake. Brush the edges of the tortilla with egg white, fold them over, and press the edges firmly together. Sauté quickly in 1 tablespoon each of heated butter and oil, and serve.

RABBIT IN COCONUT SAUCE

Yield: 4 servings

8 rabbit drumsticks
Salt
Pepper
1 onion, peeled and finely diced
1/4 cup olive oil
3 small tomatoes, skinned, seeded, and cut in small pieces
1 cup milk
1 cup whipping cream
3/4 cup grated coconut

Season the rabbit with salt and pepper. Heat the oil in a frying pan and brown the rabbit pieces on all sides. Add the onion and sauté until translucent. Stir in the tomatoes, milk, cream, and coconut; simmer for 30 to 40 minutes. Remove the drumsticks and keep warm.

Puree the sauce in a blender or food processor. Return to the pan and bring to a boil, and cook until thickened. Season with salt and pepper to taste.

To serve, pour the sauce over the rabbit.

GARLIC SCAMPI

Yield: 4 servings
4 to 5 tablespoons peanut oil
24 shrimp, peeled and deveined
4 cloves garlic, peeled and finely chopped
2 small plum tomatoes, skinned, seeded, and cubed
¼ cup fresh parsley, finely chopped
3 tablespoons butter
Salt
Pepper

Heat the oil in a frying pan and sauté the shrimp for 3 minutes. Arrange on a heated plate and keep warm.

Discard the fat in the frying pan, then melt the remaining butter in the pan and sauté the garlic for 2 minutes. Add the tomato, parsley, and salt and pepper to taste. Sprinkle this mixture over the shrimp and serve with rice.

GRILLED LOBSTER WITH RED WINE BUTTER

Yield: 2 to 4 servings
For the lobster
2 lobsters (1½ pounds each)
1 small onion, peeled and roughly diced
½ leek, cut in rings
1 small carrot, peeled and cut in large pieces
2 celery stalks, cut in large pieces
5 peppercorns
1 bay leaf
Salt
Sweet paprika
For the red wine butter:
2 shallots, peeled and finely chopped
1 tablespoon chervil, finely chopped
2 tablespoons watercress, finely chopped
1 tablespoon parsley, finely chopped
¼ cup dry red wine
½ cup butter
Pepper

Fill a lobster pot with water, add the lobsters, vegetables, peppercorns, bay leaf, salt, and pepper. Bring to a boil and cook for 15 minutes. Remove the lobsters and drain.

To make the red wine butter, put the red wine, shallots, and herbs in a saucepan. Bring to a boil and cook until the liquid is reduced by half. Add the butter. Remove the pan from the stove and swirl the butter through the mixture with a spoon. Season with salt and pepper to taste.

Halve the lobsters lengthwise. Twist the claws to break them off. Carefully loosen the meat from the tail; chop into pieces.

Preheat the broiler. Mix the meat with the red wine butter, return the mixture to shell and broil for 5 minutes.

GRILLED SADDLE OF LAMB

Yield: 4 servings
3-pound saddle of lamb
2 small Granny Smith apples, peeled and diced
1 4-ounce jar mint jelly
Lemon juice
Salt
Coarsely ground black pepper

Make several diagonal cuts in the layer of fat on the upper surface of the lamb. Place the lamb in a roasting pan and bake in a 425° to 450°F oven for 45 minutes. After cooking, season the meat with salt and pepper.

To make the mint sauce, heat the apple and mint jelly together until liquified; add lemon juice to taste. Serve the sauce with the lamb.

COUSCOUS

Yield: 6 to 8 servings
⅔ cup chickpeas
2 cups cold water
2 cups couscous
1 cup hot salted water, to taste
5 tablespoons olive oil
1½ pounds stewing lamb, cut in cubes
1 large Spanish onion, peeled and diced
2 large tomatoes, skinned, seeded, and cut in eighths
2 carrots, peeled and diced
1 medium zucchini, diced
½ leek, cut in rings
½ cup fresh pumpkin, seeded and diced
2 tablespoons tomato paste
2 cloves garlic, peeled and crushed
Salt
Pepper
Juice of 1 lemon

Cover the chickpeas with cold water and soak for 6 hours, or overnight. Drain, but reserve the soaking liquid.

Mix the couscous with the hot salt water (photograph 2) and when water is absorbed form the couscous into small balls. Set aside.

Heat the oil in a large saucepan and sauté the lamb, vegetables, and chickpeas (photograph 3). Stir in the tomato paste, garlic, salt, pepper, lemon juice, and water.

Put the couscous balls in a steamer (photograph 4) and place it in the saucepan with the lamb, vegetables, and tomato sauce. Cover and cook for 1¼ hours.

Serve the meat with the vegetables and the couscous balls; serve the sauce separately.

1

2

3

4

SWEET LAMB STEW

Yield: 6 servings
6 tablespoons peanut oil
2½ pounds shoulder of lamb, cut in 1½-inch cubes
¼ cup peeled almonds
¼ cup sugar
1 cup orange juice
Salt
Pepper
Cinnamon
1½ cups pitted prunes, halved

Heat the oil in a saucepan and brown the lamb on all sides. Add the almonds and sugar; melt the sugar and caramelize the mixture slightly.

Stir in the orange juice. Season with salt, pepper, and cinnamon. Bring the mixture to a boil. Reduce heat to a simmer and cook over medium heat for ½ hour; add the prunes and, if necessary, more water. Cook ½ hour more. Before serving, season again with salt, pepper, and cinnamon. Serve with rice.

CLASSIC CUISINE

Man has always enjoyed eating something sweet. At first, there was fruit, and then we discovered honey. Later came cane sugar, with all of its enchanting possibilities. The variety and traditions associated with baked desserts are vast and enticing. Sumptuous cakes, delicate mixed creams, tempting fruit creations, and a virtual cornucopia of cookies are all within the skills of the average cook.

The delicate meringues shown here are made from sugar and beaten egg white. Many other excellent baking recipes are provided in this chapter, along with basic dough recipes and other useful baking tips.

CREAMED DOUGH

It's considerably easier to prepare this dough when you use a hand or an electric mixer. It is important with creamed dough to grease the cake pan well. Use softened salted butter or margarine; do not use a cooking oil. The pan is then dusted with fine bread crumbs or flour. With spring-form cake pans, only the base of the pan is greased. Loaf pans can be lined with baking parchment after they have been greased, which enables the cake to be removed from the pan more easily.

To make the paper lining, place the base of the pan on the paper and draw around it; turn the pan on its side and draw around the sides. Repeat for all four sides. Now cut out the corners and fold along the base line.

Assemble all of the ingredients for the dough before you start and measure each of the ingredients exactly.

Basic Recipe for a Fruit Cake

2 sticks salted butter, softened
1 cup sugar
1 teaspoon vanilla extract
Salt
4 eggs
2 cups flour
1 teaspoon baking powder
½ cup milk
¾ cup currants
½ cup raisins

Preheat the oven to 350°F.

Using an electric mixer, cream the softened butter in a mixing bowl until smooth. This will take 1½ minutes. Gradually add the sugar and the vanilla extract. Add any spices or flavoring desired to the butter and sugar mixture. Continue mixing until the dough is fully combined.

Gradually add the eggs one at a time, allowing ½ to 1 minute of mixing before adding another. After all the eggs are added, gradually mix in the baking powder. If the dough is too firm, add 1 tablespoon of milk, only adding enough so that the dough tears as it falls from a spoon. Carefully fold in the fruit. Turn the dough into a prepared loaf pan and bake for 1 hour.

KNEADED DOUGH

The use of an electric mixer or food processor is recommended for making kneaded dough, since the ingredients can be kneaded more quickly than by hand. It is important that the butter is softened so all ingredients can be easily mixed together.

So as not to change the characteristics of the dough, only small pieces of the dough should be rolled out at a time. When rolling out the dough, slide a large knife under it occasionally so that it will not stick to the bread board. As a rule, baking sheets and cake pans do not need to be greased for a kneaded dough. The exceptions are flan or bun pans and baking sheets on which doughs made with water or milk are to be baked.

Basic Recipe for a Tart Crust

Yield: 1 6-inch crust
3/4 cup flour
1 1/2 teaspoons baking powder
3 tablespoons sugar
1 teaspoon vanilla extract
Salt to taste
1 egg
2 1/2 tablespoons salted butter, softened

Sift the baking powder and the flour together into a mixing bowl. (If cocoa is also to be added, mix it with the flour before sifting.) Add the remaining ingredients and mix with the dough hook attachment on an electric mixer, using the lowest setting first. Increase the speed gradually and mix well on the highest setting. Remove the dough from the bowl and knead it to a smooth consistency on a cool, floured surface. (Do not sprinkle much flour onto the work surface or the dough will become crumbly. Knead the dough quickly with the palm of your closed hand.) If the dough is sticky, cover it in plastic wrap and refrigerate for 1 hour.

Roll out two-thirds of the dough onto the greased bottom of a springform pan (diameter about 10 inches). Knead about 1 level tablespoon of flour into the remaining dough and form it into a roll. Place this around the edge of the dough base, pressing it on to form a "wall." The dough roll should create a "wall" 1 inch high.

Pierce the dough several times with the prongs of a fork and place it in the preheated oven. Set the oven temperature and baking time according to the individual recipe you select. (Recipes specify baking the shell before or after filling it.) When the shell is done, loosen it from the pan and remove it. The pastry can now be used to create cakes or other fruit tarts.

Kneaded pastry doughs can be frozen very successfully.

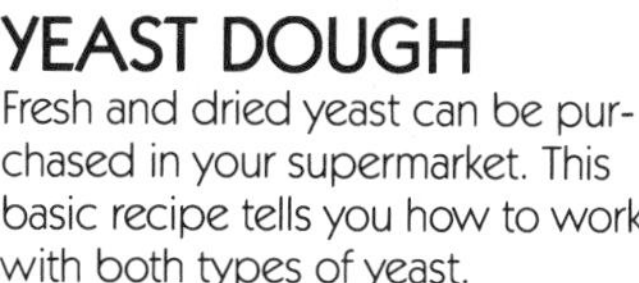

YEAST DOUGH

Fresh and dried yeast can be purchased in your supermarket. This basic recipe tells you how to work with both types of yeast.

Basic Recipe for Yeast Dough

- 1 pound flour
- 1 package dried yeast or 1 cube fresh yeast (2¾ ounces)
- 2½ tablespoons sugar
- 1 teaspoon vanilla extract
- Salt to taste
- 1 cup lukewarm milk
- 2½ tablespoons salted butter, melted and cooled

If using dried yeast, sprinkle the yeast in the bowl with the lukewarm milk and sugar. Allow the yeast to "proof" (bubble and grow) for 10 minutes. If using fresh yeast, sift the flour into a mixing bowl and make a well in the center. Crumble the yeast into this well. Sprinkle it with a little of the sugar and stir in ¼ cup of the lukewarm milk. Cover and "proof" yeast for 15 to 20 minutes. Continue as follows for both types of yeast.

Add all of the remaining ingredients given in the recipe. First mix the ingredients briefly using an electric mixer on the lowest setting, then mix on the highest setting for about 5 minutes. The dough must be smooth. Cover the dough and leave it in a warm place until doubled in size, about 30 minutes. Proceed with the processes described in the particular recipe you wish to use.

SPONGE DOUGH

Sponge dough must always be put into cake pans that have been greased and lined with parchment paper. If using a baking sheet, fold the paper on the open side of the baking sheet to form a wall so that the dough cannot spread off the pan.

Basic Recipe for Sponge Dough

4 eggs
3 to 4 tablespoons hot water
½ cup sugar
1 teaspoon vanilla extract
3 tablespoons flour
2 tablespoons cornstarch
1 pinch baking powder

Beat the eggs with the whisk attachment on an electric mixer, using the highest setting for 1 minute, or until the eggs are foamy. Add the sugar and vanilla extract, mixing another 3 minutes.

Mix the flour, cornstarch, and baking powder together and sift half of the mixture into the egg mixture, stirring it in quickly on the lowest setting. Work in the remaining flour mixture the same way.

Put the dough into a prepared pan or onto a prepared baking sheet. Bake in a preheated 375°F oven for 10 to 12 minutes.

With a knife, loosen the sponge from the edges of the baking sheet and the edges of the parchment paper immediately after baking. Lift it from the tray and place on a towel sprinkled with confectioners' sugar. Brush the parchment paper with cold water, using a pastry brush, and peel it off carefully and quickly.

CHOUX PASTRY DOUGH

This is the only dough where flour and butter are "cooked" and made into a ball with the liquid ingredients. When the dough has cooled slightly, the eggs are added. Then the dough is ready for baking.

Basic Recipe for Choux Pastry Dough

1 cup water
2 tablespoons salted butter
¾ cup flour, sifted
4 to 5 eggs

Bring the water and the butter to a full boil in an enamel saucepan with a heavy base. Remove the pan from the heat and add the flour all at once. Stir the mixture until it has formed a ball. A white skin may form on the bottom of the pan, which indicates that the mixture has heated.

Put the ball into a bowl immediately and allow it to cool for about 2 minutes. Then add the eggs. First add 1 egg (photograph below) and stir until mixed. Then add another egg and stir until mixed. Continue adding the eggs one at a time and stirring to incorporate in the mixture. If the dough is very shiny and hangs from an inverted spoon in thick clumps, the last egg may not be necessary. The dough must be so creamy that it can be piped from a pastry bag.

Grease a baking sheet and dust finely with flour. Put the choux pastry into a pastry bag with a large star tip. For cream puffs, pipe thick rosettes with enough space between them; choux pastry will spread a lot on the baking sheet. For eclairs, pipe out strips about 2 inches long, with rosettes on each end (photograph below).

Put the baking sheet into a preheated 400°F oven and bake for 10 minutes. Reduce the heat to 350°F and bake 20 to 25 minutes longer. The oven should only be opened at the end of the baking time or the pastries will collapse, and the pastries must be quite firm to the touch. Immediately cut the finished pastries in half horizontally and cool on a wire rack.

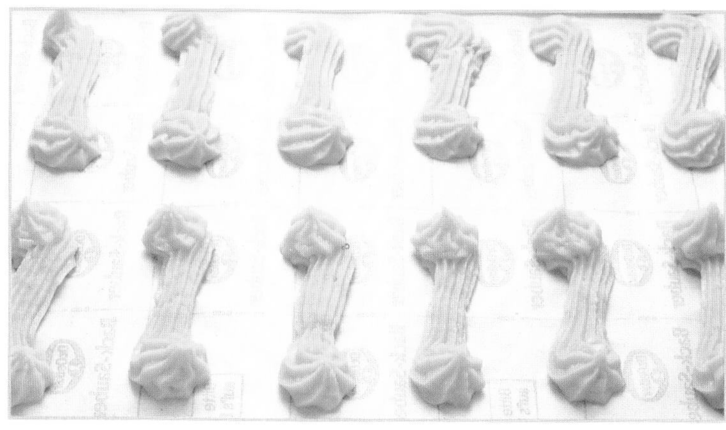

Basic Recipe for Meringues

4 egg whites
1 cup superfine sugar

Beat the egg whites to a foam, adding the sugar slowly while beating with an electric mixer on a low setting (photograph above). Increase the speed to medium until the sugar has dissolved and the foam can be cut with a knife. Place the mixture in a pastry bag. Line a baking sheet with parchment paper and, for example, pipe out spiral-shaped meringue bases with a smooth tip, or place small mounds on the baking tray, or pipe the mixture into baking pans or little shells lined with paper. This recipe will make 3 cake bases or 15 small cases or pieces.

Meringues are then baked dry. They are put into a preheated 275°F to 300°F oven for 30 minutes to 1 hour. The baking time depends on how quickly your oven browns the meringues.

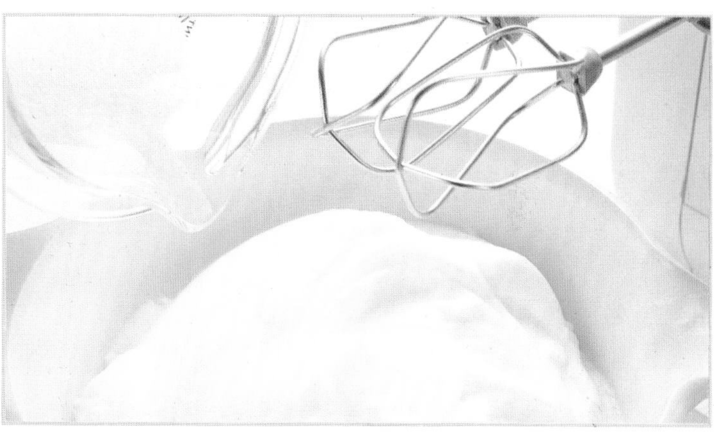

MERINGUES

Meringues are a tempting sugar-sweet pastry. They are made almost entirely from egg white and sugar.

The most common errors in cooking meringues are either the egg white isn't stiff enough, the sugar hasn't dissolved properly, or the oven is too hot.

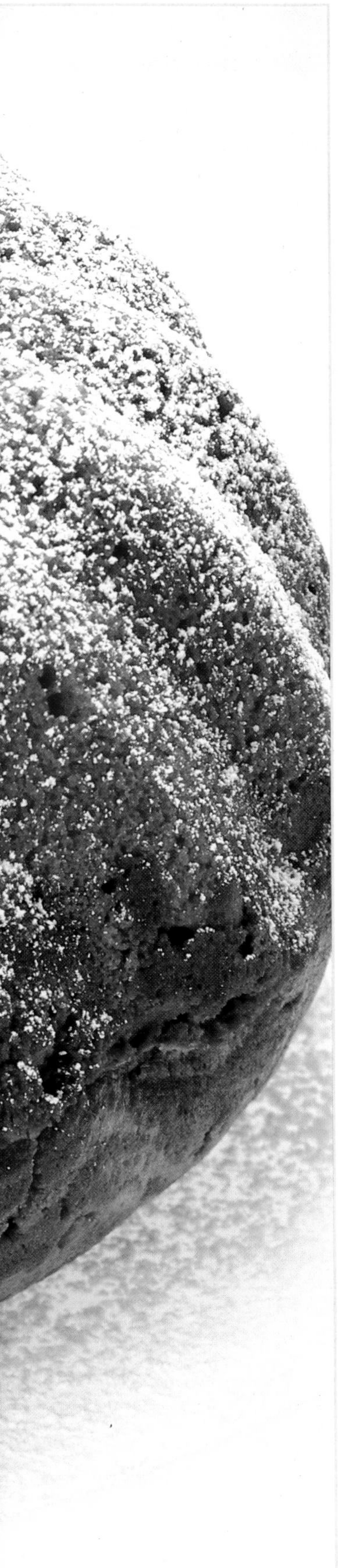

1

2

3

MARBLED CAKE

Yield: 1 9-inch cake
1 1/4 cups confectioners' sugar or superfine sugar
8 tablespoons salted butter, softened
5 eggs
1 1/4 cups flour
4 level teaspoons baking powder
2 teaspoons cocoa
2 tablespoons milk

Preheat the oven to 325°F.

Cream the sugar and the butter together. Gradually stir in the eggs. Mix the flour with the baking powder. Sift the flour mixture over the dough gradually, stirring it in after each addition.

Halve the dough and stir the cocoa and milk into one half. Grease a pound cake pan or ring pan and put in the light-colored dough (photograph 1). Spread the dark dough over this (photograph 2) and cut it into the light dough, using a fork and a spiral motion (photograph 3) to produce a marbled pattern. Bake for about 1 hour, or until a toothpick comes out clean.

SICILIAN FRUIT CAKE

Yield: 1 8-inch loaf cake
For the dough:
1/2 cup confectioners' sugar or superfine sugar
4 tablespoons salted butter, softened
2 egg yolks
1/2 cup flour
1 teaspoon lemon rind, grated
2 egg whites
For the filling:
3 level teaspoons unflavored gelatin
3 tablespoons cold water
1 tablespoon heavy cream
3 tablespoons orange liqueur
1 cup Ricotta cheese
1 teaspoon sugar
3 tablespoons chopped fruit topping
2 tablespoons semisweet baking chocolate
For the glaze:
3 tablespoons semisweet baking chocolate

Preheat the oven to 325°F.

Cream the butter and sugar together. Gradually stir in the egg yolks. Sift the flour over the dough and stir it in a little at a time. Add the lemon peel. Beat the egg whites until stiff and gently fold into the dough.

Grease an 8-inch loaf pan and fold in the dough. Bake for about 40 minutes. Remove from the oven and cool.

To make the filling, stir the gelatin into the water in a saucepan and heat, stirring constantly, until the gelatin has dissolved. Stir in the cream and orange liqueur. Mix the sugar and cheese together. Carefully stir in the gelatin solution and chopped fruit.

Cut the cake in thirds horizontally. Lay the bottom piece on a plate and spread it with some of the cheese mixture. Lay the second piece on top and spread it with the remaining cheese mixture. Top with the third slice of cake and press it on. Cover the cake and refrigerate.

To make the glaze, break the chocolate into small pieces and stir with the coconut butter in the top of a double boiler until creamy. Cover the cake with the glaze.

1

2

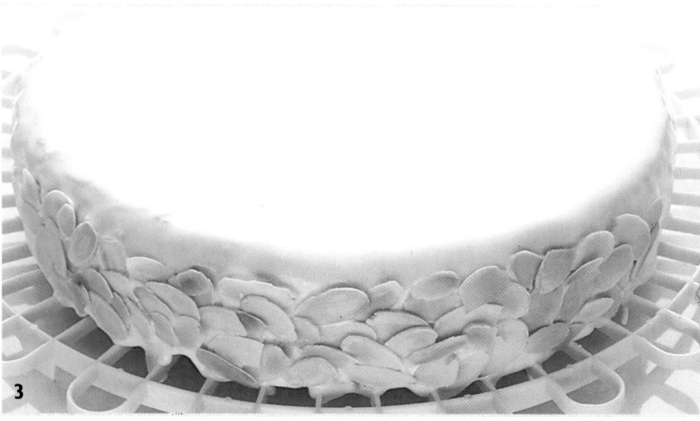
3

4

CARROT CAKE

Yield: 1 10-inch cake
For the kneaded dough:
½ cup flour
2 tablespoons salted butter, softened
1 tablespoon sugar
1 to 2 tablespoons cold water
For the carrot dough:
4 tablespoons salted butter, softened
3 tablespoons sugar
Lemon extract
1 pinch ground cinnamon
4 eggs, separated
¾ cup flour
1 teaspoon baking powder
3 tablespoons milk
3 tablespoons whipped cream
½ cup ground hazelnuts
1½ cups grated carrots
3 tablespoons sugar
For the glaze:
3 tablespoons apricot jam
½ cup confectioners' sugar
3 tablespoons cherry liqueur
For decoration:
¼ cup slivered, toasted almonds
½ cup marzipan
Red food coloring
Pistachio nuts

Preheat the oven to 325°F.

To make the kneaded dough, sift the flour into a bowl and add the butter, sugar, and water. Using the dough hook on an electric mixer, knead together briefly on the lowest setting and finish on the highest setting. Finally, hand knead the dough until smooth on a bread board. Cover and leave in the refrigerator for 1 hour.

To make the carrot dough, cream the butter and sugar together. Stir in the lemon extract and cinnamon. Gradually stir in the egg yolks. Sift the flour and baking powder together and stir into the dough a little at a time, alternating with the milk.

Mix the cream with the hazelnuts and grated carrots and stir into the dough. Beat the egg whites until stiff, beat in the sugar, and fold this mixture into the dough.

Grease a 10-inch springform pan. Roll out the kneaded dough to the size of the pan base and lay it in the pan. Add the carrot dough. Bake for about 45 minutes.

Heat the apricot jam, stirring it until smooth, and spread over the cooled cake (photograph 1). Stir the confectioners' sugar and cherry liqueur together and use this to ice the cake (photograph 2). Cover the sides of the cake with the slivered almonds (photograph 3).

To make the decorations, color the marzipan mixture with the food coloring to make it orange. Form it into a roll and cut into 12 pieces. Shape these into little carrots. Press 2 halves of a pistachio nut into the end of each carrot to make the stalk (photograph 4) and arrange them on the cake in a circle.

TREE CAKE

Yield: 1 10-inch cake
For the dough:
1 cup salted butter, softened
1 cup sugar
1 teaspoon vanilla extract
Salt to taste
3 tablespoons rum
6 eggs, 4 of them separated
¾ cup flour
¼ cup cornstarch
3 level teaspoons baking powder
For the glaze and topping:
8 ounces semisweet baking chocolate, melted
1 cup almond chips

Preheat the oven to 350°F.

To make the dough, cream the butter and gradually stir in the sugar, vanilla, salt, and rum. Gradually add the whole eggs and 4 egg yolks. Mix the flour, cornstarch, and baking powder together, sift them, and stir into the dough, a spoonful at a time. Beat the egg whites until stiff and carefully fold into the dough. Line a greased, 10-inch springform cake pan with parchment paper (photograph 1). Spread a heaping tablespoon of dough evenly over this with a pastry brush (photograph 2). Bake for 2 to 5 minutes, or until the cake is light brown. Spread another 1 to 2 tablespoons of dough over it to make a second layer (photograph 3) and bake this also. Repeat this process until all of the dough has been used. (Where possible, adjust the height of the oven rack so that the layer of cake is always 8 inches below the heating element).

Carefully loosen the finished cake from the sides of the pan using a knife. Turn the cake out onto a wire cooling rack and peel off the parchment paper (photograph 4). Return the cake to the hot oven at once, and leave it there for about 5 minutes.

For the glaze and the topping, stir the chocolate in the top of a double boiler until creamy. Spread half of the chocolate over the cake. Mix the rest of the melted chocolate with the almond chips and spread these over the top of the cake.

1

2

3

4

DUTCH BUTTER CAKE

Yield: 1 10-inch cake
For the dough:
¾ cup flour
½ cup superfine sugar
4 tablespoons salted butter, softened
2 small eggs
1 pinch salt

Preheat the oven to 325°F.

Sift the flour into a mixing bowl and add the sugar, butter, 1 egg, and salt. Mix the ingredients, using the dough hook attachment on an electric mixer, first on the lowest setting and then on the highest setting. Mix well, and then knead on a floured bread board until smooth. After kneading, cover the dough and place in a cool area for 1 hour. Turn the dough into a greased, 10-inch cake pan and smooth it, then spread beaten egg on top. Bake for 30 to 35 minutes. Remove from the oven and cool, then cut the cake into small cubes or triangles.

Tip: You can also top the cake with slivered almonds or with thinly sliced ginger.

SAVARIN

Yield: 2 6-inch savarins
For the dough:
1½ cups flour
½ package dry yeast
⅓ cup milk, heated
3 tablespoons sugar
5 tablespoons salted butter
4 eggs
½ teaspoon salt
½ teaspoon grated lemon peel
For the syrup:
1 cup water
¾ cup sugar
½ cup almond liqueur
3 tablespoons apricot jam
For the filling:
¾ cup heavy cream
1 cup strawberries

Preheat the oven to 325°F.

To make the dough, sift the flour into a mixing bowl and form a hollow in the center. Sprinkle the yeast into this hollow, pour in the heated milk and a little of the sugar and stir together. Cover the bowl with a cloth and let it stand for about 15 minutes in a warm place.

Melt the butter and add it to the dough, together with the rest of the sugar, eggs, salt, and lemon peel. Knead until smooth.

Grease and flour a 6-inch savarin pan and add half of the dough (photograph 4). Bake for 25 to 30 minutes. Remove the savarin from the pan and bake the remaining half of the dough.

To make the syrup, combine the water and sugar in a saucepan and bring to a boil, stirring constantly (photograph 2). Set aside to cool.

Brush the savarins with the syrup (photograph 3), repeating this until they have soaked up all the syrup. Heat the apricot jam in a small saucepan and stir until smooth. Brush the jam onto the savarins.

For the filling, whip the cream until stiff. Pick over and wash the strawberries, remove the hulls, and cut the large berries in half. Spoon some of the cream into the savarins and use the rest for garnish. Arrange the strawberries on the cream and serve.

1

2

3

NUTTY YEAST CAKE

Yield: 1 10-inch cake
For the dough:
¾ cup flour
½ package dry yeast
¼ cup lukewarm milk
2 tablespoons sugar
1½ tablespoons salted butter
1 egg
Salt to taste
For the topping:
½ cup raisins
3 tablespoons rum
½ cup marzipan
5 to 6 tablespoons heavy cream
1 egg yolk
¾ cup slivered almonds
For the glaze:
2 egg yolks
1 teaspoon vanilla extract
2 level tablespoons cornstarch
Cinnamon
1 cup milk, warmed

Preheat the oven to 325°F.

Sift the flour into a mixing bowl and form a hollow in the center. Crumble the yeast into the hollow, add the milk and sugar, and stir together. Let the dough stand in a warm place for about 15 minutes. Add the milk, butter, egg, and salt and knead until smooth. Cover and let rise in a warm place for 30 minutes.

To make the topping, soak the raisins in the rum. Stir the marzipan, cream, and egg yolk together. Roll out the dough and place on the bottom of a greased, 10-inch springform pan. Spread the marzipan mixture over the dough. Sprinkle the soaked raisins over the marzipan mixture.

To make the glaze, beat the egg yolk and vanilla until foamy, then stir in the cornstarch and cinnamon. Add the milk and simmer over low heat for a few minutes. Glaze the cake and bake for about 20 minutes.

1

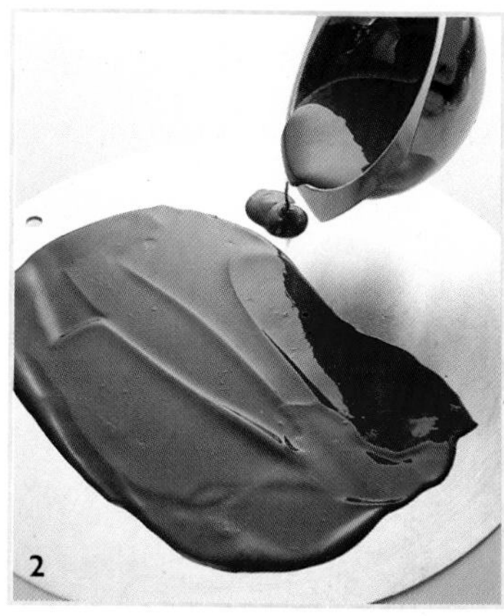
2

3

ORANGE AND WALNUT CAKE

Yield: 1 10-inch cake
For the dough:
7 eggs
¾ cup sugar
2 teaspoons vanilla extract
2 tablespoons grated orange peel
1 cup ground hazelnuts
2 tablespoons cornstarch
For decoration:
1¼ cups heavy cream
1 pinch cream of tartar
4 ounces semisweet chocolate

Preheat the oven to 350°F.

Beat the eggs with the whisk attachment on an electric mixer at the highest setting for 1 minute, or until the eggs are foamy. Mix the sugar, vanilla, and orange peel together. Sprinkle the orange peel mixture into the eggs while mixing for 1 minute; beat for 2 minutes more.

Mix the ground hazelnuts with the cornstarch and add half to the egg mixture, stirring it in quickly using the lowest setting. Work in the rest of the nut mixture the same way. Place the dough into a greased, 10-inch springform pan lined with parchment paper. Bake for 50 to 60 minutes. Remove from the oven and cool thoroughly.

Whip the heavy cream with the cream of tartar until stiff. Cover the cake completely with whipped cream. Melt the chocolate in the top of a double boiler until creamy (photograph 1) and pour it over a cake decorating plate (photograph 2). Spread thinly and allow to set. Gently scrape off large flakes of chocolate with a large spatula (photograph 3) and use these to finish decorating the cake.

WALNUT AND CARAMEL TORTE

Yield: 1 9-inch torte
For the dough:
2½ tablespoons salted butter, softened
¼ cup sugar
¾ cup flour
1 egg
1 egg yolk
½ teaspoon grated lemon peel
Salt to taste
For the filling:
¾ cup sugar
½ cup heavy cream, warmed
1 tablespoon honey
¼ cup chopped walnuts
1 pinch ground cinnamon
1 egg
For decoration:
4 ounces milk chocolate
¼ cup heavy cream
12 walnut halves

Preheat the oven to 400°F.

To make the dough, cream the butter and slowly mix in the sugar. Gradually stir in the egg, egg yolk, lemon peel, and salt. Sift the flour and fold it into the dough. Halve the dough and place on the bottom of a greased, 8½-inch springform cake pan, so that it forms a wall ½ inch high.

For the filling, melt the sugar in a saucepan and caramelize it with 1 to 2 tablespoons of cold water. Stir in the warm cream and then the honey, walnuts, and cinnamon. Remove from the heat and cool. Spread the filling onto the dough.

Roll out the remaining dough to the same size as the pan. Beat the egg and, using a pastry brush, brush it onto the walls of the dough. Cover with the second sheet of dough and brush the top with egg. Bake for about 20 minutes.

To make the decorations, heat the cream in the top of a double boiler. Add the chocolate, stirring constantly until the chocolate has melted. Remove from the heat and place over the bottom of a double boiler filled with ice water. Beat until the icing is light and cold. Put the icing into a pastry bag with a serrated tip and pipe out 12 rosettes onto the torte. Place 1 walnut half on each rosette.

1

2

3

4

FRENCH FRUIT TART

Yield: 1 10-inch tart
For the dough:
¾ cup flour
1 teaspoon vanilla extract
Salt to taste
3½ tablespoons salted butter, softened
1 egg
For the topping:
1 cup large apricots, peeled and sliced
3 medium apples, peeled, cored, and sliced
2 medium pears, peeled, cored, and sliced
For the glaze:
2 egg yolks
1 cup heavy cream
¼ cup sugar
1 teaspoon vanilla extract
2 level tablespoons cornstarch
Plus:
4 to 5 tablespoons apricot jam

Preheat the oven to 350°F.

To make the dough, sift the flour into a mixing bowl and add the vanilla, salt, butter, and egg. Mix together using the dough hook on an electric mixer, first on the lowest setting and then the highest setting. Knead the dough until smooth on a floured bread board and let it rest in a cold place for 30 minutes. Roll out the dough on a floured kitchen cloth (photograph 1) and place it in a greased tart pan.

Arrange the sliced fruit on the bottom of the tart (photograph 2).

To make the glaze, beat the egg yolk with the cream. Stir in the sugar, vanilla, and cornstarch and spread the mixture over the fruit (photograph 3). Bake for about 50 minutes.

Heat the apricot jam in a small saucepan, stirring until smooth. Glaze the tart (photograph 4) with the jam when it has just emerged from the oven.

BANANA TART WITH APRICOTS

Yield: 1 10-inch flan
For the dough:
1 cup flour
1 level teaspoon baking powder
½ cup sugar
1 teaspoon vanilla extract
Salt to taste
1 egg
4 tablespoons salted butter, softened
For the topping:
2 cups canned apricot halves
4 ripe bananas
2 tablespoons lemon juice
2 tablespoons slivered almonds
For the glaze:
½ cup confectioners' sugar
2 to 3 tablespoons lemon juice

Preheat the oven to 400°F.

Combine the flour and baking powder and sift them into a mixing bowl. Add the sugar, vanilla, salt, egg, and butter. Mix the ingredients using the dough hook attachment on an electric mixer, first on the lowest setting, then on the highest. Knead to a smooth dough on a floured bread board and then let it rest in a cold place for 30 minutes. Roll out two-thirds of the dough onto the bottom of a greased, 10-inch springform pan and press out a wall about ½ inch high around the edge. Prick the bottom several times with a fork and bake for about 10 minutes.

Drain the apricots, skin the bananas, and slice both ingredients. Mix the fruit slices with the lemon juice and almonds. Arrange the fruit mixture on the bottom of the tart.

Roll out the remaining dough to the size of the pan and place it on top of the fruit. Pinch the edges closed with your fingers or a pastry crimper. Prick the pastry lid several times with a fork. Place the tart in the oven and bake for about 35 minutes.

Sift the confectioners' sugar and mix with the lemon juice. Spread the glaze on the tart when it has just emerged from the oven.

ALMOND AND CHERRY CAKE

Yield: 1 8-inch cake
For the dough:
5 tablespoons cold, salted butter
¾ cup marzipan
¾ cup flour
½ level teaspoon baking powder
Salt to taste
1 teaspoon grated lemon peel
For the filling:
1 package vanilla pudding mix
2 cups milk
4 tablespoons salted butter, softened
4 tablespoons cherry liqueur
1 cup dark red cherries, halved and pitted
For the topping:
4 ounces white chocolate
For decoration:
⅛ cup slivered almonds
Confectioners' sugar
Cocoa powder

Knead the butter and marzipan together. Mix the flour and baking powder together and sift over the marzipan mixture. Add the salt and lemon peel and knead until smooth. Refrigerate, covered, for about 6 hours.

Preheat the oven to 350°F.

Roll out the dough very thinly on a floured bread board and cut out 3 bases with a diameter of 8 inches (photograph 1). Place the dough circles on a baking sheet lined with parchment paper and bake for 10 to 15 minutes. Trim the edges straight immediately after baking (photograph 2) and cool.

To make the filling, prepare the pudding with the milk, according to the package directions. Cool, stirring occasionally. Cream the butter and and slowly stir in the cooled pudding. Add the cherry liqueur.

For the topping, melt the chocolate in the top of a double boiler until creamy and spread onto the dough bases (photograph 3). Spread half of the cream onto one of the bases. Arrange the cherries on the cream (photograph 4) and cover with the second base. Spread this with a quarter of the cream and cover with the third base. Spread the remaining cream over the top and sides of the cake. Cover the sides with the slivered almonds and sift confectioners' sugar evenly over the top (photograph 5). Lay a paper stencil with the desired pattern on the cake and dust cocoa powder over it (photograph 6). Remove the stencil.

1

2

3

4

5

6

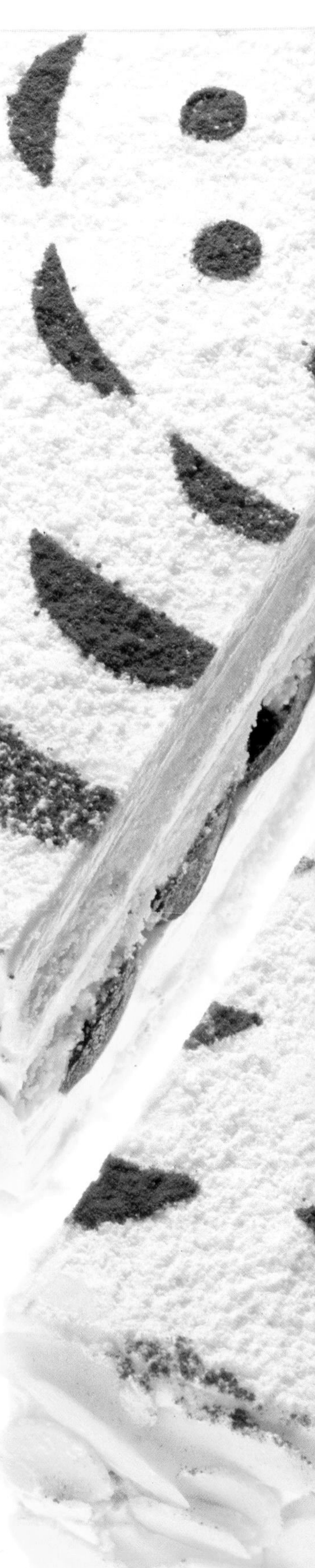

ANGEL CAKE

Yield: 1 10-inch cake
For the dough:
6 tablespoons salted butter, softened
½ cup sugar
1 teaspoon vanilla extract
2 egg yolks
Salt to taste
¾ cup flour
1 level teaspoon baking powder
For the topping:
2 egg whites
1 tablespoon sugar
1 teaspoon vanilla extract
1 level teaspoon ground cinnamon
¼ cup slivered almonds
For the filling:
2 cups heavy cream, chilled
Pinch cream of tartar
½ cup raspberry jam

Preheat the oven to 375°F.

To make the dough, cream the butter and gradually stir in the sugar, vanilla, egg yolks, and salt. Divide the dough into thirds. Roll out each third onto the greased bottom of a 10-inch springform pan.

To make the topping, beat the egg whites until stiff and spread evenly over the 3 dough bases. Mix the sugar, vanilla, and cinnamon together and sprinkle a third of the mixture and a third of the almonds onto each base. Place the bases side by side (without the sides of the springform pans) in a preheated oven and bake for about 15 minutes. Remove from the oven and cool.

To make the filling, whip the cream for ½ minute, sprinkle on the cream of tartar, and continue to whip until the cream is stiff. Spread raspberry jam and whipped cream on 2 of the bases. Layer the bases to make a cake.

RASPBERRY CAKE

Yield: 1 10-inch cake
For the dough:
6 eggs
½ cup sugar
1 teaspoon vanilla extract
½ cup flour
For the cream:
4 egg yolks
½ cup sugar
1 teaspoon vanilla extract
¼ cup flour
2 cups boiling milk
For the topping and decoration:
1 pound raspberries, picked over
2 cups heavy cream
¼ cup chopped hazelnuts or slivered almonds
Plus:
½ package red gelatin
¼ pint raspberry juice

Preheat the oven to 375°F.

For the dough, beat the eggs using the whisk attachment on an electric mixer at the highest setting until the eggs are foamy, about 1 minute. Mix the sugar and vanilla and then sprinkle onto the egg, beating for 1 minute; beat for 2 minutes more. Sift the flour onto the egg mixture and mix on the lowest setting. Place the dough in a greased, 10-inch springform pan lined with waxed paper and bake for about 30 minutes. Cool thoroughly.

For the cream, beat the egg yolks, sugar, and vanilla until white and foamy (photograph 1). Sift the flour and fold it in. Stir in the boiling-hot milk and simmer the cream in a saucepan over low heat for about 2 to 3 minutes (photograph 2). Pour the cream into a bowl and cool.

Cut the cake base in half horizontally. Spread with two-thirds of the cream and top with half of the raspberries. Spread the upper layer of the cake thinly with the cream (photograph 3) and place it with the cream side down on top of the raspberries. Spread the rest of the cream over the cake.

Whip the heavy cream until stiff and spread some of it onto the top and sides of the cake (photograph 4). Sprinkle the sides with the nuts.

Fill a pastry bag with whipped cream and pipe a wall of cream around the top of the cake. Fill this with the rest of the raspberries (photograph 5).

Optional step: Prepare the gelatin according to the package instructions and spread this over the raspberries.

STRAWBERRY TART

Yield: 1 10-inch tart
For the dough:
3/4 cup flour
1/4 cup superfine sugar
Salt to taste
4 tablespoons cold, salted butter
For the filling:
1 package unflavored gelatin
2 eggs, separated
3/4 cup heavy cream
1/4 cup superfine sugar
Juice of 1 lemon
4 tablespoons currant jelly
3/4 pound strawberries, washed and halved
Sugar
1 cup strawberry juice
1 package red gelatin

Preheat the oven to 375°F.

Sift the flour into a mixing bowl and combine with the sugar and salt. Break the butter into small pieces and add to the flour. Work it all together using the dough hook attachment on an electric mixer. Grease the bottom of a 10-inch springform pan and cover with the crumbly dough, pressing it down lightly. Prick the dough several times with a fork. Bake for about 30 minutes. Loosen the base from the pan and cool.

To make the filling, dissolve the gelatin in warm water for about 10 minutes. Beat the egg whites until stiff. In a separate bowl, whip the cream until stiff. Heat the lemon juice and add the gelatin, stirring until it has dissolved. Fold in the whipped cream and beaten egg white.

Spread currant jelly on the cake base and place a cake wall around it. Spoon the cream into this and allow it to set. Sprinkle the strawberries with sugar and set aside for 5 to 10 minutes. Drain the strawberries, reserving the juice. Arrange the strawberries on the tart. Mix the reserved strawberry juice with water and prepare the gelatin according to the package instructions. Spread evenly over the strawberries. Remove the cake wall when the gelatin has set.

1

2

3

CHOCOLATE CHERRY CAKE

Yield: 1 10-inch cake
For the kneaded dough:
3/4 cup flour
2 tablespoons sugar
1 teaspoon cocoa
3 1/2 tablespoons salted butter, softened
1 teaspoon lemon juice
For the sponge dough:
1 egg
2 tablespoons hot water
3 tablespoons sugar
1/4 teaspoon vanilla extract
1/4 cup flour
1 pinch baking powder
For the chocolate cream:
1/2 package unflavored gelatin
2 tablespoons sugar
3 tablespoons unsweetened cocoa
1 1/4 cups heavy cream
For the cherry cream:
1/2 package unflavored gelatin
4 tablespoons cherry liqueur, heated
1 1/4 cups heavy cream
1/4 teaspoon vanilla extract
1 teaspoon sugar
For decoration:
1/2 cup heavy cream
4 tablespoons chocolate flakes
Cocoa powder
Plus:
3 tablespoons raspberry jam

Preheat the oven to 400°F.

To make the kneaded dough, sift the flour into a mixing bowl and add the sugar, cocoa, butter, and lemon juice. Mix together with the dough hook attachment on an electric mixer, first using the lowest and then the highest setting. Knead until smooth on a floured bread board. Roll the dough out onto the greased bottom of a 10-inch springform pan and bake it for about 15 minutes. Loosen the cake from the base of the pan immediately after baking, and cool.

To make the sponge dough, beat the egg and water for 1 minutes, using the whisk attachment on an electric mixer at the highest setting. Mix the sugar and vanilla together, and sprinkle it on, beating for 1 minute; beat for 2 minutes more. Combine the flour and baking powder and sift half of it onto the egg mixture. Beat in quickly using the lowest setting. Work in the remaining flour in the same way. Line the greased bottom of a springform pan with waxed paper. Turn the dough into the pan and smooth it. Bake for about 15 minutes. Turn it out carefully onto a cooling rack and peel off the paper.

To make the chocolate cream, dissolve the gelatin in 5 tablespoons of warmed water. Stir the sugar and cocoa together and add to the water, bringing it to a boil. Stir constantly until the sugar has dissolved. Whip the cream until slightly stiff, and beat the gelatin syrup into it evenly (photograph 1).

To make the cherry cream, dissolve the gelatin in the heated cherry liqueur, stirring constantly. Beat the cream until slightly stiff, and beat the vanilla, sugar, and gelatin evenly into it.

Spread the cake base with raspberry jam and cover with the sponge base. Spread the chocolate cream on in a dome shape (photograph 2). Stand a cake ring, which has been greased on the inside, around the cake and fill with the cherry cream (photograph 3). Refrigerate the cake for 1 hour.

To make the decoration, whip the cream until stiff. Spread some of the whipped cream onto the side of the cake and sprinkle with the grated chocolate. Decorate the top of the cake with cream rosettes, and dust with cocoa powder.

SNOWFLAKE CAKE

Yield: 1 10-inch cake
For the dough:
4 tablespoons salted butter, softened
2 1/2 cups sugar
1/2 teaspoon vanilla extract
4 eggs, separated
Salt to taste
1/2 cup flour
1 level teaspoon baking powder
1/4 cup grated coconut, toasted
For the filling:
3 tablespoons raspberry jam
2 cups heavy cream
1 teaspoon vanilla extract
1/2 teaspoon cream of tartar
1/8 cup grated coconut
Confectioners' sugar

Preheat the oven to 325°F.

To make the dough, cream the butter, sugar, and vanilla together and gradually beat in the egg yolks and salt. Sift the flour and baking powder together. Stir in the butter mixture, a spoonful at a time. Add the coconut.

Beat the egg whites until stiff and fold into the dough. Turn the dough into a greased, 10-inch springform pan and smooth with a knife. Bake for 30 minutes. Halve the cooled cake horizontally.

To make the filling, spread the bottom half of the cake with the jam. Whip the cream for 1/2 minute. Add the vanilla extract and the cream of tartar and whip until stiff. Spread half of the whipped cream onto the bottom half of the cake, and cover with the top half of the cake. Spread the rest of the cream onto the cake and sprinkle all over with the grated coconut. Dust with confectioners' sugar just before serving.

RUSSIAN APPLE CAKE

Yield: 1 10-inch cake
For the kneaded dough:
¾ cup flour
1 pinch baking powder
2 teaspoons sugar
1 teaspoon vanilla extract
Salt to taste
3 tablespoons salted butter, softened
For the sponge dough:
5 eggs
3 tablespoons hot water
¾ cup sugar
1 teaspoon vanilla extract
½ cup flour
½ cup cornstarch
2½ level teaspoons baking powder
For the butter cream:
1 package vanilla pudding mix
2 cups milk
8 tablespoons salted butter, softened
For the apple mixture:
1 pound (6 to 8 medium) green cooking apples
2 cups water
3 tablespoons apricot jam
2 tablespoons rum
⅛ cup currants
2 tablespoons slivered almonds
Plus:
2 to 3 tablespoons apricot jam
4 tablespoons rum
2 tablespoons water
1 teaspoon sugar
½ cup caramelized almonds

Preheat the oven to 400°F.

To make the kneaded dough, sift the flour and baking powder into a mixing bowl. Add the sugar, vanilla extract, salt, and butter and mix with the dough hook attachment on an electric mixer, first using the lowest, and then the highest setting. Knead until smooth on a floured bread board, and let the dough rest for 1 hour in a cool place. Roll the dough out onto the bottom of a greased, 10-inch springform pan and prick it several times with a fork. Bake for about 15 minutes. Loosen from the pan immediately, and allow to cool.

To make the sponge dough, beat the eggs with the water using the whisk attachment on an electric mixer at the highest setting for 1 minute, or until the eggs are foamy. Beat in the sugar and vanilla extract, mixing for 3 minutes more. Mix the flour, cornstarch, and baking powder together. Sift half of the flour mixture onto the egg mixture, beating quickly on the lowest setting. Work in the remaining flour mixture the same way. Place the dough into a greased, 10-inch springform pan lined with waxed paper and smooth with a knife. Bake for 35 minutes. Remove the cake from the pan immediately and turn it onto a cooling rack. Peel off the paper. When the cake has cooled, cut it into 4 layers.

To make the butter cream, prepare the pudding with the milk according to the instructions on the package and allow it to cool, stirring occasionally. Cream the butter and slowly stir into the cooled pudding, which should be the same temperature as the butter (photograph 1).

To make the apple mixture, peel and quarter the apples, remove the cores, and cut into slices. Put the apples into a pot of boiling water and simmer gently for 3 to 5 minutes (photograph 2). Remove the apples from the liquid, drain, and cool. Carefully mix the apple slices with the apricot jam, 2 tablespoons of rum, and currants. Fold the slivered almonds into half of the apple mixture. Spread apricot jam onto the kneaded dough base and place the first sponge cake layer onto it. Stir 4 tablespoons of rum with water and sugar and sprinkle this onto the sponge layer. Spread a

third of the butter cream on top (photograph 3). Cover with the second layer of sponge cake. Spread the plain apple mixture onto this layer (photograph 4) and cover with the third layer of sponge cake, pressing it gently. Spread half of the remaining butter cream onto it, and cover with the fourth layer of sponge cake. Put 2 to 3 tablespoons of the remaining butter cream into a pastry bag with a star tip. Spread the rest of the cream over the sides and the outer 1½ inches of the top of the cake. Put the prepared apple mixture onto the cake inside this ring of butter cream (photograph 5). Sprinkle the caramelized almonds over the cream on the sides and top of the cake (photograph 6) and decorate with rosettes of butter cream.

LIME ROLL

Yield: 1 10-inch roll
For the dough:
8 eggs
1 cup sugar
1 teaspoon grated lemon peel
1 cup flour
For the cream:
1½ cups milk
½ cup heavy cream
1 teaspoon vanilla extract
6 egg yolks
1 cup sugar
¼ cup flour
½ teaspoon grated lemon peel
¼ cup lime juice
6 eggs
1½ cups butter
Plus:
1 cup marzipan
Green food coloring
Confectioners' sugar

Preheat the oven to 400°F.

To make the dough, beat the eggs with the whisk attachment on an electric mixer for 1 minute, using the highest setting. Mix the sugar and lemon peel together and add to the eggs, beating for 2 minutes. Sift half of the flour into the eggs, stirring it in on the lowest setting. Work in the rest of the flour the same way. Line a jelly roll pan with waxed paper and spread the dough evenly on it (photograph 1). Bake for 12 minutes. Remove immediately after baking and turn onto a cloth sprinkled with sugar. Peel off the paper. Roll the slab of sponge cake up in the cloth and let cool.

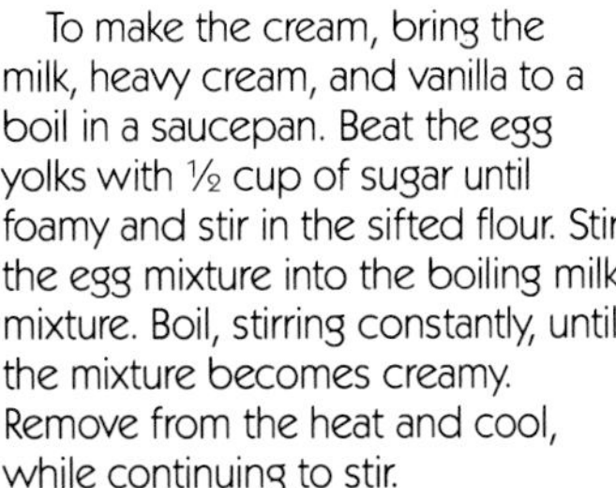

To make the cream, bring the milk, heavy cream, and vanilla to a boil in a saucepan. Beat the egg yolks with ½ cup of sugar until foamy and stir in the sifted flour. Stir the egg mixture into the boiling milk mixture. Boil, stirring constantly, until the mixture becomes creamy. Remove from the heat and cool, while continuing to stir.

Beat the lemon peel, lime juice, and remaining sugar with the whole eggs in the top of a double boiler until creamy in consistency (photograph 2). Let it rest in a cool place, stirring occasionally. Cream the butter and carefully beat in the egg cream and the lemon cream.

Knead the marzipan with the food coloring and form 6 rolls about ½ inch thick from a third of the marzipan. Carefully unroll the sponge cake (photograph 3). Spread a third of the cream onto the cake and lay the marzipan rolls at equal distances from each other on it (photograph 4). Spread half of the remaining cream over the marzipan rolls and roll up the sponge cake again. Spread a portion of the remaining cream over the roll and put the rest of it into a pastry bag with a star tip. Roll out the rest of the marzipan thinly on sifted confectioners' sugar and wrap it around the sponge roll (photograph 5). Decorate the lime roll with rosettes of cream. Refrigerate if not serving immediately.

CRUMB CHEESECAKE

Yield: 1 10-inch cake
For the dough:
¾ cup flour
½ level teaspoon baking powder
¼ cup sugar
1 teaspoon vanilla extract
Salt to taste
1 egg
3 tablespoons salted butter, softened
1 tablespoon flour
For the filling:
1 pound cream cheese
¾ cup sugar
3 tablespoons lemon juice
2 tablespoons cornstarch
3 eggs, separated
1 cup heavy cream
For the crumbs:
¼ cup flour
¼ cup sugar
1 teaspoon vanilla extract
3 tablespoons salted butter, softened

Preheat the oven to 400°F.

To make the dough, sift the flour and baking powder into a mixing bowl. Add the sugar, vanilla extract, salt, butter, and egg and beat well, using the dough hook attachment on an electric mixer, first using the lowest and then the highest setting. Remove from the bowl and knead until smooth on a floured bread board. Roll out two-thirds of the dough onto the bottom of a greased, 10-inch springform pan. Knead 1 tablespoon of flour into the rest of the dough, form it into a roll, and press around the edges of the pastry base to form a wall about 1½ inches high. Prick the pastry base several times with a fork. Bake for 10 minutes, then remove from the oven. Reduce the oven heat to 325°F.

To make the filling, stir the cream cheese together with the sugar, lemon juice, cornstarch, and egg yolk. Beat the egg white until stiff. In a separate bowl, whip the cream until stiff. Fold the egg white and whipped cream into the cheese mixture, and spread it evenly over the baked cake base.

To make the crumbs, sift the flour into a mixing bowl and add the sugar, vanilla, and butter. Rub the mixture together with your fingers to form crumbs. Spread evenly over the filling and bake for 70 to 80 minutes. Turn the oven off and allow the cake to cool in the oven for 15 minutes, leaving the oven door open.

RASPBERRY ROLLS

Yield: 4 rolls
For the sponge dough:
3 eggs
3 to 4 tablespoons hot water
½ cup superfine sugar
Grated lemon peel
½ cup flour
For the filling:
1 cup heavy cream
1 tablespoon sugar
1 teaspoon vanilla extract
¾ cup raspberries, picked over
For the raspberry sauce:
2 cups raspberries, picked over
2 tablespoons raspberry liqueur
Sugar, to taste
Plus:
1 tablespoon confectioners' sugar

Preheat the oven to 400°F.

For the dough, beat the eggs and hot water until foamy, about 1 minute, with the whisk attachment on an electric mixer, using the highest setting. Combine the sugar and lemon peel and mix for 3 minutes. Sift the flour into the egg mixture and beat it in quickly, using the lowest setting.

Cut out 4 circles with a diameter of about 8 inches from the aluminum foil, lay each over the base of a 6½-inch tart pan and press in the sides to form molds (photograph 1). Grease well and pour in the dough (photograph 2). Bake for 8 to 12 minutes. Remove immediately from the molds, wrap over a rolling pin, and allow to cool in that position.

For the filling, whip the cream, sugar, and vanilla extract until stiff and put the whipped cream into a pastry bag with a serrated tip. Fill the rolls lightly by piping in some of the cream. Add the raspberries to the rolls (photograph 3). Fold them over and decorate with the rosettes of piped cream (photograph 4). Sift the confectioners' sugar over the rolls.

For the sauce, heat the raspberries with the raspberry liqueur and pass through a fine strainer to remove the seeds. Sweeten the sauce to taste, and serve hot with the raspberry rolls.

STRAWBERRY SLICES

Yield: 8 to 10 servings
For the dough:
8 eggs
1 cup sugar
Grated peel of ½ lemon
1½ cups flour
For the cream:
1 pound strawberries, washed
1 package vanilla pudding mix
1 tablespoon cornstarch
½ cup fresh orange juice
1 pound salted butter, softened
2 tablespoons orange or almond liqueur
For garnishing:
4 tablespoons orange or almond liqueur
½ pound strawberries, washed and sliced

Preheat the oven to 400°F.
For the dough, beat the eggs until foamy, about 1 minute, with the whisk attachment on an electric mixer, using the highest setting. Add the sugar and grated lemon peel and continue to beat for 2 minutes more. Sift half of the flour over the egg and quickly beat it in on the lowest setting. Work in the rest of the flour the same way. Spread the dough over a jelly roll pan or baking sheet lined with parchment paper and bake for about 10 minutes. Turn onto a kitchen cloth and remove the paper.

To make the strawberry cream, puree the strawberries in a food processor. Stir the puree with the sugar and bring it to a boil in a saucepan. Stir the pudding mix with the orange juice and cornstarch, then add the mixture to the saucepan with the strawberry puree. Bring to a boil and continue to boil for 2 minutes. Allow the mixture to cool, stirring occasionally. Stir the butter, a portion at a time, into the cooled strawberry mixture, and then stir in 2 tablespoons of orange or almond liqueur. Cut the sponge cake slab into pieces 2½ inches wide and 8 inches long and sprinkle with 4 tablespoons of the liqueur.

Spoon the cream into a pastry bag with a wide tip and pipe it evenly onto the sponge pieces. Place 3 pieces of sponge together and press them gently together. Garnish with strawberry slices.

1

2

3

4

STRAWBERRY PUFFS

Yield: 12 to 15 puffs
For the dough:
1 package frozen puff pastry
For the topping:
2 cups milk
½ cup heavy cream
1 teaspoon vanilla extract
3 egg yolks
¼ cup sugar
3 tablespoons cornstarch
1 pound strawberries, washed and halved
4 tablespoons apricot jam

Preheat the oven to 400°F.

Allow the puff pastry to thaw at room temperature and roll it out until smooth. Rinse out 12 to 15 tartlet molds, or brioche molds, with cold water and line them with the pastry (photograph 1).

For the cream, mix the milk with the heavy cream. Set aside 5 tablespoons of the milk mixture and bring the rest of it to a boil with the vanilla. Stir the egg yolks, sugar, cornstarch, and the reserved 5 tablespoons of milk together, and pour into the boiling milk. Continue to boil until mixture thickens, stirring constantly. Remove from the heat and cool, stirring occasionally.

Spoon the cooled cream into the pastry shells (photograph 2). Bake for about 30 minutes, or until the cream is slightly browned.

In a saucepan, stir the apricot jam with 1 tablespoon of water, heat slowly until liquid, and brush half over the upper surface of the puffs (photograph 3). Allow the puffs to cool.

Arrange the strawberries on the puffs and brush the strawberries with the rest of the apricot jam (photograph 4).

PEAR PIES

Yield: 4 4-inch pies
For the pastry:
1 package frozen puff pastry
For the filling:
4 tablespoons raisins
2 tablespoons pear liqueur
$\frac{1}{4}$ cup marzipan
2 tablespoons apricot jam
4 canned pear halves
1 egg yolk, for glaze

Preheat the oven to 400°F.

Thaw the puff pastry to room temperature and roll out thickly on a floured bread board. Cut out 5 circles with a diameter of 4 inches, and 4 circles with a diameter of 6 inches. Soak the raisins in the pear liqueur. Mix the marzipan, apricot jam, and raisins together and spread over the smaller circles. Lay the pear halves on top. Brush the edges of the pastry with beaten egg yolk and place the larger circles over the smaller circles. Press the edges of the pastries together and place in a cool place for 10 minutes.

Place the pies on a baking sheet that has been rinsed with cold water and brush with beaten egg yolk. Bake for about 20 minutes. Serve warm, with a vanilla sauce.

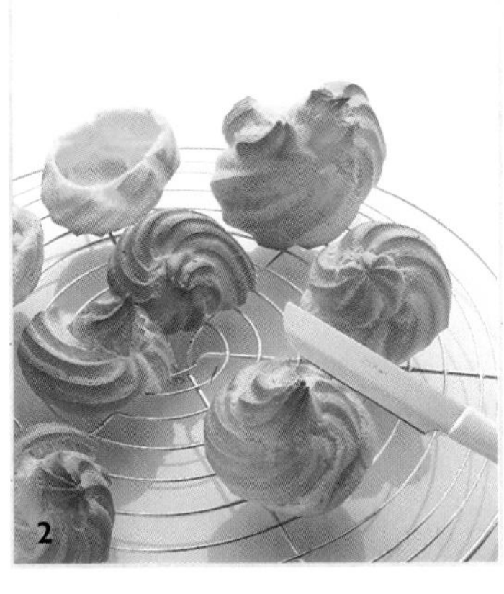

CREAM PUFFS, ECLAIRS, AND BANANA CREAM PUFFS

Yield: 1 dozen shells

For the dough:
¾ cup water
1½ tablespoons salted butter
1 tablespoon sugar
1 teaspoon vanilla extract
⅔ cup flour
1 tablespoon cornstarch
4 eggs
1 teaspoon baking powder

For the strawberry filling:
1 envelope unflavored gelatin
1 package vanilla pudding mix
1 cup milk
1 cup strawberries, washed
1 cup heavy cream
Sugar (optional)
1 tablespoon confectioners' sugar

For the pistachio filling:
1½ cups heavy cream
1 tablespoon confectioners' sugar
1 cup pistachio nuts
1 tablespoon almond liqueur

For the banana boats:
1½ cups heavy cream
1 teaspoon sugar
4 bananas

For the glaze:
¾ cup confectioners' sugar
About 3 tablespoons water
Yellow food coloring
2 squares unsweetened baking chocolate

Preheat the oven to 400°F

For the dough, bring the water, butter, sugar, and vanilla extract to a boil in a heavy saucepan. Remove the pan from the heat. Sift the flour and cornstarch together and add, all at once, to the liquid in the saucepan. Stir until a smooth ball has formed. Heat for about 1 minute, stirring constantly. Place the hot ball into a mixing bowl. Gradually mix in the eggs, using the dough hook attachment on an electric mixer at the highest setting. Stir the baking powder into the cold dough. Place the dough into a pastry bag with a wide tip. Line a baking sheet with parchment paper and pipe out mounds for the cream puffs, or strips about 3 inches long for the eclairs, or slightly curved strips for the banana boats (photograph 1). Bake the cream puffs for 25 to 30 minutes, the eclairs and banana boats for about 20 minutes. Remove from the oven and immediately cut the pastries in half horizontally (photograph 2).

For the strawberry filling, soak the gelatin in cold water for 10 minutes and squeeze out well. Prepare the vanilla pudding with the milk, following the package instructions. Stir the gelatin into the hot sauce. Puree the strawberries in a food processor, then add them to the cooled pudding and set aside in a cool place. Whip the cream with a little sugar until stiff and fold it into the strawberry mixture. Pipe the strawberry cream onto the lower half of the cream puffs and cover each one with the top half of the pastry, dusting them with confectioners' sugar.

For the pistachio filling, whip the cream with 1 tablespoon of confectioners' sugar until stiff. Chop the pistachio nuts finely and fold them into the cream with the almond liqueur. Place the mixture into a pastry bag and pipe it onto the lower half of the eclairs. Cover with the top half of the pastry (photograph 4).

4

5

6

For the banana filling, whip the cream until stiff and pipe it onto the lower half of the banana boats. Peel and slice the bananas and lay them on the cream (photograph 5). Put the tops on the banana boats.

For the glaze, stir the confectioners' sugar with 3 tablespoons of water until smooth. Color it slightly with yellow food coloring. Spread the glaze onto the upper side of the banana boats and let dry slightly. Melt the baking chocolate in the top of a double boiler, stirring until liquid. Place the melted chocolate in a pastry tube made from parchment paper. Cut off the point of the bag and use this to decorate the cream puffs (photograph 6).

1

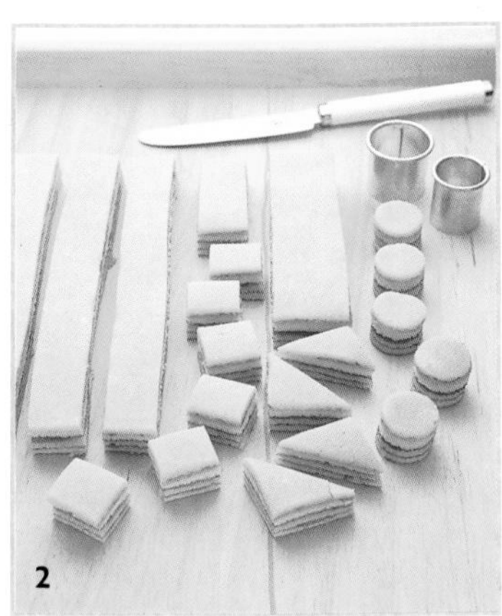

2

PETITS FOURS

Yield: About 4 dozen petits fours
For the dough:
6 eggs
3/4 cup sugar
1 teaspoon honey
1/2 cup flour
For the topping:
5 tablespoons apricot jam
5 tablespoons raspberry jam
3/4 cup marzipan
1/2 cup confectioners' sugar
For the glaze:
3 cups confectioners' sugar
5 to 6 tablespoons water
Food coloring
For garnishing:
Cake decorations
Candied flowers and fruit
Chocolate shavings

Preheat the oven to 400°F.

For the dough, beat the eggs until foamy, about 1 minute, with the whisk attachment on an electric mixer, using the highest setting. Add the sugar and honey and beat for 2 minutes. Sift half of the flour onto the egg mixture and quickly stir it in on the lowest setting. Work in the rest of the flour in the same way. Spread half of the dough onto a greased baking sheet or jelly roll pan lined with waxed paper. Bake for 10 minutes. Turn the cake out onto a cloth immediately after baking and remove the paper. Allow it to cool. Prepare the rest of the dough in the same way.

Spread apricot jam on one of the cake slabs (photograph 1) and cover with the second cake slab. Spread raspberry jam on the second slab. Knead the confectioners' sugar into the marzipan and roll it out to the same size as the cake, then place it on top of the cake. Cut the cake into assorted shapes, such as triangles, ovals, circles, or half-moons (photograph 2).

For the glaze, stir the sifted confectioners' sugar with the water. If desired, color the glaze lightly in various tints and ice the petits fours (photograph 3). Decorate with an assortment of cake ornaments (photograph 4).

3

4

APPLE PASTRIES

Yield: 6 pastries
For the filling:
1 ½ pounds apples
¼ cup raisins
½ cup sugar
3 to 4 drops lemon extract
For the dough:
1 ½ cups flour
1 teaspoon baking powder
¾ cup cream cheese
6 tablespoons milk
6 tablespoons peanut oil
¼ cup sugar
1 teaspoon vanilla extract
Salt to taste
Milk
For the glaze:
½ cup confectioners' sugar
Hot water

Preheat the oven to 400°F.

For the filling, peel and quarter the apples, core them, and cut into small pieces. Boil them gently in a saucepan with the raisins and sugar, stirring constantly. Remove from the heat and cool. Add lemon extract to taste.

For the dough, sift the flour and baking powder into a mixing bowl. Add the cheese, milk, oil, sugar, and salt. Mix for 1 minute with the dough hook attachment on an electric mixer, using the highest setting. Form the dough into a roll on a floured bread board. Roll out thinly and cut out circles with a diameter of 4 inches. Cover half of each circle with the apple mixture, brush the edges of the dough with milk, and fold the dough over the filling. Press the edges together firmly, and place the pastries on a greased baking sheet. Bake for about 15 minutes.

For the glaze, mix the confectioners' sugar with just enough water to form a thick consistency. Spread the glaze on the pastries as soon as they have been baked.

Cherries, peaches, or apricots can be used instead of apples.

NUT MARZIPAN

Yield: about ½ pound
For the mixture:
¾ cup marzipan
1 rounded tablespoon confectioners' sugar
1 teaspoon nut liqueur
¼ cup ground roasted hazelnuts
4 ounces milk chocolate
4 ounces semisweet chocolate
For garnishing:
Hazelnuts
Plus:
Confectioners' sugar

Knead the marzipan with the confectioners' sugar, liqueur, and hazelnuts. Roll the marzipan out on a bread board dusted with confectioners' sugar so that it is ⅛ of an inch thick and cut it into small squares (photograph 1). Melt the chocolate in the top of a double boiler until creamy and cover half of the candy with the milk chocolate and the other half with the semisweet chocolate.

To decorate, dip the hazelnuts in semisweet chocolate and place one in the center of each milk chocolate candy (photograph 2). Swirl the semisweet candy with the remaining milk chocolate.

1

2

3

CHOCOLATE AND MARZIPAN CANDIES

Yield: about ½ pound
For the candy:
¾ cup marzipan
1 tablespoon confectioners' sugar
2 ounces semisweet chocolate
2 tablespoons brandy
For decoration:
4 ounces milk chocolate
4 ounces semisweet chocolate
Chocolate shavings
Plus:
Confectioners' sugar

Knead the marzipan with the confectioners' sugar. Melt the chocolate in the top of a double boiler until creamy. Stir in the brandy and mix together with the marzipan. Roll the

marzipan out about ⅛ of an inch thick onto a bread board that has been spread with confectioners' sugar. Cut out assorted shapes (photograph 3) or form small balls.

Melt the milk chocolate and semisweet chocolate in the top of a double boiler and use the chocolate mixture to ice the candy. Sprinkle with chocolate shavings.

PINEAPPLE AND ALMOND CHOCOLATE CREAMS

Yield: 25 candies
For the candy:
7 ounces milk chocolate
1 cup caramelized almonds
For decoration:
¼ cup candied pineapple pieces
2 ounces semisweet chocolate, melted

Melt the milk chocolate in the top of a double boiler, then stir in the almonds. Using 2 teaspoons, place small mounds of the mixture onto the waxed paper and flatten them slightly. Place a piece of pineapple on each candy, and decorate with melted semisweet chocolate.

NOUGAT CHOCOLATE CREAMS

1

2

3

Yield: 25 candies
For the candy:
½ cup heavy cream
8 ounces semisweet chocolate
¾ cup mixed ground hazelnuts and almonds
1 tablespoon salted butter
2 tablespoons peanut butter
For garnishing:
Confectioners' sugar

Bring the cream to a boil in the top of a double boiler. Remove from heat and dissolve the chocolate in it. Stir in the ground nuts, butter, and peanut butter. Put the pan over a bowl of ice water and beat the mixture until foamy and cold (photograph 1). Spoon the mixture into a pastry bag and pipe it out into small chocolate molds (photograph 2). Dust with confectioners' sugar.

CARAMEL NUT CHOCOLATE CREAMS

Yield: 25 candies
For the candy
½ cup sugar
½ tablespoon salted butter
3 tablespoons heavy cream
⅛ cup marzipan
¼ cup slivered almonds, toasted
For the glaze:
Milk chocolate
For garnishing:
Cocoa

Melt the sugar in a saucepan over low heat, stirring constantly (photograph 3) until it turns light brown. Remove the pan from the stove and swirl in the butter and then the cream. Gently heat the mixture and stir in the marzipan and almonds.

Spread the mixture over a buttered tray or jelly roll pan to a depth of about ½ inch and allow it to cool. Cut into small rectangles about ½ inch by 1½ inches.

Melt the chocolate in the top of a double boiler until creamy and ice the chocolate creams. Dust with cocoa.

4

5

6

CHOCOLATE AND MARZIPAN CREAMS

Yield: 28 candies
For the candy:
1 cup marzipan
1 teaspoon confectioners' sugar
2 ounces semisweet chocolate
2 teaspoons cognac
For decoration:
Milk chocolate
Chocolate shavings
Plus:
Confectioners' sugar

Knead the marzipan and confectioners' sugar together. Melt the chocolate in the top of a double boiler and mix in the marzipan mixture; add the cognac. On a bread board that has been dusted with confectioners' sugar, roll out the mixture to a thickness of about ⅛ inch. Cut out crescent shapes, or roll into small balls. Melt the milk chocolate and pour over the candy. Sprinkle with the chocolate shavings.

ALMOND CHIP TRUFFLES

Yield: 35 to 50 candies
For the candy:
4 tablespoons salted butter
1 tablespoon confectioners' sugar
8 ounces semisweet chocolate
5 tablespoons almond liqueur
½ cup slivered almonds, toasted
For the glaze:
Milk chocolate
For garnishing:
White chocolate shavings

Cream the butter and confectioners' sugar together. Melt the chocolate in the top of a double boiler until creamy. Remove from the heat and cool slightly. The chocolate should remain liquid but not warm.

Stir the chocolate and almond liqueur into the butter (photograph 5) and immediately pipe it out.

Press a slivered almond into each candy and set aside to cool.

If desired, melt the milk chocolate in the top of a double boiler until creamy and decorate the truffles with it (photograph 6). Garnish with white chocolate shavings.

MERINGUES

Yield: 50 meringues
For the meringue mixture:
6 egg whites
2 cups superfine sugar
For the meringue bows and dots:
Semisweet chocolate
Pistachio nuts
For the meringue tartlets:
2 ounces semisweet chocolate
1 pound assorted strawberries, raspberries, and kiwis
¾ cup heavy cream
For the meringue snowballs:
1 pound vanilla ice cream
¾ cup heavy cream

Preheat the oven to 200°F.

Beat the egg white until stiff with the whisk attachment on an electric mixer, using the highest setting (photograph 1). Gradually beat in the sugar. Beat the mixture until it is thick enough to be cut with a knife. To make the bows and dots, fill a pastry bag with a serrated tip and pipe out the dots or bows onto a baking sheet lined with parchment paper (photograph 2).

To make the tartlets, draw circles with a diameter of 4 inches on the baking paper. Put part of the meringue mixture into a piping bag with a smooth tip and pipe out the circles in a spiral form. Put the rest of the mixture into a piping bag with a serrated tip and pipe out a wall of dots all around the edge of each tartlet.

To make the meringue snowballs, draw circles with a diameter of about 3½ inches onto aluminum foil. Put the mixture into a piping bag with a large, smooth tip and pipe out the circles in the form of a dome (photograph 3). Put the baking sheet into the oven and bake the meringues slowly for about 3 hours.

If desired, partially cover half of the bows and dots with melted chocolate (it should not be too warm) and sprinkle with chopped pistachio nuts. Spread the insides of the tartlets with melted chocolate (photograph 5).

Whip the cream until stiff and pipe it into the tartlets. Prepare the fruit and put it on top.

1

2

3

For the snowballs, loosen them from the foil immediately after baking and carefully press a hollow in the undersides with a spoon (photograph 4). Fill the hollows with ice cream and put 2 together to form a ball. Decorate with whipped cream.

PIPED COOKIES

Yield: 25 small cookies
1 cup salted butter, softened
1 cup sugar
2 teaspoons vanilla extract
Salt to taste
4 cups flour
¼ cup ground almonds
Pinch cocoa
Pinch sugar

Preheat the oven to 325°F.

Cream the butter with the sugar, vanilla extract, and salt. Sift the flour and stir it in a spoonful at a time. Mix in the rest of the flour and the almonds and knead until smooth on a pastry board. Form the dough into rolls. Use a cookie press to press out assorted shapes onto a greased cookie sheet.

Mix the cocoa with the sugar and knead it into a third of the dough. Mix a little of the dark dough with the light-colored dough and press out multi-colored cookies. Bake for about 10 minutes.

1

2

3

4

AMSTERDAM COOKIES

Yield: 25 small cookies
For the caramelized sugar
½ cup sugar
For the dough:
10 tablespoons salted butter
1 cup sugar
2 tablespoons water
1 teaspoon vanilla extract
1½ cups flour
1 teaspoon baking powder
Plus:
Peanut oil

Preheat the oven to 325°F.

To make the caramel, melt the sugar in a saucepan over medium heat, stirring constantly until it turns light brown. Pour the syrup onto an oiled tray (photograph 1), cool, and chop finely (photograph 2).

For the dough, cream the butter with the sugar and vanilla extract. Slowly stir in the water. Sift the flour and baking powder and beat it in. Fold in the caramel (photograph 3). Spoon the dough into a pastry bag and pipe out dots with a diameter of about ¼ inch onto a baking sheet lined with parchment paper (photograph 4). Bake for about 15 minutes.

SULTANS

Yield: 50 rosettes
For the dough:
$1/4$ cup raisins
2 tablespoons rum
3 tablespoons salted butter, softened
$1/4$ cup confectioners' sugar
1 teaspoon vanilla extract
1 egg
$3/4$ cup flour
2 tablespoons ground almonds
For the cream:
3 tablespoons salted butter, softened
3 tablespoons confectioners' sugar
3 egg yolks
1 tablespoon brandy
For garnishing:
1 ounce semisweet chocolate

Preheat the oven to 325°F.

Soak the raisins in the rum. Cream the butter with the confectioners' sugar and vanilla extract. Stir in the egg and almonds. Sift the flour over the mixture and mix it in. Spoon the dough into a pastry bag and pipe out small rosettes with a diameter of $1/2$ inch onto a cookie sheet lined with parchment paper. Place 1 raisin in the middle of each rosette (photograph 1). Bake for 10 to 15 minutes.

To make the cream, cream the butter and confectioners' sugar together. Gradually stir in the egg and brandy (photograph 2). Make a cone from the parchment paper and fill it with chocolate (photograph 3). Place in a warm oven and allow the chocolate to melt. Cut off the tip from the bottom of the bag and decorate half of the cooled cookies with the chocolate. Pipe a little of the cream onto each of the undecorated cookies and top with the decorated halves.

2

3

4

INDEX

C

INDEX

INDEX

G

INDEX

INDEX

INDEX

INDEX

NOTES

NOTES